Political Discourse Analysis

D1614006

'This is exactly the book we were waiting for: a clear and thorough method for analysing political discourse, written from a critical perspective and paying due attention to practical arguments. Isabela and Norman Fairclough have done a great job.'
Frans H. van Eemeren, *University of Amsterdam, The Netherlands*

'An innovative and important extension of the reach of research into political language and discourse. Sure to become an essential reference point, this book will make possible new collaborations (not to mention arguments) involving scholars of linguistics, political theorists of deliberation, discourse or ideology, and political scientists.'
Alan Finlayson, *Swansea University, UK*

In this accessible new textbook, Isabela and Norman Fairclough present their innovative approach to analysing political discourse.

Political Discourse Analysis integrates analysis of arguments into critical discourse analysis and political discourse analysis. The book is grounded in a view of politics in which deliberation, decision and action are crucial concepts: politics is about arriving cooperatively at decisions about what to do in the context of disagreement, conflict of interests and values, power inequalities, uncertainty and risk.

The first half of the book introduces the authors' new approach to the analysis and evaluation of practical arguments, while the second half explores how it can be applied by looking at examples such as government reports, parliamentary debates, political speeches and online discussion forums on political issues. Through the analysis of current events, including a particular focus on the economic crisis and political responses to it, the authors provide a systematic and rigorous analytical framework that can be adopted and used for students' own research.

This exciting new text, co-written by bestselling author Norman Fairclough, is essential reading for researchers, upper undergraduate and postgraduate students of discourse analysis, within English language, linguistics, communication studies, politics and other social sciences.

Isabela Fairclough is Senior Lecturer at the University of Central Lancashire, UK. Previously, she was Associate Professor at the University of Bucharest, Romania, and Visiting Research Fellow at the University of Lancaster. Her publications include *Discourse Analysis and Argumentation Theory: Analytical Framework and Applications* (2006).

Norman Fairclough is Emeritus Professor at the University of Lancaster, UK. He is author of numerous titles, including *New Labour, New Language?* (2000), *Analysing Discourse: Textual Analysis for Social Research* (2003) and *Language and Globalization* (2006), all published by Routledge.

Political Discourse Analysis

A method for advanced students

Isabela Fairclough and Norman Fairclough

Routledge
Taylor & Francis Group

LONDON AND NEW YORK

First published 2012
by Routledge
2 Park Square, Milton Park, Abingdon, Oxon OX14 4RN

Simultaneously published in the USA and Canada
by Routledge
711 Third Avenue, New York, NY 10017

Routledge is an imprint of the Taylor & Francis Group, an informa business

© 2012 Isabela Fairclough and Norman Fairclough

British Library Cataloguing in Publication Data
A catalogue record for this book is available from the British Library

Library of Congress Cataloging in Publication Data
Fairclough, Norman, 1941–
Political discourse analysis / Norman Fairclough and Isabela Fairclough.
p. cm.
1. Discourse analysis—Political aspects. 2. Communication in politics. I. Fairclough, Isabela. II. Title.
P302.77.F35 2012
401'.47—dc23
2011028729

ISBN: 978-0-415-49922-4 (hbk)
ISBN: 978-0-415-49923-1 (pbk)
ISBN: 978-0-203-13788-8 (ebk)

Typeset in Baskerville
by Book Now Ltd, London

MIX
Paper from
responsible sources
FSC® C004839
www.fsc.org

Printed and bound in Great Britain by
TJ International Ltd, Padstow, Cornwall

Contents

Illustrations

Figures

Acknowledgements

We are grateful to all those who have commented on talks we have given and papers related to the content of the book over the past three years. In particular, we want to thank Frans van Eemeren (University of Amsterdam), David Miller (University of Warwick), Andrew Sayer (University of Lancaster), Bob Jessop (University of Lancaster), Alan Finlayson (University of Swansea) and Teun van Dijk (University of Pompeu Fabra), for their generosity in reading various draft chapters and/or earlier papers and making valuable comments and suggestions. Some of the analyses presented in this book started as conference or workshop papers in Amsterdam, Birmingham, Bucharest, Coimbra, Lisbon, Naples, Lancaster, London, Montpellier, Palermo, Sofia and Tel Aviv, or as talks given in various Lancaster University research groups (*Language, Ideology and Power; Cultural Political Economy; Pragmatics and Stylistics*), and some ideas go back to the regular meetings of the Bucharest *Discourse Analysis* research group at Prosper ASE. We are greatly indebted to the organizers of all of these events and meetings (and particularly to Ruth Amossy, Patrizia Ardizzone, Martin Bauer, Camelia Beciu, Alexandra Cornilescu, Carmen Caldas-Coulthard, Paolo Donadio, Gabriella Di Martino, Frans van Eemeren, Carlos Gouveia, Mihaela Irimia, Bob Jessop, Clara Keating, Laura Mureşan, Claudia Ortu, Kristina Petkova, Mick Short, Jürgen Siess, Maria João Silveirinha, Isabel Simões-Ferreira, Gilles Siouffi, Sandrine Sorlin, Ngai-Ling Sum and Ruth Wodak) for their kindness in inviting us to give talks and thus offering us the chance to develop our ideas in critical discussion with others, as well as for their extraordinary hospitality. Thanks are also due to Inger Lassen for the opportunity she gave us to try out our new framework by teaching on the Doctoral Workshop in CDA at the University of Aalborg in the summer of 2011.

Isabela would like to thank Sunil Banga and Lynn Wilson, at the Lancaster University International Study Centre, and Kelly Salimian and Carmel Roche, at the Manchester University Language Centre, as well as all her colleagues and students, for two wonderfully pleasant and supportive work environments during the writing of this book. She also wants to thank the excellent teaching staff and course coordinators on Lancaster University's Linguistics Department Summer EAP Programme for the pleasure of their friendship and the chance of sharing their extraordinary professional experience and sense of humour. She is also grateful to Melinda Tan and all her new colleagues at the University of Central Lancashire for their warm welcome to the School of Languages and International Studies.

Special thanks are due to Greg Myers and Jane Sunderland (Lancaster University), Jane Mulderrig (Sheffield University) and, once again, to Frans van Eemeren, David Miller and Andrew Sayer for constant and invaluable friendship and academic support over the years; similarly, to Alexandra Cornilescu and Isabela's former colleagues at the University of Bucharest and the British Council Bucharest. Many other friends deserve our gratitude, for sharing their ideas on discourse analysis, argumentation theory or politics, and offering us their generous friendship, as well as (sometimes) the pleasure of their company on Lake District walks. In addition to those we have already mentioned, we want to thank Romy Clark, Maureen Conway, Bogdan Costea, Susan Dray, Michael Farrelly, Phil Graham, John Heywood, Anna and Costas Iordanidis, Pete Keogh, Majid Khosravinik, Diana Madroane, Simona Mazilu, Marilyn Martin-Jones, Nicolien Montessori, Liviu Mureşan, Ilinca Nicolcea, Silvia Pătru, Kathy Pitt, Marius Pleşea, Carmen Popescu, Martin Reisigl, Daniela Sorea, David Sugarman, Bron Szerszynski, Karin Zotzmann. Last but not least, a special word of thanks goes to Isabela's former students and particularly to her postgraduate students on the MA programmes in Discourse and Argumentation Studies and in British Cultural Studies at the University of Bucharest, for their unflagging and stimulating interest in argumentation theory and critical discourse analysis and for lasting friendship.

We would also like to thank Louisa Semlyen and Sophie Jaques at Routledge, as well as our copy editor, Jeffrey Boys, for their patience, good ideas and excellent editorial support.

Finally, we want to thank our intelligent, loving, hard-working and very grown-up children, Filip, Joe, Matthew, Simon and Ştefan, for all the happiness they bring to our lives. Extra thanks are due to Filip for his patience and for the countless ways in which he has helped us, encouraged us and cheered us, throughout the writing of this book.

We want to dedicate this book to the loving memory of Patricia (Paddy) Georgescu (1931–2010), a great friend and source of inspiration.

Isabela and Norman Fairclough, *Lancaster, 1 July–1 November 2011*

Permissions acknowledgements

Every effort has been made to contact copyright holders. If any have been inadvertently overlooked, the publishers will be pleased to make the necessary arrangement at the first opportunity.

Comments: 'Public must learn to "tolerate the inequality" of bonuses, says Goldman Sachs vice-chairman', No byline, *The Guardian*, 21 October 2009 ('the Content'). Copyright Guardian News & Media Ltd 2009.

Introduction

Our aim in this book is to present a new approach to analysing political discourse as a contribution to the development of critical discourse analysis (CDA). The approach we propose is characterized both by continuity with the theoretical and analytical concerns of earlier work in the version of CDA we work with and by innovation. What is new about this approach in comparison with other approaches within the field of research known as 'political discourse analysis' is that it views political discourse as primarily a form of argumentation, and as involving more specifically *practical* argumentation, argumentation for or against particular ways of acting, argumentation that can ground decision. In deciding what to do, agents consider both reasons that favour a particular tentative line of action and reasons against it, as well as reasons in favour or against alternatives, i.e. they *deliberate* over several possibilities for action. We are not suggesting that political discourse contains *only* practical arguments, or indeed that it only consists of arguments. What we are suggesting is that politics is most fundamentally about making choices about how to act in response to circumstances and goals, it is about choosing *policies*, and such choices and the actions which follow from them are based upon practical argumentation – or as Aristotle put it in the *Nicomachean Ethics* (Irwin 1999), on 'deliberation'.

The examples of political discourse which we shall discuss in the book are all taken from political responses to the financial and economic crisis which began in 2007 and continues at the time of writing (2010–11). The readership we envisage for this book includes advanced undergraduate students and postgraduate students in language, communication, discourse and argumentation studies, politics and political economy and other areas of social science, and allied fields such as media studies, as well as academic staff carrying out teaching or research in such areas. The book is therefore addressed to several academic communities (political discourse analysts, critical discourse analysts, analysts and theorists of argumentation and political analysts) and proposes something new to each of them. Let us briefly summarize the main claims we are arguing for in each case. We address to political discourse analysts and critical discourse analysts the claim that political discourse is fundamentally argumentative and primarily involves practical argumentation. Consequently, we think, analysis of political discourse should centre upon analysis of practical argumentation. In addition, we address to critical discourse analysts the claim that analysis of texts should focus upon the generic features of whole texts rather than isolated features of the text, and primarily on action, not on representations. In particular, analysis should focus on how discourses, as ways of representing, provide agents with reasons for action. Analysis of non-argumentative genres (narrative, explanation) should also be viewed in relation to the arguments in which they are usually embedded. We address to analysts and theorists of argumentation the claim that argumentation theory and analysis has not only much to offer but also much to gain from interdisciplinary collaboration with discourse analysts in theorizing argumentative genres in the political field (e.g. deliberation). To political analysts, we address the claim that an adequate treatment of political choice and decision-making in conditions of uncertainty and value pluralism demands systematic analysis of political discourse as fundamentally argumentative discourse.

Let us summarize what we see as the main contributions we are making, theoretical, methodological and descriptive. Theoretically, we are making a contribution to argumentation theory in developing an original view of the structure and evaluation of practical argumentation, which we hope will be of interest to argumentation analysts. With respect to methodology, we present a framework for analysing argumentation in a sufficiently explicit and clear way, working through a great many examples, for students and researchers to be able to use it as a model for carrying out analysis of argumentation in their own work. We hope that the book will be of value in teaching people how to analyse arguments and will work well as a course-book on advanced courses in discourse analysis. Students and academics doing research in various areas of the social sciences often wish to analyse bodies of texts of various kinds (e.g. policy texts, interviews, media texts), but commonly find it difficult to find appropriate frameworks for analysis. It is our intention to offer a practically useable framework, a method, for those who wish to analyse political discourse as argumentative discourse. Descriptively, we apply the framework in analysis of political discourse in which politicians and others are advancing ways of responding to and dealing with the current financial and economic crisis. We cover diverse aspects of the current political debate over the crisis and adequate policies aimed at overcoming it and we hope that the book will be of interest to the many researchers in politics and other social sciences who are now focusing upon aspects of the crisis. Most of them would recognize the vital importance of discourse in the development of strategies to overcome the crisis, but few currently have suitable discourse-analytical frameworks at their disposal. Finally, the book is offered primarily as a contribution to political discourse analysis, especially analysis which uses a CDA approach. Our focus on analysis and evaluation of practical argumentation is a new one, and we show how more familiar focuses (e.g. on representations, identities, narratives, metaphors) can be incorporated in analysis of argumentation in ways which account much better for their political significance and effectiveness.

We shall begin with a discussion of the crisis and political responses to it, then go on to give a rationale for the book, in the form of a set of objectives, and a chapter outline. We will also attempt to pre-empt possible misunderstandings of our position.

Accounts of the financial and economic crisis and the relevance of argumentation theory

According to explanatory critical theories of capitalism (such as Harvey 2010, Jessop 2002), crises occur when the inherent contradictions of capitalism lead to imbalances, i.e. the loss of the balances (e.g. between what is produced and what is consumed, between the funds available for investment and the demand for capital, between the number of people available for work and the demand for labour) which are necessary for the existing system to continue to function. Crises are not only inevitable but also necessary, for when imbalances develop, people have to impose some order on a situation of collapse and chaos. We can say, following Harvey (2010: 71), that crises have a rationalizing function, the function of restoring rationality where it has been undermined. In Harvey's words, crises are 'the irrational rationalisers of an always unstable capitalism'. Crises have an objective or systemic aspect (the structural imbalances we referred to), but they also have a necessary and indeed crucial subjective aspect, which is agentive and strategic. In a crisis, people have to make decisions about how to act in response and to develop strategies for pursuing particular courses of action or policies which will hopefully restore balance and rationality. It is the subjective aspect that is of particular importance in this book, because practical argumentation feeds into people's decisions about how to act. Agents' choices, decisions and strategies are political in nature, they are contested by groups of people with different interests and objectives, who are competing to make their own particular choices, policies and strategies prevail.

Many accounts of the current financial and economic crisis recognize the importance of the subjective aspect, but there is little agreement on its precise nature. Different authors accentuate different things. Foster and Magdoff (2009: 8) emphasize *action* ('the full ramifications' of the crisis 'depend on the concrete actions people take in response' to it) and indicate that action depends upon *decision*: people might undertake 'radical change', but only if they 'decide that economics is really political economy and hence theirs to choose'. Harvey (2010: 71, 236–237) emphasizes *choice* ('at times of crisis there are always options') and the dependence of which option is chosen on 'the balance of *class forces* and the *mental conceptions* as to what might be possible'. Harvey refers to the Great Depression of the 1930s as an example of how *erroneous conceptions* played a crucial role both in the emergence of the crisis and in failures to find a way out of it, and to Keynes' contribution to the 'revolutionising' of mental conceptions ('the knowledge structure') that was needed. To transcend the present crisis, he says, 'we need new mental conceptions' and a 'revolution in thinking'. Žižek (2009: 17–19) emphasizes that the outcome of the crisis depends on how the crisis is 'symbolized', which 'ideological interpretation' or 'story' or *'narrative'* 'imposes itself and determines the general perception of the crisis'. He argues that the 'central task of the ruling ideology in the present crisis is to impose a narrative which will place the blame for the meltdown not on the global capitalist system as such, but on secondary and contingent deviations' (e.g. weakness of regulation, corruption). Jessop (2002: 6–7, 92–94) emphasizes *'strategies'* and the *'narratives'* and *'imaginaries'* associated with them. Crises create the space for competing 'strategic interventions to significantly redirect the course of events as well as for attempts to "muddle through"', and which strategies prevail partly depends upon 'discursive struggles' between different 'narratives' of the nature, causes and significance of the crisis and how it might be resolved, including economic and political 'imaginaries' for possible future states of affairs and systems.

All of these accounts contribute useful insights into the nature of the subjective aspect of crises. But in order to research the crisis we need a more comprehensive view of the subjective aspect, which brings together the elements of it identified in these accounts, as well as others, in a coherent way. One notable omission in these accounts, from the perspective of this book, is that none of them mentions deliberation or argumentation. But narratives and explanations of the crisis, as well as imaginaries, cannot function as part of action unless they *provide people with reasons for acting* in particular ways. The study of narratives, explanations or imaginaries is pointless unless we see them as embedded within practical arguments, as feeding into and influencing processes of decision-making, briefly, as premises in arguments for action.

In our view, the 'subjective' aspects of crises, i.e. those aspects which have to do with the agency of political and other actors in making decisions and developing strategies and policies in response to the crisis, can most fruitfully be seen in terms of the Aristotelian account of political action as based upon deliberation that leads to decision. This entails recognizing that deliberation (and practical argumentation) is an essential part of the responses of actors to the crisis. From this perspective, in which argument is the main analytical category, the 'narratives', 'mental conceptions' and 'imaginaries' discussed in these accounts are elements of practical arguments: narratives of the crisis are incorporated within what we will call the 'circumstantial premises' of practical arguments (premises which represent the context of action); 'imaginaries' for possible and desirable states of affairs are incorporated in our account within the 'goal premises'. Practical argumentation can be seen as 'means–ends' argumentation, where the claim or conclusion ('we should do *A*') is a judgement about what means should be pursued to attain the end (goal). Practical argumentation is often characterized by complex chains, not only of means and ends (goals), but of goals and circumstances, where the goals of one action, once turned into reality, become the context of action (the circumstances) of a further action. We understand 'strategies' to be such complex chains.

All the accounts we referred to above recognize, correctly in our view, that the responses of political and other actors to the crisis inherently have a semiotic or discursive dimension: 'narrative' is obviously a semiotic category, 'imaginaries' have a semiotic character, and 'mental conceptions' are necessarily realized in semiotic forms. But unless we see narratives, imaginaries and such-like semiotic constructs as elements of practical argumentation, we have no way of showing how they affect decisions and actions or how they may, contingently, thereby have effects on the direction of social and economic change. Let us take an example. Žižek (2009: 17) claims that a narrative which 'imposes itself' in the '"discursive" ideological competition' which the crisis opens up will 'determine the general perception of the crisis'. But what interest is there in imposing narratives and determining perceptions? Is imposing a narrative an end in itself, or a means to some other end – maybe to determining perceptions? But then, is determining perceptions an end in itself? We would suggest rather that getting people to accept a particular narrative of the crisis, to see it in a certain way, is generally a political concern precisely because it gives people *a reason* for favouring or accepting certain lines of action and policies rather than others. The process of giving and receiving reasons is called argumentation. Žižek claims that a successful narrative and its determination of perception will influence the effects of the crisis, will determine whether what will emerge will be 'a radical emancipatory politics', or 'the rise of racist populism', or the emergence of a more radical form of neo-liberalism, or other outcomes, but in the absence of a consideration of the relationship between representations, decision and action he has no way of showing how this can happen.

Although 'imposing' or winning acceptance of particular representations (descriptions, narratives, explanations) and thereby shaping perceptions are concerns in politics, we would argue that they subserve a greater concern of political agents and agencies to make their proposed lines of action, their strategies and policies, prevail over others. In this sense, actions have primacy over representations, and representations are subsumed within action. Accordingly, in analysing political discourse, it is crucial to ensure that the focus on how events, circumstances, entities and people are represented does not obscure or displace a focus on what agents do; or, as we might put it, that *genres* are given at least as much attention as *discourses*. This has tended not to be the case in political discourse analysis, where the focus has tended to be on representations and discourses. But given that we are concerned with the subjective aspect of the crisis as well as its objective aspect, i.e. with how agents respond to the crisis and what effects follow from these responses, we must clearly investigate and analyse what agents *do* in response to the crisis, including what they do discursively (in what they say or write). Our claim is that in politics they primarily engage in argumentation, and particularly in practical argumentation, including deliberation. In the accounts of Harvey, Žižek and Jessop, a focus on what agents do would have to involve reference to argumentation, and narratives, explanations and imaginaries would have to be seen as embedded within arguments.

Not all accounts of crisis overlook the question of argumentation. Debray (1993) claims that there is 'an imbalance in a crisis situation': it is 'objectively over-determined' (through the 'fusion' of diverse contradictions which have 'accumulated' within the established system), 'while subjectively indeterminate' (i.e. there are various possibilities, none of which imposes itself, although not 'everything is possible'). He emphasizes the necessary 'choice' in a crisis situation between one 'road' (policy) and another, but also stresses the indeterminate nature and inherent unclearness of the crisis situation, and the inherent uncertainty of what effects actions will actually have. Moreover, the practical imperatives of politics demand immediate choices between simplified alternatives which do not do justice to the complexity of the crisis situation. While it is the task of theory to 'untangle' this complexity, from a political perspective, 'a crisis is a knot that cannot be untangled, but must be cut'. Such a choice is 'rational', in the sense that there are reasons in support of it and it is 'the end of a chain of reasoning'. However, this end is 'reached only by way of a discontinuity', 'for if reasoning consists in an analysis of conditions as they are . . . we have made a leap beyond those present conditions, a leap into the future, an anticipation, in short a policy'. Such a choice 'is not a deduction' but a 'gamble', a 'well-judged leap in the dark'. It is 'a decisive moment yet at the same time undecided; it is essentially uncertain in its results, yet it is subject to a total rational process; an indeterminate moment of determination' (Debray 1993: 102–115).

Aristotle's treatment of the relationship between deliberation, decision and action in Book III of the *Nicomachean Ethics* seems to point in a similar direction. Voluntary action follows from decisions which themselves follow from deliberation in which judgements are made about what is the right thing to do in conditions of uncertainty and human fallibility. Aristotle recognized that one circumstance in which 'we enlist partners in deliberation' is when we are dealing with 'large issues when we distrust our own ability to discern [the right answer]', and in the same paragraph he observes that we deliberate 'when the outcome is unclear and the right way to act is undefined' (1112b 9–12, Irwin 1999). More obviously still, Debray's observations accord with the Popperian (1959, 1963) view that the premises of an argument never justify the conclusion, or the conclusion never follows from the premises as a matter of inference. If it did, if there was no discontinuity or hiatus, then we would know with certainty that the conclusion was true, or that the proposed line of action was the right one, and we could confidently act in accordance with it. However, human action occurs against a background of incomplete information, uncertainty and risk, and deciding which action is appropriate always involves an element of 'gamble', however carefully well-judged. It also occurs against agents' fundamental *freedom*. Practical reasoning does not *force* agents to act in any way; agents may arrive at a judgement and yet fail to act: there is always a gap between reasoning and action.

Our emphasis on practical argumentation and deliberation is also relevant to one issue which is often raised in explanations of the crisis: that one factor which contributed to the crisis was the reliance of economists and economic and financial advisors on highly sophisticated models for economic forecasting which are now being heavily criticized for failing to recognize the inherent unpredictability of the future. One conclusion that might be drawn from the failure of economic forecasting and the failure of experts to predict the financial crisis (or indeed political crises, including the collapse of the Soviet Union and other socialist countries in eastern Europe in 1989–90, and the sudden emergence and success of democratic movements in Egypt, Tunisia and other Middle Eastern countries in the spring of 2011) is that public deliberation is a vital corrective to the proven tendency of experts to get things catastrophically wrong. For deliberation, in probing and testing proposed lines of action in terms of their possible consequences, in systematically subjecting proposals to critical scrutiny, has a crucial epistemic capacity to lessen the impact of bounded rationality, including the tendency of experts to be locked into closed ways of thinking and reasoning. From this perspective, the way we understand deliberation and the importance we ascribe to it may be of value not only in analysing political debate over responses to the crisis, but also in indicating how public debate and deliberation need to be strengthened. This can be seen as a contribution to 'deliberative democracy' as a normative ideal, but also more concretely in terms of dealing with an urgent practical political question of the day: how to avoid a repetition of the current crisis.

We have focused above on just a few accounts of the crisis, but the main point we are making can be extended to a great many others. The significance of the agency of political and other actors, of how they respond to the crisis, in affecting its outcomes is widely recognized, and so too is the significance of discourse, of how the crisis is represented, interpreted, narrated and explained, and how possible policy responses and possible outcomes are represented. But what is generally missing is a coherent way of showing how these *representations* connect with human *agency*, how they function as *reasons for action*.

Main types of account of the crisis and arguments for action in response to it

It is fairly evident that which 'narratives' of the crisis come to prevail will strongly affect which strategies and policies win out and what the effects of the crisis and the longer-term outcomes are. In the examples we shall analyse in this book, we find various interpretations, narratives and explanations of the crisis functioning as reasons for or against particular conclusions about what should be done. We now want to provide some context for evaluating particular arguments for action by identifying what seem to be the main accounts of the crisis and the main arguments from particular types of account to conclusions in favour of particular courses of action. We base this categorization partly on our observation of the argumentation which has gone on since the crisis began, and partly on the academic literature (see for instance Gamble 2009).

The primary division is between accounts of the crisis which attribute it to what we can broadly call *systemic* origins and causes, and accounts which attribute it to *non-systemic* origins and causes. Systemic origins and causes are those which arise from the nature of the economic system as such. There are two main variants: those which attribute the crisis to the form of capitalism which has been dominant especially in the USA and Britain for the past 30 years or so – neo-liberalism; and those which attribute it to the nature of capitalism as such, not just a particular form of it. Non-systemic accounts attribute the origins and causes of the crisis to peripheral attributes of the economic system rather than the economic system as such, or to the intellectual or moral failures of people with responsibility for or within the economic system. We can distinguish two main accounts which blame such peripheral attributes: market fundamentalist accounts, which blame state attempts to regulate or control markets (on the principle that markets should be left to manage themselves), and regulationist accounts, which blame inadequate regulation, either on a national scale or a 'global' (international) scale. Accounts which blame people may focus upon their failure to understand or even consider the consequences of their actions (intellectual failures) or on their selfishness, recklessness or greed (moral failures).

The primary division in arguments is between those which proceed from non-systemic accounts of the crisis to advocate measures to get back to 'normal', the '*status quo ante*' or the economic situation which prevailed before the crises, and those which proceed from systemic accounts of the crisis to advocate radical changes in the economic system. The former are not only more common but also more developed than the latter. Although arguments which advocate radical change on the basis of systemic accounts of the crisis are not too difficult to find, there is little clarity or consensus, so far at least, over the nature of the radical change that is needed. Change can be more or less radical: one version of this argument proceeds from accounts which blame the neo-liberal form of capitalism to advocate a different form of capitalism, often a form based on Keynesian principles (as advocated around the time of the Great Depression of the 1930s by the economist J. M. Keynes); another proceeds from accounts which blame capitalism as such to advocate a non-capitalist economy. Arguments for getting back to 'normal' do generally envisage some change in the *status quo ante*, though not fundamental ones, including changes in peripheral attributes of the economic system, such as more and better regulation or regulation on a 'global' as well as national scale, and in the behaviour of people with economic responsibilities (they should be less hubristic about economic models or assumptions, less greedy, and so forth). The line between such changes and what we have called radical change is not always a sharp one. For instance, those who advocate introducing particularly stringent regulation are arguably advocating a new form of capitalism, if deregulation is an essential element of neo-liberalism. There are currently two major variants of arguments for getting back to 'normal', which differ in the means advocated: those which prioritize state fiscal stimulus to sustain demand until a recovery is clearly underway, and those which prioritize the early reduction of public deficits, usually by cutting government spending rather than raising taxes.

We can summarize these distinctions as follows:

Explanations and narratives of the crisis – what's to blame?

- Systemic – capitalism as such.
- Systemic – neo-liberal form of capitalism.
- Non-systemic – peripherals of the economic system (e.g. too much or too little regulation).
- Non-systemic – people (intellectual failures, moral failures).

Practical arguments based on these explanations and narratives

- Argument for 'getting back to normal', from non-systemic accounts of crisis.
- Argument for radical change, from systemic accounts of crisis.

What we are suggesting is that different accounts of the crisis involve different descriptions, narratives and explanations of the context of action, which are present in the (circumstantial) premises of arguments. Along with the goals of arguers (in the goal premise) – and these may involve various 'imaginaries' or visions – and a means–goal premise, they provide reasons in favour of particular courses of action (the conclusion of the argument). How the context of action is represented (or narrated, explained) affects which course of action is proposed, which explains the intense competition and conflict over winning acceptance for or imposing one account (one narrative, one explanation) of the crisis rather than others.

To illustrate this range of accounts and arguments, we shall discuss three examples. The first is taken from an editorial in the *Financial Times* (2009), entitled 'The Consequence of Bad Economics', which launched a series of articles on 'the future of capitalism' (see Callinicos 2010: 12–13).

> Those who sound the death knell of market capitalism are therefore mistaken. This was not a failure of markets; it was a failure to create proper markets. What is to blame is a certain mindset, embodied not least in Mr Greenspan. It ignored a capitalist economy's inherent instabilities – and therefore it relieved policymakers who could manage those instabilities of their responsibility to do so. This is not the bankruptcy of a social system, but the intellectual and moral failure of those who were in charge of it; a failure for which there was no excuse.

This is a non-systemic account of the crisis which explicitly rejects a systemic account (this is 'not a failure of markets', not the death of capitalism, etc.) and blames primarily the people who were responsible (their 'mindset' and 'intellectual and moral failure'), as well as inadequate regulation or more exactly the absence of a proper regulatory regime ('it relieved policymakers who could manage those instabilities of their responsibility to do so'). Although it is a non-systemic account, it does attribute inherent flaws to capitalist economies ('inherent instabilities'), but represents them as 'manageable'. The editorial does not explicitly advocate a course of action and does not explicitly involve practical argumentation, but in the context of the debate over the future of capitalism which it initiates, we can interpret it as implicitly advocating some form of return to the *status quo ante*. This may seem at face value to be just epistemic argumentation over the nature of the crisis, but the implicit practical point of that argumentation – what is to be done – would be evident to those who joined in or followed the debate.

The second example is from an important speech on economic policy given in August 2010 by George Osborne, Chancellor of the Exchequer in the British Conservative–Liberal Democratic Coalition government elected in May 2010 (Osborne 2010):

> First we need to understand how Britain got here.
>
> The previous government's economic policy was based on two central assumptions:
>
> - that they had abolished the economic cycle; and
> - and that they had achieved a permanently high trend rate of economic growth.
>
> These assumptions were used to justify increased spending, persistent deficits, cheaper credit, growing imbalances and ballooning personal debt.
>
> Of course many of the same features existed elsewhere, notably the US, but they were more pronounced in Britain than anywhere else.
>
> We were left with the biggest deficit, the most indebted households, the most leveraged banks.
>
> I don't think it's unreasonable to say that this was the greatest failure of British economic policy-making for more than 30 years, since the IMF crisis of 1976.
>
> The fallacy of the first assumption – the end of boom and bust – is plain for all to see.
>
> What was said to be sustainable growth turned out to be a debt-fuelled boom that was followed by the deepest and longest bust since the War.
>
> Sadly for us all, the second assumption – an increase in the trend growth rate – also turned out to be a fallacy. [Section omitted.]

When disaster struck, the explanation was simply that a perfectly sustainable economy had been hit by a bolt from the blue that knocked 5% off the economy's sustainable level of output. [Section omitted.]

Rather than a bolt from the blue, the recession now looks wearily familiar – the bust that follows a boom.

Osborne's account of the recession involves here narrative and explanation. Mainly, there is an explanation of 'how Britain got here', i.e. as a result of Labour's mistakes, based on 'false assumptions' and 'fallacies'. Labour's explanation for the crisis is also contrasted with the allegedly genuine explanation: the crisis was the result of Labour's economic policies, not an unexpected 'bolt from the blue', which is why, implicitly, Labour is to blame. In the speech, this explanation is placed within a longer narrative of the crisis as having had three stages, spread over two years: 'inter-bank credit markets froze up' (August 2007); 'tax-payer-funded bailouts of some of the largest banks' took place (August 2008); finally, these were 'signs that fears about the liquidity and solvency of banks would become fears about the creditworthiness of the governments than stand behind them' (August 2009). Ultimately, these narratives and explanations are embedded within practical argumentation for immediate 'decisive plans to deal with the deficit', primarily by cutting government expenditure.

This account of the crisis (and specifically the recession) is a non-systemic account which puts the blame for the recession on the policies of the previous Labour government ('the greatest failure of British economic policy-making for more than 30 years'). This account has been challenged on various grounds: there is, for instance, an alternative argument that the deficit is only high because of government interventions, which were necessary and effective in reducing the severity of the crisis. Another argument observes that the policy failures attributed to the Labour government were neither specifically British failures nor, in Britain, specifically Labour failures, since the 'disaster' arose from mistakes and 'fallacies' in the economic policies of all governments, Conservative and Labour, since 1979. The course of action advocated – giving priority to deficit reduction – has also been challenged on the grounds that the claimed threat to national creditworthiness is greatly over-exaggerated and the danger of a double-dip recession or prolonged stagnation as a consequence of the proposed cuts in government spending is much greater (see Balls 2010 for some of these counter-arguments).

The third example is from an interview given by Vince Cable, the Business Secretary in the British Coalition government, to the *Guardian* newspaper (Wintour 2011):

We have had a very, very profound crisis which is going to take a long time to dig out of. It is about the deficit, but that is only one of the symptoms. We had the complete collapse of a model based on consumer spending, a housing bubble, an overweight banking system – three banks each of them with a balance sheet larger than the British economy. It was a disaster waiting to happen. It has done profound damage that is going to last for a long time.

He goes on to criticize the Labour Party:

They are in a state of denial that there is a big structural problem with the UK economy. So we stick to this short-term tit-for-tat; why has the growth in this quarter been slower, the scale of the cuts should be slower – there is genuine debate we should be having about how radical the reforms of the financial sector should be – but there is not from the progressive wing of politics a sustained critique or pressure and argument. Ultimately, it comes back to this defensiveness and an unwillingness to accept that Britain was operating a model that failed.

Cable gives a systemic explanation of Britain's crisis as a consequence of 'a model that failed', an unsustainable model of financial services that underpinned a 'golden decade of growth' that was only apparent. 'People do not understand how bad the economy is', he was reported as saying in the same interview, and politicians have not adequately explained how difficult and painful it will be 'to restructure Britain's broken economic model'. He does not advance an explicit argument on the basis of the explanation he provides, but he seems to be hinting at a course of action that includes 'radical reforms' when he laments the absence of a debate, on the 'progressive wing of politics', about 'how radical the reforms of the financial sector should be'. Although this is a systemic explanation, its representation of the systemic causes of the crisis is rather narrow: the cause was the *model*, which is characterized in terms of a set of features ('consumer spending, a housing bubble, an overweight banking system'), but apparently not the system as such. However, there are persuasive arguments which explain the high level of consumer spending as due to high levels of borrowing and the availability of loans at low interest rates, which were themselves related to structural imbalances leading to huge volumes of surplus capital and pressure to find ways (e.g. loans and mortgages) of profitably investing it. (See Harvey 2010 for a much more developed systemic explanation.)

Given the sheer complexity of the crisis, including the diversity of the forms it has taken in different parts of the world, and the vast range of political and other responses to it, a comprehensive coverage of it is clearly beyond the scope of this book. We shall limit our discussion of political responses to the crisis to British material. Given the aim of the book, this limitation is, we think, justified: it is not a book about the crisis, it is a book about an approach to political discourse analysis, which we have developed in part by following and analysing political responses to the crisis, from which we draw our illustrative examples.

Main objectives

We shall now give a fuller account of what the book is about, what our objectives are, and why we have adopted them. These are our main objectives:

1   Starting from a particular view on the nature of politics, to make a case for viewing and analysing political discourse as primarily argumentative discourse, and more specifically as involving primarily practical reasoning or practical argumentation and argumentative genres (deliberation) and activity types; to integrate analysis of theoretical (epistemic) reasoning and non-argumentative pre-genres (narrative, description, explanation) within an approach that gives primacy to practical argumentation;
2   to give an account of the character and structure of practical argumentation, and develop a framework for analysing it as well as a framework for evaluating it; this account should be compatible with philosophical accounts of practical reasoning as well as with conceptions of the nature of politics in political theory;
3   to integrate analysis and evaluation of practical argumentation into an approach to critical analysis of political discourse based upon a version of critical discourse analysis and thus expand and refine CDA's analytical framework;

4   to apply this approach to the analysis and evaluation of political discourse, specifically, political responses to the financial and economic crisis, as instantiated in different types of data: government reports, parliamentary debates, other debates on public matters, internet discussion forums, newspaper articles, and so on;

5   to provide a model for analysis that is sufficiently comprehensive, systematic and clear to be acquired and applied by students and analysts of political discourse.

With respect to Objective 1, we summed up the case for viewing political discourse as primarily practical argumentation at the beginning of this chapter. This objective rests upon a particular view of politics: politics is most fundamentally about making choices about how to act in response to circumstances and events and in light of certain goals and values, and such choices and the actions which follow from them are based upon practical reasoning about what should be done. What people do in reasoning practically is make judgements about what the best thing to do is in the circumstances, given their goals and values, and based on how they weigh together a variety of considerations, i.e. based on the normative priority that they assign to various reasons. In deciding what to do, it is rational to assess the probable consequences of one's action, where consequences can be understood more generally to include a possibly negative impact on goals and values that should (arguably) not be overridden. A reasonable decision (including a political decision) will emerge from sufficient critical examination of reasons, from considering and balancing reasons in favour but also, essentially, from considering reasons *against* a proposed course of action, i.e. from at least a minimal process of deliberation. In our view, the goal of practical reasoning is arriving at a reasonable practical judgement that can ground reasonable decision-making and reasonable action.

Objective 2 is to give an account of the character and structure of practical argumentation, and develop a framework for analysing and evaluating practical argumentation. Practical argumentation is argumentation about what to do in response to practical problems (and practical arguments are often problem–solution arguments). The conclusion of a practical argument is a practical claim or judgement about what we should do, what it would be good to do, or what the right course of action is. In the account of practical argumentation which we present in Chapter 2, the conclusion is arrived at on the basis of premises of four sorts: a circumstantial premise, which represents the existing state of affairs and the problems it poses; a goal premise, which describes (and 'imagines') the future state of affairs agents want to bring about or think ought to be brought about; a value premise, expressing the values and concerns which underlie the agents' goals (but also affects how they represent the context of action); and a means–end premise, which represents the proposed line of action as a (hypothetical) means that will presumably take agents from the current state of affairs to the future state of affairs that is their goal. Analysis is a matter of identifying within an argument its premises and its conclusion and the relations between them. We also suggest what deliberation involves: minimally, deliberation involves considering a counter-argument, i.e. looking at reasons that support the claim that the action should *not* be performed, such as negative consequences that might undermine the goals or values pursued by the agent. Deliberation can also involve considering other courses of action and reasons for and against them, and weighing all these considerations together in order to arrive at a judgement on balance.

Evaluation of arguments involves critical questioning of the acceptability of these premises and the relations between them and the claim, as well as critical examination of the claim itself. It is necessary to develop an approach to practical argumentation which is both descriptive and normative, which can both provide good descriptions and analyses of practical arguments and offer a sound basis for evaluating them. Evaluation needs to include both evaluation of arguments and evaluation of claims for action (conclusions). We can criticize a claim by showing that the action will have negative consequences that will undermine the goals and values that the agent is committed to, hence the action should *not* be performed.

The account we propose is compatible with a coherent view of politics and political decision-making, as produced in political theory. Politics on this view is about decision-making and action in conditions of uncertainty and disagreement. It is also compatible with views of practical reasoning produced in philosophy, particularly moral philosophy, and with a general theory of speech acts and of the construction of social reality by means of speech acts. We also share the underlying philosophy of reasonableness of pragma-dialectics (as one of the major dialectical approaches to argumentation), and its critical rationalist view of the essentially critical function of argument.

In relation to Objective 3, we see evaluation of practical argumentation as a bridge between the normative concerns of argumentation theory and the concerns of CDA with critique of discourse, which also involves a form of evaluation from an analytical normative standpoint. CDA aims to extend forms of critique familiar in critical social science to discourse, and we see argumentation analysis as potentially increasing the capacity of CDA to do so in offering powerful ways of analysing argumentative discourse. A concern of critical social analysts is to investigate how the political question of what is to be done in response to the crisis is addressed, how and why certain answers, certain choices of how to act, certain strategies for seeking to resolve the crisis, come to prevail over others, taking account of not only the actions and strategies of social agents, but also of how the nature and tendencies of existing social structures, institutions and relations of power bear upon such outcomes. We shall consider how the analysis and evaluation of arguments relates to and may contribute to forms of normative and explanatory critique that can be applied in investigating how the political question is addressed.

All arguments have logical, rhetorical and dialectical aspects, and need to be analysed and evaluated in logical, rhetorical and dialectical terms. A good argument is one which is good in all these respects. Rhetorical aspects are, however, integrated within a dialectical normative framework, on our approach. Following dialectical theories of argumentation, we give primacy to an external, analytical normative standpoint in the evaluation of actual argumentative practice. In so doing, we are not neglecting lay normativity, the way that social actors themselves evaluate the arguments of others and sometimes their own arguments. Participants' evaluation of arguments is for instance inherent to 'deliberation' as a genre, as we describe it. This means that the object of analysis for analysts of argumentation includes *both* people's arguments *and* their evaluation of the arguments of others from a systematic theoretical perspective, grounded in a view of human rationality. Political discourse analysis needs to incorporate both descriptive and normative standpoints. But it also needs to incorporate an explanatory viewpoint, the point of view of explanatory critique, in assessing how actual discursive practices contribute to maintaining or transforming a given social order, including existing power relations.

One of the main claims we are making in this book is that a proper understanding of the argumentative nature of political reasoning explains how agency and structures are connected: *structures provide agents with reasons for action*. Power itself provides such reasons and can only be understood in relation to how it enters agents' reasoning processes. In arguing practically, agents draw on various discourses and such selections are linked to the diverse interests of particular (groups of) social agents, and give rise to the sort of critical questions about discourse which CDA characteristically addresses (about domination, manipulation and ideologies).

Objective 4 is to apply this approach to the analysis and evaluation of political discourse, and specifically of political responses to the financial and economic crisis and thus throw some light on the broad public debate on the causes of the crisis and particularly on the strategies of dealing with its effects. Evaluation of arguments is seen as providing a sound (rigorous, non-arbitrary) basis for normative and explanatory social critique.

Finally, Objective 5 is a pedagogical and methodological one, which we regard as essential in view of our proposal that a new approach is needed in political discourse analysis. This is why we provide not only a comprehensive framework for analysing and evaluating practical argumentation, but also extensive illustration by working through a large number of examples, so that those who wish to adopt this approach in their own work can acquire sufficient competence from this book to do so. We know from experience that students wishing to use CDA are often frustrated by the eclectic and not always coherent character of existing methods of analysis and evaluation of discourse, and it is one of our objectives to provide a new and better method that can be replicated in the analysis of different sets of data.

Possible misunderstandings

In order to pre-empt possible misinterpretations, let us briefly go through some of the claims that we are *not* making and thus respond to some objections and questions that have sometimes been raised against the primacy we give to arguments. These, we think, rest on some persistent confusions which we hope to dispel. Some of these confusions rest on a failure to distinguish between the actualities of political discourse and normative models of what political discourse should be like, between a descriptive and normative level of analysis. Others arise from a mistaken conception of human rationality in which reasoning (hence argumentation) seems to play no part and the way in which power (and structural factors) can limit capacities for human agency is equally misunderstood. Others emerge from a misunderstanding of the nature of practical reasoning, from failing to grasp its relation to the genre of deliberation, as well as its relation to the world of human evaluative and emotional concerns.

First, let us briefly define a few recurring terms, which we will define in more detail later on. *Deliberation* is an argumentative *genre* in which practical argumentation is the dominant mode of argumentation. Deliberation is therefore a genre, while argumentation (including practical argumentation) can be called a 'pre-genre' (Swales 1990), but is more adequately defined in theories of argumentation either in terms of its premise–conclusion *structure* or as an *activity* of giving and receiving reasons, of justifying and criticizing claims, or a complex *speech act*. *Practical reasoning* is the mental process that corresponds to the *practical argument* as linguistic object, as premise–conclusion set.

We are *not* saying that political discourse consists only of argumentation. Other, non-argumentative genres have a significant presence in politics: narrative, description and explanation. The primacy of (practical) argumentation is a matter of its relationship to these other pre-genres which are typically embedded within (or subordinated to) it. For example, as we have indicated, descriptions, narratives or explanations of the context of action (e.g. the crisis) provide premises in practical arguments. Nor are we saying that argumentation in political discourse is always and only practical. Arguments supporting a view of how the world *is* are also common in political discourse, but again they tend to be embedded within or subordinated to practical argumentation, as the purpose of political discourse is ultimately not to describe the world but to underpin decision and action.

A particularly confused objection to an argumentative approach to political discourse goes along these lines: there is no actual deliberative democracy, no genuine democratic deliberation in politics, therefore politics does not involve argumentation/deliberation. This is obviously mistaken. In saying that deliberation is the primary genre of political discourse, we are making a descriptive statement. The structure of practical reasoning, even when an agent deliberates alone, typically involves a 'weighing' of considerations for and against a proposed action (i.e. reasons that support both the claim for action and its opposite). *Any* practical argument which involves such a balancing of reasons is an instance of deliberation (as Aristotle also saw). However, not all instances of deliberation are 'good' examples of deliberation: in both single-agent and multi-agent contexts, insufficient consideration of relevant reasons for and against a proposal may lead to a hasty, unreasonable decision. Nor is all deliberation *democratic* deliberation in the normative sense which presupposes equality of access, freedom from various constraints, etc. In saying that decisions are based on deliberation, we are *not* therefore saying that political decisions are actually made on the basis of deliberation involving all those who are affected by them, or that all participants, including ordinary citizens, have an equal chance to contribute to such deliberation, or that all relevant reasons are considered and impartially weighed. Deliberation in politics often falls short of normative standards but *it is deliberation*, hence argumentation, nonetheless. Nor are we saying that political deliberation is inherently tied to consensus or that disagreements are (or can) be resolved in practice. On the contrary, deliberation in politics is implemented in activity types (such as parliamentary debate) that are designed to lead to a reasonable and legitimate outcome precisely in the absence of consensus and disagreement resolution. We accept that 'deliberative democracy' is a normative model in politics, but we certainly do not claim that actual politics is normally consistent with that model; however, this does not mean that the nature of political discourse is not fundamentally argumentative and deliberative.

A related and persistent misconception is that it is not argumentation, not reason, but power which determines what decisions are taken, hence the study of argumentation in politics is pointless. We are of course *not* saying that political decision-making and action are always determined by the force of the better argument rather than by reasons having to do with power interests, but a bald opposition between reason and power makes no sense. Certainly those with power use their power to dominate the process of political decision-making and to take action on the basis of their interests. Nevertheless, their decisions are still based upon judgements which they arrive at on the basis of practical reasoning. Reasons for favouring certain lines of action rather than others may include such goals as holding onto power or increasing it, so power can be and often is itself *a reason for action*. If a decision is made not on the strength of the better argument but on the basis of power factors, we could say that 'bad', unacceptable reasons have prevailed, but these would still be *reasons* in a reasoning process. An unreasonable argument is still an argument. Whatever the quality of agents' reasons, whether the force of the better argument or unreasonable power considerations prevail, decision-making processes are argumentative in nature.

We also want to argue against a tendency (in discourse analysis) to declare normative models of argumentation as utopian, as unrealizable in practice, hence of no value for the discourse analyst or social scientist. On the contrary, standards of good politics are intrinsically related to standards for good argumentation; a normatively legitimate outcome in politics must satisfy standards of good argumentation (Rheg 2009). The conditions of possibility for reasonable argumentation, however, involve the 'higher order' conditions of an actual social and political context, including facts about agents (how competent or cooperative they are) and facts having to do with power: agents may not be free to challenge arguments, or power inequalities may prevent them from doing so (van Eemeren 2009b). The latter are the kind of pre-conditions for democratic public space dialogue that CDA has typically focused on (Fairclough 2000b). On the approach we suggest, they should be seen as affecting the reasonableness of an argumentative (hence political) outcome, as shaping (in ways which the analyst might want to challenge) agents' reasons for action. These reasons are premises of various types in the practical arguments that correspond to agents' practical reasoning.

Another misunderstanding relates to the role of emotion in argumentation. We are *not* saying that judgements and decisions about what to do are determined by reason rather than emotion. It is a mistake to set up reason in opposition to emotion, and to assume that reason is good and emotion is bad, as critical discourse analysts often tend to do. For one thing, not all emotional appeals in arguments are unreasonable or fallacious. Arguments can in fact be made stronger by coupling appeals to *logos* with appeals to *pathos*, as the latter might better achieve adaptation of the argument to the audience. Emotional appeals are not necessarily irrelevant and deceptive but can increase understanding of the issues being argued about. For another, devaluing emotional appeal goes with a mistaken assumption that arguments for action can and should only be based upon premises which assert beliefs about the world. On the contrary, as we argue in Chapter 2, the premises of practical arguments necessarily include what we shall call 'concerns' as well as beliefs, and concerns subsume emotions and emotional dispositions. Without a motivational and emotional investment, no belief could ever lead us to act at all, because nothing would really matter to us.

Finally, we are *not* separating facts from values. We distinguish premises which describe the circumstances of action from premises expressing the goals and values of action. Goals are explicitly informed by our values or concerns: the futures we imagine are in relation to what matters to us, such as the values we are committed to. But the way we perceive the circumstances in which we act is also informed by our values and concerns. The context of action, as a problem, is of course objective, not of our own making, but it can be described or represented in various ways. These alternative ways of representing it can even support radically different claims for action. Facts, in other words, have evaluative content, and can therefore support various normative conclusions.

Outline of chapters

Our main concern in Chapter 1 is to make a case for developing a new approach to political discourse analysis. Political discourse analysis should in our view proceed from a coherent view of the character of politics to an account of what characteristics differentiate political discourse from other sorts of discourse, and develop an approach which seeks to address what is distinctive about politics and about political discourse. We support our criticism of political discourse analysis in its current form through a (necessarily brief) discussion of two existing approaches to political discourse, and we discuss a number of contributions to political theory, both classical (Aristotelian) and modern, to support our claim that giving primacy to practical argumentation and deliberation in political discourse analysis is justified by the nature of politics.

Chapter 2 outlines an original conception of the structure and evaluation of practical reasoning, starting from existing accounts in argumentation theory and philosophy. It also discusses a number of fundamental concepts in argumentation theory and grounds the approach in a critical conception of reasonableness, in which the critical examination or testing of arguments is essential. On the view we propose (building on dialectical theories of argumentation), reasonable decisions (and actions) are likely to emerge from pursuing a dialectically adequate *procedure*, defined in normative terms, in terms of systematic *critical questioning* of all the components of arguments and relations between them.

In Chapter 3 we present an approach to CDA and discuss its relationship to critical social science and the forms of critique associated with it, and then discuss how the analysis and evaluation of arguments as we have presented it in Chapter 2 can increase the capacity of CDA to pursue its aim of extending critique to discourse. We do this by returning to an earlier analysis of part of a speech by Tony Blair (Fairclough 2000a), showing how the analysis is strengthened if we build it around the practical argument which Blair is advancing. We then discuss in more general terms how analysis of practical argumentation fits in with and contributes to normative and explanatory critique, and we look at other concepts that CDA works with (imaginaries, political legitimacy, manipulation, power) from the viewpoint of a theory of argument.

In Chapters 4–6 we move to analysis of practical argumentation in political responses to the crisis. We begin in Chapter 4 with a corpus of policy-making texts, the British Pre-Budget and Budget Reports, delivered annually to the House of Commons by the Chancellor of the Exchequer. We offer a detailed analysis of two of these: the November 2008 Pre-Budget Report delivered by Alistair Darling, Chancellor of the Exchequer in the Labour government led by Gordon Brown, and the May 2010 Emergency Budget report delivered by George Osborne, Chancellor of the Exchequer in the current government led by David Cameron. These reports mark different significant stages in the development of UK government strategy for responding to the crisis. We carry out an analysis and evaluation of these reports using the approach introduced in Chapter 2. We take as our object of analysis and evaluation not just the reports themselves, but also reactions to and evaluations of the reports by other participants in the public debate over government strategy (politicians, economists and journalists). We relate analysis and evaluation of argumentative political discourse to normative and explanatory critique.

Chapter 5 focuses on how concerns, including interests and desires, on the one hand, and moral values, duties, commitments, on the other, motivate action and enter as premises in practical arguments, by looking at a fragment of the wide-ranging public debate on whether or not bankers should continue to receive bonuses. We will see that various claims for action that have been made on this subject are underlain by either interest (in what we shall call prudential arguments) or by moral–political values such as justice and equality (in moral arguments). The latter are external reasons for action, which agents often view as reasons which should not be overridden. We develop this discussion in the final section of Chapter 6 where we discuss political promises as such reasons.

Finally, in Chapter 6 we discuss deliberation in parliamentary debate, a multi-agent institutional context where a political decision has to be arrived at. We focus on the debate in the House of Commons on the government's proposal to raise university tuition fees. We outline the main argument developed in the debate by the supporters and opponents of the motion; we show how the arguments were evaluated by the participants themselves and suggest our own evaluation. We also discuss institutional constraints on deliberation in the institutional context of parliament and how these constraints, arising from the nature of politics, lead to a contextualized view of the reasonable aims and possible outcomes of political deliberation.

In the Conclusions chapter, we pull together the strands of the arguments we have developed throughout the book and try to synthesize our main contributions to CDA, to argumentation theory and to the analysis of political discourse in social-political science.

1 Political discourse analysis and the nature of politics

This book presents a new approach to the analysis of political discourse. Its novelty resides in the integration of critical discourse–analytical concepts with the analytical framework of argumentation theory, on the basis of viewing political discourse as primarily argumentative discourse. It is based on a view of politics in which the concepts of deliberation and decision-making in contexts of uncertainty, risk and persistent disagreement are central. This is a view of politics in which the question of *action*, of *what to do*, is the fundamental question. In accordance with the critical conception of reasonableness that underlies our approach, we will define a *reasonable* decision as one which has emerged from a reasonable (dialectical) procedure, i.e. from the *systematic critical testing* of reasons, claims and arguments for action. This chapter includes a brief discussion of the current state of play in political discourse analysis and a discussion of political theory which supports the particular approach we advocate.

In our view, although some very interesting work has been done in political discourse analysis, this research area has not so far developed a clear distinction between political discourse and other sorts of discourse, or an agenda, a set of objectives, theoretical categories, and methods of analysis which would clearly distinguish political discourse analysis from other areas of discourse analysis and enable principled, systematic evaluation. To achieve this, we think, it is necessary to work from a coherent view of the nature of politics. Political discourse analysts have in many cases sought to do this, but have tended to end up with views of politics in which the question of *representation* is central, as opposed to the questions of *decision-making* and *action*, which should be in focus in our view. Of course, establishing a view of politics is not a simple matter, because there are many different views in political theory. But what we are suggesting is that there is a need for more reflection about the connection between views of politics, views of political discourse and analytical approaches to political discourse. Our own approach, which gives primacy to analysis of practical reasoning in political discourse analysis, is grounded in a view of politics which has a strong basis in classical and modern political thinking and theory.

Regarding the definition of political discourse analysis (or PDA), we adopt van Dijk's (1997b) definition, as well as his view on the significant contribution PDA can make to political science. As van Dijk observes, critical discourse analysis practitioners see the analysis of political discourse as an essentially critical enterprise. PDA is therefore understood as the analysis of political discourse from a critical perspective, a perspective which focuses on the reproduction and contestation of political *power* through political discourse, and this definition can be taken to underlie our own approach in the chapters that follow. We also adopt van Dijk's characterization of political discourse as attached to political *actors* – individuals (politicians, citizens), political institutions and organizations, engaged in political *processes* and *events* – and his emphasis that a notion of *context* is essential to the understanding of political discourse. This means that, outside political contexts, the discourse of politicians or any other 'political actors' is not 'political'. For us, as we shall argue in the chapters that follow, this is because political contexts are *institutional* contexts, i.e. contexts which make it possible for actors to exert their agency and empower them to act on the world in a way that has an impact on matters of common concern. The institutional dimension is obvious in the case of such political contexts as parliament or government (see Chapters 4 and 6 of this book), but is also present in more weakly institutionalized contexts, such as internet discussion forums (which we illustrate in Chapter 5), where citizens avail themselves of their *right* to publicly criticize government policy for failing to meet legitimate *commitments* and *obligations*. Rights, obligations and commitments are elements of the institutional fabric of society, of its deontology, and – as we shall see, it is this deontology that provides (or should provide) agents with some of their reasons for action. The prominence we give in this book to *politics as action* should be understood against the background of human institutional reality, and the possibilities it offers agents to work towards the cooperative resolution of conflict.

We agree with van Dijk that PDA can have a lot to offer political science and can contribute to answering genuine political questions, but only if – as he observes – it focuses on features of discourse which are *relevant* to the purpose or function of the political process or event whose discursive dimension is being analysed (van Dijk 1997b: 38). In our view, focusing on the structure of argumentation in a political speech is relevant in precisely this sense, as the purpose of the speech, what it is designed to achieve, may be to convince an audience that a certain course of action is right or a certain point of view is true, and this is the *intended perlocutionary effect* that is intrinsically associated with the speech act of argumentation. Likewise, being able to analyse the structure of a practical argument is indispensible (as our analyses will hopefully show) to being able to evaluate it critically in a systematic, rigorous manner, something that political scientists would also want to do. Understanding the argumentative nature of political texts is therefore key to being able to evaluate the political strategies they are a part of.

We shall begin with a discussion of classical thinking on the relationship between politics and language, specifically Aristotle's view of politics, which has been a point of reference for many political theorists and a number of political discourse analysts. We shall then discuss some recent contributions to political discourse analysis. Our objective is not to give a comprehensive overview of this area of study, which would be beyond the scope of this book, but to refer to two influential contributions in order to support our claim that current work tends not to provide a sufficiently clear distinction between political discourse and other types of discourse or to establish an agenda and set of objectives for political discourse analysis which clearly distinguishes it from other forms of discourse analysis. We shall then turn to political theory, starting from a recent attempt to define a broad and inclusive conception of politics through identifying common ground in a wide range of definitions of politics, and showing how the approach to political discourse analysis which we are advocating arises out of such a conception of politics.

Aristotle

What did Aristotle have to say about the relationship between politics and language? The following is a well-known extract from his *Politics*:

> But obviously man is a political animal in a sense in which a bee is not, or any other gregarious animal. Nature, as we say, does nothing without some purpose; and she has

endowed man alone among the animals with the power of speech. Speech is something different from voice, which is possessed by other animals also and used by them to express pain or pleasure . . .. Speech, on the other hand, serves to indicate what is useful and what is harmful, and so also what is just and what is unjust. For the real difference between man and other animals is that humans alone have the perception of good and evil, just and unjust, etc. It is the sharing of a common view in *these* matters that makes a household and a state.

(1253a 1–18, Ackrill 1987)

Aristotle makes a connection between man's political nature and the power of speech (Greek *logos*); the text seems to imply that the 'purpose' of the human power of speech (see the second sentence) is to do with man's political nature. He characterizes speech as 'serving to indicate what is useful and what is harmful, and so also what is just and what is unjust'. This is similar to a passage in the *Rhetoric* where Aristotle distinguishes three genres of rhetoric: deliberative, forensic and epideictic (*Rhetoric* 1358b, Lawson-Tancred 1991), which differ in the function of the audience, time-orientation, and objective. In deliberative or political rhetoric, one deliberates about public affairs, about what to do – what we should choose or avoid. In forensic or legal rhetoric, one seeks to defend or condemn someone's actions. In epideictic or ceremonial rhetoric one is concerned primarily with praising or discrediting another person or action. In deliberative rhetoric, an assembly of citizens are 'judging' questions about the future, 'for it is about what is to be' that the deliberator deliberates (and this differs from legal rhetoric, whose orientation is towards past events). The objective of deliberative rhetoric is to exhort towards or to dissuade from a course of action, depending on whether it is judged to be useful ('advantageous') or harmful. The function which Aristotle attributes in a general way to speech (*logos*) in the section from the *Politics* is attributed here to a specific type of rhetoric, deliberative rhetoric.

We also need to include Aristotle's *Nicomachean Ethics* to get a clear picture of his view of the relationship between politics and language. In the *Ethics*, Aristotle characterizes politics as *action in pursuit of the highest good, based upon decisions, which arise out of deliberation* (1094a, 1094b, 1111b, 1112a, 1112b, 1113a). According to him, we deliberate about actions which are within the scope of our own agency:

We deliberate about what is up to us, that is to say about the actions that we can do . . . no Spartan for instance, deliberates about how the Scythians might have the best political system. Rather, each group of human beings deliberates about the actions that they themselves can do. . . . we deliberate about what results through our agency.

(1112a 30–1112b 5)

Moreover, deliberation takes place 'where the outcome is unclear and the right way to act is undefined'; and we 'enlist partners in deliberation on large issues when we distrust our own ability to discern [the right answer]' (1112b 5–15). Furthermore, 'we deliberate not about ends, but about what promotes ends', i.e. about means:

A doctor, for instance, does not deliberate about whether he will cure, or an orator about whether he will persuade, or a politician about whether he will produce good order . . . .. Rather, we lay down the end, and then examine the ways and means to achieve it. If it appears that any of several [possible] means will reach it, we examine which of them will reach it most easily and most finely; and if only one [possible] means reaches it, examine how that means will reach it, and how the means itself is reached, until we come to the first cause, the last thing to be discovered.

(1112b 10–20)

Deliberation is closely tied in with decision: 'What we deliberate about is the same as what we decide to do, except that by the time we decide to do it, it is definite; for what we decide to do is what we have judged [to be right] as a result of deliberation' (1113a 1–10). (All references above are to the Irwin 1999 translation.)

It would seem then that, if we are to be guided by Aristotle towards a view of what distinguishes political discourse from other sorts of discourse, the political genre of deliberation ought to be given primacy. Deliberation is, as we shall argue below, an argumentative genre in which the main type of argumentation is practical reasoning. Moreover, if deliberation is an essential part of politics, then political analysis must include analysis of discourse, and particularly of argumentation.

Political discourse analysis: two current approaches

In this section we shall briefly refer to two well-established and influential contributions to political discourse analysis. Our main objective is to show how they differ from our approach and what our approach can bring that is new. Both approaches seem to give primacy to analysis of *representations*, not to the question of action. Our approach, being grounded in a view of politics where questions about decision and action are the fundamental questions, will see ways of representing reality as subordinated to the question about what to do, to action.

Chilton (2004) is an important and original treatment of political discourse analysis which is widely referred to. It is strongly anchored in cognitive science and cognitive linguistics, and is thus able to offer interesting insights on the relationship between language and politics from a cognitive and evolutionary perspective. Apart from a brief discussion (in Chapter 3) of political action as verbal action by means of performing speech acts, it does not include a view of politics as action and focuses mainly on the ways in which actors represent reality. Unlike our approach, Chilton's approach does not treat political discourse as fundamentally argumentative and deliberative in nature, but the discussion of representations could in principle be integrated within an account of deliberation and action. (In more recent contributions, Chilton (2010) has begun to develop the 'language-ethics interface' in a way that is grounded in Habermas's theory of communicative action, and this development, we find – while not focusing on argumentation – is broadly compatible with our approach.)

In the final chapter ('Towards a theory of language and politics'), Chilton summarizes his view of political discourse in terms of a list of twelve propositions (Chilton 2004: 198–205). These include some interesting claims that can be taken up in political discourse analysis, particularly if one pursues questions of representation (e.g. metaphors and binary distinctions are frequent in politics, political discourse draws on spatial cognition, political representations are sets of role-players and relations, etc.). The list does not include references to deliberation (argumentation) or to decision and choice as leading to action, which are in our view central features of political discourse (or political, deliberative rhetoric, in Aristotle's sense). The focus being proposed is therefore different from ours.

Chilton begins with a discussion of Aristotle's passage on man as a political animal in the *Politics*, which we have also quoted above, which he sees as linking together 'the main ingredients of a theory of politics and language that will serve as framework for practical analysis of political discourse' (Chilton 2004: 199). We suggest starting instead from Aristotle's views on politics in the *Rhetoric* and the *Nicomachean Ethics*. These show that Aristotle's view of the relation between politics and language is itself founded upon a coherent view of the nature of politics: *politics is action in pursuit of the highest good, based upon decisions, which arise out of deliberation*. Deliberation, decision and action are crucial in Aristotle's view and also in the account we propose in this book, but they are not in focus in Chilton's approach to political discourse. The focus on representations, particularly from a cognitive linguistics perspective, is nevertheless extremely interesting and could complement the focus on action that we advocate as primary. In our own approach we show how representations (including metaphors and other forms of rhetorically motivated representations) provide *premises in arguments for action*, and how representation issues can therefore be integrated within an account of action.

The important question of the relationship between cooperation and conflict in politics is interestingly addressed by Chilton, who refers here to political theory and notes that there are two 'strands' in definitions of politics within political studies: on the one hand, politics is a struggle for power; on the other hand, it is cooperation to resolve clashes of interest. He links this distinction to a pragmatic argument that 'non-cooperation' (lying, deceiving, dominating, etc.) in communication is possible only because there is a tacit presupposition of cooperativeness in communication. (We also propose, as we show later on, to draw on a theory of speech acts, but we link the constitutive rules of types of speech acts, in Searle's sense, or the rational presuppositions of discourse, in Habermas's sense, to a conception of reasons for action.) The question of cooperation and conflict is prominent in political theory as well, and contemporary political theory might provide a better starting point for understanding its implications for political discourse analysis. In our view, we need to move *from* political theory, from an understanding of how democratic deliberation can be at once cooperative and conflictual (and thus try to resolve disagreement or settle it in other ways if resolution is not possible), to ways of analysing and evaluating it which allow us to take these characteristics into account. The way we attempt to do this in this book is by developing an account of the genre of political deliberation which emphasizes its adversarial character, but also shows how it feeds into cooperative decision-making within institutional practices that are designed for this purpose. The normative model of evaluation of argumentation is thus contextualized in each institutional setting given the goals of institutions and a variety of institutional constraints. We find Chilton's focus on the question of cooperation and conflict to be very important and we suggest addressing it more specifically in terms of a theory of argumentation and deliberation. People's arguments are based on different but often reasonable values and value hierarchies (normative priorities), which often turn out to be hard or impossible to reconcile, and political deliberation has to find ways of dealing with these differences, while democracy has to set up institutions that can accommodate them.

Another political discourse analyst who has made a highly influential contribution is Ruth Wodak (for example Wodak 2009a, 2009b; Wodak and de Cillia 2006). Together with Martin Reisigl, she is the most prominent exponent of the discourse-historical approach (DHA). In DHA, the field of politics is viewed as segmented into a number of 'fields of action': 'lawmaking procedures; formation of public attitudes, opinion, and will; party-internal formation of attitudes, opinion, and will; inter-party formation of attitudes, opinion, and will; organization of international/inter-state relations; political advertising; political executive and administration; political control'. Each field of action is associated with a distinct set of political sub-genres (Wodak 2009a: 41, originally Reisigl and Wodak 2009: 91).

The taxonomy provided is presumably not meant to be exhaustive, as sub-genres that are most obviously oriented to action (e.g. parliamentary debates or consultations within government) are not included. Overall, this approach is classificatory or taxonomic, and it gives a persuasive picture of the sheer diversity of political discourse. However, taxonomical approaches can also lead to a rather atomistic view of politics and political discourse as a series of parts, without a coherent account of the character of the whole, without an indication of what is common to all these fields of action, or why it is that they can be classified as such and what enables agents to act on the world by participating in these sub-genres. While recognizing the potential value of an approach like Wodak's or Reisigl's, our approach to the diversity of political discourse is different. We identify a range of activity types (such as parliamentary debate, government report), implementing a limited number of argumentative genres (in this case, deliberation; another example could be negotiation) and each oriented towards a normative goal, where what is possible to achieve (hence reasonable) is constrained by the institutional context and the rationale of the institution in question, e.g. what it is designed to achieve. We can see these activity types as associated with fields of action in the sense that they all involve practical argumentation, a process in which agents give and receive reasons that attempt to justify or criticize a proposal for action which can subsequently ground decision and action.

Wodak (2009a) begins by discussing a very interesting example, a quote from a 2000 speech by Romano Prodi (former president of the European Commission) – 'The challenge is to radically rethink the way we do Europe. To re-shape Europe' – and observes (in a way that is compatible with our approach) that the 'doing' aspect of politics is important, and so are political 'visions'. She nevertheless does not view this quote as making an argument in which the 'vision' itself can be taken as a reason (premise) supporting the claim for action (as we would suggest, if we were to analyse the same example), but instead relates the 'vision' to Bourdieu's theory of the political field, i.e. to a view of 'politics as a struggle to impose the legitimate principle of vision and division' (Wodak 2009a: 1). In other words, politics seems to be about imposing representations and about how representations serve power, but there is no indication about how this can occur. Later on, in analysing the same quote, Wodak observes that politics is 'intrinsically linked with shaping, thinking and doing' (Wodak 2009a: 29) but once again the connection of representations to action via (practical) arguments is not made, as (obviously) the view of what is distinctive about politics is different.

The approach identifies six dimensions of politics. Briefly, these are said to be: (1) the staging/performance of politics (the front stage); (2) the everyday life of politics and politicians (the back stage, including *politics du couloir*); (3) the impact of politicians' personality (charisma, credibility) on performance; (4) the mass-production of politics (media, advisors, spin-doctors); (5) the recontextualization of politics in the media; (6) participation in politics (i.e. 'power, ideology, gate-keeping, legitimacy and representation') (Wodak 2009a: 24). We agree these are all interesting aspects of politics that are worth studying. What we attempt to do, however, is work from a *definition* of what is characteristic about politics (which we take from political theory) towards a view of what is distinctive about political discourse. To Wodak's dimensions of politics, we would want to add the one feature which is crucial in our view, namely that *politics is oriented towards decision-making that can ground action*. Decisions are taken in conditions of disagreement, uncertainty and risk, which make *deliberation* with others, and ideally democratic deliberation, essential in arriving at a *reasonable* decision. Although, as we have said, not all arguments are good arguments, and actual deliberation often falls short of a normative ideal, political discourse is none-the-less fundamentally argumentative and – being geared to choice and action – deliberative.[1]

The analytical framework of the DHA is different from ours; it either involves different concepts (e.g. '*topos*') or a different understanding of concepts which we also use ('argumentation', 'strategy'). For Reisigl and Wodak (2001: 46, 2009: 94), *argumentation is a strategy*, more precisely a 'discursive strategy'. They list, for example, five such strategies: nomination (reference); predication; argumentation; perspectivation (involvement); intensification (mitigation). (These are, moreover, said to be 'strategies of positive self-presentation and 'negative other presentation', which supports our view that, in current approaches, political discourse is primarily about *representation*, not action.) Strategies of argumentation are said to be realized linguistically by *topoi* and fallacies; strategies of nomination by 'membership categorization devices', metaphors, and so on. In our approach, unlike in DHA, it would not be possible to see *argumentation* as a *strategy*. Argumentation (a central analytical concept in our approach) is a verbal, social *activity*, in which people attempt to criticize or justify claims; it is a *complex speech act* whose intended perlocutionary effect is convincing an interlocutor to accept a standpoint. Moreover, it would not be possible to see argumentation as an object of the same *order*, or the same *kind*, as 'reference' or 'predication', nor place the latter categories at the same level as (or compare them with) 'perspectivation' or 'intensification', within the same taxonomy, as 'kinds of' strategy. What *we* would say instead is that, in arguing, as in any other (simple) speech acts (assertions, directives, etc.), people *refer* to individuals and objects and *predicate* properties of them: speech acts have a propositional content (as well as having an illocutionary force). Consequently, from the point of view of our approach, and from the perspective of an argumentation theory grounded in a theory of speech acts, it would not be possible to see reference, predication and argumentation as *strategies*, any more than we could describe speech acts as strategies. Given our own theoretical presuppositions, we are therefore unable to use the DHA taxonomy of strategies and we develop our own account of what strategies are, which we briefly explain further on.

Like the approach we propose, DHA also involves an explicit focus on argumentation but the way it does this, while certainly productive and influential, is different from ours. The main and most obvious difference is that there is no argument reconstruction as a basis for analysis and evaluation, hence for the purpose of normative or explanatory critique. In our view, however, a well-grounded critical perspective on political discourse requires argument reconstruction and analysis, as a basis for non-arbitrary evaluation and, if an explicit focus on argumentation is intended, then analysis should be carried out in terms of the analytical framework of some version of argumentation theory. This is why we have developed a way of representing and evaluating practical argumentation, partly drawing on informal logic and pragma-dialectics, and using concepts such as validity, soundness, argument scheme, etc.

DHA is also different from our approach in the use it makes of the Aristotelian concept of *topos*. (This is a fundamental analytical concept in DHA, and extensive taxonomies of *topoi* are provided based on surveying large samples of text.[2]) *Topoi* in DHA are sometimes highly abstract ('comparison', 'definition', 'consequence') and could, in accordance with the classical Aristotelian view, yield arguments with any conceivable content, but sometimes they are very specific in content ('*topos* of culture', of 'humanitarianism', the '*topos* of constructing the hero', '*topos* of finance', of 'burden', of the 'threat of racism', etc.). Our approach to political discourse does not use the concept of *topos* at all; instead we speak of *argumentative schemes*, e.g. the scheme we propose for practical reasoning, as ways of connecting premises to conclusions. However, we could, if we wanted, say that argumentation from negative consequences (widely involved in deliberation) involves a *topos* of consequence. In so doing, we would be in accordance with the classical Aristotelian view, as we would not go further than identifying an *abstract pattern* that can connect a premise to a claim, an *argumentative scheme*, a *warrant* (in Toulmin's 1958 sense). But we would not *also* designate as *topoi* all the *specific* types of negative consequences that may be cited in various arguments for or against a particular (political) action (i.e. negative effects on human well-being, unemployment, undesirable moral consequences, financial loss, etc.). In our view, a premise of the form 'if the action is taken, then the goals will not be achieved' can be viewed as a *topos* of negative consequence, but the sundry possible manifestations of negative consequences are not themselves *topoi*. In this respect we differ from the approach taken in DHA, which identifies a wide range of *topoi* at a very detailed concrete level. This may have the advantage of keeping a close focus on the particularities of the text, but also has the disadvantage of obscuring the (small number of) abstract argumentative schemes that lie behind particular arguments, their character as abstract *place-holders* for any conceivable content.[3]

Our understanding of strategies is also different. The treatment of 'strategies' is in fact a clear case where we should proceed from a view of politics to the distinctive character of political discourse, and then to developing an analytical approach. 'Strategy' has been recognized as an important concept and category in political and political-economic theory. Hay (2007: 67) suggests that one key feature of politics is 'the capacity for agency'; he notes that 'emphasizing agency . . . serves to bring out the strategic dimension of politics' and that, 'in so far as it involves reflexive actors', politics 'is, or has the capacity at any point to become, strategic'. The development and pursuit of political strategies, with the ultimate goal of transforming the world in particular ways, is an essential feature of political action. A strategy, on the account we develop in this book, can be understood as a plan of action for achieving a particular goal, involving sequences of means–goals relations. A goal (as we argue in Chapter 2) is a future *state of affairs* to be achieved by means of action, starting from an actual situation (usually perceived as a problem). Strategies have a partly discursive character: they are developed and formulated in discourse, and their goals (we argue later) can be conceived as discursive 'imaginaries' (Jessop 2002) and seen as future states of affairs that agents want to bring about by means of action.

However, although strategies have a partly discursive character, we would not treat 'strategy' as a discursive category. 'Strategy' is a category within theories of action, not within theories of discourse. It is *action* and, in the case of politics, political action, that may be strategic, not discourse in itself. Language is, of course, a form of action, as speech act theory has long recognized, but strategies (we argue) involve goals which are *outside* and *beyond* discourse, i.e. they involve desired *changes in the world*, not in discourse. Speech act theory can also be taken to make the same point, in talking for instance about the 'world-to-word' direction of fit of directive or commissive speech acts. The goal of performing such speech acts is an extralinguistic goal, i.e. to change the world so that it matches the orders we give or the promises we make. The 'discursive strategies' theorized in the approaches to political discourse analysis we have referred to are not strategies in the action-theoretical sense discussed above, and their goals or objectives are not goals in the sense above, as they are not future states of affairs in the world.[4]

From our perspective, then, argumentation cannot be viewed as a 'discursive' strategy in itself (as in DHA); nor can we speak about 'discursive strategies' in general. This is because, as we have said, strategies involve goals *outside* discourse, i.e. changes in the world. Moreover, it would not be possible to speak of 'discursive strategies' *as well as* political and economic strategies, or of 'discursive imaginaries' *as well as* political and economic imaginaries. In our view, changing the world so that it matches a certain political vision (imaginary) is the goal of action (i.e. a future state of affairs *in the world*, which can be described by means of language) and it is partly pursued argumentatively (discursively), by attempting to give agents (or oneself, as agent) reasons for acting in a way that will bring about that change in the real world.

In relation to this extra-linguistic goal, agents formulate strategies, as plans of action, involving sequences of means–goals relations (and sometimes several, coordinated such sequences subordinated to the same goal) where the goals of one action, once achieved (i.e. turned into reality), can become the means to further goals or can create new circumstances of action for further action in pursuit of those goals. Strategies have a discursive dimension in the sense that they are devised in processes of practical reasoning, and formulated in language, but the argumentation that corresponds to this reasoning is not in itself a strategy.

As we have said, the DHA approach is (in our view) primarily taxonomical, not analytical (at least not in the sense of analysis that we advocate) and this is a significant way in which it differs from ours. We agree that taxonomies, when they are systematic and exhaustive, can be useful and illuminating. But the disadvantage of a taxonomical approach, in general, in our view, is that it can lead to an enormous proliferation of categories of analysis, which may be so particular and detailed that they prevent a synthetic grasp of the nature of the object of study rather than facilitating it.[5] We are, however, not averse to taxonomies and we do draw on a number of them ourselves, particularly those of speech act theory (Searle 1969, 2010) and pragma-dialectics (van Eemeren and Grootendorst 1992, 2004; van Eemeren 2010); we have opted for them because, in our view, they provide systematic accounts of the relationship between language and *action* based on unambiguous and consistent principles of classification.

The approaches to political discourse that we have looked at, while very interesting and highly influential in their own right, are very different from the approach we suggest. This is because their underlying presuppositions and conceptual frameworks are different. In contrasting these approaches with ours and trying to highlight compatibilities and incompatibilities, we are not of course questioning the legitimacy of the particular focus on political discourse that they have chosen to pursue, but merely trying to clarify what our own approach is trying to do, given its grounding in a view of politics as oriented to action and underlain by practical reasoning. This is a view we take from both Aristotle and contemporary political theory. Let us now turn to how the nature of politics is discussed in political theory.

Political theory on the nature of politics

Political theory is concerned both with what politics is like and with what politics ought to be like; it is both descriptive and normative. The two are not entirely separate, because political actors in actual politics constantly evaluate political action against normative standards, assessing for instance what actually happens in (what are recognized as) political democracies against standards of what democracy ought to be like. This feature of politics must in our view be carried over into our accounts of political discourse and our ways of analysing political discourse, which does not always happen in political discourse analysis. In our approach, practical argumentation and deliberation are analysed descriptively but also evaluated in terms of normative standards, and we include in our account the ways in which political actors themselves evaluate political action against normative standards ('lay normativity') as well as the external analytical normativity of our approach.

We start our discussion of political theory with a book by Colin Hay (2007). Hay gives a list of twelve current definitions of politics or 'the political'. According to one, for instance, 'politics is concerned with the distribution, exercise and consequences of power'. Another definition sees politics as a 'set of processes and rituals' through which citizens may 'participate . . . in the process of government'. Yet another views it as a 'process of public deliberation and scrutiny of matters of collective concern' (Hay 2007: 61–62). There are sharp differences between these definitions, but Hay suggests that it is nevertheless possible to identify certain common elements which provide a basis for building 'a broad and inclusive conception of politics'. He identifies four features of politics which are common to these definitions: politics as choice, as the capacity for agency, as deliberation, and as social interaction.

All of the definitions of politics cited by Hay see political action as occurring only in situations where alternative choices might be made; if there are no alternatives, there is no politics. Politics is about making choices and decisions about what to do, what action to take in response to a situation. It is typically about making decisions is a context of scarcity: there are never enough resources to do everything, or to do what everyone wants. Politics can therefore be seen as being about the allocation of scarce resources, about 'Who Gets What, When, How?' (Lasswell 1958). In complex modern societies, there are fundamental differences of interests, purposes and values, and making decisions is therefore almost invariably an adversarial process in which participants advocate conflicting lines of action. Furthermore, political choices are characterized by uncertainty: both the nature of the situation we are responding to and how the choices that we make will affect or change the situation are inherently uncertain. This adds to the controversial character of political choices, because different agents and groups will interpret the situation in different ways, and advocate different possible lines of action in response to it even when they agree on the goals; most often there is also disagreement on the goals of action and underlying values, and on which value or goal should be given priority. Finally, political choices have to be made with greater or lesser urgency: faced with a situation of crisis, responsible political agents must act quickly, and they have to act in spite of uncertainty and controversy. Politics is premised on the capacity for agency, the capacity of actors to make a difference, to change things. Agency implies strategy: actors or groups of actors have the capacity to develop and pursue strategies for changing things in particular directions.

A similar conception is outlined by Garner (2009), who begins by citing a popular definition of politics as the process by which groups representing divergent interests and values make collective decisions. As societies are diverse, there will always be a need for a mechanism whereby different interests and values are reconciled. As scarcity is also an inevitable characteristic of all societies, the mechanism of politics is needed to decide how goods are to be distributed. Politics is then essentially a mechanism for making decisions and several questions can be asked about how political decisions are taken. First, what values are underlying these decisions? Are they informed by a concern for justice or liberty, do they serve the interests of the many or of the few? Second, who makes these decisions? Is it one person or are they made democratically? Are democratic decisions in any way better? Finally, what enables decision-makers to enforce these decisions? Can they enforce them because they have the power to do so? Or is it because they have the legitimate authority to do so? What is the difference between power and authority? (Garner 2009: 2–5.)

Because politics is concerned with decision-making, political discourse is inherently deliberative. As we will argue, deliberation involves weighing reasons in favour of one or several proposals and reasons against. Not all deliberation is 'good' or reasonable, in the sense of adequately considering and balancing as many relevant considerations as possible, and not all deliberation is democratic: it is often the case that (not necessarily unreasonable) decisions are taken by very small groups of agents on behalf of many, with no democratic participation. However, the process of arriving at a decision, to the extent that it involves a minimal weighing of options, is deliberative and argumentative in nature. We will have more to say about deliberation in the next chapters, but one possible confusion should be dispelled from the start. To say that political discourse is deliberative is a *descriptive* statement, a statement of fact, and says nothing about how normatively appropriate actual deliberative practices are, either from the normative viewpoint of a theory of argument, or from that of a theory of (deliberative) democracy. Hay also comments on this possible misunderstanding. To say that politics involves deliberation, he says, can be criticized as an 'idealized and distorted depiction' of what actually goes on in politics:

> To define politics in terms of deliberation may entail something of a value judgement – and a positive one at that. But there are a great variety of forms that deliberation may take, some more inclusive and egalitarian, some more exclusive and authoritarian, than others. To associate politics with deliberation is neither to endorse all activity which falls under that rubric, nor to commit ourselves to taking the legitimating rhetoric of formal politics at face value.
>
> (Hay 2007: 69)

Political discourse is therefore deliberative (whenever it is oriented to a normative conclusion and weighs reasons, however minimally), even when it is instantiated by particularly 'bad' or undemocratic examples of deliberation. Disagreements are not always resolved in political deliberation, even in those instances of deliberation which satisfy normative criteria for good deliberative practice, and reaching consensus is not generally an expected outcome, although it is a possible outcome. More commonly, as we shall see in Chapter 6, deliberation terminates in some procedure, such as voting, which determines which proposed course of action will prevail.

Like ancient democracies, modern democracies combine democratic and oligarchic tendencies. Politics could be more democratic, and hence in a sense more properly politics, if public practical reasoning were closer to a normative idea of deliberation than it is in practice. If political decision-making followed on from large-scale public debates, organized so that citizens could contribute substantively to discussions about what the nature of political situations actually is, what values and goals should inform decisions, what possible alternative courses of action and what arguments there are for and against particular courses of action; and if the machinery of decision-making were so designed that these debates could lead to informed decisions which citizens could partake in, then political decision-making practices would be closer to a normative conception than they currently are. There is a tendency for oligarchic forces and interests in modern democracies to represent societies as more democratic than they actually are and to represent deliberation as closer to democratic ideals than it is (what Hay alludes to above as 'the legitimating rhetoric of formal politics'). Claims that politics actually *is* democratic deliberation, or that political decisions *are* actually made in ways which arise out of and reflect public debate, may be made descriptively as part of the business of sustaining and legitimizing oligarchic power, and may even come to be taken as mere common sense in some contexts, and work ideologically in helping to sustain the *status quo* and the social relations which constitute it. But we need to be careful not to allow this possibility to blind us to an alternative possibility: that such claims can be advanced normatively as part of an effort to advance democracy.

Many political theorists place the notions of cooperation and conflict at the core of democratic politics. Mouffe (2005: 52), for example, advocates an 'agonistic' view of democracy: 'Democratic dialogue is conceived as a real confrontation. Adversaries do fight – even fiercely – but according to a shared set of rules, and their positions, despite being ultimately irreconcilable, are accepted as legitimate perspectives.' 'Agonistic' politics is an alternative to open antagonism and conflict (and the use of force), and presupposes a measure of cooperation between adversaries. Rancière (1995: 12–13) also discusses the coexistence of cooperation and conflict in relation to what he identifies as 'two origins of the political' offered in Aristotle's *Politics*: the 'good origin' in Book I, which we have referred to, 'the peculiar power of the *logos* to project a sense of the useful and of the harmful into the circle of the community and thereby to usher in a shared recognition of the just and the unjust'; and the 'bad origin' in Book IV – which says that

> the question of politics begins in every city with the existence of the mass of the *aporoi*, those who have no means, and the small number of the *euporoi*, those who have them … two irreducible components, ever virtually at war.

The 'bad origin' of politics bears upon the question of democracy. In Rancière's view, a bad democracy, according to Aristotle, 'is a democracy true to its name, where the *demos* exercises the power', and a good democracy 'comes as close as possible to the ideal regime of the *politeia*' and 'contrives to distance the *demos*'. The art of politics is to reduce the potential for conflict inherent in the division between the *aporoi* and the *euporoi* and in the power of the *demos*, and to accentuate cooperation (Rancière 1995: 15–16). Cooperation is therefore not simply a necessary precondition for democratic dialogue as Mouffe's 'agonistic' understanding of it suggests, but may also be a resource for oligarchies to limit and contain democracy. This suggests that, in analysing democratic debate as a form of practical reasoning, we should not simply be looking to identify shared sets of rules which regulate cooperation, but also looking at how and whether the terms of cooperation are open to being contested and redefined (see Fairclough *et al.* 2006 for discussion of a particular case). It is, as we shall see in Chapter 3, a manifestation of political power that people's perceived preferences and needs are often shaped for them in such a way that conflict, although real, does not even arise, and people passively (and cooperatively) acquiesce in their domination.

Bauman (1999: 78–86) sees democratic politics as the pursuit of freedom or autonomy, and the essence of politics as critical reflection. Autonomy begins with the understanding of the 'inescapably human origins of human institutions', and rejects '*de facto* validity' (the claim that institutions, practices and norms which exist are inherently valid) in favour of '*de jure* validity: validity that is the product of reflection and deliberation'. The search for *de jure* validity 'calls for critical reflection, and refrains from exempting anything, including itself, from it'. Critical reflection is 'the essence of all genuine politics' and politics is 'an effective and practical effort to subject institutions that boast *de facto* validity to the test. Democracy itself is a 'site of critical reflection, which derives its distinctive identity from that reflection'. Bauman advocates a 'reinvention of politics' based on a new forms of collective agency coming from civil society, and involving a reconstruction of public space as a space where issues of common concern can be brought to political attention, where options can be critically examined, questioned and negotiated, as a basis for decision. The 'agora' should be the space where private problems can be 'translated' into public issues and people can use the power of institutions to 'seek collectively managed levers powerful enough to lift [them] from their privately suffered misery' (Bauman 1999: 2–3). This view supports the claim we are making in this book that collective deliberation, involving the critical examination of reasons for action on matters of public concern, is fundamental in politics and political discourse. It also accords with the view (which we take from Searle and develop in the following chapters) of the political context as an *institutional* context which binds agents into a complex deontic network of relations (rights, obligations, commitments, etc.) that provide them with reasons for action. 'Reinventing politics' can thus be interpreted as the effort to ensure that people can actually exert their formally recognized rights or can effectively compel others to abide by their obligations and commitments, for instance that citizens can effectively challenge government decisions on the strength of the state's existing commitment to a set of publicly recognized, legitimate values. We illustrate this point in Chapter 5, by analysing arguments from justice produced by *Guardian* readers in a comments thread.

An 'argumentative turn' in political theory?

For quite a while, a case has been made for an 'argumentative turn' in the field of policy discourse (more specifically, policy planning and analysis) (Fischer and Forester 1993). Policy discourse, as a type of political discourse, has been recognized as fundamentally argumentative, as involving a 'process of deliberation' that 'weighs' together multiple considerations under a multiplicity of interpretative frames (see Dryzek's contribution to Fischer and Forester, Dryzek 1993: 214).

More recently, a persuasive case that analysis of political discourse needs to focus on argumentation, and particularly on the *rhetorical* properties of discourse, has been made in political theory by Finlayson (2007). According to him, political decision-making is distinctive in the way it combines two levels of contingency and uncertainty: 'the uncertainty of the world', the need to act on the basis of incomplete information, not knowing for certain what the nature of the circumstances is, what the best way to act is, or what effects any action may have; and the uncertainty caused by 'the (possibly competitive) presence of others' who think in different ways which include not only conflicting interests but the possibility of a clash of 'first principles', of basic values. Given that the reasons for taking one course of action rather than another may provide more-or-less convincing support for it but never logically determine it, and that there may be good reasons for and against a course of action, and for and against alternatives, practical argumentation with others has an essential role in political decision-making, and analysis of it has an essential role in political analysis. In addition, he observes, the logical properties of arguments are not the only ones that matter: policy-makers and analysts are also engaged in finding those arguments that will effectively persuade various groups of people, in order to create a convergence of interests and views in a world of persistent disagreement. Finlayson argues in fact for the primacy of *rhetorical* analysis: 'democracies are premised on the recognition that people disagree not only about means but about ends and even about the meaning and value of means and ends', and the field of politics abounds in 'problems without solution', in the sense of problems without one obvious solution that everyone might be brought to agree with. Hence, in the absence of indisputable truths, given fundamental uncertainty and risk, divergent interests and value pluralism, the role of rhetoric is essential in convincing others to see things in the same light as we do, so as to produce agreement around a contested claim (Finlayson 2007: 550).

Insights linking political discourse to argumentation in political theory are nevertheless not always as clear as the above observations might suggest. The questions of how policies are 'framed' and 'narrated' are sometimes discussed in studies of policy in political theory, but – as the contributions by Rein and Schön (1993) and Kaplan (1993), respectively, in Fischer and Forester (1993) show – no connection is made between frames or narratives, on the one hand, and arguments or the 'argumentative turn' that these discussions supposedly illustrate, on the other, or between frames or narratives and action. More puzzling still is the occasional conflation of argument and explanation: Parsons (2007) sets out to be an analysis of 'arguments in political science', but focuses entirely on explanations, without any reference to actual arguments. On the whole, there is considerable confusion between argument, explanation, narrative and description (particularly in political science, but also occasionally in critical discourse analysis), and the way in which narratives and explanations can contribute to the justification of a course of action has not so far been theorized. As we suggest later, in deliberative discourse, narrative, description and explanation can be viewed as subsumed to or embedded within arguments. Ways of describing (including 'framing') the situation, of explaining its causes, or of narrating a sequence of events are usually contributing premises to an argument for action, whose conclusion will be supported by certain ways of describing, narrating or explaining, and not others. Epistemic/theoretical arguments (with a descriptive conclusion, about what the situation *is*) are also usually supporting the conclusion of a more general practical argument, and are embedded in arguments about what should be done.

Political theory on deliberative democracy

Deliberation is intrinsic to democracy. According to Kenneth Burke, democracy is 'a device for institutionalizing the dialectical process, by setting up a political structure that gives full opportunity for the use of competition for a cooperative end' (Burke 1973/1941: 444, cited in Williams and Young 2009: 2). The argumentative nature of this competition for cooperative ends manifests itself variously, in public debates and controversies, and is variously aimed at disagreement resolution, compromise, collective decision-making and, on this basis, action.

Democracy can also be seen as a 'mechanism for dealing with disagreement' (Swift 2006: 203). Two conceptions of democracy can be distinguished, based on the way they manage disagreement and interpret the fundamental idea of collective decision and of equal treatment: a *deliberative* and an *aggregative* conception. According to the aggregative conception, decisions are collective and binding when they arise from arrangements that give equal consideration to the interests of each person bound by the decision. According to the deliberative conception, decisions are collective and binding when they emerge from arrangements that establish conditions of free public reasoning among those who are affected by the decision, viewed as equals. In the aggregative model, citizens' preferences are expressed by voting and each vote counts equally. In the deliberative model, citizens' preferences are not only expressed but also transformed through public reasoning, in a process where everyone has the right to advance and respond to reasons, propose issues and solutions for the agenda, and justify or criticize proposals (Cohen 1998: 185–186).

'Deliberative democracy' as a normative ideal means a democratic system where decisions are made by discussion among free, equal and rational citizens. Collective decision-making involves the participation of all those who will be affected by the decision, and this makes decisions legitimate and binding. Participation is by means of arguments (reasons) offered by and to citizens who are committed to the values of freedom, impartiality and rationality. As Elster notes, 'deliberative democracy rests on argumentation, not only in the sense that it proceeds by argument, but also in the sense that it must be justified by argument' and 'arguing is logically prior to all other modes of collective decision-making'. This is because the decision *not* to decide by public deliberation but by some other procedure is itself justified by reasons, therefore argumentatively, whatever those reasons may be, for those who make that decision (Elster 1998a: 9–10).

Supporters of deliberative democracy justify it on grounds of human fallibility. An individual's resources of knowledge and imagination are limited, and by pooling their limited capabilities together, individuals stand a better chance of making a good decision. Deliberating or discussing matters with others will 'lessen or overcome the impact of bounded rationality' (Fearon 1998: 45). Deliberating with others not only reveals information that is relevant for the choice to be made, but enables people to see matters from other people's perspective and encourages a particular mode of justifying claims, not by appeal to self-interest but in terms of the common good or the public interest. In the 'deliberative setting', the use of force-based threats is ruled out, as the only force that should count is the force of the better argument (Elster 1998b: 103). As a side-effect, deliberation develops civic virtues: public reasoning as social practice produces better and more informed citizens, with an increased sense of responsibility for a shared community. Independently of any positive consequences, however, deliberation is good in itself because it produces politically legitimate decisions. They are legitimate because they are the outcome of a fair procedure, which gives everyone (including those who will in the end disagree with the outcome) the right to advance and respond to reasons and to understand, given that reasoning is public and not private, why a certain choice was made. Those who will disagree with the outcome will see that the result was not arbitrary but justifiable. Deliberation thus tends to produce outcomes that are seen as more legitimate than those produced by voting. This is because, for one thing, public reasoning tends to produce greater consensus, as more people get persuaded that a certain outcome is good by participating in debate and may reshape their preferences (if voting takes place without discussion, this may not happen). For another, the opportunity of expressing one's view will make people more inclined to support the collective decision, even if they might disagree with it in the end (Fearon 1998: 52–60). But a decision arrived at deliberatively will not only be more legitimate, in virtue of the fair procedure, but will tend to be a *better* decision. And this is because, through its cooperative nature, the deliberative procedure is more likely to get things right, to produce better answers to problems than other procedures. Deliberative democracy has 'epistemic value', it can be a way of generating better responses to problems. This can refer to both means and goals: 'deliberation helps us to discover which are the best means to which ends, but it also helps us work out which ends are better than others' (Swift 2006: 216).

Those theorists who are pessimistic about the possibility of achieving deliberative democracy in practice observe that genuine democratic politics is very rare and only occasionally asserts itself over and above power interests. Many obstacles to the feasibility of a deliberative conception are typically acknowledged: social inequalities, power asymmetries, media distortions, public ignorance and apathy. Some are described as 'pathologies of deliberation' (Stokes 1998) and seem to contradict the belief that deliberation improves the quality of decision-making (as people may enter deliberation or cast their vote with 'pseudo-preferences' and 'pseudo-identities' created by powerful private interests). Those who have confidence in deliberative democracy point to the existence of 'outbreaks of democracy' as proof that deliberative democracy is not an impossible dream (Rheg 2009: 12). As Rheg observes, at least on some issues and some of the times, the quality of arguments and the argumentative process does makes a difference in terms of the outcome and of people's assessment of the outcome. Moreover, there is empirical evidence that the norms embodied in the ideal of deliberative democracy sometimes function as a guiding normative framework in actual public deliberation: people orient towards and hold others accountable to norms of reasonable communication, e.g. they criticize politicians for not sufficiently including citizens in deliberation and decision-making, for not thinking through the consequences of their actions, and so on.

It has been suggested (Gaus 2003) that the central problem of modern liberal-democratic societies is: how can shared political principles be justified in a deeply pluralistic world? Following Isaiah Berlin (1990), many liberal theorists start from an acknowledgment of the 'reasonable value pluralism' of modern democratic societies. People are understood as free, equal and reasonable, and as having conflicting philosophies of life, such as a religious or secular, liberal or traditionalist worldview, hence a plurality of rationally incommensurable values. This value pluralism makes it impossible to find a common framework of discussion on the basis of which disagreements might be resolved. According to Gutmann and Thompson (1996), to acknowledge value pluralism is to say that citizens reasoning together might 'recognize that a position is worthy of moral respect even when they think that it is morally wrong'. These are 'deliberative disagreements', disagreements that *can* form the object of an effort to find a morally acceptable way of resolving them in a mutually acceptable way. Not all disagreements are deliberative. If the disagreement were over a proposal to legitimize discrimination against blacks or women, then the same obligation of mutual respect would not arise, and to deliberate over the matter would be inappropriate (Gutmann and Thompson 1996: 3). In what follows we are discussing only *reasonable* value pluralism, pluralism that generates reasonable disagreements that can form the object of public deliberation.

Given the reality of reasonable value pluralism, citizens who deliberate together will have to find reasons that are compelling to other reasonable citizens, of whom many will endorse a different (religious, moral) worldview or radically different political views. According to one view, to require that justifications for political action be acceptable to others is to say that all those who are governed by collective decisions and are expected to govern their own conduct by those decisions must find the *bases* of those decisions, the substantive *political values* that underlie them, acceptable even when they disagree with particular decisions (Cohen 1998: 222). Rawls's theory of justice (1971, 2001) and his version of political liberalism as a framework for democracy were offered as a response to value pluralism. The solution advocated is to leave reasonable conflicting ethical viewpoints in play without trying to adjudicate among them, by providing principles of justice which are *neutral* in the political sense, so that all involved can accept them as offering fair terms of cooperation when viewed from their particular value commitments. Another response to value pluralism is Gray's 'agonistic liberalism' which stresses the need for compromise, for finding a *modus vivendi* among inherently clashing views (Gray 1989, 2000). Yet another response is the 'deliberative' liberal democratic conception defended by Habermas, to which we will briefly refer below.

Dryzek (2000) acknowledges that there is a conflict within theories of deliberative democracy, between those more influential versions which overstate consensus and understate conflict, such as Habermas's (1996a) and Rawls's (1971) proceduralist models of deliberative democracy, and other versions which acknowledge the irreducible value pluralism of modern societies, hence the impossibility of consensus. According to Dryzek, deliberative democracy can be rescued only if deliberation is understood as including not only dialogue oriented to achieving consensus on 'the best available course of action' but also dialogue characterized by conflict over different courses of action based on different interpretations of political situations, different goals and different values, differences which cannot generally be resolved through deliberation.

In his theory of communicative action, Habermas (1984) defines human rationality in relation to the ability to offer reasons or grounds in support of truth claims, normative claims or evaluative claims, and to handle such reasons or grounds that are advanced by other interlocutors. This is why, he claims, the concept of 'communicative rationality' can only be explained adequately in terms of a *theory of argumentation*, understood as the linguistic activity in which participants construct arguments in order to justify or criticize problematic validity claims – e.g. claims that some theoretical statement is true or that some normative statement is appropriate or right:

> We use the term *argumentation* for that type of speech in which participants thematize contested validity claims and attempt to vindicate or criticize them through arguments. An *argument* contains reasons or grounds that are connected in a systematic way with the *validity claim* of a problematic expression.
>
> (Habermas 1984: 18)

Habermas's (1984, 1987, 1990, 1996a) answer to modern pluralism is a *theory of justice*, whose aim is to reconstruct the moral point of view as the perspective from which competing normative claims can be fairly and impartially adjudicated. The justification of norms in the public sphere is tied to reasoned agreement among all those subject to the norm in question. For Habermas (who distinguishes between theoretical, normative and evaluative statements), both theoretical and normative issues hold out the prospect of *rational consensus*. (Unlike these, evaluative questions are subjective and relative in a way in which neither the statements of science nor the normative prescriptions that ought to guide us in our moral–practical life are not.) Habermas's proceduralist model of deliberative democracy views public space dialogue as a 'conversation of justification' (Benhabib 1992: 89) taking place under the constraints of an ideal speech situation, with participants being free and equal, and able to engage in reflexive questioning of previously taken for granted beliefs. In such conditions, agreement would be motivated only by the force of the better argument. The reason why participants engage in 'discourse' (seen as a second-order *argumentative* communication) is to provide justification for a particular contested claim, for instance to justify the validity of a particular norm for action. Moral–practical issues can in principle be settled by way of argumentation, through a procedure which requires all participants in communication to adopt an impartial point of view from which their own particular interests and needs count no more than those of anyone else's. For Habermas, then, moral–practical questions *can* be discussed from a *universal* standpoint of *impartiality* – from a 'moral point of view', which is rooted in the pragmatic presuppositions of rational communication.

Not everyone agrees that Habermasian *consensus* on moral–practical issues is a normative requirement that is compatible with actual democratic societies: the existence of reasonable value pluralism denies that *all* disagreements can be resolved by all parties converging on a single view. Bohman (1996) develops Habermas's proceduralist model, whose normative requirements he finds too strong, in a way that enables him to respond to scepticism about the possibility of deliberative democracy and to take into account the obstacles affecting the possibilities for deliberation: cultural pluralism, which produces deep and persistent moral conflicts; social inequalities, that limit the scope of democratic participation; social complexity, which removes decisions from public spaces where citizens might participate directly and attaches them to complex institutions.

Bohman's (1996) (non-proceduralist) 'dialogical model' of deliberative democracy aims to show how deliberation works to promote agreement and cooperation in conditions of irreducible value pluralism. Deliberation, in Bohman's view, is a 'joint cooperative activity' of exchanging reasons for the purpose of resolving problematic situations. The primary aim of deliberation is to restore cooperation among actors in problematic situations and enable coordination of action. The agents involved in deliberation should be conceived as a plural agent, composed of many agents with different perspectives and interests. The agreement reached will be a plural agreement. The normative ideal of deliberation should not be that all citizens should agree for the same reasons, but that they should *continue to cooperate and compromise* in the same process of public deliberation. A plural agreement means that each side could agree for different reasons. The outcome in this case would be a *moral compromise*, in which the reasons of all parties are recognized and taken up as part of the overall solution (Bohman 1996: 98). Such a solution, on his view, is a form of *mediation*. This, Bohman argues, is a more realistic proposal for dealing with pluralism than either Rawlsian 'overlapping consensus' or acknowledging, with Habermas, that consensus might give way to bargaining and compromise in democratic politics: the former solution brackets away disagreement, while the latter (as *negotiation*) presupposes that some common ground exists, which is often not the case.

The disagreements we will address in the analytical chapters of this book are not 'deep disagreements', they are not rooted in irreconcilable comprehensive conceptions of the good, but are underlain by a shared framework of moral–political values, freedom, equality, justice. They are grounded, rather, in different interests and different normative priorities that agents assign to (broadly shared) values. Such disagreements are still difficult, if not sometimes impossible to resolve, which is why consensus seems an implausible outcome. However, the orientation of participants in such deliberative dialogue is still towards persuading others of the acceptability of their own standpoint as one which is worthy of being accepted by all.

Conclusion

Our main concern in this chapter has been to establish the basis for developing a new approach to political discourse analysis. In our view, political discourse analysis should proceed from a coherent view of the nature of politics to an account of what characteristics differentiate political discourse from other sorts of discourse, and develop an analytical approach which seeks to address what is distinctive about politics.

Throughout the chapter we have sought, both in discussing existing approaches to political discourse and ideas within political theory, to substantiate our claim that giving primacy to practical argumentation and deliberation in political discourse analysis is justified by the particular character of politics and of political discourse. Politics is about arriving cooperatively, and through some form of (collective) argumentation (deliberation), at decisions for action on matters of common concern, it is about what to do in response to public disagreement and conflict (e.g. over such issues as the distribution of scarce social goods) and in response to circumstances and events. It is 'by definition about conflict and its peaceful resolution' (Searle 2010: 162). Politics operates not only in a context of disagreement and conflict, but also in conditions of uncertainty, incomplete information and risk, where what is often required is an immediate decision in response to some problematic situation. All of these constraints can affect the rationality of the decisions that are made. The role of deliberation is therefore crucial: carefully weighing a variety of relevant considerations, and ideally with others, in a democratic setting where a wide range of viewpoints can be expressed and taken into account, will not only produce a legitimate decision in the procedural sense, but will also enhance the rationality of the decision-making process and therefore stand a chance of producing a better, more reasonable decision. The decision will be reasonable as a result of the procedure by which it has been arrived at, even though it may not always be the 'best' decision (given unavoidable time and information limitations and other constraints). Given the undemocratic way in which politics often actually works in liberal democracies, this largely remains a normative ideal, one against which actual practice can be evaluated, and a goal for those who seek to take politics in a more democratic direction.

2   Practical reasoning
A framework for analysis and evaluation

Let us now outline the analytical framework used in this book. We will present our own proposal for the structure of practical reasoning and its evaluation and relate it to existing work in argumentation theory and philosophy. In addition, given that one of our objectives is to familiarize critical discourse analysis (CDA) practitioners with argumentation theory and offer a framework that is sufficiently explicit and detailed as to be practically usable in CDA, we will begin with an introductory discussion of a few fundamental concepts. Readers who are already familiar with argumentation can choose to skip the first three sections.

Practical reasoning and theoretical reasoning

Practical reasoning is reasoning concerning what to do. It arises in response to practical problems which are addressed to us as agents who are acting in particular circumstances and aiming to achieve various goals. By contrast, theoretical (or epistemic) reasoning is reasoning concerning what is or is not true. It arises in response to problems addressed to us as knowers with fallible cognitive capacities, trying to figure out what is the case. Theoretical or epistemic reasons are reasons for believing, while practical reasons are reasons for action. Theoretical reason is guided by a search or need for knowledge, while practical reasoning is guided by a desire or need for appropriate action. There is, therefore, a fundamental difference in purpose, and a corresponding difference in the kind of conclusion that is reached: a conclusion about what we should do, or would be good to do (a normative conclusion), in the light of our circumstances and our goals, and a conclusion about what is (probably) true (a descriptive conclusion), in view of what we know.

Practical reasoning occurs in two basic situations. Sometimes, agents start with an open question: *what should I do*, given the situation I am in and what I want to achieve? For instance, which future career should I choose among various alternatives? At other times, agents are presented with a particular possibility for action (a particular job opportunity), and they have to decide whether to take that option or not (*should I do* A *or not?*), by exploring reasons for and against, such as the probable consequences of taking it. In both situations, practical reasoning involves an imaginative effort to think of as many considerations that might have a bearing on the situation as possible. What does the agent want to achieve? What other goals does he have and how would these be affected by the action in question? What are the agent's values, what are his concerns, what does he care about? Which of these goals, values or concerns would he be willing to sacrifice by doing the action and which would he not? What constraints on his action are relevant to his decision? What might be the positive and negative consequences of the various actions that are open to him? Are there better alternatives for fulfilling his goals?

A frequent confusion is that of assuming that theoretical reasoning occurs only in connection with theoretical, e.g. scientific, matters, while practical reasoning is connected exclusively with everyday practice and decisions, or is a sort of 'practical wisdom' or 'know-how' and is therefore unrelated to theory. This confusion is based on a terminological misappropriation that ignores the way 'practical reasoning' and related terms ('practical reason', 'deliberation') are used in the philosophical tradition beginning with Aristotle. The fact is that we engage in theoretical reasoning in all sorts of trivial everyday situations, for instance when we claim that, based on today's promising weather conditions and the weather forecast, tomorrow will be a sunny day. The reasoning here is 'theoretical' or 'epistemic' because the conclusion aims to (hopefully correctly) describe a future state of the world and, depending on how the weather turns out tomorrow, the utterance will be true or false. If, on the other hand, I argue that, based on what the weather looks like now and my desire not to catch a cold by getting wet, I should take an umbrella when going out, I have engaged in practical reasoning: the conclusion of my argument is about what I should do.

It is of course true that scientists typically engage in theoretical reasoning. Physicists testing out hypotheses or arguing in favour of various claims, e.g. that string theory can adequately unify general relativity and quantum physics, are engaged in this type of reasoning. But scientists also engage in practical reasoning all the time, for instance when they try to figure out what to do in order to fix the flawed mirror of the Hubble telescope. In order to arrive at some decision for action, they would have to reason from a diagnosis of the problem and of the possibilities at their disposal (so theoretical reasoning would be involved as well), as well as from a desire, need or obligation to make the telescope work properly. Clearly then, the difference between theoretical and practical reasoning is not one of content (scientific vs. mundane; knowing that vs. knowing how) or context (academic vs. lay), but one having to do with (a) purpose – arriving at true (or at least rationally acceptable) belief *or* deciding on the right course of action, and (b) the nature of the conclusion: a descriptive or normative conclusion. Both types of reasoning occur in both everyday contexts and in highly specialized professional contexts.[1]

In this book we are using practical reasoning in the sense in which it is used in contemporary argumentation theory and philosophy, for instance in the work of Audi (2006), Walton (1990, 2006, 2007a, 2007b) and Millgram (2005), in the tradition that begins with Aristotle, continues with Kant and Hume and leads a variety of contemporary theories, such as those surveyed by Raz (1978) and Millgram (2001).

Types of argument: deductive, inductive, conductive

An argument is a set of statements (explicit or implicit), one of which is the conclusion (claim) while the others are the premises. The conventional view is that the premises give reasons in support of the conclusion, or attempt to justify the conclusion, and the conclusion purportedly follows from the premises. This definition, focusing on formal *structure*, is used in logical approaches. But argumentation is also understood as a social and rational *activity* of attempting to justify or refute a certain claim, and aiming to *persuade* an interlocutor (a *reasonable* critic) of the acceptability (or unacceptability) of a claim (van Eemeren and Grootendorst 1992, 2004); on this view, argumentation is a *complex speech act*. It is also seen as an inherently *dialogical* or *dialectical social practice*, whose aim is the *rational persuasion* of an interlocutor by giving reasons; in other words, it is 'manifest rationality' (Johnson 2000). The last two definitions, used in dialectical approaches, focus on argumentation as social practice and interaction, and on persuasion as its intended purpose or point. People advance argumentation (give reasons) in order to change other people's beliefs about what is the case or what would be good to do, so a theory of argumentation is inextricably linked with a theory of action, and should be seen (as pragma-dialectics explicitly does) as part of a theory of speech acts (of action by means of language).

Ever since Aristotle, a distinction has been drawn between two types or modes of argumentation: inductive and deductive. In a deductively valid argument, the conclusion *necessarily* (and therefore certainly) follows from the premises: if the premises are true, the conclusion will also be true. It is not possible for the premises to be true and for the conclusion to be false (the premises *entail* the conclusion). But valid deductive arguments can be constructed on false premises: an argument can be *deductively valid* without being *sound*. A *sound* argument, however, is one which is both deductively valid *and* has true premises. The following argument (from Lepore 2000: 11):

> All fish fly.
> Anything which flies talks.
> So, all fish talk.

is deductively valid, because it is not possible both for its premises to be true and the conclusion to be false. If, for some reason, the premises *were* true, then the conclusion would have to be true. However, the argument is not sound (because the premises are *actually* false). Unlike soundness, validity has nothing to do with the actual truth of the premises.

In inductive arguments, we speak not of validity but of inductive strength or force, and not of certainty but of probability. In an inductively strong argument, there is a high *probability* that the conclusion is true, if the premises are true. In other words, given no other information except that contained in the premises, it would be more reasonable to expect the conclusion to be true than to expect it to be false. It is, for instance, very probable that, since most children have loved the *Harry Potter* novels and films, and your child is probably no different from most children in most respects, your child will also love them. It is by no means certain, though: the conclusion of this argument might turn out be false, even from true premises (the argument may be unsound). Your child might turn out to be one of a minority of children who hate *Harry Potter*, while being a typical child in most other respects. Inductively sound arguments are inductively strong arguments with true premises. Unlike deductively sound arguments, they may have false conclusions from true premises (as in this particular example).

In deductive arguments, the major and minor premise are always linked together: each is necessary and together they are sufficient to support the claim. The two premises 'Poirot is Belgian' and 'Belgians are foreigners' are together, and not separately, not independently, supporting the conclusion 'Poirot is a foreigner'. Inductive arguments (e.g. empirical generalizations) exhibit a *coordinative* pattern where several premises of the same type are also linked together: 'Tom likes *Harry Potter*, Alex likes *Harry Potter* novels, Kate likes *Harry Potter*, and so do other children I know, therefore children like *Harry Potter*'. All these premises have to be taken together in order to support the conclusion, as each would be too weak by itself to do so, but each is relevant to the claim. The strength of this inductive argument comes from the enumeration or accumulation of relevant examples: the more children seem to confirm the claim, the stronger its probability. Take away some premises and the argument becomes weaker. By contrast, the deductive validity of the *Poirot* argument above does not depend on anything empirical, but solely on the meanings of the terms. The conclusion is logically contained in the two premises, or the conjunction of the premises deductively entails the conclusion. Take away either of the two premises and the conclusion is not merely weakened but no longer follows from the remaining premise.

A third type of argumentation is sometimes recognized, distinct from either deduction or induction, namely *conductive* argumentation (Bickenbach and Davies 1997; Govier 2001). In conductive arguments, the support pattern is said to be *convergent* (also called *multiple* argumentation) and the premises are put forward as separately or independently relevant to the claim (if they are taken together, the argument will be stronger, but each premise can provide sufficient justification even in the absence of the others). Practical reasoning is usually discussed as an example of such reasoning. As a conductive argument, practical reasoning involves the 'weighing' of *pros* and *cons*, of various considerations that are thought to have a bearing on the claim, and the conclusion is drawn 'on balance'. In conductive argumentation the premises are not of the same kind, as they are in inductive argumentation. Widely different considerations, from different if not altogether incommensurable spheres of life, often seem to be relevant in deciding what to do, and some will be reasons for the conclusion, while others will be reasons against. How well the claim for action is supported will depend on how a certain person will weigh these reasons together and how thoroughly and imaginatively she will explore as many relevant considerations as possible, including different and possibly conflicting goals, likely consequences, moral implications, different conceptualizations of the context of action, coherence with an overall plan of action, including a broad life plan, and so on. The sufficiency criterion for practical arguments, as Bickenbach and Davies (1997: 10) suggest, can be approximated to a Habermasian ideal of 'communicative rationality', i.e. it goes beyond the merely instrumental rationality of finding the best means to one's goals, or the most cost-effective solution, and involves a process of weighing possible goals and values against each other in a process that is as extensive as possible and aims to decide whether what we value or aim for *is worth* valuing or aiming for (we will return to this discussion in discussing reasonableness).

Let us imagine how someone might reason practically when faced with a particular difficult choice. Should the person in question take up a job opportunity in London? She can think of several desirable goals that such an option might enable her to achieve, having to do with a successful and enjoyable academic career, financial rewards, enjoying the cultural attractions of London, being close to certain old friends, and so on. But she can also think of a number of reasons against such a decision, again having to do with other goals that are important, which the decision might have an adverse impact on: other family members would be affected, their lives might be disrupted, existing emotional attachments to places and people would be placed under strain. Such considerations are often impossible to quantify and measure against each other. The agent would have to weigh a multiplicity of considerations in favour and against accepting the job and come up with a conclusion embodying the 'best' option, *on balance*. The situation is particularly difficult where several goals and concerns are all important to the agent, and whatever choice she makes in the end, something important will have to be sacrificed. Confronted with the same choice, and even with exactly the same range of considerations, different people may arrive at different conclusions, depending on what they care about most, what hierarchies of goals and values they have, or what reasons matter comparatively more or *override* other reasons *for them*.

Plausible arguments

Walton (1991, 1992a, 1993, 2001a, 2006, 2007a) has theorized a type of argument which he calls *plausible* argument, distinct from deductive and inductive arguments. Plausible argumentation is based on *presumption* and is therefore in principle *defeasible*: the conclusion is inferred tentatively from the premises, it 'seems' to be true, based on all the evidence available, and is therefore reasonable to believe, but it is subject to defeat by the various particular features of a given situation. A presumption is a 'qualified, tentative assumption of a proposition as true that can be justified on a practical basis provided there is no sufficient evidence to show that the proposition is false' (Walton 2006: 72). For example, drawing a conclusion on the basis of the testimony of a witness may be a reasonable thing to do, but when more compelling evidence comes to light, we might want to revise this otherwise plausible inference.

Plausible argument is appropriate where a tentative conclusion needs to be drawn, in conditions of uncertainty and incomplete knowledge and often under constraints of time, as a provisional basis for further reasoning and/or action. A lot of the propositions we use in everyday arguments are presumptions, as opposed to firmly established conclusions of previous arguments. Presumptions come into play in the absence of firm evidence or knowledge. Without presumptions no argument could ever move forward, as people would endlessly challenge each other's premises or be forced to produce ever more evidence. We would for example, never be able to accept an experienced doctor's recommendation that a medicine which has so far helped thousands of patients might be good for us as well in a similar situation. The reasonable inference that takes the doctor's professional authority as premise would be blocked, defeated by the knowledge that there is a possibility that the doctor might be wrong. Thus, hoping and asking for absolute certainty, for infallibility, we would find ourselves paralysed by uncertainty and inaction. Usually, in such situations, we wisely accept the doctor's advice, on a presumption that he is an expert and knows what he is doing. However, the conclusion of a plausible argument is always defeasible *in principle*, even in those cases where the presumption in favour of it is very strong.

Practical arguments are plausible arguments. In reasoning practically, agents come up with a claim for action as a presumptive means to an end or goal. The claim can be accepted presumptively unless there are stronger, overriding reasons against it. All other things being equal, a job opportunity that is attractive in various ways, say financially, ought to be accepted. But if this decision undermines goals which are more important to the agent than financial considerations, then the presumption in favour of accepting the job as the right action will disappear. The argument will be invalid, that is, it is possible for the conclusion to be false while the premises are true: it may be true that the job is financially attractive and financial security is something I want, but, if accepting the job clashes with goals that are more important to me, then I should not accept it. Practical reasoning is essentially defeasible. Even when a claim for action seems reasonably supported, some additional premise (expressing some new information, some better alternative means that is brought to our attention, a competing goal or moral principle, some undesirable consequence of action we had not thought of before) may lead us to revise the argument or to reject the original claim. Bearing in mind that new considerations of this sort can always come up, until they do, if we have paid sufficient attention to all considerations we could think of, if the claim has survived our attempts to find (overriding) reasons against it, we can presumptively accept the proposal for action as a reasonable one, as the right thing to do.

Our proposal for analysing the structure of practical reasoning

This book makes an original proposal about the structure and representation of practical reasoning in political discourse. We start from two existing proposals (Audi 2006 and

Walton 2006, 2007a), from which we take over important insights, but we develop these insights in a different direction and suggest a different structure. Mainly, we suggest a different view of agents' goals (as future states of affairs, underlain by values or concerns) and a factual, circumstantial premise that is not present in existing accounts; this circumstantial premise can include institutional (socially constructed) facts. To pre-empt misunderstanding, let us say from the start that the circumstantial premise is *not* divorced from what agents value, but is in fact selected as a relevant premise and under a certain linguistic formulation *precisely* in relation to what agents value or care about. Besides arguing, in our view, from goals and circumstances, agents argue from goals and the possible consequences of the action they are contemplating, so we are also proposing a second practical reasoning scheme, which takes agents' goals and the possible negative consequences of action as premises and may conclude that the action should not be performed. We also relate the two schemas and suggest that this integrated version represents the minimal structure of (single-agent) deliberation.

According to Audi (2006: 92–99), practical reasoning has a *cognitive-motivational* structure. It is an *inferential* process,[2] whereby agents infer judgements favouring action from premises expressing motivation and (instrumental) cognition. (Instrumental beliefs are means–end beliefs, i.e. by doing something I will attain a certain end.) Practical *reasoning* (as a *process*) is a way of responding to a practical problem or question and a practical *argument* is a premise–conclusion *structure* that corresponds to that reasoning. The conclusion of a practical argument, called a practical *judgement*, is the agent's *answer* to the problem (question). However, concluding that an action is the right one need not be followed by an *intention* or *decision* to act, nor by the *action* itself. Arriving at the judgement that I ought to stop smoking may or may not be followed by an intention to stop, a decision to stop, or by the action of stopping smoking. There are therefore four categories of responses to a problem: a cognitive response (drawing the conclusion is making the practical *judgement* that I ought to do *A*); an intentional response (drawing the conclusion is forming an *intention* to act); a decisional response (drawing the conclusion is making a *decision*); a behavioural response (drawing the conclusion is the *action* itself) (Audi 2006: 87).

The simplest schema for practical reasoning, according to Audi (2006: 96) involves desires and instrumental beliefs as premises:

1   major premise – the motivational premise (I want φ);
2   minor premise – the cognitive (instrumental) premise: my doing *A* would contribute to realizing φ;
3   conclusion – the practical judgement I should do *A*.

To use one of Audi's examples, suppose I am confronted with a problem that I want to resolve, e.g. my friends have quarrelled over their failure to organize their children's weekend. I might reason as follows: given that I would like to reconcile my friends (my goal, major premise) and given that, if I offer to look after their children over the weekend, I might resolve my friends' conflict (minor premise, means–goal relation), I should perhaps offer to look after their children (conclusion). Practical reasoning is very often, as here, a problem–solution type of argument. The action advocated in the claim as the means towards the goal is the solution to the identified problem. Unlike Walton (see below), Audi does not mention values as premises, but he does indicate (implicitly) how an argument like the one above is in fact informed by values. As he says, my goal is to reconcile my friends because I *care about* (in other words, value) marital harmony and friendship (Audi 2006: 4). As we will argue later, something only becomes a problem to resolve *because* of certain things that matter to us, because of what we value or care about. We 'see' problems around us partly because of the concerns (values) we have.[3]

Walton (2007a) distinguishes between instrumental and normative (value-based) practical reasoning. The former structure is simpler: if you want to get the train, you ought to buy tickets. The latter makes reference to some value underlying the goal:

> I have a goal *G*.
> *G* is supported by my set of values, *V*.
> Bringing about *A* is *necessary* (or *sufficient*) for me to bring about *G*.
> Therefore, I should (practically ought to) bring about *A*.
>
> (Walton 2007a: 35, emphasis added)

To use Audi's example again, I want to reconcile my friends (goal) *because* I value friendship and marital harmony, and this is why I will offer to perform an action that might lead to this goal.

Let us say a few things about *necessary* and *sufficient* conditions. Let us imagine our (recent and successfully accomplished) goal of going to London to see Beckett's play *Waiting for Godot*, starring Ian McKellen and Patrick Stewart. What should we do in order to achieve this goal? It would be first *necessary* to buy tickets for the play; this would be a *necessary* condition for achieving the goal. But buying theatre tickets is not a *sufficient* condition as well. It will not ensure that we get to see the play, unless we are also prepared to travel to London on that day, get train tickets, actually show up at the appropriate time at the theatre, etc. Doing something that is necessary in view of a goal may not be sufficient to fulfil that goal, but doing something that is sufficient in view of the goal may not really be necessary, if other better or easier means are available. Suppose that queuing at the box office early on the morning of the play in order to get some of the tickets which are released without fail on the day of the performance would be *sufficient* to get us the tickets. Would it follow that this is what we should do? Most probably not, as long as we are aware that easier alternatives are available, such as booking tickets online or by phone in advance. If there is an obvious alternative means that is far better than the action *A* that we first envisaged (even if *A* were in itself sufficient to realize the goal), then it would be unreasonable to conclude that we should do *A*. A typical situation is one in which several separate and connected actions are all necessary and together presumably sufficient in view of a goal, but we can imagine alternative sequences of such connected actions that will also lead to the same goal. We will have to choose, depending on how we weigh alternative means, consequences of action (e.g. comparative financial costs of alternative means of transport), and so forth. According to one such sequence, at least, in order to see the play it is necessary to book theatre tickets on-line, then buy train tickets, then take the train to London, show up at the right time at the theatre, etc., and provided that the performance is not cancelled and everything goes according to plan, these might together provide a sufficient set of conditions for seeing the play. So, presumably, this is what we will have to do, unless we can think of further considerations why we shouldn't (why we shouldn't book on-line, or why we shouldn't take the train).

On the basis of the examples we have given so far, it would seem that we can identify the goals of action with what agents want (this may include *wanting* to do their duty in a situation). My goal is to see *Waiting for Godot*, and this is something I *want* to do. If values are explicitly involved, they can be taken to indicate why the goal is desirable. I desire to reconcile my friends or to see this play because of such-and-such values that are important to me.[4] However, we think it is misleading to identify goals with what is desired by the agent. There is a clear sense in which the goal is *not always desired*, strictly speaking, by the agent. I may decide to do an action because my goal is to fulfil a promise that I have made, abide by a contractual obligation I have entered into, or some other suchlike reason, although my desires and inclinations strongly point the other way. If I decide to perform an action, in spite of my current desires, and only because I promised to do it or feel it is my obligation to do so, I would be clearly acting *against* my current desires and inclinations. I would not be motivated by what I want but by some normative reason which, if I actually do the action in the end (if I fulfil my promise), will effectively override my other desires.

In order to make sense of such situations, it is a good idea to look at some recent discussions of practical reasoning in philosophy. We will do so in more detail later in this chapter, but for our present purposes a distinction between *internal* and *external* reasons for action is essential. What is involved in saying to myself 'I ought to recycle all these newspapers'? For one thing, the sentence could mean that, given my goal of behaving in an environmentally friendly way, as something I desire to do, and my belief that recycling paper will help achieve that goal, I am motivated to recycle rather than throw everything away. There is a direct route from my desires to the claim and, if I do recycle my newspapers, then that behaviour can be explained in terms of my desired goal and the belief in the existence of an appropriate means–end relation. My reasons to recycle my newspapers are *internal*, they are real psychological motives, here having to do with what I want, and they can explain why I choose to recycle. But there is another interpretation available. I could in fact use the same sentence even when I do not have any particular desire to behave in an environmentally friendly way. I could say I know I ought to recycle but I can't be bothered to do it, it's too complicated. In this case someone could still say I have a reason to recycle my newspapers (and I ought to do it), but that reason could not be interpreted as a an internal motivation I have, but as an *external* reason, an external constraint, in the sense that 'there is a reason' why I ought to do it, although that reason doesn't actually motivate me or prompt me to act accordingly. A very interesting view of the relationship between external reasons such as duties and obligations and internal ones (wanting to fulfil them) is suggested by Searle (2010) and we will return to this discussion at this end of this chapter when we explain his theory of institutional facts.[5]

To account for situations in which agents do not desire the goal they nevertheless (feel they) ought to bring about, we make the following theoretical proposal: the goal premise should not be equated with what the agent wants but should be understood as a *future, possible state of affairs* that the agent envisages, compatible with his *concerns* (as expressed in the value premise). These concerns can be his actual wants and desires, or concerns to fulfil (and thus comply with) duties, requirements, obligations, norms, rules, laws, i.e. what he *ought* to want. We take this understanding of goals as possible states of affairs from possible world semantics and a particular theory of modality (Kratzer 1981, 1991).[6] Modal verbs (including deontic *should*, *must* and *ought to*, which are of interest to us here because they figure in practical claims) are discussed there in terms of different types of premises from which speakers reason. Deontic modals involve reasoning from *circumstantial* premises, specifying what the facts are, and *normative* premises, variously relating to what is desirable, what is good, what is morally required, what the law requires, what other people require, what the agent's desires, plans and wishes are, and so on. In terms of practical arguments, we can say, therefore, that, given a set of actual circumstances and a future state of affairs that corresponds to the agent's concerns (i.e. a state in which his desires, obligations, etc. have been realized), the agent ought to do *A*. The envisaged action (as means) is thus intended to take the agent from the current set of circumstances to a future situation, one which matches (at last in some respects) a certain normative ideal.

This view of deontic modality as involving normative and circumstantial premises does not fit in very well with either of the two accounts we have been discussing, as neither Audi nor Walton incorporate a factual, circumstantial premise into the structure of practical reasoning. For them, people reason from goals, means–goal and (in Walton's schema) value premises. When beliefs enter the picture, they are seen only as instrumental beliefs, expressing the means–goal premise. The context of action is not taken into account as a premise, although it is sometimes alluded to as being a 'problem' that needs solving, or by saying that agents take knowledge of the context of action into account. We think the semantic account of deontic modality is correct, and that the primary two premises that are involved in practical reasoning are a *circumstantial* and a *normative* premise (the latter corresponds in our account to the goal premise, underlain by the value premise).[7] We suggest that practical reasoning is of this form: given the circumstances I find myself in and a certain goal (this may be a future situation I desire or one that I don't particularly desire but think I ought to bring about), and given that I am or ought to be concerned with the realization of this goal, I ought to do *A*. In other words, I know what the circumstances are, and I know what the future outcome should be: these are *two states of the world*, one immediately present, the other an imagined future in which what I want or what is morally required (what I ought to want) has been achieved. What I *don't know* is what means will take me from the current situation to the future one, and I will *conjecture* that action *A* might be that means, based on my knowledge of the world, past experience, imagination, etc. So, we suggest, the action I eventually conclude in favour of is the one that appears to *connect* the present circumstances to the future ones, the one that can *transform* my current circumstances in accordance with the *source of normativity* specified in the value premise.

If we are correct, and if the conclusions of practical arguments are based on these two types of premises, *circumstantial* and *normative*, then Audi's and Walton's accounts are incomplete, to the extent that premises referring to the circumstances or context of action do not figure within the cognitive-motivational structures they advocate and goals are simply equated with the agent's desires. The understanding of goals we propose is in terms of future states of affairs generated by some source of normativity, and the latter is specified in the value premise. Our view of the status of the means–goal premise also derives from this understanding of circumstances and goals as states of affairs. When we reason practically, the means appear to us as a *conjecture*, a *hypothesis* that could presumably lead us from our circumstances to our goals, from one state of affairs to another. If we nevertheless become aware that the action may not lead us to our goals, or might even compromise our goals, then we might want to revise the claim. It might be more reasonable *not* to do the action.

Let us say a few words about the relationship between consequences and goals. Actions have intended and unintended consequences. The intended ones are the goals of action (there may be a sequence of such goals terminating in a long-term, final goal). But consequences can also be unintended and therefore unforeseen, and such consequences can be more or less desirable, or may be 'costs' that agents would not want to incur. A distinction should be made, we suggest, between consequences of action that have a negative impact on the goal, while still making that goal possible to attain (these are costs that can be reasonably traded off against the benefits of achieving the goal), and consequences of action that compromise the goal of action (so that it is no longer achieved) or other goals of the agent that he would not want to compromise. We suggest that agents operate with *hierarchies of goals and hierarchies of values* and they are willing to accept some costs but not others, depending on how these affect highly ranked goals and values, i.e. goals and values that (in their view) should not be overridden.

Let us also further explain our view of goals and values. We have been making a distinction between goals which agents effectively desire and goals which they do not desire but nevertheless can shape what they do. Your goal can be a future state of affairs in which your present desires are fulfilled, a future state of affairs in which some value you care about is more fully realized (friendship, politeness, kindness, freedom), and can also be a moral or an institutional order, governed by moral principles or norms, or by laws, rules, regulations. We can say, for instance, that, in view of your goal, i.e. in view of what is moral or legal, or just friendly, polite or kind, you should not cheat your customers. You should not cheat them, even if you feel strongly inclined to do so. The goal in this case, as a future situation in which your behaviour is honest, is one which may clash with what you in fact *want* to do, and this supports our argument that goals are not to be equated with what the agent wants. In addition, let us note that it is possible to invoke more than one source of normativity for the same action. You should not cheat your customers, in view of what is *moral*, what is *legal*, in view of your long-term *interests*, or in view of other values (it is not *nice* or *kind* to cheat your customers). The claim can thus be made against the background of a moral order (informed by shared moral values or by universalizable rules of conduct), an institutional order (generated by laws or rules), against a background of various other values (kindness, generosity), *or* simply in view of what your actual desires and preferences are. We can say that in view of what the world *ought to be like* according to these norms, values, laws, desires, as sources of normativity, we ought to do *A*. But it is often the case, and moral principles, duties, promises, laws illustrate this situation, that in addition to a concern for acting in accordance with these reasons, the *fact* that we have these reasons, that they exist objectively in the social world (that there *are* such obligations and laws, that promises *were* made, etc.) and are consequently binding on us as agents, is also a reason. It is, as we show, later, recognition of such a reason that can create a corresponding concern to act accordingly, although it may not. We propose to include such reasons in the circumstantial premise as (social, institutional) *facts*.

The structure of practical reasoning that we suggest is shown in Figure 2.1, where the hypothesis that action *A* might enable the agent to reach his goals (*G*), starting from his circumstances (*C*), and in accordance with certain values (*V*), leads to the presumptive claim that he ought to do *A*. It is often the case that the context of action is seen as a 'problem' (and is negatively evaluated in view of the agent's existing values or concerns) and the action is seen as the solution that will solve the problem. As the conclusion that the action might be the right means to achieve the goal or solve the agent's problem follows only presumptively, we have represented the link from premises to conclusion by means of a dashed line.[8]

The way we see practical reasoning differs from other accounts in the following ways.

1. In our view, practical arguments take *circumstances* and *goals* as premises. Agents combine knowledge of their circumstances and of their goals with a presumptive means–end relation that might take them from the circumstances they are in to the future state of affairs which is their goal. Agents choose certain actions over others not just in view of the goal, but also because they find themselves in particular circumstances and not others. The context of action restricts the range of actions that can be thought of and the choices that can be made. The action that emerges as (presumably) the right action, is supposed to transform the present set of circumstances so that they match the agent's goal, which is itself informed by the agent's values (either his actual values or the values that he – or some other arguer – thinks he ought to have). Thus, current circumstances will be brought more in line, so to speak, with the source of normativity that underlies the action.

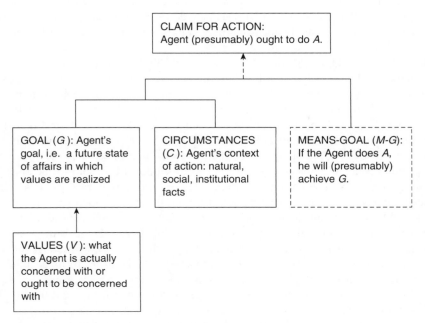

Figure 2.1 Our proposal for the structure of practical arguments.

2. We began by suggesting that goals should not be identified with what the agent wants in any simple manner. To say that a premise of the form 'I want φ' expresses the agent's goal is misleading. We suggested instead (following modal semantics) that agents' goals are *(possible) future states of affairs*. The goals we have are futures we imagine. The relation we stand in with respect to these imagined futures may be one of actual desire (we actually want to bring about that state of affairs). But we may also think that we *ought to* desire them, because they are normatively appropriate, they correspond to moral values that we think are right, and so on. We often give ourselves goals that we don't actually desire but we think are right, appropriate, worthy of being pursued. Many goals (such as conforming to a moral or legal order) are in fact typically imposed on people as external constraints, independent of their desires. If agents act in accordance with what is moral or legal, they will of course do so because in some sense they want to, however reluctantly (as all intentional action presupposes that the agent *wants* to do the action, however weakly). But there is an important difference, one that is worth preserving, between action which springs from one's desires and action that springs from recognition of an external reason, therefore from what the agent thinks he ought to do, even when he may not really desire the final outcome.

3. Both Walton and Audi illustrate practical reasoning with examples of action formulated from a first-person-singular perspective ('My goal is . . .'/'I want φ'). However, this type of example tends to obscure a very important fact about practical judgements. Deontic modality ('He ought to do A') is speaker-oriented (as opposed to subject or agent-oriented) (Bybee *et al.* 1994). The source of modality (obligation) is the speaker of the sentence, not the putative agent of the action proposed. In the Walton and Audi examples, the agent (subject) and the speaker coincide, which is one of the reasons why goals seem to be identical with what the

agent wants. If we devise examples in which a *speaker* is arguing that an *agent* ought to do *A*, then it will be easier to see that the agent may not actually desire a particular goal but, *in the arguer's view*, he *ought to* desire it. Similarly, the agent may not actually care about a particular value but, *in the arguer's view*, he ought to care.

4. According to Walton's (2006, 2007a) schema for value-based practical reasoning the goal premise is supported by the value premise. This understanding of the relationship values and goals is taken from Atkinson *et al.* (2004), for whom values determine goals. A more encompassing concept than value is that of 'concerns' (Blackburn 1998), which we explain later. I act to help you because I am concerned about your well-being, I value it, or it matters to me. We agree that the goal premise is supported by the value premise, as the goals we set ourselves are obviously a function of what matters to us, our values, our concerns. Arguers can explicitly invoke an audience's known values in support of a claim for action, and ground their argument in these known commitments, as part of a rhetorically effective strategy. Our suggestion is that values restrict the set of actions that are compatible with the goals, seen as desirable or normatively appropriate states of affairs, by excluding all those which are not compatible with the value in question. Values also restrict the goals that can be imagined or desired by an agent. An agent can get rich (goal) by various means, but only some of these means may be compatible with the set of values he adheres to. In his search for appropriate means, the agent will choose from among those means that are compatible *both* with the goal and the values that inform the goal. Our values or concerns – and by this we understand both our actual values or concerns and those we think we ought to have – are sources of normativity that shape our goals and the action we take to realize them.

As we explain in more detail below, we will draw a distinction between values in the sense of *actual concerns*, i.e. what the agent may actually care about or value (e.g. his health, the interests of his family, honesty, fulfilling his promises, etc.) and values in the more *objective* sense of socially recognized *moral values* or other types of *value commitments* that individuals are bound by in virtue of being part of a moral, social and institutional order. In the latter category we include the *fact* that honesty is a socially recognized norm, the *fact* that the agent made a promise or is bound by an obligation. Such facts belong (in our view) to the circumstantial premise and may also be *actual concerns* of the agent, things he *actually* values: the agent may actually want to act honestly or fulfil his promise. But the agent may also recognize that he is bound by such moral values or commitments and still fail to act accordingly. In such cases, the moral value or commitment in question (as an external, objective reason) has not been internalized as an actual concern or motive.

5. Regarding values or concerns, we argue that, besides informing goals, they also inform the selection and description of the relevant circumstances. Circumstances are described in ways that fit in with the claim that is being made. We not only imagine goals in relation to values, but we 'see' problems around us in relation to our values. The 'facts' that people reason from are not divorced from what they value but have evaluative content. Often, the situation is described in highly value-laden terms, but even when this is not apparent, the circumstances of action in a practical argument are inherently seen as a *problem* to be resolved, and are therefore negatively evaluated from the point of view of the agent's goals. The facts of the matter are only a problem in relation to the agent's concerns or values; for a different agent, with different concerns, the situation might call for a totally different type of action or no action at all.

Depending, for example, on how the current situation in the UK is described (e.g. as a state of economic bankruptcy brought on by decades of excessive spending encouraged by previous Labour governments, or by decades of neoliberal Thatcherite financial deregulation), certain claims for action (e.g. cutting spending and borrowing or, on the contrary, intensifying state intervention) will be more reasonable than others. Alternative descriptions of the situation are the direct result of different systems of value and may be drawn from different discourses. Not only the description, but the selection of what counts as relevant circumstances are determined by the arguer's concerns or values. Our concerns explain our action, they explain why we act in one way and not another, and justify it, by giving us reasons to pursue certain goals and take certain means towards them.

6. In a previous section we said that practical reasoning is conductive in the view of some theorists, and that it is represented as multiple (convergent) argumentation, as each reason counts separately for or against the claim. In the example we discussed there (taking up a job opportunity or not), there were several possible goals that could be attained and several others that would be negatively affected, several positive consequences and several negative consequences, and the decision depended on how the agent weighed all these reasons against each other. To say that arguers have to arrive at a conclusion on balance, by weighing various considerations, can only mean, in our view, that they balance considerations *in favour of the claim* against considerations that *go against the claim*, and which therefore support a *counter-argument* whose conclusion is the negation of the original claim. For example, by doing *A* in circumstances *C*, I can achieve goals *G1* and *G2* (so two distinct arguments will support the claim). But if I do *A*, negative consequences will arise that will go against other important goals I have, *G3* and *G4* (there will be two arguments that support the counter-claim). Which of these goals is more important to me, which would I not be prepared to sacrifice? It is only in this sense that practical reasoning can involve *weighing* of reasons and can lead to a conclusion that is drawn *on balance*: what we balance in fact are considerations belonging to *different* arguments. In such cases, we suggest, when an argument is weighed against a counter-argument, practical reasoning is one and the same as deliberation (more about this later). In weighing goals against other goals, and values against other values, practical reasoning (seen as deliberation) displays a rationality which is more than instrumental, and is oriented towards comparatively assessing goals and values, in an attempt to decide which should override others, which are more worth pursuing than others.

If we look at a simple practical argument, however, when people reason from a single, *given* goal, the structure is not convergent. Agents seem to be starting from an assessment of the context of action (the real world) and a goal they want to achieve (or think they ought to achieve), as a future possible situation, and with some tentative idea about what means (action) might take them from the current circumstances to their goal. These premises have to be taken *together* in order to support the claim for action, which is why the argumentative structure is coordinative or linked. This is how we have represented it in the schema above.

7. We want to integrate 'institutional facts', such as theorized by Searle (2010), into the practical reasoning schema, as reasons that people have, whether they act on them or not. Once you make a promise, you have a reason to act accordingly, whatever your desires, and the same can be said about duties, obligations and other forms of commitments people undertake which constrain their action. We suggest placing such external reasons in the circumstantial premise: they are *facts* that speakers argue from in saying that agents *ought to be concerned* with their realization and therefore do *A*. In the case of promises or moral norms or laws, the fact that the agent made a promise or is bound by a law or moral norm typically override any other possible consideration of what the context is or might require, or what the agent's actual concerns are. When we say, for instance that, *regardless of other circumstances* and *regardless of what he actually wants*, the agent ought to do *A* because he promised, we regard the fact that the agent *made a promise* as the only relevant fact or reason.

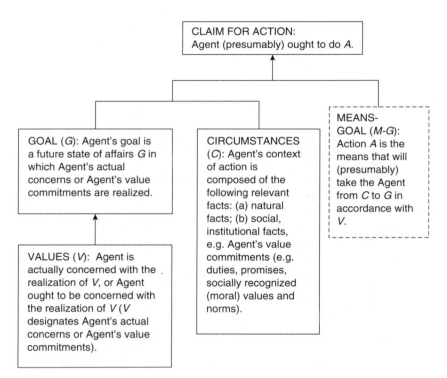

Figure 2.2 The structure of practical reasoning: a more detailed representation.

The structure we propose in Figure 2.1 can account for arguments which say that, given the agent's *actual* concerns or desires, and given his *actual* goals, as well as his circumstances, he ought to do *A*. But it also aims to account for arguments which say that, given that the agent is bound by a promise or moral value (these are institutional or social facts belonging to the circumstantial premises), and given that he *ought to be concerned* with the realization of this promise or moral value, he ought to do *A*. In this case, we suggest, the value (commitment, duty) in question enters the argument as a social or institutional fact, but not necessarily as an actual concern as well, as the agent may recognize the objective and binding nature of his promise or of a socially recognized, legitimate moral value and still fail to be actually concerned with its realization (or be motivated by it).

To sum up, any moral value (or institutional fact, such as promises) has to be *internalized* by the agent as a *concern*, in order to actually motivate his action (in order for the agent to actually *do* the action). But even when the agent is not concerned to act morally (or to fulfil his promises), moral values, duties, commitments, norms and other such reasons are still there, as *external* reasons which the agent *has*, even if he chooses not to be concerned with their realization.

Figure 2.2 gives a slightly more detailed representation of the structure of practical arguments that sums up these theoretical points. The value premise may refer either to the agent's actual concerns (what he actually values) or to what the agent ought to be concerned with (what he ought to value), either in his own view or according to another arguer (the arguer and the agent may or may not be one and the same person). For instance, it may state that the agent *actually* values or *is actually* concerned with fairness or with keeping his promises, or it may state that he *ought to be* concerned with fairness or with keeping his promises, i.e. he ought to want to abide by his pre-existing value commitments (specified in the circumstantial premise). These external reasons may or may not be turned into actual motives in the end, but the agent can be nevertheless said to *have* them in virtue of being part of a social, moral and institutional order in which *fairness* and *promises* enjoy collective recognition. (We use 'value commitments' here to refer to external reasons such as promises, duties, moral values and norms that the agent is bound by.)

8. From a critical rationalist perspective, agents do not move *from* premises *to* a claim for action that is allegedly *supported* or *justified* by those premises. There is always a *gap* between premises and conclusions, a *leap*, as we cannot reason logically, inferentially from premises about what is known to claims about what is unknown. A more accurate view of what goes on would be then the following. People come up with a tentative choice, a judgement, an idea, as possibly the right thing to do, and then think of its implications for various spheres of life. What consequences would this option have, as far as they can anticipate? How would it affect their other aims and concerns? In order to *increase the rationality* of their final decision, people have to think of challenges to their original hypothesis, i.e. the hypothesis that the action is the right one. If we think about it in this way, we can say that a claim for action can be provisionally accepted if it survives our critical attempts to refute it by imagining what considerations would count against it. Instead of launching into unwise action, we derive the implications of our tentative choice or decision, and if these are undesirable, we allow (in Popper's words) our hypotheses to die in our stead. If unacceptable consequences have been exposed, we might abandon the hypothesis and look for a better one. Criticism, not justification, is the way in which rational argument can advance our search for both scientific truth and rational decision-making (Miller 1994, 2005, 2006).

According to Miller (1994, 2006), the typical situation, as far as practical decision-making is concerned, is one in which an agent is faced with several possible courses of action and the available evidence does not indicate that any of these is clearly the wrong way forward. How can the agent eliminate some of these alternatives and choose one? How can the agent use the information he has in order to decide rationally? How can he compensate for all the information he does not and could not possibly have? What the agent can do is to subject these alternatives to thorough criticism in an attempt to find reasons *against* the proposed course of action (*not reasons in favour*), and thus eliminate the worst alternatives. The agent should then adopt the practical proposal that has best survived the most testing criticism that he has been able to direct at it. Because alternative proposals for action cannot be tested empirically as long as no action has yet been undertaken, the agent will examine these proposals critically by using the relevant theoretical (e.g. scientific, empirical) knowledge at his disposal. It is also rational to try to compensate for all the knowledge that he does currently have and could not possibly have by allowing for continuous piecemeal adjustments and revisions of the action if things turn out unexpectedly. Rational decision making does not *guarantee* that the 'right' or 'best' decision has been arrived at. What can be said, however, is that, having resulted from a rational procedure, the conjecture in question can be provisionally accepted. 'Rational decision making is not so much a matter of making the right decision, but one of making the decision right' (Miller 1994: 43; see also Miller 2006: 119–124).[9]

9. In light of the above discussion, our suggestion is that there are two types of practical arguments. One is the argument from circumstances and goals, which cannot justify a claim except tentatively, presumptively: the argument is always open to defeat if new relevant considerations come to light. The second one is an argument from consequences, which takes

the probable consequences of the action as a premise (if I do A, the following consequences, which are negative in light of my goals, are likely to occur) and infers, given the agent's commitment to achieving the goals, that the action should not be performed.

Agents hypothesize that a certain means (action) might connect their present circumstances to their goals, or might take them from the present to the desirable or normatively appropriate future. This corresponds to the structure of practical arguments we represented in Figure 2.1. Next, what they have to determine is whether the proposed action will not have unintended consequences that will compromise their goal rather than achieve it. In the light of everything they know, they should try to explore all the probable consequences of action that would count as reasons against it. If the proposal for action seems to survive criticism, they can provisionally adopt it. How can this argument from negative consequences be integrated with the main practical reasoning schema? We suggest the following representation, where the practical argument from negative consequences is a *counter-argument* to the practical argument from goals and circumstances. As we show further on in this chapter, pointing to consequences of action that undermine the goal can be used to rebut or reject the original claim, i.e. show the claim is unacceptable or false; such consequences are premises in a *counter-argument*. If consequences are exposed that undermine the stated goals of the action, then *not doing* the action is a more rational decision if one maintains one's commitment to those goals. This counter-argument is not presumptive but deductively valid (if the premises were true, then the conclusion would also be true). The question is of course whether the premise that such-and-such negative consequences will occur or have occurred *is actually* true. If, for instance, negative consequences have already emerged and compromised the goal, then the original claim has been conclusively rebutted; more often, however, the consequences that figure as premises in such argument are only probable, they are predicted to occur, but it is by no means certain that they will.[10]

We suggest that the two types of practical argument can be represented and connected as in Figure 2.3.

10. Finally, let us say a few words about *deliberation*, which will be in focus particularly in Chapter 6. In our view, deliberation is an argumentative *genre* in which practical reasoning is the main type of reasoning. The view we propose on the relationship between practical reasoning and deliberation is the following. Agents deliberate either by themselves or together with others. In both single-agent and multi-agent contexts, deliberation involves balancing considerations in favour of one proposal for action against considerations that support various alternatives (minimally, the alternative of *not doing* the proposed action, but also *other* actions). Deliberation involves therefore considering *alternative practical arguments*, supporting *different claims* and examining and weighing considerations that support these alternative claims. This is what agents deliberating together are doing. But this is what agents reasoning practically on their own are often doing, when they are trying to make a reasonable decision by considering reasons that support various possible courses of action, or count *against* the proposal they originally thought of. They do not always do it very well, and sometimes they do not do it at all, and a hasty and unwise decision may result from the absence of a minimal deliberative process, for instance from failing to think of the possible consequences of action or better alternatives. Sometimes, agents can revise and refine their decision as events unfold, sometimes they cannot, and the consequences of a bad decision sometimes cannot be undone.

Deliberation involves therefore 'balancing' *several* practical arguments, in favour of *different* claims for action, against each other. Minimally, it involves weighing reasons in favour of a claim against reasons against it (reasons supporting the counter-claim), or balancing each argument against a *counter-argument*. Saying that practical reasoning is 'conductive' (as we said

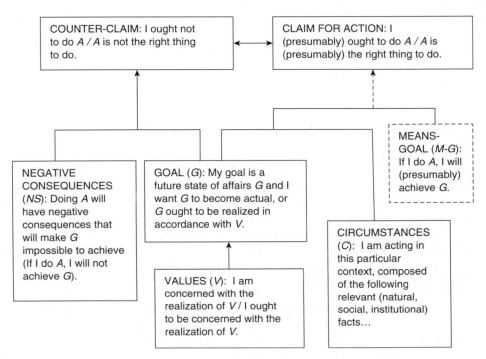

Figure 2.3 Deliberation: argument and counter-argument.

earlier) already involves seeing practical reasoning as a form of deliberation. The structure of practical reasoning we represented in Figure 2.1 does not yet involve deliberation, only the one we represented in Figure 2.3 does, although only in a minimal sense, as it does not consider several alternatives, with their associated goals and values, but only reasons against doing the action. Considering the probable impact of a proposed action on *other* goals – not just the stated goal of action, but other goals that might be affected, including other agents' goals – involves *deliberation over goals, not just over means*. Instrumentally, we may deliberate over whether a hypothetical action will be the right means in view of a certain goal; but we may also expand the deliberative context beyond this purely instrumental rationality and wonder whether perhaps we should not be considering *other* goals and shape our action to fit in with those goals. This may involve deciding *against* the action, if it seems likely that it will compromise those other goals, even if it seems to achieve the goal we started with. Or it may involve deciding on alternative action, alternative means, as being better suited to meeting a revised conception of what our goals should be.

In Chapter 4, we will say more about deliberation over means and over goals. In Chapter 6 we will continue to develop our view of deliberation as genre and suggest in what way multi-agent deliberation in highly institutionalized contexts such as parliament differs from the simple model of single-agent informal deliberation.

Argument evaluation

The normative question 'what properties make an argument a good one?' has received various formulations from various theorists, depending on the particular perspective adopted on argumentation in general: logical, rhetorical, dialectical, and which one of these three is thought to be the dominant perspective that can integrate and ground the others. We follow Blair (2003) and others in regarding these perspectives as *complementary*: all arguments have logical, rhetorical and dialectical aspects, and can be evaluated from a logical, rhetorical and dialectical perspective. We will take the view that a 'good' argument is one which is, at the same time, good from all three perspectives. Let us say a few words about argument evaluation from all of these perspectives.

The logical perspective: rational persuasiveness

According to the informal logical perspective, including the fast-expanding discipline of 'Critical Thinking' (Johnson 2000; Johnson and Blair 2006; Bowell and Kemp 2005; Govier 2001, etc.), a good ('cogent') argument is a 'rationally persuasive' one, i.e. an argument that provides 'good reasons' or 'rational support' for the conclusion, such that belief in the conclusion is 'justified'. 'Rational persuasiveness' is an epistemic notion that takes into account the fallibility of human knowledge claims, and replaces 'soundness' as a cogency criterion. A sound argument is a valid argument with true premises, but it is not always easy to tell which premises are true and which are not. An argument can be rationally persuasive without being sound and premises can be rationally acceptable without being true. It is now reasonable for physicists working at the Large Hadron Collider in Switzerland to believe that the particle they call the Higgs Boson exists and to try to test this hypothesis experimentally, but it is by no means certain that the Higgs Boson does exist and in fact it may not. In other words, reasonable belief is not one and the same as true belief, but is belief which, given the evidence we have at a certain time, it is reasonable to hold. Soundness is therefore not necessary for cogency.[11]

'Rational persuasiveness' is not only distinct from 'soundness' but also from mere 'persuasiveness' (the province of rhetoric). An argument may be persuasive, but not *rationally* persuasive. People are all the time actually persuaded by arguments that they should not be persuaded by, for instance by fallacious appeals to popularity or novelty. Such arguments are not *rationally* persuasive for them because the reasons that are being offered (you should buy this product because it is new, or because everyone else is buying it, and whatever is new and popular should be bought) are not good reasons. Fortunately, not everyone is easily persuaded by bad reasons, and a bad argument which is persuasive for a person will not necessarily be persuasive for another person as well.

In informal logic, a good argument is defined in terms of three criteria: premise acceptability, relevance and sufficiency. From the perspective of an epistemic subject, premises must be rationally acceptable, relevant to the claim, and together must provide sufficient support (or adequate grounds) for the claim. Premise acceptability is an *epistemic* notion, concerning the relationship of premises to audiences, and is a weaker notion than truth (an objective notion, concerning the relationship of premises to the world, independently of people's beliefs). If in a given context we have *good reasons* to believe a premise (e.g. it is grounded in evidence, supported by reliable testimony or authority or by cogent argumentation), then it is rationally acceptable. Sometimes, premises may be acceptable and relevant but insufficient to establish the acceptability of the claim, for instance in an inductively weak argument, in which a general conclusion is hastily drawn on the basis of insufficient evidence. Or premises may fail to be relevant to the claim. Such is the case of many fallacies, such as fallacious *ad hominem* appeals (when an appeal to the personality of the arguer is irrelevantly brought to bear on the acceptability of his claim) or irrelevant emotional appeals (when appeals to emotion that are not relevant to the claim are used in place of relevant rational appeals).

Being able to dismiss an argument as a bad argument does not entail that the argument's claim is unacceptable. A weakly supported claim, one for which there is little or even no evidence, or one which is supported by an invalid or in other way fallacious argument, may very well be a true claim. In other words, to say that an argument is not good is not the same as showing that the conclusion is false. The conclusion may well be true, but it may be inadequately supported by the argument in question. In order to have sufficient grounds for dismissing the conclusion, one would have to be able to do more than simply knocking down the arguments that claim to support it. One would have to provide a rationally persuasive *counter-argument*, one that supports the opposite standpoint (the denial of the conclusion) (Govier 2001: 81–82). We have seen that, for practical claims, negative consequences that undermine the goal can serve as premises in such a counter-argument.

The dialectical perspective: dialectical reasonableness

From a *dialectical* perspective, argumentation is a *dialogical* exchange of moves between two or more interlocutors. Argumentation involves dialogue because it always arises in response to some difference of opinion, some expressed or anticipated doubt or criticism. For pragma-dialectics (van Eemeren and Grootendorst 1992, 2004; van Eemeren 2010), the normative *goal* of this dialogue is the *resolution of a difference of opinion in a reasonable* way, or 'on the merits'. Thus, argumentation is best understood as a *procedure* for testing the acceptability of a standpoint in light of critical questioning, and this procedure is developed on the basis of a critical rationalist conception of reasonableness. According to the philosophy of critical rationalism (Miller 1994, 2006), the function of argument is essentially critical, not concerned with justification.

A pragma-dialectical approach in argumentation theory is a *normative* approach that takes an *external*, analytical perspective on its object of study. Unlike descriptive theories, which can yield models of the empirical internal normativity that is regarded as sound in practice by participants themselves, normative theories such as pragma-dialectics construct an external (a priori) normativity, by stipulating a set of norms defining optimal argumentative behaviour. Pragma-dialectics constructs an ideal model of argumentative interaction ('critical discussion'), in relation to which actual practices can be assessed. Argumentation theory on this view is part of 'normative pragmatics', i.e. language use and verbal interaction viewed from a *critical* perspective. As a complex speech act, or a type of social verbal action, argumentation has a goal, a purpose or point. Each argumentation is viewed as part of a discussion between (two or more) parties who try to *resolve a difference of opinion in a reasonable way*. It is in relation to how they (instrumentally) contribute to this goal that actual argumentative moves are to be assessed (van Eemeren and Grootendorst 2004; van Eemeren 2010). (Note that 'critical discussion' in pragma-dialectics is *not* an empirical object, is not actual argumentative dialogue, but an abstract theoretical construct. Any actual argumentative dialogue, implementing any argumentative genre and activity type, can be reconstructed as critical discussion.)

In pragma-dialectics, the abstract theoretical model of 'critical discussion' embodies the critical ideal of reasonableness. Critical discussion is defined in terms of specific stages and in terms of a set of dialectical rules (or norms of argumentative conduct), which the argumentative moves that are relevant at every stage must comply with in order to promote the goal of a reasonable resolution of the difference of opinion.[12] These rules define therefore an ideal procedure for conducting argumentation, against which argumentative reality can be evaluated, and they are designed to ensure maximum opportunity for the critical examination (testing or questioning) of standpoints. Unreasonable or fallacious argumentative moves are those which violate these rules and thus obstruct the goal of the procedure. In other words, the aim of the procedure is to enable the resolution of a difference of opinion on the merits, by delivering a standpoint that is tenable in the light of systematic criticism, a standpoint that has successfully answered all the critical questions that have been directed at it, a *reasonable* standpoint. Specific critical questions are attached to each of the three argumentation schemes defined in pragma-dialectics.[13]

In this book we are drawing on a distinction (made in pragma-dialectics) among *concrete speech events* (e.g. a particular debate between two presidential candidates, or a particular debate in parliament), communicative *activity types* which they instantiate (e.g. presidential debate, parliamentary debate) and (abstract) *genres* of communicative activity (deliberation, negotiation, adjudication, etc.) Argumentation always takes place in context, and the context is often an institutional context, with its own purposes, rules and procedures, and offering various institutional preconditions, constraints and opportunities to arguers. What counts as reasonable argumentation in such cases depends partly on the institutional context, so the model of 'critical discussion' should be contextualized in an empirical way in relation to communicative activity types in order to do justice (in the analysis) to the specific demands and criteria of particular kinds of institutional contexts (for instance, different activity types have different institutional rationales or goals; what is possible to achieve may also be also different) (van Eemeren 2009a, 2010: 129–151). In simple terms, it would not be reasonable to hold arguers responsible for argumentative moves which they are either forced to make or cannot make due to the constraints placed on them by the institutional context; nor would it be reasonable to hold them responsible for failing to achieve outcomes that cannot be achieved. (In Chapter 6 we will present our own view of the features of deliberation in parliamentary debate that arise from the nature of the institutional context.)

Critical discourse-analysts might view the pragma-dialectical model of critical discussion and its definition of reasonableness as utopian, as unrealizable in practice, hence of little potential value to the critical concerns of social science. To do so would be misconceived. The dialectical rules for critical discussion can be naturally viewed in relation to the ideals of deliberative democracy. They define a 'first order' set of conditions for reasonable discussion, whose adoption in actual practice is, however, dependent on the fulfilment of 'higher order' conditions (van Eemeren 2009b). The norms for reasonable discussion *presuppose* that participants actually want to resolve a disagreement and they are capable of reasoning. Thus, 'first order' conditions are embedded in, and presuppose 'second order' conditions, involving appropriate attitudes and competences. In addition, there are 'third order' conditions that must be met, having to do with the social-political context, that should be such as to enable participants to 'claim the rights and responsibilities' associated with their roles, for instance give them the power and freedom to question and challenge arguments. Primarily, they involve ideals of equality, non-violence, freedom, intellectual pluralism, the absence of constraints arising from unequal power. These conditions may be counter-factual in actual practices, but this should not lead to a rejection of the normative model as a standard against which actual practices can be assessed and improved. There is, after all, no other way of coping with the overwhelming problems of the modern world than by 'promoting a culture of critical discussion' (van Eemeren 2009b: 48–49).

Other dialectical approaches

Walton's (1989, 1992a, 2006, 2008a) dialectical framework is also based on the view that argumentation takes the form of a dialogue and has a critical function. A dialogue is seen as a type of 'goal-directed conversation' in which (minimally) two people are participating by taking turns. It is a 'connected sequence of moves' (speech acts) in which participants ask and answer critical questions in order to test the (tentative, provisional) acceptability of a claim (Walton 2006: 2). Walton attaches a set of critical questions to every argumentation scheme. In the case of the appeal to expert opinion we cited earlier (the doctor advising on the right medication), the argumentation scheme looks as follows (Walton 2006: 133):

- *Major Premise:* Source E is an expert in subject domain S containing proposition A.
- *Minor Premise:* E asserts that proposition A (in domain D) is true (false).
- *Conclusion:* A may plausibly be taken to be true (false).

Critical questions:

1 *Expertise Question:* How credible is E as an expert source?
2 *Field Question:* Is E an expert in the field that A is in?
3 *Opinion Question:* What did E assert that implies A?
4 *Trustworthiness Question:* Is E personally reliable as a source?
5 *Consistency Question:* Is A consistent with what other experts assert?
6 *Backup Evidence Question:* Is E's assertion based on evidence?

According to Walton (2006), putting forward a presumptive statement (in plausible argumentation) is a move in a dialogue that lies between an assertion (which incurs a burden of proof – the proponent is supposed to support it with reasons, if challenged) and an assumption (which carries no burden of proof). Presumption is not a substitute for knowledge, but enables agents to proceed with action in contexts of incomplete knowledge, uncertainty and risk, in all those situations when there is not enough evidence to indicate clearly which course of action will be appropriate. In advancing something as a presumption, the proponent is *reversing the burden of proof:* it is now the respondent that has the obligation to disprove or rebut it. To advance a statement as a presumption is somewhat like saying: 'I think this is true, or this seems to me to be true, based on all the evidence available to me. Correct me if you think I'm wrong.' The burden of proof, which rests originally with the proponent, is thus shifted from the proponent (who openly acknowledges the presumptive, tentative nature of his statement and its inherent fallibility) to whoever doubts the statement. It is the interlocutor's task to ask critical questions that point to the particular conditions in which a claim based on a presumptive scheme is in principle likely to default. We take this view of the allocation of the burden of proof to mean that plausible arguments are evaluated in a dialectical process in which what is important is not how strongly the claim seems to be justified (by the proponent) but how well it can withstand criticism and deal with reasons *against* it.

For instance, in order to accept an argument based on an appeal to expert opinion, a critical question will be whether or not the individual is an expert in the actual field under discussion. If the answer is yes, then the argument has survived critical testing based on this question, and a new question can be asked (and so on, until there appears to be no other reason why the conclusion cannot be provisionally accepted in those circumstances). However, if the answer is no, then the inference to the claim is defeated (Walton 1992a, 1996, 2007b). The question indicates that in all circumstances when appeal to expert opinion is based on the views of an expert whose field of expertise is other than the relevant one (e.g. a linguist pontificating on nuclear physics), the argument, although based on a plausible argument scheme, will default. This does not mean that the linguist's view may not be in fact correct, but only that the argument *from authority* in this particular case is not reasonable; the claim cannot be validly supported in *that* way.

Walton classifies dialogues according to the goals of the dialogue, the goals of the participants and the situation at the commencement of the dialogue. There are six primary dialogue types in his view (not all of them involving argumentation to the same extent), as follows:

- *persuasion dialogues* (e.g. a discussion of the benefits vs. dangers of GM food);
- *information-seeking dialogues* (e.g. interviews or asking for and receiving directions);
- *inquiry dialogues* (e.g. scientific or philosophical reasoning);
- *negotiation dialogues* (e.g. trade union vs. management wage negotiations);
- *deliberation dialogues* (e.g. public deliberation among citizens on what solution to adopt to solve a problem of common concern); and
- *eristic dialogues* (e.g. quarrels).

Each type of dialogue has its collective goal, as a framework governing both participants and all their moves, but each participant also has his own goal. For example, in persuasion dialogue, the cooperative goal of the dialogue is disagreement resolution but each party is also actively promoting or advocating their own viewpoint and attacking or criticizing the other as strongly as they can. An argument is reasonable in a framework of dialogue if it contributes to the collective goal of the dialogue, if it is a cooperative move in view of that goal. But within this cooperative framework there is also room for each participant to seek his own goal (Walton 2006: 183, 2007a: 60).

The rhetorical perspective: effectiveness

There is a lot of confusion surrounding the definition of rhetoric. Generally, it is defined as the study of *persuasion,* and *adaptation to the audience* in order to achieve persuasion is essential to this definition. Plato held a negative view of rhetoric, by contrast with dialectic. While dialectic was for Plato a cooperative search for truth, by means of dialogue, or questions and answers, rhetoric was the art of arguing both sides of an issue, as if they were both equally acceptable (which for Plato they could not be), thus making even a bad argument look cogent, and deceiving the audience in matters of truth. The negative meaning surfaces in the postmodern appropriation of 'rhetoric' in the sense of 'creating truth', i.e. Foucault's 'regimes of truth' or 'epistemes' understood as rhetorical constructs, as exercises in power, whereby particular communities or groups of people are hegemonically imposing their own particular standards onto the rest of society and declaring them universal and acceptable for all. The same negative meaning appears in ordinary linguistic usage, where 'rhetoric' is most often used in a negative sense, to mean words without substance, spin, language intended to deceive and manipulate. To say that a political speech is 'just rhetoric' means that the reasons provided in support of a claim are not good reasons but can be nevertheless effective in persuading the audience. This would be the case of arguments which tap into widely shared feelings, desires, instincts or sensitivities. Advertising and political discourse abound in appeals to emotions and social instincts, and often attempt to create effective bonds of trust between arguers and audiences by adapting rhetorically to their emotional sensibilities. Such appeals are often irrelevant to the claim being made and disguise a failure to produce relevant arguments of a less emotional nature.[14]

For Aristotle, unlike Plato, rhetoric was the legitimate counterpart of dialectic and it had to do with the 'ability in each case to see the available means of persuasion'. As Aristotelian scholars emphasize, Aristotle defined rhetoric as an 'art', a *technē* (*Rhetoric* 1.2.1), more specifically *an art of civic discourse*. As an art, rhetoric is thus 'morally neutral' and can be used for both good and evil purposes (Kennedy 1994: 8, 57). On this view, supported by many modern theorists of rhetoric (Tindale 1999), the conventional association between rhetoric and deceit, sophistry and manipulation is simplistic and wrong.

Van Eemeren (2010: 66) suggests viewing rhetoric as the 'study of aiming for effectiveness' in argumentative discourse. It is important, as he also warns, not to understand this as *actual* persuasive effectiveness or success, as this would turn the study of rhetoric into a purely empirical, descriptive enterprise. To judge whether an argument is a good one, one would have to investigate empirically whether it has actually managed to persuade a substantial number of people for whom it was intended. This would be independent from any other normative criteria. An argument could be then rhetorically effective, therefore good by this standard, while being logically or dialectically weak. Clearly, unless there is some other type of normativity that we can associate with rhetoric, not just *actual* effectiveness, any argument designed to successfully persuade any particular audience that *actually succeeded in doing so* would be a good argument, regardless of the argument's intrinsic qualities. Similarly, arguments that fail to persuade would be regarded as bad arguments, whatever their other merits. The rhetorical perspective would then collapse into relativism, and this in fact is an objection that has often been aimed at various rhetorical approaches (for instance by van Eemeren and Grootendorst 2004).[15]

Aiming for rhetorical effectiveness is not in itself sufficient to make an argument good, as an argument could be designed to be rhetorically effective while being logically and dialectically flawed. According to Blair (2003), the logical, rhetorical and dialectical perspectives are to a large extent independent from each other, and being a good argument from one of these perspectives does not say anything about how 'good' the argument is overall. There are, according to him, several types of possible relationship between these three perspectives. There is an interdependence between logic and dialectic: for an argument to be dialectically acceptable it has to be logically acceptable as well, and an argument cannot be regarded as logically adequate unless sufficient support is provided for the claim, i.e. unless the argument is dialectically adequate as well. But rhetorical effectiveness does not presuppose dialectical completeness, and the converse is also true: a dialectically satisfactory argument could fail to be rhetorically effective (its dialectical completeness may result in an argument that is too complex, too tedious, too difficult to understand). Moreover, logically flawed arguments can be rhetorically effective (fallacious arguments are often very persuasive), while logically valid or sound arguments may fail to be so (they may be formulated in terms that do not resonate with the audience). Overall, logical and dialectical adequacy seem to go together but there is no relation between satisfying norms of rhetoric, on the one hand, and satisfying norms of logic and dialectic, on the other, hence always a potential tension or conflict between these two orientations.

The rhetorical and dialectical perspectives are combined in the pragma-dialectical concept of *strategic manoeuvring* (van Eemeren and Houtlosser 2002b), which refers to the 'argumentative predicament' of having to pursue two aims (a rhetorical and a dialectical aim) simultaneously, of having to combine *effectiveness* with *reasonableness*. In other words, arguers are committed to resolving the disagreement in a reasonable way but also, hopefully, resolving it in their favour. Maintaining a balance between these two orientations is not always easy; for instance, the pursuit of rhetorical effectiveness may take place at the expense of reasonableness, in which case strategic manoeuvring is 'derailed', and the process of resolving a difference of opinion on the merits is compromised (van Eemeren 2010: 40–41).

Argumentation that is rhetorically effective can nevertheless be, at the same time, dialectically acceptable, or reasonable. It is this particular combination between rhetoric and dialectics which is achieved in successful, non-fallacious strategic manoeuvring that, in our view, can rescue rhetoric from its equation with mere actual persuasiveness. A normative, non-relativistic conception of rhetoric is possible if a concern for effectiveness is combined with a concern for reasonableness along the lines suggested by the pragma-dialectical concept of strategic manoeuvring. It is also implicit, we think, in the concept of 'rational persuasiveness', as distinct from mere persuasiveness.

So far, we have looked at rhetoric as the art of aiming for effective, persuasive arguments. This is a *goal-based* view of rhetoric and is widely shared amongst argumentation theorists. Kock (2007, 2009), however, goes back to Aristotle and Protagoras, and to an entire tradition of argumentation theorists that includes Perelman and Olbrects-Tyteca (1969), to defend an alternative, *domain-based* definition of rhetoric, as the proper and original definition of rhetoric, ignored in many contemporary conceptions. For this tradition, rhetorical argumentation is intrinsically connected with deliberation over what to do when several alternatives are possible, with choice and action related to matters of common concern. Indeed, Aristotle says in the *Rhetoric* that rhetoric is 'a certain kind of off-shoot of dialectic and of ethical studies, which it is just to call politics' (1.2.7), and in the *Ethics* he calls rhetoric a subdivision of politics (Kennedy 1994: 55). For Aristotle, rhetoric is relevant to those domains, like the moral, political and legal, where people deliberate together over matters that are within their agency; people do not deliberate over matters of epistemic truth. Almost always, however, there will be several reasonable and divergent arguments on any issue, grounded in competing but legitimate values and goals, and reasonable disagreement may persist indefinitely, without the possibility of ultimate consensus, and without the prospect of one party retracting his original standpoint (Kock 2007).[16]

Recuperating Aristotle's original domain-based definition of rhetoric, as opposed to the more limited one in terms of persuasive aims, as Kock advocates, will help the clarification of the ambiguity we have noted in the meaning of rhetoric. The negative view of rhetoric, we suggest (in the footsteps of Kock's argument), arises from situations in which the rhetor is using his skills to persuade people of the acceptability of a standpoint that is unacceptable, either because it is false (in epistemic argumentation), or because it is wrong (in practical argumentation). These are situations where a reasonable resolution (on the merits of the case) is in principle possible and rhetorical argumentation may be precisely designed to obstruct that resolution. In matters of epistemic truth, as well as on a variety of moral–practical issues, where there is an independent intersubjective standard of evaluation, it is in principle possible to resolve the disagreement and to expect the withdrawal of the 'false' or 'wrong' standpoint. It is not reasonable for disagreement to persist in such cases, although of course it may: both arguers cannot win the argument, although of course both will try to win and may remain entrenched in their original positions. In situations of *reasonable disagreement*, however, it cannot be expected that one of the arguers will retract his standpoint, no matter how long the argumentation should continue. These are the issues that are relevant to politics and ethics in particular, which – as Kock reminds us – Aristotle viewed as the proper domain of deliberative rhetoric. Disagreement may in such cases *reasonably* persist because of the different ways in which reasonable agents weigh different considerations that are relevant to them, because of their different hierarchies of (otherwise reasonable) values and goals. This situation creates a space for rhetoric to highlight what should be comparatively more important, in the arguer's view, to appeal to the audience's feelings and moral sense, make them see new connections between the issue being advocated and their experience, and imagine alternatives, in the hope of changing their priorities, thus making them adhere to a standpoint that is not obviously the only one that they could or ought to choose. It also opens up a space for trying to make a weak argument, or a worse alternative, look better than it actually is.

Rhetoric and values in the political domain

Rhetoric becomes free of its negative connotations when it is associated with its proper domain, that of deliberation, practical choice and action, and with *reasonable disagreement* over alternative choices. Political philosophers, following Isaiah Berlin, refer to such situations as *reasonable value pluralism*. As we have said, not all value pluralism is reasonable: a racist argument about how to deal politically with an ethnic minority can be conclusively rejected by questioning its various premises, and its proponent cannot defend himself by invoking value pluralism or his legitimate right to differ. Many moral–political issues do admit of rational consensus over what the best choice of action would be, and some arguments over what to do can be unambiguously evaluated, in the sense that of two contrary positions both cannot remain in play indefinitely. Following Habermas, we can say that such claims (and associated arguments) can be assessed in terms of a right/wrong distinction. Agreeing on the existence of reasonable value pluralism does not therefore entail a relativist stance.[17]

If rhetoric is placed, as it should be, within a context of choice and action, where several reasonable alternatives are possible, and not an epistemic context (where argumentation is oriented towards truth), then it becomes possible to see how more than one opinion can be *legitimately* possible, and how adapting to the beliefs and values of the audience and producing an argument that is comparatively better, rhetorically speaking, than another, might give an arguer a considerable advantage in mobilizing the support of a greater proportion of the audience. This is the characteristic situation of politics, where different but fundamentally reasonable positions might be at stake. The rhetorical perspective is therefore particularly relevant to our concerns with political arguments, which are inherently fallible and put forward in a context of incomplete knowledge, uncertainty and risk, where a multiplicity of contingent factors can causally affect the most carefully planned strategies of action, and are also underlain by persistent and irresolvable conflicts of value and interest.

As we said in Chapter 1, some of these persistent disagreements are underlain by conflicts of interest, but occur within a broadly shared framework of moral and political values. This is the kind of disagreement that we are focusing on in this book. Other irresolvable disagreements are deeper and more intractable. Such 'deep disagreements' (typically part of 'comprehensive' moral conceptions) are underlain by incommensurable fundamental principles and values, incommensurable 'framework propositions'. Argument cannot proceed because there is in such situations no common ground that can be identified and thus the conditions that are essential to argumentation are undercut (Fogelin 2005).[18]

With regard to the issue of relativism, our position is essentially that of Lukes (2005). Relativism, in his view, 'embodies a non sequitur': 'acknowledging the facts of moral diversity and value pluralism does not entail abstention from judging others (and their judging us)', nor does it entail that there is no privileged value perspective. The fact that there is no one worldview and set of values that everyone adheres to 'does not render us unable to make universally applicable judgments'. Recognition of the fact that 'there is no single best way for humans to live' or that 'there are many such best ways' is not incompatible with making moral judgements and thus recognizing the authority of moral standards and the reality of moral disagreements. Relativism actually 'denies the reality of moral disagreements'. It claims that disagreements are apparent because there is no one shared framework of reference, each position is *right* relative to its own set of norms and values, and there is no way of resolving the disagreement in favour of one position. Its message is not tolerance, as its proponents claim, but abstention from judgement, denial that people have the right to judge others (Lukes 2005: 135). A non-relativistic position, which Lukes advocates, would distinguish, among a wide diversity of practices, those that are right and those that are wrong. One can do so either by adopting a Kantian perspective and wondering whether a given practice could be universalized without contradiction, whether it could be justified to all those affected, or by taking the Aristotelian line of virtue theory and asking whether it would push those affected below the threshold of one or more human capabilities. Whatever approach one takes, some practices will pass these tests and some will not (Lukes 2005: 140–142).

In this chapter we have said that practical arguments are underlain by values, which inform both the goals that people set for themselves and their understanding of the context of action. People give priority to different values, hence different goals and different under-standings of the context of action. Some value differences are unreasonable and cannot withstand critical examination. For instance, some values are indefensible from a purely instrumental point of view, because they contradict the agent's goals: valuing a life of leisure is not reasonable if your goal is to get high grades. But some value differences are unreason-able in a deeper, non-instrumental sense: a racist conception cannot remain indefinitely in play alongside one which rejects racism. Disagreement over this issue is unreasonable and a reasonable resolution can be legitimately expected. Sometimes, however, people disagree in a reasonable way and the disagreement is also irresolvable. Such disagreements often depend on the way people rank the values and goals that matter to them. Reasonable disagreement, we suggest, is generated by conflicting but reasonable values and goals or by different rankings of the same values and goals. This situation is typical in politics, where political parties have fairly different and often not obviously unreasonable strategies for deal-ing with problems in light of different values and goals or in light of different rankings or priorities of values and goals. Certain political values and goals will rank higher as priorities for a left-wing party than for a right-wing one, and both left-wing and right-wing goals and values can sometimes (though not always) be argumentatively defended as reasonable. Critical testing, especially by looking at the *consequences* of political action, and how it affects various other legitimate goals and concerns, is an important resource for social critique.

This brings us to the normative foundations of CDA: which values can be argumenta-tively successfully defended in a process of critical discussion/deliberation? CDA has sometimes been relativistic about these values (defending a normative standpoint from which *all* differences should be given recognition) or too closely attached to a left-wing point of view, which has rendered it vulnerable to the charge of being ideological and biased. We want to ground CDA normatively in a set of values that closely approximate a list of univer-sal human rights, or duties/obligations that we have towards our fellow beings (rights and duties being two sides of the same coin), and more precisely in a list of human capabilities that define a concept of human flourishing or well-being, such as those envisaged by the 'capabilities' approach in ethics (Nussbaum 2000, 2006) and those versions of social theory inspired by the capabilities approach (Sayer 2011). The ethical foundations that we ground CDA with are not relativistic, in the sense that we do not think that one should give recogni-tion to just any value that particular communities happen to hold. Not any difference should be given recognition: in particular those that infringe human rights, hinder human capabil-ities or violate fundamental duties we have towards each other should not be among those that can ground good practical arguments.

Alternative frameworks of moral principles that can ground rational action are formulated by Audi (2006, Chapter 9) and Freeman (2005, Chapter 9), both based on W. D. Ross's original list of *prima facie* duties (Ross 1930).[19] The duty of *justice* or *fairness* towards others is, for example, a fundamental moral obligation on this list. Such fundamental moral considerations can conflict with each other (not just with self-interested reasons), and deciding what to do in such cases will involve deciding which one should be given priority, which should override others. The rationality involved in such deliberation over reasons is in such cases not a purely instrumental (or means–end) rationality but also involves deliberation over the appropriate ends of action.

Evaluating practical reasoning in a dialectical framework

In pragma-dialectics, practical reasoning is subsumed under causal argumentation schemes, as *means–end*, *instrumental* or *pragmatic* argumentation, in which a certain act is presented as the means to reach a given goal. The claim of a means–end argument is to be evaluated in terms of the following critical questions, where the first question amounts (we suggest) to asking whether the action is sufficient in view of the goals, the second inquires about the consequences of action and the last one amounts to asking whether the action is necessary in view of the goals:

- Will the action that is being advocated really lead to achieving the goal?
- Will the action have other effects than the intended goals?
- Will other actions, different from the one that is being envisaged, also lead to the fulfilment of the goal? (van Eemeren *et al.* 2002: 102–103; Garssen 2001: 91–92)[20]

These questions, we think, highlight the essence of practical reasoning, as reasoning aimed at producing practical *effects*, or having *consequences*, or *causing* some change in the world, and also point to the nature of causality: an action can have multiple effects, intended but also unintended; it can misfire or fail to achieve its intended goal; and the same effect might result from different actions (causes).

Walton, as we have seen, suggests a particular argument schema for practical reasoning, involving a goal premise, a means–goal premise and (optionally) a value premise, and a more detailed matching set of critical questions. The conclusion is provisionally acceptable, subject to rebuttal by critical questioning, by asking any of the following set of questions (see Walton 2006: 301, 2007a: 33; Walton *et al.* 2008: 96 for various alternative formulations of these questions):

- Are there alternative courses of action apart from *A* that would also lead to the goal? (Other-Means Question)
- Is *A* the best (the most acceptable) among these alternatives? (Best-Means Question)
- Are there other goals that might conflict with the action and whose achievement should have priority? (Other-Goals Question)
- Is it really possible to do action *A* in the circumstances? (Possibility Question)
- What bad consequences of the action should be taken into account? (Side-Effects Question)

Walton (2006: 327–329) introduces a few more variables into the practical reasoning schema. First, in real-life contexts, people frequently alter a plan of action in light of the observed consequences of what they are doing. 'Feedback' is a feature of practical reasoning and involves continuous monitoring of one's action and modifying one's plan based on incoming information. Second, agents often have conflicting goals and this is the source of all practical dilemmas. Sometimes it is easy to decide which goal to sacrifice but sometimes it is not and, whichever course of action is taken, something of value will be lost. Third, practical reasoning often involves several agents, and a process of deliberation amongst several people might be appropriate in order to decide what to do. These lead to the formulation of three additional critical questions:

- Does new information (through feedback) give good reasons to revise the previous conclusion that has been taken to represent the practical course of action? (Feedback Question)
- Does the conclusion (the course of action so far considered) conflict with other goals of the agent? (Agent's Multiple Goals Question)
- Are other agents involved, and if so, does the relation between all of these agents' goals indicate that a discussion amongst all these agents would be practically useful? (Multiple Agents Question)

In Walton (2007b: 221–222), the critical questions are revised as follows:

- What other goals does the agent have that might conflict with his goal *G*?
- How well is the goal supported by (or at least consistent with) the agent's values?
- What alternative courses of action apart from the one advocated that would also lead to the goal should be considered?
- Among these alternatives, which is the best in light of considerations of efficiency in bringing about *G*?
- Among these alternatives, which is the best in light of the agent's values?
- What grounds are there for arguing that is it practically possible to do the action in the situation?
- What negative consequences of the action that might have even greater negative value than the positive value of *G* should be taken into account?

Walton claims that practical reasoning is inherently defeasible. In conditions of incomplete information, uncertainty and risk, agents are forced to go ahead with a defeasible line of action and are usually prepared to modify it in light of emerging consequences or if the context of action changes. The conclusion of a practical argument is inherently subject to revision as new information comes in, e.g. if the action misfires in some way, if the agent becomes aware of value conflicts, or of conflict with other goals he pursues or other agents' goals. Critical questions indicate various possible problems with the argument. There are at least two main ways of challenging an argument, according to Walton: one is 'to ask questions that raise doubts about the argument', and the other is 'present a rebuttal or counter-argument', which is a stronger form of attack (Walton 2006: 27).

We will say more about the evaluation of 'deliberation dialogue' (Hitchcock *et al.* 2001; Hitchcock 2002; McBurney *et al.* 2007) in Chapter 6.

Our proposal for the evaluation of practical reasoning

We agree with dialectical approaches that critical questioning of arguments offers a productive way of systematically evaluating argumentative practice. Consequently, we adopt a dialectical approach, which subordinates rhetorical considerations to a primarily dialectical perspective. Although our analyses in this book (with the exception of part of Chapter 6) are not explicitly based on the pragma-dialectical model, we take over from pragma-dialectics the definition of the general *goal* of argumentation, as involving the *reasonable resolution of a difference of opinion*, as well as the pragma-dialectical critical conception of *reasonableness*. Because our focus is on *practical* arguments and particularly on *deliberation*, we want to further specify this goal as involving a *reasonable decision*. A reasonable decision results therefore from following a reasonable procedure. The decision itself may not be the 'best' or 'most rational' but it will have been arrived at in a reasonable way, by following a dialectical procedure of systematic critical testing.

Certainly, we do not claim (and neither does pragma-dialectics) that disagreements are always resolved in practice. In our view, it is often the case that actual argumentative practice not only falls short of the ideal of reasonableness but takes place in contexts in which, due to a variety of institutional constraints and empirical factors, such as divergent and irreducible conflicts of interests and of values, disagreement resolution in the strong sense of consensus (i.e. parties agreeing on *one* standpoint) is not only improbable but its improbable nature is actually captured in the institutional logic of the practices in question. As we show in Chapter 6, deliberation in parliamentary debate does *not need to lead to agreement on one view* and is not – as activity type – defective in any way for failing to yield such agreement amongst all participants. Its legitimate outcome is a collective *decision* which is legitimately based on the view shared by a majority at the end of a deliberative process. However, we think, the fact that many disagreements are not resolved in politics (including deep disagreement over value systems) does not deny that the fundamental normative orientation of political argumentative practice, of what and participants are hoping to achieve, their goal, *is* towards reasonable disagreement resolution, by means of persuading others of the reasonableness of their own standpoint. If this was not their aim, the whole practice of argumentation would lose its rationale, its point.

We are also drawing on Walton's dialectical approach. In particular, regarding possibilities for systematic critical questioning, we agree with his proposal (based on Pollock 1995) to distinguish between challenging the argument and challenging the conclusion, i.e. between attempting to defeat the argument and attempting to rebut its conclusion. Walton (2007b) makes this distinction more explicit by saying that practical reasoning can be criticized in *three* main ways. One is to challenge one or several of the premises, showing that they are not rationally acceptable (or true). (For instance, we suggest, it may not be acceptable that the situation is a problem that calls for action, or it may not be rationally acceptable that it is to be described in such-and-such terms. If a premise can be shown to be false, then the argument will be unsound.) Another is to try to defeat the argument by asking critical questions that can defeat the inferential link between premises and claim. (I may think that a certain action *A* is a *necessary* means towards a goal, but if an alternative, better means *B* emerges that will also fulfil the intended goal, then the inference that I should do *A* is undercut and the argument is defeated.) A third way is to produce a *counter-argument* aiming to reject (rebut) the original claim.

Walton (2007b) does not explain how defeating and rebutting relate to his critical questions, for instance which questions can do either or maybe both. We would like to suggest the following development and clarification of this distinction, based on our view that being able *to defeat an argument* is much less significant than being able to *rebut its claim*, given that *a claim can be true or false independently of the quality of the argument that allegedly supports it*. Basically, we suggest, questioning whether the action being proposed will have *negative consequences* that will undermine the stated goal (or other goals the agent wants to pursue, or other agents' goals) is the only really interesting critical question, as it is the only one that can rebut the argument's claim (and also defeat the argument's validity). Questions about the existence of alternative actions are of course also important, but the existence of alternatives cannot in itself rebut the claim. It can show that the argument in favour of doing action *A* seen as a *necessary* means towards a goal is *invalid*, but pointing to alternatives could only rebut the claim if the action chosen could be shown to have a negative impact on goals, while the alternatives would not have such consequences, i.e. if the claim in favour of that action could be rebutted. To defend an alternative action would amount to showing that this alternative, as a hypothesis, is more reasonable, as systematic criticism (in terms of its impact on goals) has not revealed, or has not *yet* revealed, reasons against it. So, we suggest, the distinction between rebutting and defeating points to a sharp division between two types of critical questions: questions that aim to defeat the argument, by which we understand attempting to show the argument is invalid (and therefore unsound) or unsound (though valid), and questions that aim to show that the argument's conclusion is false (unacceptable) by indicating the existence of a rationally persuasive argument (a *counter-argument*) whose claim is the *denial* of the original claim (i.e. the agent *should not do* the action).

Let us explain the view above in more detail and give some examples. We said that not all critical questions we can aim at an argument can indicate that there is something wrong with the argument's conclusion, which we take to be the main point of criticism. It is essential to observe that showing that the action is not *necessary* or *sufficient* in view of the conclusion (the claim for action) does not point to the existence of a counter-argument but merely defeats the argument; in other words, it does not indicate that *not doing* the action is the right thing to do. For instance, an action may not be in itself *sufficient* to realize the goal, without thereby indicating that it should not be performed. If I want to learn Italian, I may think that I ought to enrol on an Italian language course. The fact that simply enrolling is not *sufficient* for learning the language does not mean that I shouldn't enrol. Similarly, enrolling on a course is not strictly speaking *necessary*, in view of the goal, as there are other alternatives available, such as using a language course on CD. But once again, the fact that there are alternatives (even easier, cheaper alternatives) does not show that I should not enrol, that my decision to enrol is irrational, or incompatible with the goals. For the claim to be rebutted, we suggest, there would have to be a rationally persuasive counter-argument saying that enrolling in an Italian language course is not what I should do because, in the process of doing so, *negative consequences would arise that would make the goal of learning Italian impossible to achieve*. It is highly improbable that such a rationally persuasive argument can be made.

Let us imagine another example, closer to the kind of text we are analysing in this book:

> The government's goal is to pull the country out of recession. (Goal)
> If the government cuts public spending, then the goal will be achieved. (Means–Goal)
> Conclusion: The government should cut public spending. (Recommended Action or Means)

Is this argument valid? No, because we can imagine a situation in which the conclusion above would be false, although the premises would be true, for instance if some other action (some alternative means) would *also* lead to the goal, or even would lead to the goal more efficiently.[21] So, while it may be true that spending cuts will deliver the goal (i.e. the strategy is sufficient for the realization of the goal), some other strategy might do this more efficiently. In this case, the conclusion would be false. The inference to the claim would be defeated, the argument would be invalid and therefore also unsound (a sound argument is a valid argument with true premises).

However, the argument would be valid if the premise 'If the government cuts public spending, then the goal will be achieved' was formulated as 'Cutting public spending is *necessary and sufficient* in order to achieve the goal'. If this premise was actually true as well, then the argument would be both valid and sound. In this latter situation, however, if anyone were to advance such a strong means–goal relation, we might want to question the actual truth of that premise. We might either say that there are many alternatives or that it is by no means certain that the proposed action can deliver the goals, i.e. that a lot more is needed besides spending cuts, for instance a strategy for economic growth and job creation. Showing that the action is either not necessary (because there are alternatives) or not sufficient (because it does not lead to the goals, or at least not in itself) would defeat the argument in favour of the conclusion. The argument would be unsound (having a false premise, in spite of being valid) *but this would still not rebut the claim, as a claim might be rationally acceptable (true) even if it supported by a bad (invalid or unsound) argument.* In other words, the conclusion that the government ought to cut public spending to achieve the goal *may not follow from the argument*, but neither does it follow that the government *should not cut public spending*. It might be reasonable to go ahead with public spending cuts *in combination with* another action (a growth strategy) which *together* might be sufficient to realize the goal. By contrast, if spending cuts should endanger the goal of the action or other related goals (if, instead of recovery, there should be a double-dip recession, with massive unemployment, etc.), then it might be wise *not* to go ahead with spending cuts: the conclusion would be in this case rebutted by counter-argument. The counter-argument has taken as premises the *consequences* of the action on the stated goal.

We suggest that whether the argument itself is valid or not does not ultimately matter. The one thing that matters is whether the conclusion is true or not, and it is only examination of the consequences of action and their impact on goals that agents are otherwise committed to that can rebut the conclusion. Briefly, an argument that is defeated may still have a rationally acceptable claim (though one that, in that particular case, is inadequately supported), but to rebut a claim is to be able to construct a rationally persuasive counter-argument. In talking about the consequences of action on goals we should bear in mind the understanding of goals on our approach, as future states of affairs compatible with a particular normative source (specified in the value premise). Normative sources can involve moral principles, so the impact on goals should be taken to include consequences in moral terms (e.g. how the action affects or undermines moral concerns) and should not be understood in simple cost–benefit material terms.

There seem therefore to be two types of critical questions and we shall illustrate both types, particularly in our discussion in Chapter 4: questions that challenge the argument (its soundness, its validity, or both, see (a) and (b) below), and questions that can rebut the claim and show that *not doing the action is more reasonable* (c).

(a) *Critical questions that challenge the rational acceptability of the premises (or their truth)*. If an argument is based on a false assessment of the situation, or on a mistaken view of some means–goal relation, then this might lead to a hypothesis for action which does not correspond to what the facts actually are. The argument will be unsound, but it does not necessarily mean that the conclusion should be rejected as unreasonable. It could be reasonable but inadequately supported. If I am mistaken about the deadline for submitting student reports and, thinking the deadline is tomorrow, I conclude I ought to do them today, it does not follow that, once I realize that the deadline is in a week's time, it is unreasonable to do them today. The argument is valid and unsound, but its conclusion is not rebutted.

(b) *Critical questions that can defeat the argument.* These challenge the inference from the premises to the conclusion and can indicate that the argument is invalid. If, for instance, such questioning reveals the action is not necessary, that there are better alternatives, then the claim that the agent should do the action *A* will no longer follow from the premises. The argument will be invalid and will not support the claim that the agent should do *A*. It will not follow *from that argument* that the agent should do *A*, but neither will it follow that the agent should *not* do *A*, that doing *A* is irrational in view of the agent's goals. The claim may still be reasonable, unless rebutted by a counter-argument.

However, we might want to argue that the action should *not* be performed, given its impact on various goals and values. This would illustrate the second type of questions, discussed below.

(c) *Critical questions that can rebut the claim.* These focus primarily, we suggest, on the *consequences* of action, consequences that undermine the stated goal of the action or other goals that the agent is or ought to be committed to (such as the legitimate goals of other agents). In light of these consequences, it is not the original proposal for action that should be adopted but its opposite. Negative consequences of this sort are part of a counter-argument supporting a counter-claim. We suggest that, from the point of view of the evaluation of the rationality of action, these are in fact the only interesting questions: if an action undermines the goal of action, then it should not be performed. Similarly, if an action leads to the goal stated in the goal premise (is sufficient) but has negative consequences on *other* goals that are important to the agent or to other agents, then again it might be wise not to go ahead with the action. These two situations are not identical. In the former, the stated goal of the action is not achieved, so – if the agent is committed to the goal – it is clear that the action should not be performed. In the latter, the goal is achieved, but with a negative impact on *other* goals. For instance, in the argument about government action we suggested earlier, the government might achieve their goals by cutting public spending but at high costs in terms of *other* goals they ought to be committed to (e.g. high employment, as a publicly recognized, legitimate goal). We can imagine therefore the premises of this argument being true but the conclusion being false, once the additional considerations of a negative impact on other goals (not mentioned in the argument) are taken into account. Any action will have consequences or costs of some kind and there should be a distinction between consequences or costs that can be accepted, or traded off against positive consequences, and costs that are unacceptable. If the costs of doing *A* are not significant, then it will not follow that the agent should not do the action. If, however, the goals that are being endangered should not be overridden (and such goals can include the fulfilment of overriding concerns but also of duties, obligations, publicly recognized norms, etc.), then *not doing* the action might be more rational.

To conclude, a proposal for action (the conclusion of a practical argument) can be rationally acceptable even if the argument that allegedly supports it is invalid or unsound. The invalidity or unsoundness of the argument itself does not indicate that the conclusion of that argument is false, but merely that it does not follow from the premises. If, on the other hand, a practical conclusion is rebutted by constructing a cogent counter-argument, then the conclusion is false. It is only questioning the possible negative consequences (and only those consequences that result in goals being compromised, not just any minor side-effects) that can rebut the claim. From the perspective of the rationality of the proposed action, therefore, many of Walton's critical questions are less significant than they seem to be, as they cannot practically refute the claim that the action is right, but only suggest that it does not follow from a particular argument.

We have suggested a somewhat different picture of what critical questioning can and cannot do, based on granting special weight to questions about the consequences of (proposed) action. We also want to suggest a few more possibilities for critical questioning, in line with the structure of arguments we have suggested in this chapter. These, we want to emphasize, are only important to the extent that they can be connected with the question about consequences. We have, for example, argued for the inclusion of premises referring to the circumstances of action in the practical reasoning schema. The circumstances of action can be described in various ways to support different courses of action and this reflects the different concerns or values that inform the argument. Critical questions pertaining to the circumstances of action might target the rational acceptability of these alternative descriptions. We can therefore ask:

- Is the situation described in a rationally acceptable way? (Definition of Circumstances Question)

For instance, is it described in a way that introduces a possible bias for which no burden of proof has been assumed, e.g. some persuasive definition that has not been convincingly argued for? Is it true that the situation is really a problem to be solved?

We also suggest further questions related to the value premise, by analogy with the questions aimed at the goal premise:

- Are the values that underlie the action rationally acceptable? (Acceptable Value Question)
- Should the agent consider other values? (Other Values Question)
- Do the stated values conflict with other values of the agent? (Agent's Multiple Values Question)

Let us finally say a few things about the way practical arguments can 'ground' action. We have said that practical reasoning is inherently defeasible and can be accepted provisionally if it has withstood critical questioning. We have been implicitly arguing for viewing the function of arguments as essentially *critical*, rather than having to do with justification. Arguments cannot justify claims, at least not in the sense in which the conclusion *follows* from the premises (unless they are deductive arguments). As we have seen above, in practical arguments, as in all arguments, the acceptability of a (practical) claim is independent from the 'goodness' of the argument that allegedly supports it. In order to criticize a claim for action we should therefore look at its *consequences*, not at the way in which it is allegedly supported. The claim for action does not follow from the premises except as a hypothesis, a conjecture that the action might be the right one, and this hypothesis is always open to revision in light of criticism. However little doubt or scepticism arguers may show in everyday situations, and however emphatically they may advance their arguments, a practical claim for action can only be advanced tentatively, subject to defeat or rebuttal by critical questioning. People no doubt do support or justify their claims with reasons all the time, often with allegedly 'good' reasons, but this should be understood in light of a conception of human fallibility, of agents acting in conditions of partial and uncertain knowledge and of risk.

Some theorists speak about good arguments as being 'well-grounded'. For Audi (2006: 214), 'rationality is *well-groundedness*' and a good practical argument is an argument which is 'grounded in the right sort of way in the right kind of reasons'; rationally defensible values are among such 'right' reasons. In light of our remarks in this section on the impossibility of justification, this can only mean that the acceptability of such reasons, their apparent 'rightness' or 'well-groundedness' has emerged in a process of critical examination. It is the procedure itself (as method) that, in the absence of certainty (or 'grounds'), can deliver a reasonable standpoint. The reasonableness of arguments, including practical arguments of the sort made in politics, should be seen as being 'located in the self-correcting capacities of a discussion procedure and not in the security of substantive starting points' (van Eemeren *et al.* 1993: 170–171). Rationality is attached to a *procedure* that ensures maximum opportunity for the critical examination of arguments, it resides in the *method* of arriving at a practical judgement (or decision). Thus, we can of course go on saying that a practical argument that has resulted from careful consideration of possible consequences and their impact on goals, of the context of action, of goals and values, and so on, can be a *good*, rationally persuasive argument, that it can 'ground' or 'justify' action, but by this we can only mean that its conclusion has resisted our attempts to find reasons *against* doing the action, as opposed to being supported by reasons *in favour*. We are therefore generally sceptical about 'well-groundedness' to the extent that we always act against in a context of uncertainty, risk and incomplete information.

However, there is another sense in which it nevertheless makes sense to talk about 'well-groundedness', a sense in which Audi (2006) is right: the sense involved in talking about moral, external reasons for action. A morally justified action is 'well-grounded' in a different sense from a purely instrumental action. So is, as we shall see below, an action which is prompted by an institutional reason, such as an action that conforms to some particular rule or regulation (not necessarily moral). Such reasons conflict not only with self-interested reasons, but also amongst themselves: there are various reasonable normative *hierarchies* that can be reasonably defended in various contexts, and often no obvious way of solving a conflict of obligation or duties, no obvious *priority* of one moral principle over others. It is in such situations that what we have called the fundamentally 'presumptive' and 'conductive' nature of practical reasoning is most obvious: several reasonable arguments, favouring different courses of action, and grounded in different moral (or other external) reasons will have to be weighed together and compared in order to decide (Audi 2006, Chapter 10).

To conclude, our approach is grounded in a critical notion of reasonableness: a reasonable standpoint is one that has emerged from a systematic dialectical procedure of critical testing or questioning. (We share this underlying philosophy with both pragma-dialectics and with critical rationalism.) Similarly, a reasonable decision is one that has emerged from such a procedure of critical examination. In speaking of 'rational decision-making' or 'increasing the rationality' of a decision-making process we are talking therefore about a rational *procedure* that can yield a reasonable decision (which nevertheless may turn out not to have been a 'good' decision, however reasonable it seemed at the time). We are not invoking a means–end rationality (seen as a purely instrumental orientation to given goals, or as the pursuit of the most 'cost-effective' means towards the goals) but talking about a procedure which involves the critical examination and 'weighing' of non-instrumental reasons (moral, institutional reasons) as well. Acting on such reasons may be reasonable (and rational in a non-instrumental sense) while possibly going against instrumentally defined goals. For instance, agents can decide to fulfil duties and obligations that go against what they desire or may entail substantial 'costs'. Another way of expressing this is by saying that the rationality of practical reasoning in politics is partly instrumental (as politics pursues goals) but also more-than-instrumental, as it can involve deliberation on the goals of action themselves. Agents should not only evaluate means instrumentally, in relation to *given* goals, but should also ask: 'are these goals reasonable or worthy of being pursued?', and should not only ask: 'what should I do given what I want?', but also 'what ought I to want?'

Philosophical approaches to practical reasoning

All current approaches to practical reasoning in philosophy begin by discussing Aristotle, Hume and Kant on practical reasoning, and position themselves in relation to them. Let us just say a few things at this point that will put our own discussion into a broader perspective, with the caveat that we are not philosophers and may unduly simplify highly subtle and complex arguments.

Aristotle's views on practical reasoning are found in his *Nicomachean Ethics*, where he writes about practical syllogisms and deliberation. Famously, he says there that 'We deliberate not about ends, but about what promotes the ends', that is, we deliberate not about ends, but about means (a doctor does not deliberate whether he will cure the patient, but only about what remedy he should prescribe in order to cure him). This can be easily misunderstood. As Audi (2006: 28) shows, Aristotle's position is that deliberation is relative to some end or goal that is *given* in that context, and cannot therefore be at the same time the subject of deliberation in *that* context. This does not mean that we cannot choose to deliberate about goals: we can compare goals, choose among competing goals, see how one particular goal fits in with other goals we have, how one goal we might want to pursue in the short-term is likely to serve or undermine our long-term goals. In political discourse, for example, deliberation is often about which ends to pursue at society level, and each political party will argue in favour of its own vision for the future.[22]

David Hume's conception of reason is usually taken as the paradigmatic example of the instrumentalist conception of practical reasoning. To quote a famous passage from Hume's *Treatise of Human Nature*, 'Reason is, and ought only to be the slave of the passions, and can never pretend to any other office than to serve and obey them' (Hume 1739, 1967: 415). In other words, reason's role is *instrumental* in relation to desire, and it is desires ('the passions') that *motivate* us to act. To the extent that we can talk of practical *reason* at all, its role is only to inform us of the existence of possible objects of desire and of what means are available to satisfy those desires. We cannot reason about desires (such as the desire to avoid pain), we simply have them, and no desire is irrational. For Hume therefore, reason is not motivationally practical, in the sense that by itself it cannot prompt action: it is desire, not belief that is basic to action. But (unlike for Kant) reason is not normatively practical either, in the sense that by itself it cannot tell us which desires or ends are good or bad, or what we should or should not do or want (Audi 2006: 47). In fact, given the instrumental role reason plays, for Hume there is no such thing as a theory of practical *reasoning*.[23]

Instrumentalism is the 'default' theory of practical reasoning. It views all practical reasoning as means–end reasoning: in order to get what they already want, people have to figure out the means. Once achieved, our goals become means towards further goals and so on, but ultimately all goals 'bottom out' – philosophers say – in intrinsic (non-instrumental) desires (for instance a desire to avoid pain). Instrumentalism has become increasingly attractive to many philosophers because, as Audi (2002) argues, it holds out the prospect of naturalizing practical reason, of naturalizing the notion of normative reasons for action and, through this, hopefully, the moral domain. This project fits in very well with the naturalization of theoretical reasoning that cognitive science and biology set out to achieve long ago. Vogler (2002) defends instrumentalism by looking at the structure of action (instead of focusing on desire as psychological motive). All intentional action, she argues, displays a means–end structure (alternatively a part–whole structure) and can be broken down into smaller components by asking 'why are you doing *A*?'. The answer always indicates a means–end or part–whole relation, as a non-optional, obligatory structure for all intentional action (even for those actions which we think we are doing for their own sake, as they are a part of a whole). All simple intentional actions are performed as part of chains of action leading to an end-point or as a part of another more complex action.

Rationalist philosophers, following Kant, however, reject the claim that the moral 'ought' can be ultimately explained in terms of natural desires or aversions. For them, the moral 'ought' expresses an imperative of pure reason independent of desire. For Kant, practical reason is autonomous (not instrumental). It enables us to see what we ought to do and motivates us to act accordingly even when we have no independent desire to do so. Moral judgement (as instantiated in categorical imperatives) is the paradigmatic case of practical reason as motivationally practical (Audi 2006: 212). It is therefore moral judgement or belief (e.g. that stealing is wrong) and not desire that primarily motivates us to refrain from stealing, and our beliefs about what is right and wrong constrain our desires: 'Reason is given to us as a practical faculty, i.e. one which is meant to have an influence on the will' (Kant 1959: 10, cited in Audi 2006: 57).[24]

Among contemporary philosophers that have reflected on practical reasoning, Audi's (2006) account is part-Aristotelian and primarily Kantian. On his view, practical reasoning can take judgements of duties (principles, norms), not only desires, as premises; the belief that it is my duty to do *A* can also motivate action (as internal reason). By contrast, Blackburn (1998) takes a Humean view: all action is motivated by a combination of belief and desire, but desires are ultimately basic. It is our beliefs and our *concerns* (our emotional, evaluative attitudes towards those things we care about) that together issue in action, and everything we do can be traced back to some concern we have, as the final motivator of action. Beliefs can lead to action only through the mediation of a concern (I believe that you are in pain and I act to help you because your being in pain matters to me, because I care about the way you feel) and have no motivating force on their own unless coupled with a sense that something is of value, or desirable, or that we care about it in one way or another (Blackburn 1998: 90–91).

Our concerns (e.g. a concern for the happiness of our children), as things that matter to us and affect us when we try to decide what to do, are emotionally invested. Among our concerns, our values are very important. Unlike desires, which may be unstable and contradictory, values represent our stable, fundamental concerns or dispositions to act. We would not be willing to give them up as easily as we may renounce particular desires. Within the field of our concerns, values can be regarded as those concerns that we are also concerned to preserve, those that we regard as constitutive of our identity. Values inform agents' desires and goals, or can enable agents to take a critical stance with respect to their desires and goals (Blackburn 1998: 67).

Regarding deliberation, Blackburn points out that, in considering reasons for action, we do not stand over and above our concerns, somehow surveying our conflicting desires from the standpoint of reason. Our survey of the situation and our engagement with it are done *in light of our concerns*: whatever features of the context we notice and pay attention to, whatever ends and means we choose, all these are selected from within our 'individual profiles of concern and care'. It is the concerns we have that determine both, on the one hand, our beliefs about what problems need to be overcome and about what means are likely to succeed, and, on the other hand, the goals we set ourselves. Concerns are features of the deliberating agent and not the object of deliberation (Blackburn 1998: 252).[25]

Most work on practical reasoning in philosophy has been done so far in the field of moral philosophy. According to Millgram, moral theories (whether they are rule-based, consequence-based or virtue-based) pair off with particular theories of practical reasoning. 'Theories of practical reasoning are the engines of strong moral theories', they drive moral theories and it is possible to claim that 'the right way to do moral philosophy is to start by working out your theory of practical reasoning' (Millgram 2005: 1–4). A theory of practical reasoning has implications not only for moral philosophy, but also for philosophy of mind, philosophy of action and for social science, as it raises such problems as freedom of the will, the structure of action, the link between agents' reasons for action and social change, the fact–value and is–ought distinctions, the relationship between emotion and reason, and so on.

Instrumentalism, also referred to as the 'calculative' view of reason, underlies a consequence-based, utilitarian approach to ethics, where utility or happiness are viewed as a complex of goals (Millgram 2005). Kantian moral theorists are disturbed by what they see as undesirable implications of instrumentalism. If instrumentalism is true, and if desires are the ultimate motivators, there can be no rational basis for ethics. There is no sense in which we can say that an individual ought to behave morally if he has no desire to do so. All moral reasons (being honest, keeping one's promises, etc.) are external reasons, on an instrumentalist picture, and therefore they cannot be reasons for action at all. On the other hand, if keeping one's promise (however much that may conflict with one's other desires and plans) effectively motivates an agent, then the instrumentalist fundamental proposition that all reasons are desire-based is false (Vogler 2002: 188–189). A calculative view of practical reasoning allows for the existence of rational agents who cynically exploit others in pursuit of their own ends, it allows for what Vogler calls a 'reasonably vicious' agent: being immoral is not a failure of rationality. The refutation of the calculative, instrumental view often turns on the conviction that we need to exercise some form of *non-instrumental reason*, i.e. practical reason that aims *to set or evaluate ends*, rather than merely find means to ends which we already happen to have (Vogler 2002: 3) and that non-instrumental practical reason is essential to living an ethical life.

A Kantian view of practical reasoning is a more-than-instrumental one, and a more demanding one, because the view of rational action and agency are different. Immoral behaviour is, on this view, a failure of rationality. We can know which actions are right or wrong on grounds of pure reason alone (and not by looking at their consequences): these are the actions that pass the tests of the categorical imperative of universalizability. Millgram argues that the over-demanding and exceptionless character of a moral judgement which this view entails indicates that Kantian moral theory does not allow for practical judgements which are defeasible (but possibly only valid deductive arguments). On the contrary, Aristotle recognized that in practical reasoning (which he called deliberation), justified exceptions are endless and practical inferences are *characteristically* defeasible (Millgram 2005: 17). Moreover, knowing when a practical argument is defeated, therefore knowing when to abstain from action is, for Aristotle, the mark of the virtuous man. Practical syllogism is at the core of Aristotle's conception of virtue and an account of virtue begins with an account of correct deliberation (Millgram 2005: 136–138).

The philosophical debate on practical reasoning is far-ranging and the main dispute between Humeans and Kantians, between instrumentalists and rationalists, and between inductivists and deductivists is not settled. There are many contemporary approaches to practical reasoning, and we have referred to Blackburn (1998) and Audi (2006) representing a Humean and respectively a Kantian view. Millgram (2005) defends *practical induction* or *practical empiricism* as an alternative theory to instrumentalism. It is a theory that allows reasoning to adjust and modify ends. Often, he says, we need to find out first what ends we want, and the best way is to learn by experience. From experience, we may learn that the desires and goals we have so far had are not conducive to our well-being or that of others, or that they clash with other goals we value or other desires we have, or are not coherent with our broader plans. We will be thus prompted to revise our goals, to modify our desires. Practical induction means that experience teaches us what is important and what matters, and leads us to revise our motivational system, reorganize our priorities, so as to make what we want more coherent with our broader longer-term plans and with the goal of a coherent life (Millgram 2005: 316–320). On the other hand, Popperian philosophers (Miller 1994, 2006) would not deny the role of experience but would argue nevertheless that practical reasoning can only be deductive, and that all inferences, theoretical or practical, are so.

An extremely persuasive view of practical reasoning is developed by Searle, as part of his theory of the construction of social reality (Searle 1995, 2010). Although our analysis and evaluation of practical arguments in the chapters that follow draw on many of the insights into practical reasoning that we have discussed above, our understanding of practical reasoning is most indebted to Searle's theory and we try to give a brief preliminary account of it in the next section.

Social reality and agents' reasons for action

According to Searle (2010), the distinctive feature of social reality is that humans have the capacity to impose functions (*status functions*) on people and objects, i.e. functions that cannot be performed by these people and objects just on the basis of their physical nature. For instance, a certain plastic rectangle can be a bank card and it cannot be a bank card just in virtue of its physical properties, just in virtue of being a plastic rectangle. A certain person can become Prime Minister, but he cannot have this function just in virtue of his physical properties as a human being. Something more is needed for objects or persons to fulfil the functions that are assigned to them. The performance of status functions requires that there be a *collectively recognized* status that the person/object has and it is only in virtue of that collectively recognized status that the person/object can perform the function in question. So there must be collective acceptance or recognition of the object/person as having that status, i.e. *collective intentionality*. (Collective acceptance does not imply approval: people collectively recognize things which they may hate.) Institutional reality comes into being by acts whereby status functions are assigned to people and objects and these status functions exist in virtue of collective intentionality (often embodied in written documents). These acts are performative speech acts of the type '*X* counts as *Y* in context *C*' (what Searle calls a constitutive rule) – e.g. 'such and such counts as a £20 note in our society' – and, in Searle's (1969) well-known typology of speech acts, belong to the class of *declarations*. Declarations are those speech acts that create the very reality they represent and all institutional reality (family, marriage, universities, private property, money, government etc.) is, Searle argues, created by this type of speech act.[26]

Status functions carry *deontic powers*, i.e. they carry rights, duties, obligations, requirements, permissions, authorizations, entitlements etc. Having a *bank card* and *bank account* in which I keep *money* which is my own *private property* enables me to do a variety of things, but also constrains my actions (I can dispose of my own money in a way that I cannot dispose of someone else's money). It is, Searle argues, *because status functions carry deontic powers that they provide the 'glue' that holds human civilization together* (Searle 2010: 9). How do they do that? Deontic powers have a unique trait: once recognized, they provide us with *reasons for action that are independent of our inclinations and desires*. If I recognize an object (your bank card, your bank account, your money, your house) as your property, then I recognize that I have a (*desire-independent*) reason not to take it or use it without your permission, not to steal it, etc. And if I do misuse your

card or steal your money or damage your property, I understand that I risk facing consequences, and that I may be lawfully punished, as your right to your property is collectively
recognized by others and enshrined in a collectively recognized system of laws.

What is the explanatory value of looking at society in these terms? Searle's answer is that
such an understanding shows how 'human institutional reality locks into human rationality'
by providing people with reasons for action (Searle 2010: 124) and makes possible an understanding of how power functions in society. In collectively recognizing status functions we
accept a series of obligations, rights, duties, responsibilities, etc. Status functions are the *vehicles of power* in society, and the whole point of creating institutional reality is to 'create and
regulate power relationships between people' (Searle 2010: 106). To recognize something as
your obligation or someone's right is to recognize a reason for action that is independent
from your desires and inclinations, a reason you *have* (in virtue of collective recognition of
institutional facts) regardless of whether you want to act in accordance with it or not. The
deontic powers assigned to people and objects make possible desire-independent reasons for
action. Institutional structures enable people to do things which they could not otherwise do,
but they also provide a deontology that constrains them to do things which they would not
otherwise do. The fact that many people would not want to break the law or would willingly
and without coercion abide by social norms should not obscure the fact that the reasons are
there, and people have them, in the sense of recognizing them, whatever attitude they adopt
towards them, whatever their inclinations to abide or not by them. Institutional reality can
continue to function because it provides *free* rational agents (agents that could choose to act
in different ways) with reasons for action, in the sense that it constrains them to act in ways
in which they may be disinclined to act. Searle criticizes the internalist (Humean) view that
equates motivation with internal reasons such as desires. In his view, reasons that are independent from what we desire, such as obligations, promises, duties (all the deontic powers
that flow from collectively assigned and recognized status functions) motivate people to
act, and they do so whether they give rise or not to a desire to act in accordance with that
reason. It is recognition of such reasons that may lead to the formation of a desire to observe
their binding force, but *the desire derives from the reason we recognize*, and not vice-versa (Searle
2010: 131).

We find that Searle's social ontology is compatible with that of critical realism (which
underlies CDA) but has the advantage of clearly showing the mechanism whereby social
institutional reality is created and reproduced through language, with the purpose of creating and regulating relations of power. It also shows how institutional reality connects with
human agency by providing people with reasons for action. On the whole, it offers a very
plausible explanation of the relationship between agents and structures, and of the role of
language in the creation and reproduction of social reality, including power relations. We
have used Searle's conception of the relation between desire-independent and desire-
dependent reasons for action in thinking about the structure of practical reasoning and in
analysing various arguments from collectively recognized norms and values, and we will
draw on it at various points throughout the book.

Is–ought, facts and values

The conclusion of a practical argument is a normative *ought*-statement or an evaluative statement of the type *action* A *is the right action*. Is it possible to start from descriptive premises and
reach a normative/evaluative conclusion? The 'is–ought' problem, first formulated by

Hume, says that a prescriptive (normative) statement cannot be derived from a descriptive one. The fact that something happens to be the case (e.g. the Catholic Church has existed for a very long time) is insufficient grounds for concluding that something ought to be the case (e.g. the Catholic Church ought to be treated with respect). Another normative premise must be added to make the argument valid and make the conclusion follow, e.g. 'anything that has existed for a long time ought to be treated with respect'. This additional premise seems to be outside the scope of rationality altogether, its grounding seems to be purely arbitrary. Some people would accept it, while others would say it is false (not everything that has existed for a long time ought to be treated with respect). It would appear that it is only from a combination of descriptive and normative premises that a normative conclusion can be validly derived, not from facts alone, and the rational acceptability of the added premise is not self-evident.

Other examples seem less problematic. It seems quite reasonable to infer, from the fact that smoking damages health, that people ought to avoid smoking. The normative premise we would have to add (anything that damages health ought to be avoided) seems uncontroversially true. Similarly, from the fact that a lot of people in the world are suffering from hunger, it is reasonable to infer that governments ought to do everything in their power to end this suffering. The additional premise (suffering from hunger is wrong) seems again uncontroversial. However, the same logical problem bedevils these arguments, as a normative or evaluative premise has to be added in order to make the arguments valid; moreover, this premise cannot itself be derived from facts alone, or so the argument goes, so we seem to be left with infinite regress.

But is it really impossible to derive such *ought*-statements from *is*-statements? Words like 'suffering' and 'damaging', which we have used to describe what is actually the case, have an in-built normative, evaluative component. To use such words is not only to describe but to *warn* against smoking and suffering, or to *recommend* a certain type of action: whatever causes suffering or damages health ought to be avoided and this is *because of natural facts about human beings*. Such facts (that smoking is damaging or hunger is bad) are not value-free, they have evaluative, normative content, and this is in virtue of what people are (as biological and social beings). (If human beings were immune to the effects of smoking or hunger, then such 'facts' would not exist.) It is because of what we are (fact) that anything that damages health or causes suffering ought to be avoided (prescription). The is–ought gap can thus be bridged by natural facts about human beings. The arbitrariness we noted above seems to have disappeared.[27]

The attempt to ground *ought*-statements in what is natural for human beings, what helps or hinders their 'flourishing', is not without problems. What makes people flourish often turns out to have damaging consequences – on other people, on the environment, etc. Also, while human beings have much in common as biological beings and social beings, there is also a lot of cultural and individual diversity in terms of what makes them flourish. However, the naturalistic belief that moral truths can be grounded in facts about human physical reality, and that there is no unbridgeable gap between factual (scientific) questions and evaluative or moral ones, is a powerful one and is gaining more and more support from cognitive and biological science. On this view, in enabling us to understand what helps or hinders human well-being in an objective sense, science holds the key to moral questions (Harris 2010).

A way of linking *is* and *ought*, facts and values is therefore to deny that such distinctions exist: 'facts' are imbued with evaluative/normative content and evaluative/normative statements are naturally grounded in facts about human beings. This is the line we have also taken here, in placing 'concerns' (as evaluative attitudes) at the root of the goals agents set for themselves, but also behind what they select as relevant circumstances (facts) and the particular description under which these facts enter arguments. (In Chapter 3 we will say more about so-called 'persuasive', evaluative/normative ways of defining the context of action.) We are also denying that facts can be divorced from values in saying that critical questioning of arguments can refer to the rational acceptability of values and of goals, as well as the rational acceptability of the value-laden descriptions of the context of action. This is another way of expressing the insight that values are not beyond the scope of reason, they can be argued about, as they are not merely subjective preferences (Sayer 2011). Reasoning about values, on the view that we propose, a view we share with Sayer, is grounded in a conception of human well-being: it is (partly) in relation to how the values that underlie arguments promote or hinder human well-being that those arguments can be evaluated as reasonable or not. In other words, 'it is in the context of capability, vulnerability and precarious well-being or flourishing ... that both values and reason in everyday life need to be understood' (Sayer 2011: 6).

Searle (2008) has his own answer to the *is–ought/fact–value* distinctions (and he takes the former to be the linguistic formulation of the latter). He also rejects this dualism, as being one which no one would really accept in real life: when we are the subject of aggression, when our rights are violated, we make very clear connections between facts and values. We say that whoever acted abusively against us did something wrong and ought not to have done it; we do not accept that what happened can be explained or justified in terms of the malefactor's different or equally justifiable set of values. In other words, we would not accept that the move from 'He cheated me' to 'He ought not to have done it' is motivated by a subjective and arbitrary premise, one that cannot be rationally defended. On the contrary, we would say that 'Cheating *is* wrong', and this is a *fact*, not just some evaluative attitude some people happen to have.

Searle – for whom 'ethics is really a branch of the much more interesting subject of practical reason and rationality' (Searle 2008: 22) – argues that the *is–ought* question is a question about whether or not there are 'objective' reasons for action. The question can thus be reformulated as follows: Can there be reasons for action that are binding on a rational agent just in virtue of the nature of the fact reported in the reasons statement, and independently of the agent's desires, values, attitudes and evaluations? (Searle 2008: 165). The answer is yes: such reasons are the 'desire-independent' institutional facts that arise from the performance of speech acts, e.g. the public commitment to truth incurred in making statements, the public commitment to future action undertaken in making a promise, the rights, duties and obligations that follow from declarative speech acts, and so on (we have explained these in the previous section). These self-created reasons are objective, they are *facts*, reasons that people *have* for doing what they *ought* to do, whether they actually end up doing it or not, and whatever their subjective attitudes may be. They are *internal* or *constitutive* of the speech acts people perform, and of the intentional acts associated with those speech acts. The derivation of *ought* from *is* thus becomes, for Searle, a trivial and straightforward matter (what people ought to do is a constitutive part of, already contained in, the institutional facts in question).

Conclusion

In this chapter we have laid out our own conception of practical reasoning, different from that of other theorists and we have suggested an original schema for practical reasoning. We have argued that practical arguments typically take *goals* and *circumstances* as premises (and also *values* that underlie goals). From given and known circumstances and goals, agents conjecture that a certain action might enable them to transform current circumstances in accordance with some values or concerns. This hypothetical means will have to be compatible with both goals and circumstances, as well as with the values that inform the agent's conception of what the circumstances are and what the goals should be. Premises having to do with the *negative consequences* of action enter into a counter-argument that has the denial of the original claim as its conclusion.

The circumstances of action were said to include empirical circumstances but also social, institutional facts (duties, commitments, socially recognized moral values). External reasons for action have to be internalized by the agent in order to lead to action (the agent has to recognize the binding nature of promises, duties and moral principles, and has to *want* to act in accordance with them), but are not reducible to wants and desires. They may ground a motivation to act in accordance with them, but they do not always do so (agents may choose to disregard commitments and norms that they are otherwise bound by). The empirical *facts* that people reason from are inseparable from their values (i.e. there is no fact–value distinction). Facts are selected as relevant premises and presented under a certain (usually rhetorically convenient) description in relation to the action being advocated. Even in those cases when the description of circumstances seems to be 'neutral', the circumstantial premise remains a premise that describes a *problem* to be solved, and – as a problem – inherently contains an evaluation of the facts. Goals, we suggested, should not be simply equated with what agents want, but should be seen as imagined, future states of affairs that are compatible with various sources of normativity (desires, moral values, etc.); a specification of this normative source constitutes the value premise.

In arriving at a view of the structure of practical arguments, we started from philosophical accounts of practical reasoning, in particular the distinction between internal and external reasons, between desire-dependent and desire-independent reasons, a theory of speech acts and action by means of language, of the construction of social institutional reality, the fact–value distinction, as well as from a semantic theory of deontic modality. Our account is also informed by a critical rationalist view of the essential critical function of argument and of human rationality. In beginning to develop a view of practical reasoning as deliberation, we have drawn on Aristotle but also on contemporary political theory, in particular a conception of reasonable and unreasonable value pluralism, hence reasonable and unreasonable disagreement, and a non-relativist perspective in matters of value judgement.

In a dialectical framework, critical questions are used to test the reasonableness of the proposed action. Principally, these questions will refer to the likely impact of the action on various goals (the goals of the agent or of other agents, including goals defined in terms of moral concerns), but may also involve alternative means, the rational acceptability of stated goals and values, etc. These questions can defeat the argument (e.g. show that the conclusion does not follow) and this is distinct from the situation in which the argument's conclusion can be rebutted or rejected: in this case, the conclusion that follows is that the action should *not* be performed. In our view, questions related to the consequences of action are the most interesting from a critical perspective as, unlike other questions, they can help the critic rebut the conclusion, the proposal for action itself.

Regarding the evaluation of arguments, we have adopted a dialectical perspective. Rhetorical considerations are not neglected but are integrated within a primarily dialectical approach. Taking a critical perspective on the variety of instances of practical reasoning put forward in every domain of life has an inherent legitimacy, one that is built into the nature of practical arguments and the dialectical nature of the context in which argumentation occurs. It is part of the logic of practical arguments that they are *presumptively reasonable* and can default. The presumption that by performing an action a certain effect (goal) will be achieved may have to be reassessed if there is a strong probability that the action will back-fire and achieve undesirable effects, or if emerging consequences throw into doubt the wisdom of the action. Practical arguments are often advanced with great certainty but by nature they can only be put forward tentatively and provisionally and are inherently subject to defeat, due to human fallibility and other limitations. While critical questioning can challenge them, it can also lead to the production of stronger arguments. Critical discussion and critical testing of proposals for action can lead arguers to revise their proposals and replace them with new ones, in light of the progressive uncovering of various considerations against them that affect their rational acceptability.

3 Critical discourse analysis and analysis of argumentation

In this chapter we present an approach to critical discourse analysis (CDA) and discuss its relationship to critical social science and the forms of critique associated with it, and then discuss how the analysis and evaluation of arguments as we have presented it in Chapter 2 can increase the capacity of CDA to pursue its aim of extending critique to discourse. We shall do this by returning to an earlier analysis of part of a speech by Tony Blair (Fairclough 2000a), showing how the analysis is strengthened if we build it around the practical argument which Blair is advancing, asking what aspects of the earlier analysis need to be retained and how they can be connected to the analysis of practical argumentation. We shall discuss in more general terms how analysis of practical argumentation fits in with and contributes to normative and explanatory critique, and we will look at other concepts that CDA works with (imaginaries, political legitimacy, power) from the viewpoint of a theory of argument.

CDA began to develop as a separate field of teaching and research in the 1970s and 1980s (Fowler *et al.* 1979, Fairclough 1989). It subsumes a number of versions and approaches which differ in sometimes major ways (see for example Fairclough and Wodak 1997; Wodak and Meyer 2009; van Dijk 1997a on these differences). The account of CDA which we shall present here does not attempt to cover these differences; it is based upon a particular approach to CDA (Fairclough 1989, 1992, 1995, 2000a, 2003, 2006, 2010; Chouliaraki and Fairclough 1999) and especially the more recent versions of this approach.

CDA has sought to extend the critical tradition in social science to include discourse. 'Discourse' is basically social use of language, language in social contexts, although those who use the term tend to be committed to certain more specific claims about the social use of language, e.g. the claim that discourse contributes to the 'construction' of social reality. But there are various understandings of discourse, and ours is built into the particular version of CDA which we present below. CDA has aimed both to change linguistics and other areas of language study by introducing critical perspectives on language, drawn from critical theory in the social sciences, which were previously absent, and to contribute to critical social analysis a focus on discourse which had previously been lacking or underdeveloped. This includes a better understanding of relations between discourse and other elements of social life, including social relations (and relations of power), ideologies, social institutions and organizations, and social identities, and better ways of analysing and researching these relations.

Critical social science

Critical social science differs from other forms of social science in that it aims not only to describe societies and the systems (e.g. political systems), institutions and organizations which are a part of them but also to evaluate them in terms of ideas of what societies should be like ('the good society') if they are to cultivate the well-being of their members rather than undermine it. Evaluation is linked to a concern to understand possibilities for, as well as obstacles to, changing societies to make them better in such respects.

Critical social science tends to be open to the idea that discourse is part of its concerns and ought to be given more detailed and systematic treatment than it generally has, because it has long recognized the importance of ideas and concepts in social life, which are manifested in discourse (Fairclough and Graham 2002). Social reality is 'conceptually mediated' (Marsden 1999): in addition to social events, social behaviour, social practices, there are always ideas, concepts, representations and indeed theories of them, which are, on the one hand, produced in social life and effects of social life and, on the other hand, have effects on social life, both helping to keep existing forms in existence and helping to change them. So ideas need to be socially explained and social life needs to be explained in part ideationally, in terms of the effects of ideas. And since ideas (concepts, representations, theories) are manifested in particular types and forms of discourse (and different ideas of, say, justice are manifested in different discourses), this claim can be extended to discourse: the types and forms of discourse which exist need to be socially explained and social life needs to be explained in part in terms of the effects of discourse.

Critical social analysis includes critique of particular areas or aspects of social life. Various forms of critique are generally distinguished and these differ in different approaches to critical social analysis. We shall focus upon two fundamental characteristics of critical social analysis – it is *normative*, i.e. it evaluates social beliefs and practices as true or false, beneficial or harmful, etc., and it is *explanatory* – and we will distinguish normative critique and explanatory critique. Normative critique evaluates social realities against the standard of values taken as necessary to a 'good society', which raises the question of what a good society is. One answer is that a good society is one which serves and facilitates human 'well-being'. There are various views of what constitutes well-being; one which has recently been influential defines it in terms of a range of human 'capabilities' – a range of distinctively human abilities that 'exert a moral claim that they should be developed' (Nussbaum 2000: 83). Explanatory critique seeks to explain why social realities are as they are, and how they are sustained or changed. Both types of critique are necessary in critical social research, which starts from judgements that the society or aspect of social life in focus is significantly but avoidably damaging to human well-being in particular respects. But while normative critique is directly concerned with such judgements in evaluating behaviour, actions and social practices as being, for example, just or unjust, fair or exploitative, racist or non-racist, sexist or non-sexist, and beliefs as being true or false, explanatory critique seeks to explain, for example, why and how existing social realities endure despite their damaging effects. Explanatory critique seeks understanding of what makes a given social order work, which is clearly necessary if it is to be changed to enhance human well-being: another aim of critical social science is to identify what might facilitate such change as well as obstruct it. See Sayer (2011) for an account of critique and well-being (including the 'capabilities' approach) along these lines.

Both forms of critique extend to discourse, though differently. Normative critique includes critique of unequal relations of power and forms of domination which are damaging to well-being and which may be manifest in discourse, e.g. in manipulative discourse when it is an integral part of some form of domination. Explanatory critique includes both explanations of particular types and forms of discourse as effects of social causes and explanations of social phenomena such as the establishment, maintenance or change of a social order as partly effects of discourse. An example will make the character of explanatory critique clearer.

It is widely recognized that neo-liberalism was established and accepted through a successful strategy centred initially in universities and think-tanks to change capitalism in a liberal direction, which became a real possibility in the crisis of the 1970s. This strategy included a neo-liberal discourse which has been crucial in the establishment of neo-liberal economies and their endurance despite a series of crises (see for instance Bourdieu and Wacquant 2001). Explanatory critique would seek social explanations of how and why this discourse emerged as part of this strategy and how and why it was relatively successful, and also explanations of the transformations of international capitalism since the 1970s, which include neo-liberal discourse as a causal factor. Part of the concern is with ideologies: with ideas, beliefs and concerns manifest in discourses, as well as enactments of such discourses in practices and genres and inculcations of them in identities and styles (for these terms, see below), which contribute to establishing, sustaining and reproducing social orders and relations of power. In ideology critique, critical social science seeks causal explanations of the normalization, naturalization and institutionalization, as well as pervasiveness and endurance within populations, of particular beliefs and concerns. It seeks to explain them in terms of material and social relations in particular forms of social life, with such questions as: Why do these particular beliefs and concerns endure? Why do they have powerful resonance for many people? Why are they so little challenged? What effects do they have on continuities and changes in social life? This is ideology in its critical sense, tied particularly to the question of how social orders which are significantly detrimental to human well-being can nevertheless endure. It is to be distinguished from ideology in a descriptive sense (Fairclough 2010: 23–83), the understanding of the different positions of political parties and groups, or the different outlooks of individuals or social groups, as so many 'ideologies', a sense which we shall not use in this book.

CDA cannot in itself carry out normative or explanatory critique, but can contribute a focus on discourse and on relations between discourse and other social elements to interdisciplinary critique. And in bringing CDA and argumentation theory and analysis together we are seeking to draw the latter into such interdisciplinary collaboration. How then do the two forms of critique relate to analysis and evaluation of argumentation? The latter amounts neither to normative nor to explanatory social critique, but it offers a particularly effective way of helping CDA to systematically extend these focuses of critique into analysis of texts. It poses critical questions which lead into and contribute to analysis of relations of power and domination manifested in particular bodies of texts, it shows how particular beliefs and concerns shape practical reasoning and, contingently, decisions and actions on matters of social and political importance, and it poses critical questions about how contexts of action, values and goals are represented in the premises of arguments which can feed into critique of ideology.

Critical social science seeks to give an account of the causes of social change. It treats reasons for action as one type of cause. Reasons for action are premises of practical arguments. They are part of the causal powers (Fairclough *et al.* 2004) of people as social agents (i.e. their powers to bring about change). But in addition to agentive causes of social change, there are structural causes and CDA is committed to the aim which characterizes critical social science more generally, of trying to clarify how agentive and structural causes relate to each other, i.e. to clarify the dialectic of structure and agency (Giddens 1984, 1987). For CDA in particular, this aim includes for instance trying to clarify the relationship between the causal effects of 'orders of discourse' (structures of a particular sort, which we will say more about below, see Fairclough 1992, 2003) and of the agency of people as social actors and producers of texts. For instance, in the case of practical reasoning, we have identified beliefs, desires and values as premises in practical reasoning, but an adequate account of the causes of social change would need to also ask why particular sets of beliefs, desires and values appear in particular instances of practical reasoning, how for instance they may arise from particular groups or classes of people being positioned in particular social–material relations. This moves us from the agency of people involved in practical reasoning towards structural factors and causes. Among people's reasons for action are reasons that express various external (structural, institutional) constraints on what they can do (we have discussed this in Chapter 2). They have duties, obligations, commitments, for instance obligations to abide by rules and laws and to respect the rights of other people. Analysis of practical reasoning offers the advantage of showing how the power of social and institutional structures manifests itself in the reasons for action that people recognize. In our view, *structures constrain (or enable) agency by providing people with reasons for action.*

The analysis and evaluation of practical reasoning will not tell us everything about social change; it will not tell us for instance whether action based on this reasoning will be effective in achieving social change, or what other facts about the world will make it succeed or fail to do so. But it can make a substantive contribution to both normative and explanatory critique (in ways which we explain further on in this chapter). It can, for instance, offer a principled way of criticizing powerful arguments that are not easily challenged, arguments that draw on dominant discourses and ideologies at the expense of an impartial consideration of other interests and perspectives, as being unreasonable, or as being grounded in unreasonable and rationally indefensible values and goals. It can thereby offer a principled way of evaluating normative claims and decisions made on the basis of deliberative practices which may not come up to the standards of rationally persuasive argumentation and thus fall short of an ideal of communicative rationality. This represents a substantive enhancement of the capacity of CDA to undertake critical analysis of texts in politics and other social fields.

Critical discourse analysis

We said above that 'discourse' is basically social use of language in social contexts. But the term is commonly used with different senses, even within our particular approach to CDA. It commonly means (a) signification as an element of the social process; (b) the language associated with a particular social field or practice (e.g. 'political discourse'); (c) a way of construing aspects of the world associated with a particular social perspective (e.g. a 'neo-liberal discourse of globalization'). These different senses are often confused, so it is helpful to use a different term at least for (a). The term 'semiosis' can be used for this most abstract and general sense (Fairclough *et al.* 2004) and this has the further advantage of suggesting that discourse analysis is concerned with various 'semiotic modalities' of which language is only one (others are visual images and 'body language').

Semiosis is a social element, a part or an aspect of social life, which is *dialectically* related to others (Fairclough 2001, 2010). Relations between elements of social life are dialectical in the sense of that, although they are different elements which social analysts would generally find it necessary to differentiate, they are not fully separate from each other. It is easiest to see this in cases of social change such as the transformation of capitalism into neo-liberal capitalism which we referred to above: neo-liberal economies appeared first as neo-liberal ideas and a neo-liberal discourse, which were then (because of the existence of favourable circumstances and conditions) successfully turned into new economic realities, neo-liberal economies.

It would be quite misleading to say that all the systems and practices and activities which constitute neo-liberal economies are just ideas or just a discourse, because they clearly have a partly material character. But on the other hand there is a sense in which they are partly ideas and discourse: their material features are ideas and discourse 'made real', and we can say that they incorporate, or in Harvey's (1996) terminology, 'internalize' neo-liberal ideas and discourse. CDA is not just concerned with the semiotic element of neo-liberal economies, it is concerned with working in an interdisciplinary way (for instance with economists and political economists) to identify and understand the relations between semiotic and material elements. The nature of such relations can vary between institutions and organizations and in different places, and can change over time; it needs to be established through analysis. In the case of political responses to the crisis, although our focus in this book is on analysis of argumentation, from a CDA perspective this would be just one part of interdisciplinary research into relations between: public debate; political decisions (policies, strategies); actions in response to the crisis; economic and broader social outcomes. Such research would centre upon the relations between the semiotic (discourse in the most general sense) and the material. (Note that the term 'dialectical' is predominantly used in this book in the way which we explained in Chapter 2, for one of three major aspects of argument, logical, rhetorical and dialectical, and refers to argumentation and its evaluation as an essentially *dialogical* process. It is important not to confuse these two senses of the term.)

Social life can be conceptualized and analyzed as the interplay between three levels of social reality: social *structures*, *practices* and *events* (Chouliaraki and Fairclough 1999). Social events are concrete individual instances of things happening, people behaving in certain ways, people acting (including acting by means of language). Social structures are the most abstract of the three, they are structures, systems and mechanism which social scientists postulate as causal forces in terms of which events and practices can be explained. Capitalism, for example, is a social structure (or rather an interconnected set of structures). The relationship between social structure and social events is not seen in this account as a direct one but as mediated by social practices, which are relatively stable and durable (but more open to change than structures) ways of acting, ways of representing and ways of being associated with particular identities. One example is practices of public political discussion and debate in which people debate responses to the crisis. So we can say that structures directly shape practices, and practices directly shape events, but structures do not directly shape events. However, the relations between them are more complex: practices shape but do not determine events, and changes in the character of events can cumulatively lead to changes in practices, which can lead to changes in structures.

Structures, practices and events all have a partly semiotic character. Events in their semiotic aspect are texts, including spoken as well as written texts, electronic texts, and 'multimodal' texts which combine language, image, music, body language, etc. In the case of practices, ways of acting include *genres*; ways of representing include *discourses*; and ways of being include *styles*. Genre, discourse and style are semiotic categories. In distinguishing semiotic aspects of ways of acting, representing and being in these terms we are seeking to identify ways which have a measure of stability over time. Genres are semiotic ways of acting and interacting such as news or job interviews, reports or editorials in newspapers, or advertisements on TV or the internet. Part of doing a job or running a country is interacting semiotically or communicatively in certain ways, and such activities have distinctive sets of genres associated with them. Discourses are ways of representing aspects of the world which can generally be identified with different positions or perspectives of different groups of social actors (e.g. different political parties). Styles are ways of being, social identities, in their semiotic aspect – for instance, being a successful manager is partly a matter of developing the right style.

Social fields, institutions and organizations are constituted by multiple social practices held together as networks, and the semiotic dimension of such a network is an *order of discourse*, which is a configuration of different genres, different discourses and different styles (Fairclough 2000a). So politics, for example, is a social field constituted by a network of social practices including those associated with activities within political parties, the functioning of parliaments, elections and public spheres in which politicians communicate and interact with citizens. Semiotically, this network of practices includes various genres which, we are arguing, are primarily though not exclusively forms of argumentation and especially practical argumentation, such as parliamentary debate, political interviews on radio and television, and political speeches. It also includes different styles, for instance the styles of political leaders as opposed to the styles of citizens who contribute to public debate, though these will not be given much attention in the book.

The social field of politics also includes discourses which represent in varying ways the many areas and aspects of social life which are focuses of political thought, debate, deliberation and action, corresponding to different positions and perspectives within the political field. For example, there are different political discourses about the economic system and economic and business activity, about the provision of social welfare and protection for citizens, and about international politics and development aid. Sometimes these discourses can be broadly identified with the political right versus the political left – for example we might identify a group of liberal economic discourses which is broadly associated with the right, and socialist (including Marxist) economic discourses broadly associated with the left – but often the positions are more complicated, especially now that the division between left and right is not as clear-cut as it once was. In terms of our concerns in this book, one important difference between arguments is in premises which represent aspects of the crisis in different ways; the lines of action that people argue in favour of or against are of course strongly dependent upon the premises they argue from. If we are to discern politically significant differences in political argumentation over responses to the crisis, we need to be sensitive to significant recurrent differences in how the crisis is represented, which are associated with different discourses. Indeed one output of the analysis might be conclusions about what are the politically significant discourses drawn upon in representing the crisis; these would no doubt include significant families of economic discourses – (neo-)liberal, Keynesian, Marxist, etc. In part, the analyst is recognizing discourses which are already familiar and established in the political field, but the identification of which discourses are significant in debates over political responses to the crisis is a result of the analysis.

Discourses which originate in a particular social field or institution (e.g. neo-liberal economic discourse, which originated within academic economic theory) may be *recontextualized* in others (e.g. in business, the political field or the educational field), or originate in one place or one country and be recontextualized in others. Recontextualization can sometimes be a sort of 'colonization' of one field or institution by another (that would be a way of interpreting the recontextualization of neo-liberal economic discourse in the former socialist countries of eastern Europe after 1989), but it can also sometimes be an 'appropriation' of an external discourse which may be incorporated into the strategies pursued by particular groups of social agents within the recontextualizing field (Chouliaraki and Fairclough 1999). Often it is both, as it arguably was with neo-liberal discourse in Eastern Europe (Iețcu 2006a, 2006c). Arguments which are widely drawn upon are elements of discourses, and they too can be recontextualized. An argument can be understood as a process, when the focus is on someone advancing a particular argument on a particular occasion, but also as a product: in the process of argumentation, over time, certain arguments come to be recurrent and come to achieve the relative durability and stability we associate with practices and discourses. They can be drawn upon by arguers and they can be recontextualized.

Discourses may, under certain conditions, be *operationalized* or 'put into operation', put into practice: they may be *enacted* as new ways of acting and interacting, they may be *inculcated* as new ways of being (new identities), and they may be physically *materialized*, e.g. as new ways of organizing space, for example in architecture. Enactment and inculcation may themselves take semiotic forms: a new management discourse (e.g. the discourse of 'new public management' which has invaded public sector fields like education and health) may be enacted as management procedures which include new genres of interaction between managers and workers, or it may be inculcated as identities which semiotically include the styles of the new type of public managers. We should emphasize that these processes of operationalization are not inevitable, they are contingent possibilities which depend upon a range of factors and conditions, both material and semiotic (Fairclough *et al.* 2004). With respect to our concern with practical argumentation in political responses to the crisis, we would be particularly concerned with the question of which proposed lines of action in arguments are enacted. Practical arguments make judgements about what the best line of action should be, and these can be the basis for decisions, and decisions can be implemented in actions. But not all judgements lead to decisions and actions, and whether they do or not depends upon various conditions, such as the relative power of different social agents or agencies, as well arguers' ability to mobilize support.

Operationalization of discourses may in certain cases be a form of action based upon decisions which in turn are based in practical reasoning. It is possible for individuals to conclude that they should start acting in new ways or change their identities in certain ways, on the basis of beliefs about what the state of the world is and goals of achieving different states of affairs, and to decide to do so and actually do so. But such processes do not always have a purely individual character. In many cases, organizations of various sorts come to such conclusions about changes in ways of acting and identities which, for instance, their employees should undergo (e.g. shop assistants should ask customers 'How has your day been so far?'). This connects practical reasoning with the 'technologization of discourse' discussed in Fairclough (1992): seeking to bring about changes in discourse as part of an attempt to engineer social, cultural or institutional change, applying what Rose and Miller (1989) call 'technologies of government' to discourse.

As we said earlier, CDA works through interdisciplinary cooperation with other areas of critical social science, and the version of CDA we are using has been used in collaboration with various areas and theories (e.g. politics, management, education studies, media studies, cultural studies; and theories of the political field, power, ideology, hegemony, public space, citizenship, instrumental and communicative rationality, capitalism, 'new sociology of capitalism, organizational change, Marxism, critical realism, etc. – see Fairclough 2010 for a range of these), which have more recently included 'cultural political economy' (CPE, Jessop 2004, 2008; Jessop and Sum 2001). CPE claims that economic and political systems, institutions, relations, practices, etc. are socially constructed and that there is a cultural dimension to their social construction which is interpreted in terms of discourse. CPE works with a distinction between structures and strategies, and strategies are seen as coming to the forefront in times of crisis, when existing structures appear not to work adequately, and the different strategies of social agents to transform existing structures in particular directions suddenly proliferate. Strategies have a semiotic dimension: they include 'imaginaries' for future states of affairs which social agents seek to bring into being, for instance economic imaginaries for ways of operating economically which are different from what exists, and these imaginaries are discourses of a particular sort. Certain imaginaries, certain discourses, will be, in CDA terms, operationalized, put into operation, made material and real, whereas most will not. So apart from the variation and proliferation of strategies and discourses (including imaginaries), a major focus is upon selection and retention, i.e. how some are chosen over others, implemented and institutionalized. CPE has worked especially with the version of CDA that we use, which provides it with the means of handling semiotic issues, whereas CPE offers CDA a way of contextualizing discourse analysis within a version of political economy which handles material and institutional dimensions of political economy as well as the semiotic dimension. We believe that argumentation analysis can make a significant contribution to CPE, by providing a systematic and coherent way of operationalizing the CPE categories of structure and imaginary in analysis of texts (we discuss this in the section on imaginaries below).

Let us now move towards the question of how the analysis and evaluation of argumentation can help CDA to improve the way in which it pursues its aim to extend critique to discourse, by discussing textual analysis within CDA.

Developing CDA's framework for textual analysis. An argumentative perspective on discourses as 'ways of representing reality'

The main publication on textual analysis within the version of CDA we are working with is Fairclough (2003) (see also Fairclough 2004). Textual analysis in CDA comprises (a) interdiscursive analysis, and (b) language analysis. Fairclough (2003) is organized around the distinction between genres, discourses and styles: each has a section of the book devoted to it, and various aspects of analysis of (lexical, grammatical and semantic) features of language are assigned to each section depending on whether they are most relevant to analysis of genres or discourses or styles. Each chapter applies the analytical categories which it deals with to material which bears upon a number of current research themes in the social sciences.

Interdiscursive analysis of a text identifies the genres, discourses and styles that are drawn upon, and mixtures of different genres or different discourses or different styles that it contains, including mixtures that are novel. An example of such a combination in the case of genres would be the various forms of interview (including political interview) on television, which tend to produce many combinations, some novel and some not, of features of interview genres with features of conversational genres. An example of such a combination in the case of discourses is the political discourse of Thatcherism which is analysed in Fairclough (1989/2001) as a 'hybrid' discourse combining elements from other political discourses; the same is true of the political discourse of 'New Labour' in Britain (Fairclough 2000a). This approach rests upon the claims that: texts are shaped but not determined by existing orders of discourse in which genres, discourses and styles are articulated together in relatively established and conventional ways; social agents in producing texts may combine genres and/or discourses and/or styles in unconventional ways; and such innovative combinations can be semiotic aspects of social changes taking place in behaviour and action, which may ultimately be established as changes in social practices and in orders of discourse.

The section on genres in Fairclough (2003) includes a short discussion of arguments with some analysis using Toulmin's (1958) categories of Grounds, Warrant, Backing, Claim, which is clearly insufficient in the light of the claims we are making in this book. Here we claim that argumentation, and practical argumentation in particular, is the primary activity that is going on in political discourse, and analysis of argumentation can make a major contribution to strengthening textual analysis in CDA. We shall illustrate this contribution by returning to an analysis of part of a speech by Tony Blair which was published in a book on the political discourse of New Labour in Britain (Fairclough 2000a), a book which works with a framework of analysis similar to that in Fairclough (2003). We will provide an analysis of the argument developed in Blair's speech and focus on the critical evaluation of the argument, by addressing the question of *representation*. A considerable amount of research done in CDA involves analysis of representations of social action, actors or various other aspects of the world (analysis of discourses) *without however connecting these representations to agents' action via agents' practical reasoning*. We want to indicate (here and throughout the book) how representations enter as premises in arguments and how arguments based on such representations can be critically evaluated.

Let us first discuss the CDA approach to representation from the point of view of argumentation theory. Here is an extract from a speech which Blair made to the Confederation of British Industry in 1998, which is analysed in Fairclough (2000a: 25–29):

> We all know this is a world of dramatic change. In technology; in trade; in media and communications; in the new global economy refashioning our industries and capital markets. In society; in family structure; in communities; in lifestyles.
>
> Add to this change that sweeps the world, the changes that Britain itself has seen in the 20th century – the end of Empire, the toil of two world wars, the reshaping of our business and employment with the decline of traditional industries – and it is easy to see why national renewal is so important. Talk of modern Britain is not about disowning our past. We are proud of our history. This is simply a recognition of the challenge the modern world poses.
>
> The choice is: to let change overwhelm us, to resist it or equip ourselves to survive and prosper in it. The first leads to a fragmented society. The second is pointless and futile, trying to keep the clock from turning. The only way is surely to analyse the challenge of change and to meet it. When I talk of a third way – between the old-style intervention of the old-left and the laissez-faire of the new right – I do not mean a soggy compromise in the middle. I mean avowing there is a role for Government, for team work and partnership. But it must be a role for today's world. Not about picking winners, state subsidies, heavy regulation; but about education, infrastructure, promoting investment, helping small business and entrepreneurs and fairness. To make Britain more competitive, better at generating wealth, but to do it on a basis that serves the needs of the whole nation – one nation. This is a policy that is unashamedly long-termist.

The analysis of the extract in Fairclough (2000a) focuses on a number of aspects which are important from a critical point of view. All of the issues discussed are to do with how aspects of reality are represented and how representations draw on the discourse of the 'Third Way'. There is no discussion of genre because the book is organized in a way which separates analysis of discourses from analysis of genres, and the extract is not discussed as argumentation. Yet this is a clear example of practical argumentation and the analysis would be more complete and more coherent if analysis of representations were incorporated within analysis of practical argumentation. This is because *ways of representing the world enter as premises into reasoning about what we should do.* Unless we look at arguments, and not just at isolated representations, there is no way of understanding how our beliefs feed into what we do.

The analysis in Fairclough (2000a) focuses on the representation of 'change', more precisely on the representation of the world as involving change. Mainly, the focus is on 'change' as a nominalization, hence on a representation of change as an objective phenomenon that exists in the world, as a fact ('this is a world of dramatic change'). 'Change' is metaphorically represented as a force of nature, like a tidal wave which 'sweeps the world' and can 'overwhelm' us. Its nature is similar to that of time: trying to prevent it is like 'trying to keep the clock from turning'. 'Change' appears as the subject of sentences ('this change that sweeps the word'), as an entity with causal powers (it can 'overwhelm us'), or as an object (something we can seek to 'resist'). But it is not explicitly associated with any human agency: there are no claims in which 'change' is a verb with a human agent as its subject, (e.g. 'Bankers with the support of governments have changed our capital markets'). Apparently, 'change' just happens, it is a fact of life. In addition to 'change', 'the new global economy' is also represented as an existing factual entity which appears as the subjects of sentences (the new global economy is 'refashioning our industries and capital markets').

The approach we advocate in this book would focus on the argument for action that is being made, starting from a description of the context of action and a desirable goal, informed by values. The text illustrates a form of deliberation, an agent reasoning practically, apparently weighing options before arriving at the right course of action. This monological deliberative process is similar to deliberation in a multi-agent context. When we deliberate alone we are supposed, ideally, to think of the strongest objections to a proposal for action, in the same way in which several agents, supporting different proposals, would argue against each other.

As we explain in Chapter 6, deliberation is a genre, an argumentative dialogue type which starts from an open question – *what should I (we) do?* – and then proposes various courses of action, on the basis of an analysis of circumstances and of the goals that agents want to achieve. Each possible course of action is discussed primarily in terms of its consequences for the achievement of the goal or other goals that the agents would not (or should not) want to compromise. Evaluation may involve different perspectives, and these may not always be easy to weigh against one another. Courses of action can also be discussed in terms of whether they are easily achievable or indeed possible from the present circumstances, what constraints on action there are (is there some reason that cannot be overridden?), but the question of possible negative consequences is paramount, because discovery of probable negative consequences may lead agents to reject a tentative proposal.

In terms of the structure of practical argumentation which we proposed in Chapter 2, the first two paragraphs, describing the context of action according to Blair, would be assigned to the circumstantial premises. The main premises that describe the circumstances of action assert that that the world has been changing, Britain has been changing, and change poses a challenge. The claim is in the third paragraph and is signalled by the paragraph opening, 'The choice is' and the list of possible courses of action, namely, 'to let change overwhelm us' (i.e. inaction, doing nothing), 'to resist it' or 'to equip ourselves to survive and prosper'. Blair gives reasons for rejecting the first two options, by pointing to the undesirable consequences of the first and by negatively evaluating the second: 'The first leads to a fragmented society'; the second is 'pointless and futile', it is like 'trying to keep the clock from turning.' The only option that stands up to critical examination is the third: to 'equip' ourselves in view of achieving our goals, also expressed as 'the only way is surely to analyse the challenge of change and meet it'. The goals that this third option makes possible are 'to survive and prosper'; later on re-expressed as 'making Britain more competitive, better at generating wealth' (goal premise). The goal is said to be a long-term one ('unashamedly long-termist') and based on a concern for 'serving the needs of the whole nation – one nation' (this is the main value premise allegedly informing the goal and therefore the action; 'fairness' is also mentioned as a value later on). The proposed action (as means), i.e. 'analysing the challenge of change and meeting it', will therefore take us from the existing state of affairs (as problem or 'challenge') to a state of affairs in which we survive and prosper, generate wealth and serve the needs of the whole nation. The claim is initially very general and vague ('analyse the challenge of change and meet it'), but Blair goes on to formulate it in more specific terms: the action he advocates is in fact 'a third way – between the old-style intervention of the old left and the laissez-faire of the new right'. What this involves, he goes on to explain, is not a 'soggy compromise' but a new role for government: a government that promotes education, infrastructure, investment, helps small business and entrepreneurs and ensures fairness. The goal premise is also expressed as pursuing 'national renewal' and trying to create 'a modern Britain' in paragraph 2. An apparently open choice amongst different actions turns out to be an advocacy of the Third Way as policy (the word 'policy' is used in the last sentence).

A succinct reconstruction of the argument would have to include circumstantial premises, goal premises, value premises and a claim for action. If we look at the speech as deliberation, we would have to indicate what alternative proposals have been considered and why they have been rejected. These elements can be systematized as follows:

Claim (solution)	We should 'analyse the challenge of change and meet it'; 'equip ourselves'; adopt the 'policy' of the 'third way'.
Circumstantial premises (problems)	'This is a world of dramatic change', of 'change that sweeps the world'; there is a 'challenge [of change]' that the 'modern world poses' (these premises are supported by examples of change in different areas). Britain has seen a lot of changes in the 20th century (supported by examples). Change is a challenge that the modern world poses.
Goal premises	Our goals are 'national renewal', a 'modern Britain'. Our goals are to 'survive and prosper'; 'make Britain more competitive, better at generating wealth'.
Value premises	We must achieve our goals 'on a basis that serves the needs of the whole nation – one nation'. [National unity and a concern for people's needs are relevant values.] A concern for prosperity and survival [implicit in the goals of action] Fairness [underlies the role of government according to the proposed policy]
Means–goal premise	'The only way' of meeting goals starting from current circumstances is by 'analysing the challenge of change and meeting it', i.e. by adopting the 'third way.' [If we adopt the Third Way we will meet our goals / solve the problem.]
Alternative options	The other two options are 'to let change overwhelm us' and 'to resist (change)'.
Addressing alternative options	Alternatives can be rejected on account of negative consequences (a 'fragmented society') or as unreasonable or even irrational ('futile', 'pointless', like 'trying to keep the clock from turning'), i.e. by arguments from negative consequences and argumentation by analogy. [Just as it is futile and pointless to try to keep the clock from turning, so is it futile and pointless to try to resist change.]

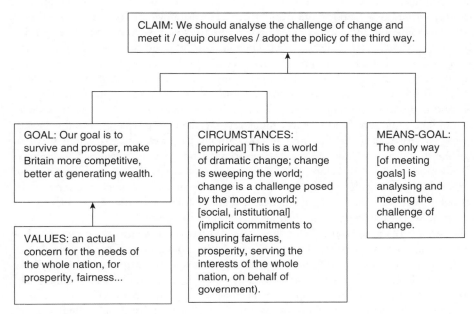

Figure 3.1 Blair's argument for accepting 'the challenge of change'.

The Means–Goal premise expresses a particularly strong relation here: '*if and only if* we adopt the means, can we reach the goals'. It not only says that the advocated means is necessary and sufficient in view of the goal, but also that there is no alternative, that this solution is the only one that will deliver the goals. We explain how such a relationship differs from merely saying 'if we adopt the means, we will reach our goals' in our analysis in Chapter 4.

We can represent the practical argument succinctly as in Figure 3.1. The practical argument is therefore saying that, in the arguer's view, given what the circumstances are and given what our goals are, underlain by our concerns or values, the proposed action or policy is necessary and sufficient to address the circumstances and meet our goals. However, merely reconstructing the argument, while essential, is not enough. Identifying premises and claim correctly gives us a snapshot of the structure of the text, as a prerequisite for evaluation, but does not do justice to the argumentative *process*, to the way it unfolds sequentially, as a process of reasoning, of deliberation. Practical reasoning involves here considering three possibilities for action, i.e. deliberation over possible several courses of action. As we said in Chapter 2, deliberation minimally involves considering what reasons would support *not* doing the action (i.e. a counter-claim), but may also involve other alternatives (doing something else, not just refraining from action). Deliberation can be seen as a procedure for arriving at a common course of action by examining various proposals for action in light of reasons for and against each proposal. Deliberation is a normative model, a genre, and to evaluate an actual argumentation against such a model does not claim of course that particular arguments are *good* instances of deliberation.

As we shall see in Chapter 6, deliberation usually starts with an *open practical question* (*What should we do?*), which is left implicit in Blair's speech. The next stage involves a critical examination of the *context* of action (in business practice, this can take the form of and analysis of 'strengths, weaknesses, opportunities and threats', 'feasibility' analyses, etc.). In Blair's speech, this assessment of the context of action takes up the first two paragraphs (the world is swept by change, change is a challenge, etc.). Then, a range of options is *proposed* by the participants, or (when deliberation does not involve several agents, as here) by the arguer. Blair mentions three such possible choices. The next stages (*considering* or *commenting* on proposals and *revising* them) involve a critical discussion of these options, with participants pointing out desirable and undesirable consequences, and constraints on action (what is or is not possible, allowed, required), and may lead to participants revising their proposals or even their goals. Blair gives reasons against the first and second options, and advocates rejecting them in favour of the third option. Choosing the third proposal is advocated (*recommended*) at the next stage. Deliberation involves therefore choosing among proposals or options, in response to an open question, in a particular context of action, after careful and thorough examination of each proposal. A more accurate representation of the argument, including these alternatives and the way in which Blair deals with them, is therefore as in Figure 3.2.

On the surface, Blair's speech can therefore be reconstructed as a report of previous deliberation (where implicit proponents of alternative views are not co-present but their views are addressed, evaluated and rejected). Blair attempts to both justify his proposal in terms of how successfully it will deal with present challenges and enable Britain to achieve desirable goals, and also to show that alternative proposals will not lead to those goals (will have negative consequences that will defeat the goals) or are in other ways are unreasonable, hence unacceptable. Would we want to say that, on the basis of these formal features, this text is a good example of deliberation? If not, why not? As we have seen, deliberation involves the critical examination of options in the light of criticism. It also involves an analysis of the circumstances and may involve a critical discussion of goals and values as well. Deliberation is typically about means, with goals and other premises taken for granted, but if discussion reveals disagreement about goals, agents can decide to deliberate on the goals of action before deliberating about means. The test is whether the proposals being advanced, and the reasons that support them, can withstand systematic critical examination in view of the normative goal of the practice. In argumentation, the goal is to arrive at a reasonable choice 'on the merits', and thus resolve disagreement on a reasonable basis. How is Blair representing the alternative proposals and on what grounds is he rejecting them? How is he defining the context of action and the goals? Would these representations be found rationally acceptable? Has his own proposal, the one that has been adopted, emerged from a process of critical examination in light of its probable consequences?

Many people would probably agree that it is highly implausible that Blair has chosen the third option on the basis of a genuine analysis of the situation and an assessment of several alternatives. Rather, he wants to legitimize a particular policy, and he therefore represents the existing state of affairs, the goals and the alternative arguments in a way which is rhetorically designed to support his preferred conclusion. Consequently, he is not deliberating here in any real sense, weighing several options and choosing one after careful consideration of consequences and means–goal relations. Nor is he reporting a process of deliberation he has previously been involved in. These, however, are psychological claims that can at best be indirectly supported by evidence. What we need is an analytical framework that allows us to evaluate Blair's speech as a practical argument starting from the properties of the text as such. A dialectical theory of argument is capable of doing just that.

Once we look at the practical argumentation developed in this speech as an instance of (or report of) deliberation, we come to realize that the normative structure of the practice,

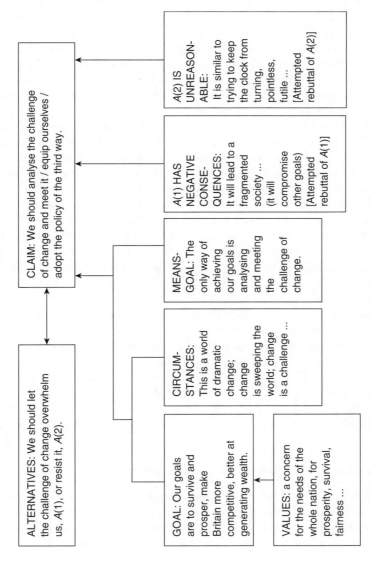

Figure 3.2 Blair's argument for the Third Way. Deliberation over alternatives.

of the genre itself, requires the presence of certain structural features. Are these features present in this particular deliberation or not? As we have said, the structure of deliberation requires the arguer to address alternative options, alternative claims for action. In practical conductive argumentation, as we said in Chapter 2, agents weigh different goals, different means of achieving them, different consequences and values, supporting a proposal for action but also its opposite or alternative proposals, and arrive at a practical judgement on balance. In multi-agent deliberative dialogue, these alternatives or counter-arguments are actually put forward by other participants. In a monological text like this one, the alternatives are represented by the arguer, as the standpoints of other participants that he has to address in order to show that *his conclusion still follows*, after these other arguments have been dealt with.

How are these alternative choices represented? The first choice is described as one in which we 'let change overwhelm' us, i.e. we do nothing and passively concede defeat. The second one involves 'resisting' change, but is 'pointless and futile', it is like 'trying to keep the clock from turning'. The third one involves adaptation and leads to success: 'equip ourselves to survive and prosper'. Given the way Blair represents these alternatives, the 'choice' is really no choice at all. It is obvious that the only reasonable choice is the third one: 'the only way is to analyse the challenge of change and meet it'. But the reason why the claim seems to follow so inevitably from the premises is that the premises have been formulated in such a way as to make the conclusion inevitable.

What is wrong with Blair's alleged weighing of options now becomes clear: *all the options are formulated in ways which favour his own conclusion.* This would not happen in real face-to-face dialogue: the other participants would formulate their arguments in ways that would favour *their own* conclusions, or at least would not prevent their own conclusions from following from their premises. The structure of deliberation provides for the presence of alternative arguments and counter-arguments formulated in terms that advance the rhetorical goals of the participants who advocate them. This may include evaluative terms, metaphors, persuasive definitions (which we explain below), amounting to different ways of representing the context of action, the goals or other reasons. Such counter-arguments and alternative arguments, with their associated claims and premises *formulated in terms that actually lead to those claims*, are absent in this text. Blair is not addressing real alternatives, real options, but his own representations of those alleged alternatives. Consequently, there is no actual deliberation, no actual weighing of alternative options in this text, although there appears to be. Actual deliberation is avoided by representing alternatives in rhetorically convenient ways (in pragma-dialectical terms, we can say that the argument attempts to be rhetorically effective at the expense of being dialectically adequate). Another significant dialectical failure is the absence from Blair's argument of any indication that his own proposal has been critically examined. The way in which the preferred option is formulated does not allow us to suspect any possible negative effects or costs. The argument is thus heavily biased in favour of a foregone conclusion and is a good illustration of typical (and fairly vacuous) New Labour 'spin'.

Representations of the world as persuasive definitions

Let us say a few words about the use of value-laden terms and so-called 'persuasive' (biased) definitions in arguments. Premises containing persuasive definitions ('taxation is theft') are extremely important in argumentation. This is because they direct arguers towards certain conclusions and not others. The same is true for emotive terms. In normal circumstances, it would be strange to say: 'Jerry is a coward, and is therefore to be admired.' The definition of 'coward', as well as the emotional connotation of the word, contain a negative evaluation that normally suggests a conclusion that is the opposite of the one above. Persuasive definitions are essential in allowing arguers to pursue their rhetorical goals. They are almost always *re-definitions* of terms that already have a definition and are deployed to serve the interest of the definer. They are what Skinner (2002) calls 'rhetorical re-descriptions' of reality.

The key to the dialectical approach to persuasive definitions, according to Walton (2007a), lies in *understanding them as arguments*, with a burden of proof attached. They are in fact claims that are open to challenge by the other party, who is expected and should have the opportunity to ask critical questions. They cannot be assumed to be shared, unproblematic commitments at the beginning of argumentation. A reasonable discussion cannot *proceed* from a definition of 'abortion as murder' or of 'capitalism as an unjust system of government that allows the greedy rich to exploit the working poor', but needs to defend these definitions first. If no attempt to critically question and thus test the acceptability of these definitions is made by the participants, if such definitions are put forward or accepted as the one and only possible way of understanding the matters in question, as uncontroversial truth (for instance as definitions which are not normally open to objections, such as *lexical, theoretical* or *stipulative* definitions), then the dialogue in question holds the potential for deception and manipulation.[1]

The same observation applies to the use of so-called emotive or loaded terms in an argument, i.e. terms that have a positive or negative emotional connotation as part of their lexical, dictionary meaning ('terrorist' vs. 'freedom-fighter'). Walton cites Bertrand Russell's example: 'I am firm, you are obstinate, he is a pig-headed fool' (Walton 2006: 220). The use of such terms is generally condemned as putting a spin on the argument but, since persuasion is a legitimate function of argumentation, a critical perspective on such choices needs to distinguish between those cases in which loaded terms are used legitimately to defend a particular standpoint, when it is clear that there is also a contrary standpoint in play, and both are open to critical questioning, and those cases in which loaded terms and definitions are used deceptively, as if no other possible viewpoint is possible, as if they were neutral, fact-stating propositions beyond any conceivable doubt.[2]

We have insisted on the question of definitions and evaluative terms from an argumentation theory perspective for the obvious reason that it relates to the CDA view of discourses as ways of representing reality. Premises describing the context or the goals of action are fundamental to practical reasoning, and different people will describe the context and the goal in different ways, depending on how adequate and extensive their knowledge of the facts is, but also depending on their evaluative (including ideological) orientation towards this context and their particular interest in changing it. In assessing the circumstances of action, something may be a 'fact' for someone but not for someone else. The most difficult part of figuring out what to do is often getting to understand the circumstances of action, as a prerequisite to imagining a future state of affairs or a solution, and agents may disagree on the right action partly because they define the context of action in radically different ways and imagine goals in radically different ways, in relation to different and often incompatible values or concerns.

An alternative way of talking about the same difficulty we noted above is in terms of 'framing' the context of action. This 'framing' is often done in terms that serve arguers' rhetorical interests. People's claims for action follow from their own descriptions of the context and may not follow from the ways in which their opponents define the situation. Re-describing or re-framing reality in a rhetorically convenient way is part of a strategy of action. Such situations are frequently discussed in cognitive semantics in the terms originally proposed by Lakoff and Johnson (1980, 1981) and Lakoff (2002, 2004). Cognitive linguists insist that *metaphors* or *frames* determine how people see or conceive reality, therefore – in our terms – how they conceptualize their goals, their circumstances and consequently, how they act. Analysis of metaphors or frames, we suggest, can be integrated into a theory of practical reasoning, as a special case of practical reasoning in which the premises (or the claim) involve a (metaphorical) definition. (We will return to this discussion briefly in Chapter 4.) The advantage of looking at these phenomena in terms of a theory of practical reasoning is that of seeing how re-framing or re-describing the situation functions within people's plan of action, how it gives people reasons for action and fits within a particular action strategy.

Several representations of the context of action, but also of other parts of the argument in Blair's speech, lend themselves to a discussion in the terms we have sketched above. Definitions, we said, should be seen as incurring a burden of proof, as requiring the arguer to justify the particular equivalence being proposed, in all those cases when the definition is not obviously uncontroversial. What justification is provided for viewing the second alternative, 'resisting change', as 'pointless' and 'futile', similar to 'trying to keep the clock from turning'? Why should we accept these evaluative terms and this metaphorical definition? Are they beyond dispute? Similarly, why should we accept the definition of the circumstances of action in terms of a process of 'change sweeping the world', i.e. as an objective, natural, agentless, inevitable phenomenon, or the definition of change as a 'challenge'? No burden of proof is assumed for these persuasive definitions and evaluative terms, which nevertheless clearly steer the argument in a particular direction and support a particular conclusion. If change was represented as a 'danger' or a 'threat', then maybe we could convincingly argue that we must resist change, but not if change is a 'challenge': if change is indeed a challenge, then this *entails opportunities* that must be taken advantage of. If trying to resist it is like trying to stop time, then again, only the conclusion that we must accept change seems rational. Similarly, who could question the goals of action, if the goals are formulated in terms of a wealthier Britain? Moreover, we are told, these equivalences are something that we all recognize ('this is simply a recognition of the challenge [of change] . . .'); 'we all know' this is what the world is like. Eventually, the argument's conclusion (the third option) will thus follow naturally from these persuasive, rhetorically motivated representations (of 'change' as a positive 'challenge', of alternative options as unreasonable, of goals as wholly uncontroversial and beneficial). It may, however, not have followed from representations formulated in other terms, by other agents, but whatever representations those agents might have used in their arguments, we cannot find out from Blair's speech, although the speech allegedly represents those other agents' views.

Instead of questioning representations in isolation, what we suggest therefore is questioning representations as parts of premises of arguments. The same observations apply to all types of premises in practical arguments and to the claim itself, so we will focus on the circumstantial premise for the sake of simplicity. Does a particular representation of the circumstantial premise withstand critical questioning? Is it for instance rationally acceptable that Britain's 'industries and capital markets' are indeed being 'refashioned' by a type of agentless, objective process of change, beyond human control, analogous to natural phenomena (e.g. a tidal wave)? One might want to question this and suggest that, rather, the changes that have 'refashioned' Britain's financial industry and 'reshaped our business and employment' were a matter of *deliberate* policy, not agentless processes of change, and have turned out to be a major cause of the current crisis. What is the role of human agency in these processes of change? If some of these changes (e.g. the deregulation of capital markets) have been caused by the decisions and actions of political leaders, governments and businesses, are those agents not responsible for making further decisions and developing further policies which can reverse some of these changes or produce different effects? Can Blair's representation of the circumstances be sufficient to support his argument for action given that he says nothing about the causes of the key changes in trade and capital markets and about their possible impact, i.e. offers no explanation and no justification for them?

To conclude, it is clear that the extract from Blair's speech is an instance of practical argumentation. In not treating it as such, the analysis in Fairclough (2000a) missed what is primary in political discourse: addressing the question of what to do in response to problematic events and circumstances, given certain goals and values. Because, in that analysis, representations of social reality are not seen in their immediate connection to what agents are trying to achieve and to the actions they are advocating as means towards their goals, *critique of representations appears isolated and disconnected from critique of action*. Moreover, orders of discourse (as structures) are not seen in their proper relation to *agency*, because this fundamental insight is absent: that discourses provide agents with premises (i.e. beliefs about the circumstances of action, instrumental beliefs, values and goals) for justifying, criticizing and, on this basis, deciding on action, i.e. *discourses provide reasons for action*.

Normative critique in CDA. An argumentative perspective on manipulation

Let us now move to a more general assessment of how argumentation analysis and evaluation fit into the two forms of critique, normative and explanatory social critique, as they appear in CDA, and what precisely they add to such critique. Two focuses for CDA in the critique of discourse have been manipulation and ideology. We see the former as an issue for normative critique and the latter as an issue for explanatory critique. In this section and the next we discuss these in turn.

Manipulation can be seen as an issue in evaluation of arguments. In the Blair extract we have re-analyzed in this chapter, one of the reasons why the representation of the context of action is not rationally acceptable is that Blair fails to differentiate between changes which are established facts (e.g. the end of the British Empire) and changes which are a matter of decision and open to further decision and revision (e.g. changes in the rules of international trade and in the regulation of capital markets). We might take this as a deliberate deceptive intention, but how can we assert with any confidence that, in conflating two types of changes and thus making them appear equally objective and inevitable, Blair is trying to 'manipulate' the audience? Maybe he is not aware of what he is doing, maybe he is making an 'honest mistake'?

Van Eemeren (2005: xii) argues that 'manipulation in discourse boils down to intentionally deceiving one's addressees by persuading them of something that is foremost in one's own interest through the covert use of communicative devices that are not in agreement with generally acknowledged critical standards of reasonableness' and we agree with him that manipulation is 'always intentional and always covert' and that the arguer is violating the sincerity (responsibility) condition of the speech act of argumentation: a proposition is presented as an acceptable justification of a claim while the arguer does not really *believe* that it constitutes an acceptable justification. Yet, how do we know whether Blair *intended* to deceive or not? How do we know whether he is being *insincere*? In order to give a conclusive answer we would need to have access to Blair's psychological motives, and we do not.

One form of manipulation is *rationalization*, a deceptive argument addressed by Audi (2006) from an epistemological perspective. His discussion is compatible both with the pragma-dialectical speech act approach (referred to above), which points to the *sincerity* or *responsibility* condition of speech acts as a *constitutive* rule, as well as with Habermas's (1984) view of sincerity as a *presupposition* of rational discourse. Audi shows on what grounds we may characterize an instance of practical reasoning as a rationalization and why such an argument fails to meet normative criteria for good argumentation. In a rationalization, the reasons that are ostensibly offered in support of a claim are *not* the reasons that support the claim from the viewpoint of the arguer; the arguer believes the claim for *other* reasons. Rationalizations can be fairly good arguments when considered from an outside, third-person perspective and without any knowledge of the wider context of argumentation and debate. This is why they can be persuasive and achieve their deceptive intent. Often, the claim can be validly inferred from the premises and, if the premises are acceptable, the argument will be sound. The problem is epistemic: from the viewpoint of the arguer, the stated premises do not support the claim. The arguer *knows* that his commitment to the claim is based on *other* reasons, on covert reasons. *For him*, the claim is not inferable from the premises, although it might seem to be inferable for an audience. Let us note that not only arguments but also explanations can be rationalizations, as when a false, insincere reason (in the sense of cause) is provided to explain an action ('I avoided paying tax because the government wastes people's taxes anyway'). In this book we are only dealing with rationalizations that are arguments.[3]

A good example of rationalization was the justification of the Iraq war of 2003 on the grounds of an allegedly well-documented belief that Iraq had weapons of mass destruction (WMDs), that it posed a threat to the world through its connections to global terrorism, as well as on the basis of an alleged desire to bring democracy and freedom to the Iraqi people by freeing them from an oppressive dictatorship. These reasons were put forward by the Blair and Bush administrations as good reasons, sufficient to make the case for war. They were often asserted together in multiple argumentation, i.e. each reason was deemed to be in itself sufficient to justify the claim for action. Opponents of the war denied that these were real reasons or real concerns (and in the case of WMDs, they also denied that this particular premise was true or sufficiently supported by evidence). They argued that the real reasons for going to war were different and had to do with American geostrategic interests and with the UK's commitment to support those interests; briefly, that the public argument was a rationalization, put forward with the intention to deceive and manipulate the public.

In his evidence to the Chilcot Inquiry on Britain's role in the Iraq war, in January 2010, Blair defended himself by claiming that the reasons he gave for going to war were real reasons and that there was sufficient evidence at the time for believing them. He said that, on the basis of the intelligence then available, it was 'beyond doubt' that Iraq was continuing to develop its weapons capability. The intelligence reports he had acted upon were 'absolutely strong enough', 'extensive, detailed and authoritative'. This amounts to saying that the argument, while not being sound, as it later on turned out, was nevertheless rationally persuasive for Blair at the time when it was made, given all the evidence available.

This line of defence has been strongly challenged. One of the members of the public at the Inquiry said in an interview:

> I, like millions of other Britons at the time, suspected Blair was wrong about the threat that Saddam posed. I don't say that now with the luxury of hindsight. All that is different now is that history has proved us right. It is incredible that Tony Blair . . . refuses to

accept any possibility that he could have been wrong. He seems to refuse to accept any other interpretation of the intelligence at the time. At one point he was asked about the phrase "beyond doubt". Mr Blair said that he believed the intelligence beyond doubt. But one of the members of the panel shot back "beyond your doubt but was it beyond anyone's doubt?" There was audible applause from the public at this point.[4]

This particular comment highlights an important problem for the evaluation of arguments: an argument can be rationally persuasive for a person even if it is unsound, if the person has good reasons to accept the claim. If, on the basis of reports which I have every reason to consider reliable, I draw a conclusion which seems justified but is in fact (as it later turns out) false, I can only be accused of making an honest mistake. This is in fact how Blair has tried to defend himself, and the question 'was it beyond anyone's doubt?' aims to challenge precisely the legitimacy of this line of defence. In other words, Blair cannot reasonably use the excuse of an honest mistake, as plenty of doubt was voiced *at the time* by MPs and the media, as well as by the weapons inspectors and other authorities, as to whether Iraq actually had any WMDs. There was no reliable evidence at his disposal that could make the argument rationally persuasive for him, either in 2003 or later.

In defending himself along the lines of human fallibility, Blair has tried to persuade his critics that he was not being insincere in his argument for war. He was not manipulating public opinion, he genuinely believed that the premises were true, that Iraq possessed WMDs and had links with Al-Qaeda. The argument, in other words, was not a rationalization. As we have said, the judgement that an argument is a rationalization or that it attempts to manipulate depends upon being able to plausibly claim an intention to deceive, which is not possible simply on the basis of argument analysis. This intention cannot be simply read off an argument and, however strongly we may feel that this is what is going on, judgements of this sort can only be made tentatively. However, they can acquire some confirmation by comparison with other evidence. For example, the arguer may give different reasons for the same claim in private from the ones he has given in an official capacity in public, the sort of discrepancy often revealed by Wikileaks. Or a comparison of arguments in various contexts might indicate a broad strategy or plan of action which the reasons given for the claim do not seem to fit in with. Audiences may draw on their knowledge of the world to assess whether the reasons offered are likely to be sincere or not. For instance, given the 'special' Bush–Blair relationship, Blair's declared commitment to support Bush, or given America's known interests in the Middle East, is it really plausible that these were *not* reasons for action, but that a concern for the Iraqi people was? Such judgements require therefore a broader dialectical context, an extended context of dialogue, across various space–time locales, as well as an understanding of the social and political context of actors – what it is likely that they are trying to do, how what they say is supposed to fit in within their strategies of action.

We have illustrated normative critique by an example of manipulation of public opinion and said that it can be discussed as involving rationalization, as a type of defective argument. Viewing manipulation in these terms offers a sounder basis for analysis and evaluation of discourse. Whether or not arguers are sincere or not (as an ethical issue) is only one aspect of normative critique. It corresponds to Habermas's 'truthfulness' criterion as a presupposition of rational discourse. But discourse can also be normatively assessed on the basis of the criteria of truth and normative appropriateness. According to Habermas's (1984) account of normative critique (an account which is explicitly grounded in argumentation), a person who makes an assertion is, in so doing, (implicitly) making a claim that it is valid, in the sense of being true, and can be defended if necessary. Similarly, a person who proposes a course of action (implicitly) claims that it is valid in the sense of being in accordance with norms for rational action and can be justified if necessary. A 'validity claim' is 'equivalent to an assertion that the conditions of validity of an utterance are fulfilled' (Habermas 1984: 38). The communicative rationality of assertions and proposals depends upon them being 'susceptible to criticism and grounding', and the more they can be defended against criticism, the more rational they are. Validity claims are open to challenge and, when they are challenged, they should be defended in argumentation, which Habermas defines as 'that type of speech in which participants thematize contested validity claims and attempt to vindicate or criticize them through arguments' (Habermas 1984:18). Such validity claims are the claim that a proposition is true (in theoretical argumentation); the claim that an action (or proposed action) is right in the sense of being in accordance with norms of action (practical argumentation), and the claim that the speaker is speaking truthfully or sincerely. Our main concern is with practical argumentation, and the approach we have developed to evaluating practical argumentation through critical questioning is equivalent with the critical questioning of the validity claim to the rightness of the (proposed) action. Questioning the acceptability of premises that claim to represent reality is equivalent with questioning the validity claim to the truth of propositions. Furthermore, as our discussion of rationalization above has illustrated, our approach includes questioning the sincerity of the arguer, which is involved in assessing whether arguments offered for proposed lines of action are rationalizations. This is equivalent with questioning Habermas's third validity claim, 'truthfulness' or sincerity. Overall, the legitimacy of critical questioning is grounded in these validity claims' status as *presuppositions* of rational discourse, or as *constitutive* speech act conditions.

Evaluation of arguments that contributes to normative critique can involve critical questioning of the value premise (its rational acceptability or normative appropriateness) or criticizing the proposed action in view of its consequences on human well-being or on other agents' legitimate goals and other publicly recognized concerns. It thus relates primarily to validity claims to normative appropriateness. Evaluating the properties of deliberation and debate as public space dialogue can also contribute to normative critique. Is such dialogue inclusive and democratic, are people free from influences that might distort the argumentative outcome? The latter issue has been amply addressed in CDA (Fairclough 2000b: 182, 2003: 80), in terms of a normative framework for public space dialogue, and a theory of argumentation can enhance that conception by viewing public space dialogue as essentially argumentative and governed by a dialectical normative conception of good argumentative and deliberative practice.

Explanatory critique in CDA. Critique of ideology and evaluation of argumentative discourse

Let us now come back to the Blair speech analyzed earlier with a focus on explanatory critique and critique of ideology. Can the Blair extract be said to be ideological in any respect? Can we relate such a claim to the analysis of the practical argument as deliberation that we have suggested? In social life, certain arguments come to be recurrent and achieve the relative durability and stability we associate with practices and discourses. They can be drawn upon by arguers, they can be recontextualized, and we can regard them as parts of particular discourses. Let us consider Blair's text once again in the light of these observations.

We have suggested that the goal premise appears initially in paragraph 2, as the goal of achieving 'national renewal' and 'a modern Britain', then in paragraph 3, as 'to survive and prosper' (in a context of 'change'), then as 'to make Britain more competitive, better at generating wealth'. The latter is the most specific formulation of the goal, the only one specific enough to be recognized as a policy, and it is indeed referred to as a 'policy'. These are alternative specifications of the goal of action. It is not clear from the text whether they should be seen as equivalent or as chained together in a sequence of goals, but they are certainly presented as fundamentally compatible, part of a coherent vision. Blair does not make an explicit claim that surviving and prospering in a context of change amounts to (or results from) being more competitive and better at generating wealth, nor does he need to. While some members of his audience, as well as analysts, might raise the question of whether the move from surviving and prospering to being more competitive and better at generating wealth is justified, or whether these goals are self-evidently compatible or indeed equivalent and part of a coherent and uncontroversial vision, it can also be reasonably expected that audiences will accept this move without question, as obvious or just 'common sense'. Why?

We suggest that members of the audience would be recognizing here an argument which Blair is drawing upon and implicitly drawing upon it themselves. Blair is evoking a neoliberal argument, without spelling it out completely. It is present in the focus on promoting competitiveness, in the fact that Blair takes changes in markets which result from self-interested and reversible decisions by business and governmental elites to be no different from changes which are simply facts about the modern world, and in the dismissal of state intervention in the economy. The argument can be summed up as follows: self-regulating markets are the best means of creating wealth and prosperity, which is our goal; government interventions and 'heavy regulation' only prevent them from doing so, and governments should therefore accept the decisions of the markets and not 'interfere', and should restrict themselves to creating conditions for competitiveness; these conditions include removal of government 'interference' in markets in the form of rules and regulations, opening state enterprises to market forces (i.e. privatizing them) and cutting the overall costs of labour including wages and welfare benefits. The state should no longer be a 'welfare state' but a 'competition state' (Jessop 2002).

This argument – and more broadly the discourse which it is a part of – was pervasively drawn upon, constantly repeated and extensively recontextualized during the heyday of neo-liberalism (Fairclough 2005). Explanatory critique would seek to explain the emergence of this discourse and arguments associated with it, and the dominant position they came to have in the wake of the crisis of the 1970s, and to explain the subsequent transformation of capitalism in a neo-liberal direction in a way which includes the effects of this discourse. Insofar as this discourse, including this overall argument, can plausibly be shown to have been a causal factor in these changes in capitalism, as well as serving particular interests while presenting them as being in the general interest, they can be regarded as ideological. It is in this sense that we might say that Blair's discourse is includes ideological elements.

What can analysis and evaluation of argumentation contribute to the conclusion that Blair's discourse can be regarded as ideological in this respect? From a dialectical perspective, Blair's moving from 'surviving and prospering' to 'making Britain more competitive' and 'better at generating wealth' can be challenged on various grounds. First, no justification for the move is provided. Second, it can be argued that an exclusive focus on increasing competitiveness and wealth might in fact compromise the goal of 'surviving and prospering', by creating extreme forms of inequality (negative consequences) that might undermine that goal, or by affecting other important goals and concerns (for instance, ecological sustainability). Third, there are other conceivable ways of 'surviving and prospering' which Blair does not address which may be preferable to the one he offers, such as ensuring that growth and wealth creation are limited to forms which are sustainable both ecologically and economically (e.g. avoiding speculative bubbles which may implode and cause major economic and social damage), and that the wealth created should be fairly distributed and used for socially beneficial purposes. There may be other more legitimate values or concerns (sustainability, equality) that ought to underlie the goals: not any future state-of-affairs in which prosperity is achieved may be a legitimate one, but one in which such prosperity is fairly distributed and ecologically and economically sustainable. Applying analysis and evaluation of argumentation to large samples of public political discourse, broadening the dialectical context (as we put it earlier), could be used to establish whether the exclusive focus on the goal of increasing competitiveness and the capacity for wealth creation to the exclusion of other possible goals is widespread, and whether this understanding of national survival and prosperity is widely taken for granted and allowed to go unchallenged.

The theory of ideology is concerned in general terms with the question of how beliefs and concerns which are associated with the interests of particular social groups come to be general beliefs and concerns, and how they come to have effects on social life. Ideologies are part of the way in which the dominance of dominant social groups is achieved, maintained and renewed through particular directions of social change. The capacity of ideologies to have such effects depends upon them not being recognized as such, being 'naturalized' (Fairclough 1989) as a part of common sense. Explanatory critique aims to explain people's beliefs and concerns as partly due to structural causes affecting their form of social life, and differing according to their positions in social life and the social relations they are positioned within. One aspect of the latter is that, where there are asymmetries of power, beliefs and concerns of dominant social groups which correspond to their own interests can come to be accepted by other social groups, whose interests they do not correspond to, as part of a perceived general interest. Since people may not be conscious of the social origins of their beliefs and concerns, individual decisions and actions can be partly explained as resulting from their own intentions but also partly explained as resulting from structural causes. People's reasons, as we have seen, may be provided by discourses and associated arguments, seen as constitutive parts of such discourses and products of argumentative discursive practices. Social changes, such as changes in the form of capitalism, as well the continuity of existing forms, can be explained in part as the effects of people's social agency, of the decisions they make and the actions they take, but social agency is also structurally constrained, and decisions and actions are partly based upon beliefs and concerns which have structural causes that people may not be conscious of. Insofar as such beliefs and concerns and the discourse they are manifested in have effects on social life, they are ideological.

We can see ideology as one focus within a broader attempt to understand and explain the capacity of discourse to have causal effects on social life, to contribute to changes in social life. Of course, not all beliefs and concerns, and not all discourses are ideological in the sense of supporting certain power interests and many are effects of people's own beliefs and interests rather than transferred effects of those of others. Moreover, social life has a reflexive character and people can come to examine their own beliefs and concerns and those of others and consciously seek to change them. It is increasingly the case in modern societies that the effects of discourse on social life are matters of calculation and design, and that there are people who deliberately aim to produce such effects (see the discussion of 'technologization of discourse' in Fairclough 1992). We said above that the effects of ideologies depend upon them being naturalized, but this does not mean that they are necessarily or even normally naturalized for everyone: they need to be naturalized for a significant number of people, and for a sufficient number of people, to have these effects. The situation in the heyday of neo-liberalism, in which neo-liberal discourse was widely (though by no means universally) taken for granted as common sense, can in this sense be regarded as a rather remarkable achievement of those architects of neo-liberalism who consciously worked for its realization. So in focusing on ideologies we recognize that the ideological effects of discourse are an aspect of its capacity to have causal effects on social life and that these effects are often intended. We must distinguish the intentional acts of people who seek to promote discourses which might work in an ideological way from the non-intentional character of ideologies, as manifested in the beliefs and actions of people for whom they appear as common sense. Discourses and arguments which correspond to particular interests but are taken for granted by a sufficient number of people as corresponding to a general interest can be effective in ways which those who take them for granted do not intend.

Critical analysis aims to produce explanations of social life which both identify the nature and causes of what is 'wrong' in it and produce knowledge which could (in the right conditions) contribute to 'righting' or at least mitigating these 'wrongs'. But explanations, interpretations, evaluations of social practices (both lay and specialist accounts) already exist within social contexts, because a necessary part of living and acting in particular social circumstances is interpreting and explaining them, and human beings reflexively assess the social activity they participate in. Furthermore, it is a feature of the social world that interpretations and explanations of it can have effects upon it, can transform it in various ways. In our approach to practical argumentation, interpretations and explanations of the crisis, produced by various agents, feature as reasons for acting in one way rather than another in response to the crisis. A critique of some area of social life must therefore be in part a critique of interpretations and explanations of social life and of the practical argumentation in which they feature as premises, as objects of research. It must therefore be in part a critique of (argumentative) discourse.

In analyzing discourses which are part of social life, the critical social analyst is also producing discourse. On what grounds can we say that this discourse is more rationally persuasive than the discourse that is the object of critique? The only basis for claiming superiority is providing explanations which have greater explanatory validity or power and greater predictive power. This is a matter of both quantity – how comprehensive the scope of explanations is – and quality – good explanations must be such that we can defend them and justify them if challenged and they can predict comparatively better what we can expect to happen or to discover in the real world. One aspect of the matter of quantity is the extent to which existing lay and non-lay interpretations and explanations are themselves explained, as well as their effects on social life, in terms of what it is about an area of social life that leads to these interpretations or explanations emerging, becoming dominant and having practical effects on social life (Marsden 1999; Fairclough and Graham 2002). Such interpretations and explanations can be said to be ideological if they can be shown to be in a sense necessary – necessary to establish or keep in place particular relations of power (Bhaskar 1979). A possible case in point is explanations of the crisis which play the 'blame game' in terms of the mistakes or moral flaws of bankers, politicians, regulators, rather than in terms of the (systemic, structural) logic of capitalism or its neo-liberal variety.

From the perspective of explanatory critique, one important question about practical argumentation is how reasons for action (one type of cause) contribute to causing social change, and another is how arguers' reasons for action are shaped by structures. Neither question can be fully addressed through analysis and evaluation of argumentation alone. But such analysis can make an important contribution to CDA and to interdisciplinary explanatory (and normative) critique. Analysis of argumentation shows, for example, how particular beliefs and concerns shape practical reasoning and, contingently, decisions and actions on matters of social and political importance, and it poses critical questions about how contexts of action, values and goals are represented in the premises of arguments, all of which can feed into critique of ideology. It shows whether argumentation is reasonable or unreasonable in anticipating alternative arguments and dealing with challenges, or in failing to do so, and this can indicate cases where particular representations of circumstances, values or goals seem to be taken as given and beyond question. These may be cases where arguers are drawing upon discourses which have been imposed by powerful social groups (an effect of 'power behind discourse') and which are of ideological significance. Institutional, external reasons are also important from the perspective of explanatory critique. Whether such reasons are drawn from institutional facts associated with status functions and deontic powers, or from ideological discourses which have been imposed and naturalized, they are reasons which are provided by *structures*, based in and shaped by relations of power. As we argue throughout this book (and in more detail later in this chapter), these are obvious cases where structures constrain agency, and the way they do is by providing agents with reasons for actions.

Our approach to argumentation analysis can be integrated within a normative (as opposed to merely descriptive) approach to social science, and particularly within an approach that recognizes 'lay normativity', the evaluative character of people's relation to the world, as a fundamental feature of social life which should be addressed by social scientists (Sayer 2011: 2). In Sayer's view, when social science disregards the fact that we are social beings *'whose relation to the world is one of concern . . .*, as if it were merely an incidental, subjective accompaniment to what happens, it can produce an alienated and alienating view of social life' (original italics). This is a view of values as 'beyond the scope of reason', as a matter of subjective preference, a view which ignores the grounding of values in people's objective capacities for suffering and flourishing. Things matter to people because of what people are, as biological, social and cultural beings. Lay normativity is distinct from analytical, external normativity: as analysts, 'we could just report that some group claims to feel happy or oppressed, but we are also likely to want to know whether their claims are warranted', which we cannot do without 'evaluating their judgements' (ibid.: 2–6). And if our aim is to engage in critical social science, that aim requires not only a normative but also an explanatory standpoint. The social scientist should seek not only to evaluate judgements, beliefs and practices, but also to explain why judgements are made, why beliefs are held, why practices exist, and also to identify cases where they 'help to maintain existing circumstances . . . that support those beliefs' and 'also are likely to be favourable to dominant groups' (ibid.: 220–222).

As analysts, we distinguish between interpretations of the social world, such as produced by participants, and analyses such as our own. We also distinguish between lay normativity and the external normativity of our analytical approach. In actual argumentative practice (as our analyses in Chapters 4, 5 and 6 will show), the analyst encounters not just participants' arguments but also their analyses and evaluations of other participants' arguments: actual argumentative practice itself has a normative character, in the sense that, as well as arguing, arguers evaluate the arguments of others. Such analyses and evaluations of arguments are sometimes produced by specialists, e.g. economists discussing economic arguments, and sometimes by members of the public with no particular specialist competence in the field at issue. (We illustrate these two situations in Chapters 4 and 5 respectively; both are instances of lay normativity in relation to our analytical approach.) Taking an external, normative perspective, as a CDA practitioner or argumentation theorist, does not intend to disregard lay normativity but makes a deliberate decision to view it against the framework of a particular theoretical model, and thus make evaluative decisions that are systematically motivated. Lay evaluations and analysts' evaluations do not, of course, have a radically different character; one can find lay challenges to arguments corresponding to all of the normative standards associated with the normative model. (Empirical research has shown, for example, that the pragma-dialectical normative model is intersubjectively acceptable to ordinary arguers and consistent with norms of reasonableness that they have already internalized, van Eemeren 2010: 36.) In proposing our own view of the structure and evaluation of practical reasoning, we have tried to contribute to the further specification of the normative framework of a pre-eminently dialectical approach. Such an approach can contribute to explanatory critique in providing a systematic basis for addressing participants' evaluation of each other's arguments, as an aspect of the reflexive assessment of social life, which explanatory critique aims to explain. And it contributes to normative critique by offering a systematic basis for the evaluation of actual argumentation practices from an external normative perspective.

In the last part of this chapter we will discuss the relevance of argumentation theory for understanding two concepts which originate outside CDA but have been significant concerns within this version of CDA (imaginaries and political legitimacy) and the concept of power, which is of fundamental importance for CDA as for any form of critical social science.

Imaginaries as discourses and goal premises

Discourses as ways of representing the world do not only describe what social reality is but also what it should be. The latter corresponds to what social theorists working within Cultural Political Economy (CPE) have called 'imaginaries' (Jessop 2002, 2008). This is an extremely interesting concept but, although CPE incorporates a version of CDA, there has been so far no clear way of working with it as an analytical category in discourse analysis. We think that relating it to a conception of human rationality and of practical reasoning in particular offers such a way.

What is currently said about imaginaries in CPE tends to conflate an important distinction, between discursive (semiotic) representations of the *actual* world, on the one hand, and imaginaries proper, as discursive (semiotic) representations of a possible, *non-actual* (or not-yet-actual) world, on the other. In the account we propose here, we start from the premise that both representations of the actual world and 'imaginaries', as representation of the non-actual, are semiotic in nature, they are discourses. A representation of the economic system currently in place in the UK and a vision of how this economic system might be transformed both stand in relation to the actually existing economy, just as my representations of what my situation is and how I would like it to be both stand in a relationship to the actual world. But they are distinct in what they are used to describe: one is used to represent the *actual world*, the other is used to represent a *future possible world*. It is only the latter discursive representation that is an 'imaginary'.

CPE seems to talk of 'economic imaginaries' or 'imagined economies' as designating both alternative, competing representations of the actually existing economy, and future visions or projects, competing for selection and retention, and eventually capable of more-or-less shaping the actual world. We argue for a clear distinction between these two types of representations. The competing vocabularies in which people talk about the capitalist economy as it exists today in western states, for instance, are not 'imaginaries' because they aim to describe the actual world. If we were to use 'imaginaries' to cover both senses we would lose a distinction which is clear in the structure of practical reasoning, where these two sorts of semiotic representations always appear as *distinct types of premises*. Imaginaries, as future visions, capable of guiding action, are assigned to the *goal* premise, while semiotic representations of the actual world are assigned to the *circumstantial* premise. This distinction accords perfectly with CPE's acknowledgement of the performative power of imaginaries:

> Imaginaries are . . . creative products of semiotic and material practices with more or less performative power. This is why they have a central role in the struggle not only for 'hearts and minds' but also for the reproduction or transformation of the prevailing structures of exploitation and domination.
>
> (Jessop and Sum 2012: 86)

But it also explains *why* imaginaries have this power: *because they give people reasons for action*, they *are* reasons for action, premises of practical arguments. An explanation of how visions can motivate or inspire action, of how one can move from vision to action and attempt to change the world is only possible if the whole discussion is placed with the framework of a theory of practical reasoning.

Our aims in this section are twofold. First, we want to arrive at a definition of 'imaginaries' as a semiotic construct that can be of real use to the discourse analyst. This will involve an attempt to place 'imaginaries' within a schema for practical reasoning. Second, we want to relate 'imaginaries' to an ontology that is capable of explaining how language can be a form of action and create institutional reality. Let us address the first issue by looking at a text produced by the UK centre-left organization Compass (www.compassonline.org.uk). The text, entitled *Building the Good Society. The Project of the Democratic Left* and used in a printed leaflet during the 2010 national electoral campaign, is signed by Jon Cruddas and Andrea Nahles (no date) and begins as follows:

> Europe is at a turning point. Our banks are not working, businesses are collapsing and unemployment is increasing. The economic wreckage of market failure is spreading across the continent. But this is not just a crisis of capitalism. It is also a failure of democracy and society to regulate and manage the power of the market. (. . .) The future is uncertain and full of threats; before us lie the dangers of climate change, the end of oil and growing social dislocation. But it is also a moment full of opportunities and promise: to revitalise our common purpose and fulfil the European dream of freedom and equality for all. To face these threats and realise this promise demands a new political approach.
>
> On the tenth anniversary of the Blair–Schroeder declaration of a European Third Way, the Democratic Left offers an alternative project: *the good society*. This politics of the good society is about democracy, community and pluralism. It is democratic because only the free participation of each individual can guarantee true freedom and progress. It is collective because it is grounded in the recognition of our interdependency and common interest. And it is pluralist because it knows that from a diversity of political institutions, forms of economic activity and individual cultural identities, society can derive the energy and inventiveness to create a better world.
>
> To achieve a good society based on these values we are committed to:

- restoring the primacy of politics and rejecting the subordination of political to economic interests;
- remaking the relationship between the individual and the state in a democratic partnership;
- creating a democratic state that is accountable and more transparent;
- strengthening our institutions of democracy at all levels including the economy;
- reasserting the interests of the common good, such as education, health and welfare, over the market;
- redistributing the risk, wealth and power associated with class, race and gender to create a more equal society . . .

We can use the account of the structure of practical reasoning in Chapter 2 to identify a number of arguments. The first includes the following premises and claim:

Circumstantial premises	[First paragraph, from] 'Europe is at a turning point. Our banks are not working . . .' [to] 'it is also a moment full of opportunities and promise'. [Circumstances also include the existence of suitable opportunities for action: it is possible for us to do what we want.]
Goal premises	[Our goals are] 'to face these threats and realise this promise'.
Claim	[The goal] 'demands a new political approach', [subsequently defined as the] 'alternative project: the *good society*'.

Up to this point, the argument justifies the need for a new approach to politics and can be represented as in Figure 3.3.

Goal premise	[Our goal is] 'to achieve a good society based on these values'.
Value premises	'This politics of the good society is about democracy, community and pluralism'. [Justification of the acceptability of the value premise:] 'It is democratic because only the free participation of each individual can guarantee true freedom and progress. It is collective because it is grounded in the recognition of our interdependency and common interest. And it is pluralist because it knows that from a diversity of political institutions, forms of economic activity and individual cultural identities, society can derive the energy and inventiveness to create a better world.'
Claim	[This is what we ought to do and we are committed to doing, in view of achieving the goal]: 'restoring the primacy of politics and rejecting the subordination of political to economic interests'; 'remaking the relationship between the individual and the state', etc.

From this point onwards, a new claim is made, which justifies a set of actions designed to turn the project (i.e. the imaginary or vision) of the good society into reality. Achieving the good society is the goal premise, the actions are the means. An extended discussion of the values underlying this project is included at this point (see Figure 3.4):

We have identified two interconnected arguments with two claims. The first claim is that a new political project is required, and is justified in terms of what the context is (crisis, threats but also opportunities) and what the goals are (i.e. to respond to these threats and fulfil possibilities). In the second argument, this political project (the imaginary of the Good Society) is taken as given (not argued for), as a goal of action, and a set of actions is proposed

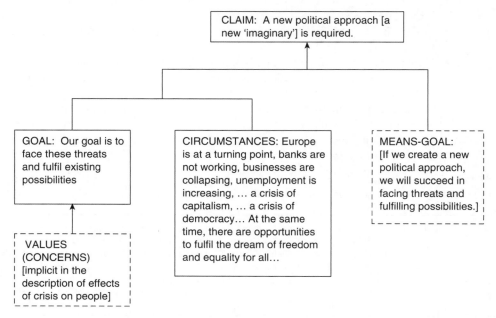

Figure 3.3 Compass: the argument for a new political approach.

as being capable of turning the imaginary of the Good Society into reality (and thereby successfully responding to the circumstances of 'threats' and 'opportunities').

Compass has implicitly engaged in a process of deliberation over what the goals of action ought to be and what actions are required to realize these goals and is here advancing its own political project (proposal) in response to the implicit open question 'what should be done, given the circumstances, in order to meet our shared goals'? However, instead of advancing a specific action or set of actions, as means towards shared goals, uncontroversial goals, Compass is suggesting a redefinition of the goals themselves: we need to develop a new political approach, a new project or vision, a new goal. The text nicely illustrates deliberation both about goals and about means. In other words, before considering what action (as means) will solve current problems, we need to decide whether the goals of action, as we currently understand them, are appropriate. Compass is 'offering an alternative project', the Good Society, as the result of implicit deliberation over goals. (Implicitly, having considered several possible goals, it has concluded that a change of goals is needed in order to solve current problems; adopting *a new goal* is the *means* to solving the problem – Figure 3.3). Subsequently, this project, once identified and put forward, becomes a goal premise from which a specific course of action follows and is proposed in the second argument (Figure 3.4).

We have said that 'imaginaries' (the 'Good Society', the 'Big Society', etc.), function as goal premises in arguments and can thus motivate action. Some imaginaries have been around for a long time, for instance the 'knowledge-based economy'. There seem to be several distinct ways in which we can talk about the 'knowledge-based economy', not all of them in terms of goals. We can say: *Our goal is to achieve a 'knowledge-based economy', therefore we ought to invest more money in education and research.* But we can also say: *The economy of the UK is a*

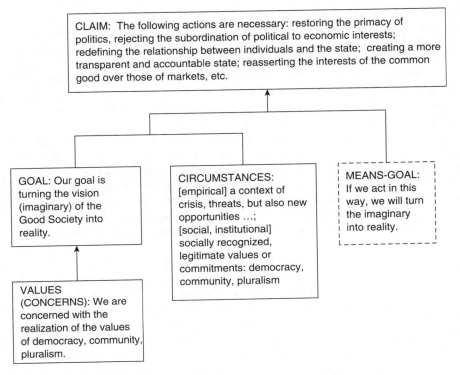

Figure 3.4 Compass: how to turn the imaginary of the Good Society into reality.

'*knowledge-based economy*', *therefore, if our goal is to compete internationally, we ought to invest more money in education and research.* In the former example, the imaginary of the knowledge-based economy is clearly a goal. In the latter example, the description of the economy as a knowledge-based economy is taken as a description of what the economy is actually like, therefore as a circumstantial premise, not as a goal to achieve in the future. This seems to contradict our view that imaginaries are (non-actual) goals of action. In order to account for this puzzle, which we think underlies the confusion we mentioned earlier regarding the status of imaginaries, let us briefly refer once more to Searle's social ontology, which we introduced in Chapter 2.

The distinction we have defended so far amounts to one between what is 'imagined' – as in 'imagined community' (Anderson 1991), or as in seeing the state system as an 'imagined political entity' (Jessop 2002) – and what is 'imaginary' (the 'Good Society' imagined by Compass, or the 'Big Society' imagined by the Conservatives). An imagined community is the result of a collective act of imagination, but is nevertheless a community that actually exists, so is 'real' in a sense in which the imaginary of the 'Good Society' is not real, or not real yet. The same goes for other imagined entities or relationships ('marriage' is an imagined relation, but not an 'imaginary' relationship for actually married people). We can relate this distinction to Searle's social ontology and say that imagined entities or relationships of this kind are *institutional* facts and are ontologically subjective but epistemically objective. What we have called 'imagined' but not 'imaginary' (marriage, but also promises, money, government) are social institutions of various sort. They are created in a process whereby people impose certain so-called status functions on other individuals and objects, followed by collective recognition of those status functions. Status functions are assigned by speech acts of declaration ('*x* counts as *y* in context *c*') and carry deontic powers, i.e. they confer or impose rights, obligations, entitlements, etc. The purpose of assigning them is to regulate relations of power in a society. They hold society together because they give people reasons for action that are independent of their desires (Searle 2010). David Cameron's collectively recognized status as Prime Minister gives other people reasons for acting in accordance with his decisions that are independent of those people's actual desires.

Where do 'imaginaries' fit within this social ontology, in our view? We have said that imaginaries belong to the goal premise in arguments for action, and that this premise motivates action. Given these goals (visions, projects), whose realization we want, and given the circumstances we are in, the following type of action is recommended. But what would the consequences be of talking about these visions *as if they were reality?* What would follow if, instead of being the goal premise, the vision were to shift to the circumstantial premise, the one that claims to represent how reality is, as in the example we gave above, involving the knowledge-based economy?

The suggestion we are advancing here is the following. The 'performative' power of the 'imaginary' has to do with a shift in its place within the argument: from the goal premise to the circumstantial premise. The mechanism is the following: the arguer is performing a status-function declaration which represents the 'imaginary' as 'actual' and he attempts to get it collectively recognized as a factual representation. How does such an 'imaginary', represented as actual fact, differ from an 'imaginary' which functions as a goal premise? In the following way: the 'imaginary' as goal can motivate and guide action, being a reason for action, but it has no deontic powers. No system of rights, duties, obligations, authority follows from it as long as it is represented as non-actual, i.e. as long as it stays in the goal premise. However, representing the 'vision' as institutional *reality*, instituting it by declaration and trying to get it collectively recognized, *can*, if this recognition is successful, eventually shape reality. An institutional reality that is collectively recognized assigns deontic powers to people and gives them reasons for action. The 'performative' power of an 'imaginary' has to do with whether or not, in practical reasoning over action, in relevant contexts (having to do with persons, settings, procedures, etc. – which themselves must have the appropriate status functions), the 'imaginary' is collectively recognized as (institutional) fact (e.g. enshrined in new regulations, laws, discourses and genres, etc.), generating a deontic system, and thus enabling and constraining human action. The success of this collective recognition has to do both with how the vision resonates with various audiences (whether it is taken up, accepted, whether it manages to persuade) – and this is partly to do with its intrinsic qualities (such as the quality of the argument in its favour) – but also has to do what has been called in CDA (Fairclough 1989) the *power behind discourse*. It depends on whether the vision is supported by groups of people who have the power to decide and impose it as a view of what the world is.

In the speech by Blair that we analyzed earlier, 'the new global economy' is an imaginary (an imagined economy) that is being treated as fact (as part of the objective, empirical context of action). In so doing, in representing goals as facts, Blair is arguably advancing the interests of particular agents and organizations. The achievement of these interests depends on collective recognition (e.g. in laws, contracts, etc.) of a certain imagined economy as the way the economy is. As we have said, whether or not a representation achieves collective recognition depends on a variety of factors, partly having to do with the arguments that support it, partly with power issues independent of those arguments. This is precisely where the value of Searle's ontology lies, in seeing status functions, including the very possibility of assigning them by declaration, as the vehicles of power. Being able (i.e. having the power resources) to declare that a certain imaginary is a fact and to enforce its collective recognition and the recognition of its deontic powers is one of the manifestations of power in society.

Besides imaginaries, other significant concepts used in social science could be viewed from an argumentative perspective. The understanding of the structure of practical arguments that we propose in this book, and particularly of the value premise, and its relation to how people formulate goals and represent the circumstances of action, could (we suggest) be particularly relevant to the perspective of the 'moral economy', as developed in social science by Sayer (1999, 2000, 2007, etc.). The concept refers to the moral dimensions of economic and social systems and a focus on practical arguments would offer a clear discourse-analytical understanding of the way in which moral values (fairness, equality, justice, greed, thrift, etc.) underlie and legitimize action: they motivate (are reasons for) action because they are premises in practical arguments. We are not exploring this connection in an explicit way in this book; an early attempt to link moral economy with argumentation was made in Ieţcu (2006b, 2006c).

Legitimation: an argumentative perspective

In CDA (Fairclough 2003 included), the concepts of 'legitimation' and 'legitimacy' have been used in a very broad and undefined sense. Any reason offered in support of an action, *any justification*, has sometimes been regarded as an example of legitimation (van Leeuwen 2007; van Leeuwen and Wodak 1999; Wodak *et al.* 1999). We suggest, however, that legitimation is not quite the same thing as justification, it has a narrower scope than justification, it is a particular type of justification. We often speak of legitimation in connection with courses of action: we ought to do *x* (or action *x* is legitimate) because it conforms to certain norms or values that we adhere to. Most often we speak of legitimation in connection with power (or sources of authority in general), e.g. a system of power may be considered legitimate or may legitimize itself (and its actions) because it has resulted, for instance, from free democratic elections, or because it conforms to tradition or custom, or because it accords with widely shared values and beliefs. In all these cases, the justification involved in legitimation seems to have one particularity, namely to invoke *publicly shared* and *publicly justifiable*, and sometimes even highly formalized, codified, institutional systems of beliefs, values and norms, in virtue of which the action proposed is considered legitimate. Justifications of action which do not invoke such shared systems of rules or shared norms cannot be properly said to be legitimations. We are *justifying* a claim to action both in saying 'MPs shouldn't fiddle their expenses because they are breaking the law' *and* 'MPs shouldn't fiddle their expenses because they could end up in prison', but only the reason used in the former example (they are breaking the law) indicates that the action is not legitimate; the latter only says that, in view of their interests, i.e. prudentially, they shouldn't fiddle their expenses. In referring to the law we are invoking a *second* level of justification: adhering to the law itself is a reason that can be publicly justified. We take this understanding of legitimation as involving a multi-layered structure of justification from political theory (Beetham 1991) – see Ieţcu-Fairclough (2008).

A widely referred-to theoretical statement on legitimation in CDA is an article in *Discourse and Communication* by Theo van Leeuwen (2007). A lot of empirical research has drawn on this framework, which is why we want to discuss it briefly here. According to van Leeuwen (2007), legitimation involves an answer to the spoken or unspoken question 'Why should we do this?' or 'Why should we do this in this way?' On this basis, he distinguishes four major categories of legitimation: (a) authorization; (b) moral evaluation; (c) rationalization; and (d) mythopoesis. For instance, we should do *x* because experts advise it (authorization), because it is the honest thing to do (moral evaluation), because it is useful or effective (instrumental rationalization), etc. (Note that 'rationalization' is not used here to mean what it means in argumentation theory, a defective argument, but a type of legitimation based on a 'rational' reason, such as utility or factual truth.)

Van Leeuwen correctly identifies the type of reasoning that underlies legitimizing statements as being of the form 'we ought to do *x* because of *y*', in response to the implicit question 'why should we do *x*'?, or 'why should we do *x* in this way'? However, he does not relate legitimation to argumentation. Argumentation is hardly mentioned at all, with the effect that the exact nature of legitimation remains a mystery. More importantly, the typology does not capture the crucial fact that judgements of legitimacy are always *in relation to* a background of norms, beliefs and values that are *themselves* 'legitimate' in some sense, i.e. they can be publicly justified, they are 'worthy' of being collectively recognized. When we say 'we should do *x* because it is useful', we would not be able to legitimize the action if the reason, utility, were not in itself considered a good thing. As we have said, there are two distinct levels of justification involved: a justification of action in virtue of some reason and a justification of that reason in virtue of a publicly recognized system of norms, values, beliefs.

In addition, legitimation is not distinguished from explanation. Many of van Leeuwen's examples are in fact explanations, yet legitimation can only be related to argumentation, because it is only in arguments (not in explanations) that we are giving reasons in support of a *controversial* proposition that stands in need of justification. By contrast, in explanation, the proposition that is being explained, the *explanandum*, is *already* accepted as a fact, and therefore, logically, cannot be justified (or *legitimized*) by the *explanans* (instead, it is the *explanans* that can be controversial). Van Leeuwen's framework does not capture the inherent link between legitimation and argumentation (nor the existence of more than one level of argumentative justification) but has, nevertheless, an insightful starting point and indicates (if only implicitly) some of the values, norms or criteria that are used in public justification (moral, utilitarian, instrumental) and some of the argumentative schemes involved in public justification (argumentation from authority, practical arguments from consequence or from moral values, and so on).[5]

In political theory, unlike in discourse analysis, legitimation is widely seen as an argumentative process involving the public exchange of reasons, or public deliberation. As we said in Chapter 1, according to a purely proceduralist conception of democratic legitimacy, democratic decisions are legitimate when they result from fair procedure (correct voting procedure in which every citizen has had a say). Decisions emerging from such procedures are legitimate, whatever the quality of the outcome. Thus, people who disagree with a decision and consider it wrong would have to recognize it as legitimate as long as it has resulted from fair procedure. Other conceptions of democratic legitimacy (Peter 2010; Swift 2006) think that a purely procedural view is insufficient: the epistemic quality of the outcome is also important (i.e. is it a reasonable decision?). Deliberative democracy involves a public exchange of reasons and thus generates new knowledge and a better understanding of social problems. It is therefore likely to lead to decisions that are also *good* decisions, not merely decisions that are legitimate in procedural terms.

According to one type of views on political legitimacy, the epistemic value of deliberative decision-making arises precisely from its procedural features. A decision will be better depending on how fair and inclusive the procedure has been, on how thoroughly the reasons and proposals advanced have been subjected to criticism. Conceptions of this sort argue for combining procedural features with features that refer to the *quality* of outcomes of democratic decision-making. These mixed, 'rational proceduralist' conceptions of democratic legitimacy (Peter 2008) are underlain by a concern that the fairness of the democratic decision-making process is not sufficient to establish the legitimacy of its outcomes, as fair procedures (e.g. majority vote) may sometimes lead to irrational or undesirable outcomes. The ideal outcome, on this view, is a *rationally justified decision* – a decision everyone has reasons to endorse. If conducted in accordance with the norms that define it, democratic deliberation is capable of reaching such rationally justified decisions (Peter 2010).

The 'rational proceduralist' conception is most congenial to a dialectical theory of argumentation. The normative frameworks of dialectical theories are designed to distinguish between reasonable and unreasonable argumentation. In the form of critical questions or rules of argumentative conduct, they specify procedural conditions that have to be met by reasonable arguers and arguments. In pragma-dialectics (van Eemeren and Grootendorst 2004, van Eemeren 2010), the dialectical procedure – as we understand it – is so designed as to produce a reasonable, rationally acceptable outcome as a result of the *discussion procedure*. In other words, methodically following the procedure will deliver reasonable decisions or reasonable beliefs. If the objective is to resolve disagreement in a reasonable way, as in pragma-dialectics, the procedure is designed to avoid obstacles to resolution or 'false' resolutions. The constraints imposed on the quality of the outcome by the procedure itself are, on this view, sufficiently high to prevent unreasonable outcomes. (Let us reiterate that disagreement resolution is a normative orientation of argumentative activity; it does not follow that agreement is always reached or that it is always possible. Depending on institutional context, specific activity types will not be deficient if they fail to result in disagreement resolution amongst all participants – see Chapter 6 for the case of parliamentary debate.)

Political theorists who adopt a substantive view of democratic legitimacy (Cohen 1998) advocate looking not just at the quality of the procedure but at the quality (rational acceptability) of the reasons adduced in favour of a certain choice. It is only by going beyond merely procedural legitimacy that decisions arrived at by deliberation can have a cognitive, epistemic dimension, can be the 'right' solutions to problems (however fallible and revisable these 'right' solutions may be). A deliberative decision will be reasonable insofar as the arguments that justify it will take into consideration in an optimal way the relevant aspects of the problem, think through the consequences of various proposals, subject possible solutions to critical questioning, answer objections and counter-arguments. What this means is that, in political deliberation, 'normatively legitimate outcomes must satisfy standards of reasonable argumentation' (Rehg 2009: 13). If such standards are met, deliberation will stand a better chance of delivering an outcome that is both procedurally and substantively legitimate, an outcome that is rationally persuasive by virtue of having withstood a process of critical testing. To say that public deliberation should satisfy standards of argumentative reasonableness is not to say that individual participants, as individuals, must satisfy such standards: deliberative reasonableness is a collective product emerging from dialogue amongst individuals.

An essential distinction is drawn in political philosophy between legitimacy and perceived legitimacy (Swift 2006: 220). A political regime may be perceived as legitimate without being in fact legitimate: perceived legitimacy could be resting on false beliefs that would not stand up to critical examination. Political theorists also speak about a descriptive (empirical) and a normative conception of legitimacy. All discussions of legitimacy go back to Weber (1978), who understood legitimacy in the descriptive sense: power is legitimate if people *believe* it to be legitimate. Other theorists, however, insist on 'good reasons': there must be some 'reasonable consensus' (Rawls 1993), or 'rationally motivated agreement' or 'rational consensus'

(Habermas 1984, 1996a), some normative basis for judgements of legitimacy, beyond what people happen to believe. According to Habermas, '*legitimacy means a political order's worthiness to be recognized*'; it says that 'there are good arguments for a political order to be recognized as right and just' (Habermas 1996c: 248). A normative claim is legitimate if it is the object of an agreement among all parties, as free and equal, at the end of a process of deliberation that is free from deception and the distorting constraints of power, and thus embodies the general, public interest (Habermas 1996b, 1996c). For Beetham, a given power relationship is not legitimate because people believe in its legitimacy, but because it can be argumentatively justified and defended as being in accordance with established rules (norms, values) and these rules can themselves be publicly justified. (In addition, for him, there has to be evidence of consent) (Beetham 1991: 11).

We can reformulate the above views as saying that legitimation is a type of argumentative justification, public justification, in which an action can be justified in terms of reasons and those reasons can themselves be justified as collectively accepted and recognized (as 'worthy of being recognized'). A particular kind of the latter reasons, Searle (2010) would say, are the duties, rights, obligations, commitments, moral values and norms that agents (individuals, the state or the political system) are bound by.

Power as a source of agents' reasons for action

Finally, we want to say a few words about power, an ever-present concern in CDA, and the way in which (in our view) it connects to analyses of argumentation. The main reason is to dispel a persistent confusion which can be formulated as follows: decisions in politics are *not* taken by means of argumentation, but are determined by power, hence the study of argumentation in politics is a useless enterprise. This objection rests on a fundamental misunderstanding which we can answer as follows. Political discourse is fundamentally argumentative in nature, and in particular it is almost always a case of practical argumentation (with other types of argumentation and other genres subsumed to and embedded within practical argument). However, not all argumentation is reasonable and very often political decisions are made not on the strength of the better argument but on the basis of other reasons. One such reason is power. *Power provides agents with reasons for action*: reasons to obey legitimate authority, or reasons to avoid or seek particular outcomes; reasons that are legitimate or reasons that are only perceived as legitimate (as a consequence of the ability of systems of power to naturalize values and beliefs that have not been critically examined). Briefly, power *is* a reason in practical arguments, which is why the study of power in politics cannot be divorced from the study of arguments and decision-making on the basis of arguments.

We shall begin with the standard distinction between 'power to' and 'power over', then move on to a discussion of theories of power drawing particularly on Lukes (2005). We shall also return to a distinction in Fairclough (1989) between 'power in discourse' and 'power behind discourse'. We shall then discuss Searle's (2010) view of power, which is of particular interest for the question of how power factors enter as reasons (premises) in practical argumentation.

'Power to' is a general human capacity to bring about change, to act in ways that bring about changes in reality. Both individuals and collectivities (e.g. governments) have this capacity, and it is important to see it as a *capacity* and not reduce it to its exercise: the capacity exists whether or not it is exercised and whatever means of power (wealth, military force, etc.) may be used in exercising it. 'Power over' is a specific form of 'power to': someone's capacity to cause, undergo or resist change may include (and be increased by) their power over other people. 'Power over' is an asymmetrical relation between people, and having power over others means being able to get them to do what you want them to do, to get them to do things which they otherwise would not do (Lukes 2005: 69–74).

Lukes advances a 'radical' view of power (in the sense of 'power over') as a 'three-dimensional' view in contrast to 'one-dimensional' and 'two-dimensional' views. In the one-dimensional view, power over others is a matter being able to prevail over them in decision-making. The two-dimensional view is an advance over the one-dimensional view in that it sees power (over) as not only the capacity to prevail in decision-making, but also the capacity to limit the scope of decision-making to exclude issues whose airing would be detrimental to those who have power. Both views focus on behaviour, conscious decision-making and conflict. The three-dimensional view criticizes both of these views for their restricted focus on observable behaviour and decision-making. Not all cases of exclusion of potential issues from the political agenda can be seen as effects of conscious, individual, intentional decisions: the 'bias of the system' can be mobilized and reinforced in ways that are not consciously intended by agents. This 'bias' is in fact not as much the product of a series of individually chosen acts, but rather of the 'socially structured and culturally patterned behaviour of groups, and practices of institutions' (Lukes 2005: 25–26). The third dimension adds therefore the (non-intentional) effects of group behaviour, institutional practices and systems in limiting the scope of decision-making. Moreover, overt conflict is not essential to power: power may be exercised over others by shaping or determining their preferences or perceived needs in such ways that conflict does not arise. Lukes's third dimension of power refers therefore to cases of domination where people are subject to domination and acquiesce in that domination, either by actively adopting the beliefs and values that oppress them, or simply by being resigned to them. It thus introduces a distinction between subjective interests and *real* interests, and the possibility that people may be unaware of their real interests (Lukes 2005: 27–29). What is of particular relevance to us in our book is the connection with ideology which suggests itself here. To speak about the third dimension of power, Lukes says, is to speak of 'interests imputed to and unrecognized' by social actors, of the 'power to mislead' people about what is in their interest, distort their judgement, for instance by 'naturalizing what could be otherwise' (Lukes 2005: 146, 149).

Discourse and power was the central theme of Fairclough (1989), where a distinction was drawn between 'power in discourse' and 'power behind discourse'. 'Power in discourse' is a matter of some people exercising 'power over' others in discourse. This can take various forms. It includes powerful participants controlling and constraining the contributions of less powerful participants and can sometimes amount to a form of coercion. An example would be the power of producers of newspaper articles or television programmes to determine what is included and excluded, how events are represented, and thus potentially affect how audiences see aspects of the world and act towards them. The idea of 'power behind discourse' is that orders of discourse, the semiotic aspect of social practices, emerge and are sustained or changed within particular (asymmetrical) relations of power and through the application of power. 'Power behind discourse' is consistent with Lukes's radical 'three-dimensional' view of power, but not with the other two views. It is an aspect of 'power over', which Lukes defines in strong terms as 'the ability to constrain the choices of others, coercing them or securing their compliance, by impeding them from living as their own nature and judgement dictate' (Lukes 2005: 85). In his terms, the 'inculcation and policing' of social practices (and concepts, norms, roles, etc.) – which would in our view include orders of discourse – is part of the 'mechanisms' of domination (Lukes 2005: 101).

In our treatment of external reasons in practical argumentation, we have adopted Searle's account of desire-independent reasons as based on institutional facts, status functions and deontic powers. A common way to exercise power, according to Searle, is 'to give people reasons for actions that they would not otherwise have'. There are various possibilities here, according to him, and one is to exercise power by getting the subject to *want* something that he would not have wanted, for instance by presenting a limited range of options as the only ones available so that the subject is not aware of alternatives (Searle 2010:146–147). Searle argues that 'all political power is a matter of status functions, and for that reason all political power is deontic power': it involves rights, duties, obligations, authorizations, permissions, privileges, authority and so on. A characteristic feature of deontic powers is that they do not have to involve the use or threat of force. If I make a promise to you, as Searle explains, then you have a deontic power over me, because I have created a binding reason on myself for acting according to my promise and you can expect me to do so. I can be held responsible for breaking the promise precisely because undertaking a commitment to do the action I promised to do is a *constitutive* rule of the act of promising. However, given agents' freedom, i.e. their capacity and motivation to break the rules, the political power of the state is also backed by force (Searle 2010: 148).[6]

Deontic powers are cases in which the power exercised consists of a certain type of *reasons for action*, i.e. reasons that are independent of what people's actual desires and inclinations are, reasons that people *have*, in an objective sense, whatever their actual motivations might be. Searle suggests that 'the entire system of status functions is a system of providing desire-independent reasons for acting' and the system works because it provides people with reasons for action that they recognize and accept. A political system that did not have the capacity to create desire-independent reasons would collapse, given agents' freedom (Searle 2010: 139–141). People do recognize the binding force of obligations, duties, commitments, moral norms: in a shop, most people have a desire-independent reason not to steal the merchandise, a reason which goes beyond the merely prudential reason (desire) of not getting caught and arrested. The threat of force is often (and in this case, always) in the background, as a potential deterrent, but the point is that it is not because of this reason that most people refrain from stealing.

Power can give people prudential reasons for action (they do not steal because they do not want to be arrested: the threat of violence is a prudential reason) but crucially it gives them desire-independent reasons: people accept or recognize a certain institutional arrangement. Here, Searle says, the question of how institutional reality is *legitimized* is crucial, as institutions work only to the extent they are recognized or accepted, and people must think there is some ground, some good reason, for accepting that institution. Most institutions are taken for granted, and no justification is demanded or offered, but institutions can also be challenged (Searle 2010: 140). Earlier in this chapter we said this recognition depends on a process of public justification. This, we may add, opens up the space for manipulation (which Searle does not discuss). We can see it as an attempt to provide people with reasons that they would otherwise not have, possibly with reasons that would in fact not be in their interests and would not be *rationally* persuasive for them, although they might be quite effective in actually persuading them. We can regard the massive public relations industry which serves government, businesses, and other types of institutions, seeking to win support for particular policies and influence public opinion, as being involved in a continuous effort to secure the necessary acceptance of status functions, to create the *perception* of legitimacy.

To sum up, to exert power over an agent is to give him reasons for action that he would otherwise not have. Such reasons can be either prudential (when people obey authority to avoid violence) or deontic, when people recognize and accept their external (moral, institutional) force. Acting in accordance with an order given by someone in a position of authority, or with institutional rules and norms, when action is prompted by recognition or acceptance of status functions, involves deontic reasons. Because deontic reasons presuppose acceptance or recognition, the questions of how acceptance is achieved or whether it is justified or not, are essential questions. Agents might be induced to perceive as legitimate social arrangements which cannot withstand a process of public justification. The type of power involved in this process, in the naturalization of beliefs and values which would not, if critically examined, survive scrutiny, is Lukes's third type of power: the ideological power of systems.

Finally, let us say a few words about the relationship between power and legitimacy in light of our remarks above, and in relation to our proposal (in Chapter 2) for the structure or practical reasoning. Politicians commonly include amongst reasons for proposed actions objective, desire-independent reasons of the sort which, according to Searle, are based upon status functions and deontic powers. An example (which anticipates a discussion in Chapter 4) is arguing that 'we should do *A* because it is fair', where achieving a fair outcome is one of the arguer's goals, a motive or reason for acting in a certain way, but also, at the same time, *a socially recognized commitment that the agent has and therefore is expected to act in accordance with*. Being fair is widely recognized as an obligation that the government or politicians have, a commitment they are bound by as a consequence of holding political positions and as a necessary condition for the legitimacy of government policy, decision or action. It is a desire-independent reason that is binding on political agents in virtue of their status function and is independent on whether they want or not to act fairly. In giving a reason of this sort, a politician is seeking to claim legitimacy for the action proposed. As we suggested in the section on legitimation, giving a reason can legitimize, rather than just merely justify, a proposed action only if there is also a further reason for that reason, a reason that can be publicly defended: 'we should do *A* because it is fair, and fairness is a publicly shared value to which we are *committed*', i.e. we have an *obligation* or *duty* to be fair. The fact that politicians generally give reasons of this sort suggests that their power to pursue a proposed line of action depends upon their ability to legitimize it and thereby persuade audiences to accept it in virtue of the audience's recognition of the legitimacy of the underlying value. An appeal to fairness can legitimize political action because fairness is a publicly justifiable or publicly recognized, legitimate value. In addition, its invocation suggests that the politician is one who honours the (institutional, objective) obligation attaching to his status function.

Conclusion

Our main objective in this chapter has been to argue that the analysis and evaluation of argumentation can increase the capacity of CDA to pursue its aim of extending forms of critique familiar in critical social science to discourse and texts. We began by presenting our approach to CDA and discussing its relationship to critical social science and to normative and explanatory critique. We then carried out a reanalysis of part of a speech by Tony Blair which was originally analysed in Fairclough (2000a), with the objective of showing that it is an example of practical argumentation, that analysing it as such significantly strengthens the original analysis, and that the critical force of the analysis of representations (e.g. the representation of 'change') which was really the sole concern of the latter is substantially increased when we recognize that these representations are part of the premises of the practical arguments and analyse them as such, rather than analysing them in isolation, as has often happened in CDA (including in Fairclough 2000a). We suggested that an analysis of persuasive definitions and evaluative terms in various premises, as well as a normative framework for analyzing deliberation, can provide a clearer understanding of what is going on in this speech: rhetorically motivated representations (including metaphors or particular ways of 'framing') should not be seen as isolated features of the text but as having an argumentative function of steering the argument towards a certain conclusion and precluding other conclusion from being arrived at.

We then moved to a more general discussion of how analysis and evaluation of argumentation can contribute to normative and explanatory critique and to critique of manipulation and ideology. Regarding normative critique, we suggested that examining argumentation can provide a sounder basis for analysis of manipulation in discourse and we illustrated this with an analysis of rationalization as a normatively defective argument. In subsequent chapters we will address other argumentative issues that can feed into normative critique, such as argumentation based on false premises, or on unacceptable values and goals, or on inadequate deliberation. Regarding explanatory critique, we noted that, in arguing, people draw on different discourses in the way they represent premises and claims. Such selections are linked to the diverse interests and social positions (e.g. positions in relations of power) of particular groups of social agents, and give rise to the sort of critical questions about discourse which CDA characteristically addresses (about domination, manipulation and ideologies). Deliberation that restricts consideration of alternatives or represents alternative actions in ways which make them seem unreasonable (illustrated by Blair's speech), and thus unreasonably steers the argument towards one possible conclusion, can be regarded as ideological if it is geared to supporting certain power interests.

We continued with a discussion of two concepts that have tended to figure prominently within CDA and critical social science (imaginaries and political legitimacy), claiming that they can be more adequately dealt with in CDA than they have been hitherto if we see them as essentially involving argumentation. We suggested that imaginaries are in fact goal premises in arguments. Goals are the 'motivational' premises of practical arguments and this is why imaginaries or visions can motivate and inspire action. We also suggested that imaginaries can have performative power, or can transform the world, when they are collectively recognized as representations of *actual*, not merely possible states of affairs, thus acquiring an associated deontology from which various practical consequences follow. As for legitimation, it is inherently an argumentative practice and is different from ordinary justification in the sense of involving a double level of justification; certainly it is different from explanation, with which it is persistently confused. As regards power, we have suggested how discussions of 'power in discourse' or 'power behind discourse' can be related to a theory of practical reasoning. Power itself is a reason for action, or more specifically, it provides agents with (either self-interested or deontic) reasons for action. For instance, in providing agents with reasons to want what they would otherwise not want, or obscuring the existence of various alternative possibilities for action, power manifests itself as ideology.

4   The economic crisis in the UK

Strategies and arguments

In this and the following three chapters we shall move to analysis of practical argumentation in political responses to the crisis, beginning with a corpus of policy-making texts, the British Pre-Budget and Budget Reports, delivered annually to the House of Commons by the Chancellor of the Exchequer. We are offering a detailed analysis of two of these: the November 2008 Pre-Budget Report delivered by Alistair Darling, Chancellor of the Exchequer in the Labour government led by Gordon Brown, and the June 2010 Emergency Budget Report delivered by George Osborne, Chancellor of the Exchequer in the Coalition government (Conservatives and Liberal Democrats) which was elected in May 2010 and is led by David Cameron. These reports mark significant stages in the development of UK government strategy for responding to the crisis. The Labour government's strategy was to try to reduce the depth of the recession by stimulating the economy (and 'allowing borrowing to rise' for this purpose), whereas the Coalition's strategy is to try to create conditions for private-sector-led growth by taking rapid measures to cut the budget deficit, primarily through reducing public spending. We shall carry out an analysis and evaluation of these reports using the approach introduced in Chapter 2. From the perspective of critical social analysis and CDA, it is more illuminating to take as our object of analysis and evaluation not just the reports themselves, but also reactions to and evaluations of the reports by other participants in the public debate over government strategy. We will therefore also look at how the arguments of Alistair Darling and George Osborne were evaluated in various contexts by politicians, economists and journalists (economic and political commentators). This focus is of course necessarily selective and represents only a section (though a significant one) of (mainly elite) opinion. In Chapter 5 we will analyse a comments thread in the *Guardian* which represents a section of lay opinion.

Budget and Pre-Budget Reports

In Labour governments between 1997 and 2010, the Chancellor of the Exchequer (on behalf of the Treasury) presented two major economic forecasts to Parliament: a Pre-Budget Report (PBR) in autumn and a Budget Report in spring. Both these reports came as an extended full text and a shorter speech in Parliament and in what follows we will refer to the speeches, not the full reports. Both the full texts and speeches of the Budget and Pre-Budget Reports for 1997–2010, as well as the current government's Budget speeches and full texts, together with the recent Spending Review, are available at http://www.hm-treasury.gov.uk/. (The practice of having a PBR, in addition to the Budget Report, was abolished by the current government in 2010.)

We have analysed the 2008 PBR in two earlier papers (Fairclough and Fairclough 2010, 2011a) and we will offer a revised analysis in this chapter. In the latter paper we also gave an overview of the content of all PBRs. There is no space to do this again here. Let us just mention that, according to the first PBR (delivered by Gordon Brown in 1997), Britain's 'unenviable history' for the last 40 years had been one of 'boom and bust', or 'stop-go', marred by a 'failure to take the long-term view'. There was, therefore, a 'real choice' to be made, between, 'muddling through as we have done for decades from one stop-go cycle to another', or 'breaking with our past, burying short-termism and securing long-term strength'. As a step towards these long-term goals, in 1998, the Government elaborated the Code for Fiscal Stability, with two rules: (a) the Government will borrow only to invest (the 'Golden Rule'); and (b) public sector debt will be held at sustainable and prudent levels (the Sustainable Investment Rule). All subsequent PBR and Budget speeches without exception until 2008 claimed that the two rules had been consistently met.

In the 1999 PBR, the Government set itself the aim of 'locking in' the stability it had successfully delivered since taking office in 1997. The Chancellor argued in favour of leaving behind the 'sterile century-long conflict between enterprise and fairness', between the left and the right, and advocated the 'third way' of 'pursuing both enterprise for all and fairness for all' in order to 'set the course for a Britain of stability and steady growth'. As is well known, by 2001, the media carried reports of Brown's declaration (in another context) that he had definitively abolished 'boom-and-bust' (later qualified as 'Tory boom-and-bust'). In 2006, in the last PBR delivered as Chancellor, Brown noted with satisfaction that, of all major economies, Britain had sustained the longest period of uninterrupted growth and he predicted that growth would continue, with the UK second only to the USA in terms of national income per head.

The 2007 PBR (delivered by Alistair Darling) acknowledged 'increased international economic uncertainty' and 'turbulences in international financial markets', originating in the American mortgage market, whose global impact was 'as yet unclear'. The British economy, however, had grown for 60 consecutive quarters, inflation and unemployment had remained low, and the Government was meeting both its fiscal rules. Borrowing was forecast to be £38 billion in 2007–08 and was set to fall every year for the next five years (the forecast for 2012 was only £23 billion). The economy was expected to grow by 3 per cent in 2007 and 2–2.5 per cent in 2008, with unemployment remaining low, and substantial spending increases were announced in education and public health. In the March 2008 Budget speech, Chancellor Darling acknowledged a change in context ('difficult and uncertain times', a 'world economic slowdown') and reaffirmed the 'core purpose' of the Budget, to secure and maintain 'stability' and 'equip' Britain for the times ahead, as well as build 'a fairer society', 'a fair Britain in which everyone can succeed'. He expressed his conviction that Britain was 'better placed than other economies to withstand the slowdown in the global economy', 'more resilient and better prepared to deal with future shocks'. This 'hard-won stability', he claimed, was the result of the reforms undertaken by Labour governments: making the Bank of England independent and consistently adhering to the 'tough fiscal rules' of the Code for Fiscal Stability, which had managed to 'deliver sound public finances in the medium term'. The Budget advocated continued adherence to fiscal discipline, as the action that would continue to deliver stability and other long-term goals. As always, the 'core values' underlying the Budget for 2008/2009 were 'fairness and opportunity, founded on stability and strength'.

How can a text of this type be analysed in terms of the structure of practical arguments that we proposed in Chapter 2? In the 2008 Budget speech, for example, the Chancellor is saying that, given a certain set of circumstances and a set of goals, underlain by certain values, a certain type of action is recommended, or is the right one. The *circumstances* of action involve global economic uncertainty and undeniable economic slowdown, but also Britain's unique strengths (low unemployment, low inflation, excellent business and financial environment, stability and resilience to shocks, fundamentally strong public finances), which allegedly make it well-equipped to meet these challenges. The *goal* of the government's policies is to 'secure a strong, sustainable future', a future of stability and continued growth, based on the *values* of fairness, opportunity, responsibility. The main *action* that will deliver economic stability will continue to be strict adherence to the Code for Fiscal Stability. Fiscal discipline, as a line of action that the Government has consistently defended over the past decade, is now giving Britain the much needed 'flexibility' (i.e. creating favourable *circumstances*) to respond adequately to the new global economic challenges (*circumstances*) and enables the government to meet its *goals*. This illustrates rather nicely our view of strategies, and how they relate goals to means and circumstances. Fiscal discipline was once advocated as the means towards certain goals (e.g. stability); once such goals become reality, and what was previously imagined turns into reality, into new circumstances of action, it is possible to formulate new goals and new actions towards those new goals. It is possible to respond adequately to the new global challenges because previous goals (stability) have been achieved.

The 2008 Budget also contains an extremely interesting set of economic forecasts from which we quote below, and which we will contrast both with more recent forecasts and with economic reality. None of the forecasts for 2009, 2010 and 2011 has come even remotely close to reality. In 2008, debt and borrowing at the end of 2011 were forecast to be very low, a fraction of what they became in that year, and lower than in 1997, 'even taking into account the turbulence in financial markets'. The section on economic forecasts ended by declaring that 'by 2011 we will have seen the longest sustained expansion of investment in public services since 1945' and that this was 'an achievement to be rightly proud of'. These (epistemic, theoretical) arguments can be discussed along the familiar lines of Popper's (1959, 1963) critique of induction, a critique which has in fact been revitalized by the onset of the financial crisis itself. Taleb (2007) has for instance used the metaphor of the 'Black Swan' (the high impact–low probability event, the 'outlier', the 'unknown unknown') to highlight the epistemic arrogance of political and economic predictions based on statistical, probabilistic methods.

The November 2008 PBR marked a radical departure from the usual description of current circumstances, projected objectives and strategies for action. This Report was explicitly set against the backdrop of an already full-fledged and 'unprecedented global crisis', caused by 'failings in the global financial system'. In this new context, the economic forecasts of the previous Budget and Pre-Budget Reports were discarded, together with their associated plans of action. Economic growth was now forecast to slow to 0.75 per cent in 2008, and to minus 1.25–1.75 per cent in 2009, before recovering to 1.5–2 per cent in 2010. Borrowing was forecast to rise sharply in the short term, to £78 billion in 2008/09 and £118 billion in 2009/10, i.e. 8 per cent of GDP. Thus, UK net debt, as a share of GDP, was predicted to increase from 41 per cent in 2008/9, to 48 per cent in 2009/10, 53 per cent in 2010/11 and 57 per cent in 2013/14. Consequently, the underlying budget deficit would be 2.8 per cent of GDP in 2008 and 4.4 per cent in 2009, but would then decrease yearly until reaching balance again by 2015/16. The 2008 Report reviewed alternatives and made the case for allowing borrowing to rise as the only type of action that would protect families and businesses, and presented a detailed set of measures geared to this fundamental goal.

The 2008 Pre-Budget Report: an overview

We will now focus on the 2008 PBR, presented to Parliament on 24 November 2008, by Chancellor Alistair Darling. We begin with an overall presentation of its content, trying to identify the main normative claims that are made and the various types of reasons offered to support them, but also the rhetorical choices made, e.g. particular linguistic formulations of premises, in relation to a particular strategy of action. It is significant, for example, that the circumstantial premises are formulated in terms of 'exceptional' circumstances, or as 'global financial turmoil'. The latter suggests similarities with the effect of natural calamities where no human agency and responsibility can be imputed. Such choices, involving rhetorically convenient representations in the circumstantial premises, can be challenged within a dialectical argumentative framework, rather than treated as isolated features of texts, as often happens in CDA (see Chapter 3).

What discourse analysts can do with texts of this sort is to identify the practical arguments in the text, i.e. identify the claims to action, the goals, circumstances, values which support the proposed action, and then evaluate the argument by asking critical questions, following the dialectical approach we presented in Chapter 2. Let us look at the following abridged version of the 2008 PBR:[1]

1   Mr Speaker, my Pre-Budget statement today is made against a background of economic
2   uncertainty not seen for generations. These are extraordinary, challenging times for the
3   global economy. And they are having an impact on businesses and families right across
4   the world.
5
6   Mr Speaker, in these exceptional economic circumstances, I want to take fair and
7   responsible steps to protect and support businesses and people now – while putting the
8   public finances on the right path for the future.
9   That is what I will do today. My central objective is to respond to the consequences
10 of this global recession on our country, both now and in the future, so that we are ready
11 to take full advantage of the recovery of the world economy. My aim is to provide sup-
12 port and protection for families and businesses when they need it most. To maintain our
13 commitment to investing in schools, hospitals and the nation's key infrastructure. And to
14 put in place the measures necessary to ensure sound public finances in the medium term
15 so that as a country we live within our means. Not one single initiative, but a compre-
16 hensive plan, to support families, business and the economy.
17   And because of the wide ranging measures I am announcing today and the many
18 strengths of the British economy, I am confident that the slowdown will be shallower
19 and shorter than would have been the case. I am also confident that the UK, as an adap-
20 table and open economy, will be well positioned to benefit from a return to growth in
21 the world economy.
22   (...) But monetary policy – interest rates – on their own are not enough to stimulate the
23 economy, as most people recognise. So we need action now – to boost economic activity –
24 together with the real help I will announce today, to help us emerge quicker. And emerge
25 stronger – from these difficult times, and face the future with confidence. (...)
26
27 Mr Speaker, every country in the world is facing the impact of this crisis on their own econ-
28 omy. There is a growing international consensus, although unfortunately not in this House,
29 that we must act now to protect people and to help pull our economies out of recession.
30   For there is a choice. You can choose to walk away, let the recession take its course,
31 adopting a sink or swim attitude, letting families go to wall. This is the no action plan. Or
32 you could, as I have decided, as have governments of every shade around the world, to
33 support businesses and families, by increasing borrowing, which will also reduce the impact
34 and length of the recession.
35   I will do whatever it takes to support people through these difficult times. That's why
36 my Pre-Budget Report today represents a substantial fiscal loosening – to help the

37   economy now – with a £20bn fiscal stimulus between now and April 2010, around one
38   per cent of GDP.
39   Before I describe the detail of how the Government will support people, let me turn
40   to the fiscal framework which will help us ensure fiscal sustainability. The Government
41   introduced the Code for Fiscal Stability in 1998, committing itself to conducting fiscal
42   policy in accordance with a clearly stated set of principles. Our objectives are, and
43   remain, to support the economy, to ensure medium-term sustainability and maintain
44   public investment. (...) But today Britain – like every other country in the world – faces
45   an extraordinary global crisis, which means significantly lower tax revenues, both now
46   and in the medium term. In the current circumstances, to apply the rules in a rigid
47   manner would be perverse and damaging. We would have to take money out of the
48   economy, making a difficult situation worse.
49   So it is right that in this Pre-Budget Report we do all we can to support the economy,
50   but also ensure fiscal sustainability in the medium term. This all means that borrowing
51   will be significantly higher than forecast. (...)
52   If we did nothing Mr Speaker, we would have a deeper and longer recession, which
53   would cost the country more in the long-term. In these exceptional circumstances,
54   allowing borrowing to rise is the right choice for the country, as the CBI, the Institute
55   of Directors, Institute for Fiscal Studies, the IMF, and many others, have all said in
56   recent weeks.
57
58   Mr Speaker, we will continue to invest in public services – just as we have done over the
59   last ten years. (...) By continuing to make efficiency savings, we can help fund the action
60   needed to help families and businesses. But we will also ensure spending continues to
61   rise from £584bn last year to £682bn in 2010/11. (...) As businesses and families across
62   the country carefully watch what they spend, it is only right that the Government works
63   even harder to make savings.
64
65   Mr Speaker, I now turn to a wide range of measures which I am taking to support the
66   economy and the people of this country. They will help businesses, support home-
67   ownership and boost people's incomes now. Bringing forward capital spending, on
68   major projects, supports jobs and businesses. It is right that, at this time, we re-prioritise
69   investment, from within the existing three-year limits, so that more money is being
70   spent now, when the economy is weaker. (...) Mr Speaker, this spending will help put
71   money into the economy in the coming months. But to prevent the recession deepen-
72   ing, we also need to take action to put money into the economy immediately.
73   I have looked at a range of ways which might achieve this. I have decided that the
74   best and fairest approach is a measure which will help everyone. To deliver a much-
75   needed extra injection of spending into the economy right now. I therefore propose to
76   cut VAT from 17.5 to 15 per cent until the end of next year. (...)
77   But along with these immediate steps to help businesses and families now, I am also
78   announcing measures to ensure sustainable public finances in the medium term. I con-
79   sidered a number of options to raise revenue in future years. And I have chosen those
80   which are fairest – and affect those who have done best out of the growth of the last
81   decade. (...) So again from April 2011, I intend, only on income over £150,000, to intro-
82   duce a new rate of income tax of 45 per cent. This higher rate of tax will only affect the
83   top one per cent of incomes. (...) But I also believe it is right that, as we all benefit fairly
84   from the exceptional measures we take today, we should all share fairly the burden of
85   the future.

86   Taken together these steps will ensure that there is extra money flowing into the
87   economy now when it is needed most, but we can reduce borrowing as growth returns.
88   And as a result of my decisions today to provide support now and balance the books in
89   the future, I will bring the current budget back into balance by 2015/16. (...)
90
91   Mr Speaker, these are exceptional times and require exceptional measures. It requires
92   action now to help people – and action now to build a stable economy. We have made
93   our choice. Helping businesses. Helping homeowners. Helping people into work.
94   Boosting incomes. All only possible because this Government has taken the deliberate
95   decision to support people and businesses through these difficult times.
96   And I commend this statement to the House.

The text contains several formulations of the same basic argument on what ought to be done in response to the crisis. The first occurs in lines 1–21 in our excerpt (the introductory section of the speech, which gives a summary of the main argument), where there is a brief description of factual circumstances, immediately followed by an announcement of the Chancellor's 'objectives' or 'aims'. The circumstances are said to be 'exceptional': a 'background of economic uncertainty not seen for generations'. Other aspects of the circumstances are Britain's 'many strengths' as an 'adaptable and open economy'. The goals are of several kinds. There are immediate goals, i.e. 'to protect and support businesses and people now'; medium-term goals, i.e. 'maintain our commitment to investing in schools, hospitals and the nation's key infrastructure', 'putting in place the measures necessary to ensure sound public finances', and also more distant goals, such as eventually being ready to take advantage of 'economic recovery' (later reformulated as 'pulling the country out of the recession'). Given these *circumstances* and *goals*, the speaker announces his intention to take a number of 'fair and responsible steps' (i.e. concrete *actions*) informed by the *values* of fairness and responsibility. This is the core of any normative practical argument: given certain *circumstances* and certain *goals*, a certain type of *action*, informed by certain *values*, is advocated in the *claim* as the right thing to do, and – as in this case – can be followed by public expression of intention, commitment and decision to act. The means–goal premise is implicit (as it often is) and so is the practical judgement which is the claim of the argument. The claim is expressed here as an intention to act (a commissive speech act, I will do *x*); later on it is expressed as a practical judgement (doing *y* is the right thing to do).

From the start, the speaker makes it clear that what is presented is 'not a single initiative' (not a single action) but a 'comprehensive plan' (lines 15–16), a 'wide ranging' set of (inter-connected) 'measures', intended to take the country from the current (undesirable) situation to a future situation in which the effects of the recession have been overcome. We will refer to this 'plan' as a *strategy*, emerging from a certain description of current *circumstances* and a certain future vision or *goal*, informed by certain *values*, and (later on in the text) further supported by an assessment of the *consequences* of the proposed action and those of possible *alternative* actions.

The argumentation advances simultaneously on two distinct planes in this text: there is 'practical reasoning' (what needs to be done, including reports on previous deliberation) and there is 'theoretical reasoning' (what is predicted to happen based on present circumstances or decisions). Practical reasoning is mostly reported: the text is a 'report' of a process of collective practical reasoning (deliberation) and is thus at one remove from the original process of deliberation itself. This is practical reasoning that has already resulted not only in a *normative conclusion (judgement)* but also in a *collective decision* and *commitment* to act that are now being communicated to the public. Theoretical reasoning involves mostly prediction (economic forecasts), but also an exploration of predicted consequences of action, both of the action which the government is advocating and the alternative action defended by the government's opponents. The predicted consequences of the government's action are said to be a shallower and shorter recession, with less severe impact on the population, while those of the opponents' action are said to be 'a deeper and longer recession, which would cost the country more in the long-term' (52–53). As we show later, these predictions are used (in implicit arguments from positive or negative consequence) to evaluate the practical claim being put forward. If we do *x*, then the following negative consequences will occur; these consequences are undesirable, therefore we ought not to do *x*.

After this initial formulation of the main argument, Darling turns to a detailed description of the international situation (omitted from our extract). A narrative of uninterrupted beneficial growth in the past decade is followed by an account of how the crisis arose and an explanation of its causes ('the root of today's problems are failings in the global financial system'), with narrative and explanation integrated within the overall argument. He then gives an account of what has already been done to combat the effects of the crisis (a 'scheme' to 'recapitalize banks') and makes an assessment of Britain's strengths in the face of this unprecedented 'global turmoil'.

Lines 22–25 contain another formulation of the main argument, this time with a more precise assertion of the *need to take action* (exactly what action is still not specified at this stage): 'So we need action now' (claim) in order 'to boost economic activity' and 'help us emerge quicker' and 'stronger' from these 'difficult times', and 'face the future with confidence' (goals and circumstances). This is followed by a section containing the economic forecast for the following years, with recovery already forecast to be underway in 2010 (GDP growth will be positive once again, between 1.5–2 per cent, the Chancellor says). The claim, circumstances and goals are reasserted and made more specific in lines 27–29. As 'every country is facing the impact of this crisis on their own economy' (circumstances), 'we must act now' (claim) 'to protect people and to help pull our economies out of recession' (goals). At this point, the claim is also supported by an argument from authority ('there is a growing international consensus' that this is what we must do), and a counter-claim is introduced (the action proposed should not be performed) and disavowed. 'There is a choice', the speaker says, namely, 'you can choose to walk away, let the recession take its course, adopting a sink or swim attitude, letting families go to wall' (30–31). This is what the Chancellor calls 'the no action plan', attributing it to an unspecified group of politicians (presumably the Conservatives). He then defends the *decision to act*, in order 'to support businesses and families, *by increasing borrowing*', which will 'reduce the impact and length of the recession' (positive consequence). So in line 33 the main type of action that will bring about the goals and other positive consequences is (finally) explicitly formulated as 'increasing borrowing', not for investment but for current spending.

Between lines 39 and 48 the argument addresses a potential objection to the claim it makes, arising from previous strategies (the 1998 Code for Fiscal Stability, which placed limits on borrowing and allowed borrowing for investment, not for current spending) which are now seen to clash with the course of action advocated. This potential objection is addressed by appealing to the new 'extraordinary' circumstances in which 'to apply the rules in a rigid manner would be perverse and damaging', 'making a difficult situation worse', not better. In other words, the goals have not changed, only the context of action has changed, which is why the strategy of action has to change as well. In the new context, adhering to previous strategies would produce negative consequences (costs) that would outweigh the benefits. As we saw in Chapter 2, if an action can be shown to have negative consequences that go against its intended goals, then the claim in favour of that action is rebutted. Negative consequences can emerge as *actual* negative consequences, as events unfold in the real world, in which case they conclusively falsify or rebut the original claim, or they can emerge as *probable* negative consequences, in a process of critical discussion aimed at exploring the possible effects of the proposed action *before* the action has been undertaken. In the latter case, it is always possible to challenge criticism based on the invocation of negative consequences by doubting that such consequences are really probable.

In lines 49–56, the 'rightness' of the chosen action and of the goals are reasserted ('it is right that . . . we do all we can to support the economy', 'allowing borrowing to rise is the right choice for the country') and the claim is also independently supported by an argument from authority ('as the CBI, the Institute of Directors, Institute for Fiscal Studies, the IMF, and many others, have all said . . .') and by pointing to the alleged negative consequences of the alternative strategy (the counter-argument) ('If we did nothing . . ., we would have a deeper and longer recession, which would cost the country more in the long-term'). In other words, the 'no action' plan will not deliver the goals. The argumentative defence of the main claim for action is followed by a section expressing the government's commitment to continue investing in public services, a choice justified in terms of the negative effects that cutting public spending would have (based on past evidence) and also in terms of the positive effects that it would bring (creating jobs, stimulating the economy). This section is followed by an expressed commitment to find more 'efficiency savings' and 'improve value for money', yet 'without putting public services at risk' (£30bn of efficiency savings will be made by 2010/2011).

From this point onwards, the speech (over half of it, omitted here apart from lines 65–85) details a 'wide set of measures' (specific actions) aimed at 'supporting the economy and the people'. Thus, the government's strategy, as it emerges from this speech, involves several types of action: increasing borrowing, increasing public spending, making savings and implementing a set of concrete measures aimed at supporting businesses and the population. Some of these are medium-term (bringing capital forward to create jobs in infrastructure, re-prioritising investments), but most are immediate measures to 'boost people's income now' (cutting VAT, increasing the personal tax allowance, cutting corporation tax, increasing child benefit and pension credits). They are intended to increase spending power for the economy and for individuals in the short term but are also explicitly geared to longer-term goals ('preventing the recession deepening'). In the second half of the report, the strategy is summed up in various ways: 'Taken together these steps will ensure that there is extra money flowing into the economy now when it is needed most', while borrowing can be reduced in the future 'as growth returns' (86–89). The Chancellor reasserts his decision is 'to provide support now and balance the books in the future' and undertakes a commitment 'to bring the current budget back into balance by 2015/16' (as a long-term goal).

Two aspects of this half of the report are of particular interest from an argumentation point of view. First, this is where the main value premise of the argumentation ('fairness') is asserted repeatedly. For instance, 'I considered a number of options . . . and I have chosen those which are fairest'; '. . . as we all benefit fairly from the exceptional measures we take today, we should all share fairly the burden of the future'. There are also a few occurrences of 'rightness' in the sense of 'fairness' ('as businesses and families . . . carefully watch what they spend, it is only right that the Government works even harder to make savings'). Second, there are several occurrences of this statement, with minor variations: 'And this is only possible because I have rejected advice to take no action' (or 'This is only possible because I am prepared to take action now'; 'All these measures are only possible because we have taken a deliberate decision to support business, protect jobs, and help homeowners'). This statement is used to refer to the measures aimed at 'putting money into the economy', giving money back to consumers and businesses in order to stimulate demand, and its function seems to be to reinforce the argument by pointing to the positive consequences of the strategy of action and to how it will contribute to realizing the goals. All the projected benefits of these measures will only become possible because the government has decided to take one type of action and not another and because it is committed to certain goals and not others. So, what these various reformulations are saying in fact is that the action will lead to the goals and have other positive consequences and, at the same time, that the government's deliberate commitment to the goals and its determination to avoid negative consequences require the action. From a logical point of view, this amounts to saying that the government's strategy is necessary and sufficient in view of the goals. In Fairclough and Fairclough (2011a) we tried to capture this strong (biconditional) relation by including a separate efficiency premise (following Bowell and Kemp 2005). Here we represent this as part of the means–goal premise which, in this case, says that the action is not merely necessary and not merely sufficient, but necessary *and* sufficient in view of the goal: there is no other alternative than the one being proposed and this alternative will deliver the goals.

The concluding sentences (lines 91–96) review the circumstances ('these are exceptional times', 'difficult times'), reassert that 'action' and 'exceptional measures' are needed and restate a number of goals and actions. The actions have to do with helping people, while the goal is a 'stable economy'. The result of deliberation in government is again reported and the Budget is 'commended to the House' for debate. The conclusion of the deliberative process which is being reported here is expressed alternatively as a normative judgement ('allowing borrowing to rise is the right choice', 54; 'we have made our choice', 92–93), an intention and commitment ('I will do whatever it takes to support people through these difficult times', 35), as well as a decision that has been taken in government ('this Government has taken the deliberate decision to support people and businesses through these difficult times', 94–95).

Argument reconstruction

We will now focus on the argument in support of action and identify the premises involved. The two diagrams represent the argument as it advanced initially (lines 1–16) and was reformulated later (lines 27–56). In the premises we suggest below we are preserving the original wording, while in the diagrams, for the sake of brevity, we are reformulating the arguments more succinctly. In lines 1–16, the argument has the following elements:

Claim	[The right thing to do is] to 'take . . . steps', 'to put in place' a plan of 'wide ranging measures': 'not one single initiative, but a comprehensive plan'
Circumstances	These are 'extraordinary, challenging times for the global economy', 'economic uncertainty not seen for generations', having an 'impact on businesses and families'.
Goals	The goal is to respond adequately to the recession: 'My central objective is to respond to the consequences of this global recession on our country, both now and in the future'. Short-term goals: 'to protect and support businesses and people now'; 'medium-term' goals: to 'maintain our commitment to investing in schools, hospitals, key infrastructure'; 'to ensure sound public finance, 'putting the public finances on the right path'; long-term goals: place Britain in a position to 'take full advantage of the recovery of the world economy'.
Values / concerns	Our [the government's] values are 'fairness' and 'responsibility'. Our (implicit) concerns: people's well-being, people's 'needs' – we want to support them 'when they need it most'.
Means–goal	[The action is sufficient in view of the goals] In these circumstances, if we put in place this plan of action, we will achieve our goals: 'And because of the wide ranging measures I am announcing today . . . I am confident that the slowdown will be shallower and shorter than would have been the case' and the UK will 'benefit from a return to growth in the world economy'.

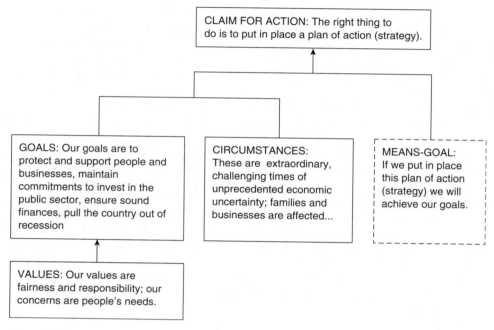

Figure 4.1 Chancellor Darling's first argument for action in the 2008 Pre-Budget Report.

At this stage, the argument can be represented as in Figure 4.1.

In lines 27–56, the argument is developed to include not only a more explicit reiteration of the claim, with the claim now made specific (the right action is 'allowing borrowing to rise') but also additional support for the claim, in the form of arguments from authority (which are not practical arguments but support the same practical claim), and an assessment of the costs of not acting as proposed (which are part of a counter-argument) and of failing to modify one's action in light of the new circumstances. Circumstances have changed, Darling says, and to stick to a previous policy (as the Code for Fiscal Stability would require) would do more harm than good. The claim is therefore multiply supported by four arguments, of which two arise in response to an already advanced counter-claim (the Conservatives' 'no action' plan) and a possible, anticipated objection, that the government is being inconsistent with its own past policies, which would support the counter-claim.

The means–goal premise says that the action will deliver the goals but also that the action is necessary in view of the goals. This is because the alternative (the 'no action' plan) has allegedly been examined and found to be unacceptable. Only the advocated means will therefore lead to the goals, and no alternative can deliver the goals more efficiently. The necessary *and* sufficient character of the strategy will be re-emphasized throughout the text: the goals are *only* possible because the Government has chosen to act in this way ('This is only possible because I am prepared to take action now'; 'All only possible because this Government has taken the deliberate decision to support people and businesses through these difficult times', and so on).

As we said in Chapter 2, negative consequences that compromise the goal of action or other goals which should not be compromised can rebut the claim for action.[2] We suggested that they support a counter-claim (part of a counter-argument), a claim that the action should not be performed. Darling is invoking here the alleged negative consequences of the proposal *not to act* (the Conservatives' strategy, as he represents it) in order to support his own argument. If the Conservatives' claim can be rebutted by pointing to its unacceptable consequences, then Darling's own argument will presumably be strengthened.

These are the main elements of the argument for increasing borrowing as it is developed between lines 27 and 56:

Claim	'We must act now . . . by increasing borrowing'; 'borrowing will [have to] be significantly higher than forecast'; 'allowing borrowing to rise is the right choice for the country'.
Circumstances	'Every country in the world is facing the impact of this crisis on their own economy', these are 'difficult times', 'exceptional circumstances'. Britain 'faces an extraordinary global crisis, which means significantly lower revenues . . .'.
Goals	Our goals are to 'protect people and pull our economies out of recession', 'prevent the recession deepening'; 'support the economy but also ensure fiscal sustainability in the medium term'. 'Our objectives are, and remain, to support the economy, to ensure medium-term sustainability and maintain public investment.'
Values	Our values are 'fairness and responsibility', we are concerned to 'protect', 'support' and 'help' people.
Means–goal	[The action is sufficient in view of the goals] Increasing borrowing will 'boost the economy', 'will also reduce the impact and length of the recession'.
	[The action is necessary in view of the goals, no other action can deliver the goals more efficiently] 'There is a choice, . . . the no action plan' and this choice is unacceptable.
Counter-claim	[as represented by speaker]: The right thing is not to act, 'walk away', 'let the recession take its course' – the 'no action plan'.
Dealing with counter-claim	[Not doing the action will undermine the goals and values; the costs would outweigh the benefits] The 'no action plan' will compromise the goal of action ('If we did nothing, we would have a deeper and longer recession, which would cost the country more in the long-term') and other agents' goals (people will 'go to the wall'). The 'no action plan' compromises values that should not be compromised (it is underlain by questionable values; instead of a concern with people's needs, a 'sink or swim' attitude).
Anticipated objection	Increasing borrowing contradicts the provisions of the 1998 Code for Fiscal Stability, which placed limits on allowable borrowing (and, implicitly, in allowing borrowing to rise the government is being inconsistent in its policies).
Dealing with objection	Circumstances have changed and therefore 'to apply the rules in a rigid manner would be perverse and damaging', 'making a difficult situation worse'.
Argument from authority	'There is a growing international consensus, although unfortunately not in this House' that this is the right course of action, 'governments . . . around the world' have already decided to increase borrowing; 'the CBI, the Institute of Directors, Institute for Fiscal Studies, the IMF . . . have all said [this]' (and, if there is a consensus among governments and authorities, or if they have all come to this conclusion, then the claim is right.)

The argument developed in lines 27–56 is represented in Figure 4.2. Certain parts of the argument are implicit in these lines (they have been expressed explicitly in other sections, such as government's concerns for and commitment to fairness and responsibility).

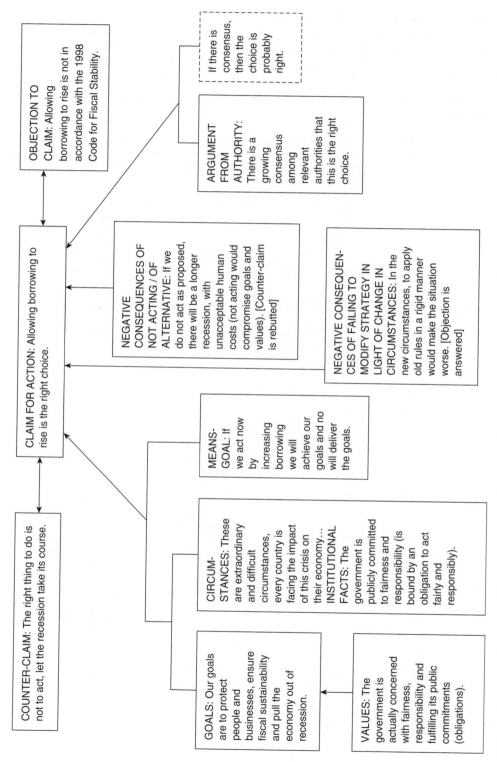

OBJECTION TO CLAIM: Allowing borrowing to rise is not in accordance with the 1998 Code for Fiscal Stability.

If there is consensus, then the choice is probably right.

ARGUMENT FROM AUTHORITY: There is a growing consensus among relevant authorities that this is the right choice.

CLAIM FOR ACTION: Allowing borrowing to rise is the right choice.

NEGATIVE CONSEQUENCES OF NOT ACTING / OF ALTERNATIVE: If we do not act as proposed, there will be a longer recession, with unacceptable human costs (not acting would compromise goals and values). [Counter-claim is rebutted]

NEGATIVE CONSEQUENCES OF FAILING TO MODIFY STRATEGY IN LIGHT OF CHANGE IN CIRCUMSTANCES: In the new circumstances, to apply old rules in a rigid manner would make the situation worse. [Objection is answered]

MEANS-GOAL: If we act now by increasing borrowing we will achieve our goals and no will deliver the goals.

COUNTER-CLAIM: The right thing to do is not to act, let the recession take its course.

CIRCUM-STANCES: These are extraordinary and difficult circumstances, every country is facing the impact of this crisis on their economy... INSTITUTIONAL FACTS: The government is publicly committed to fairness and responsibility (is bound by an obligation to act fairly and responsibly).

GOALS: Our goals are to protect people and businesses, ensure fiscal sustainability and pull the economy out of recession.

VALUES: The government is actually concerned with fairness, responsibility and fulfilling its public commitments (obligations).

Figure 4.2 Deliberation over alternatives in Chancellor Darling's 2008 Pre-Budget Report.

Argument evaluation

We now turn to a dialectical evaluation of Darling's arguments in the 2008 PBR, in terms of critical questions aimed at the premises, at the argument as a whole and at the claim. We will do this briefly here, as a more detailed discussion of both strategies of action, of the previous Labour government and of the current government, will follow later. Rhetorical analysis is incorporated into a fundamentally dialectical evaluation in our approach.

Let us begin with the circumstantial premise. Is the existing situation described in a rationally acceptable way? Darling's account of the situation tells us that these are 'exceptional circumstances', 'extraordinary, challenging times', but also that Britain is well-placed to withstand these challenges. The circumstances are being defined in a way that supports a certain type of action and not another. What is selected as a relevant fact and the inherently evaluative words that are used to describe the facts already point towards a certain conclusion. For instance, Darling mentions the fall in tax revenues as a relevant fact and this will connect later to a claim about the need to inject money into the economy. There is no acknowledgement of any responsibility of the UK government for the current situation, of past policy mistakes as facts that future reasoning needs to start from. If there were, then maybe a radically different policy would be a sensible course of action. Nor is there any acknowledgement of the responsibility of capital, as a structural feature of capitalism that it is indifferent to 'externalities', e.g. the social consequences of its activities. On the contrary, Britain is said to be at comparative advantage: past policies and fiscal stability will enable her to cope better than other countries. This description of the state of the economy is consistent with the government's broader attempt to legitimize its past and future action, yet it has been severely questioned. Economists, the media and the wide public have pointed to the profound imbalances that have built up over time in Britain's economy. Far from giving it 'resilience to shocks' and 'flexibility', Britain's overly inflated financial sector and its comparatively weak manufacturing sector (neglected by Labour governments over the last 13 years – Elliott 2010a) have in fact made it particularly susceptible to the crisis.

Speaking of Britain's alleged advantages, Martin Wolf, the *Financial Times* economics editor, has described the situation in the following terms: 'The UK has a strategic nightmare: it has a strong comparative advantage in the world's most irresponsible industry'. The influence of the financial sector, with its 'light-touch' approach was 'surely malign' and Britain needs to ask itself a 'painful question: how should the country manage the cuckoo sitting in its nest?' (Wolf 2009). The government, Wolf says, 'bears substantial responsibility for the vulnerability of the economy and public finance', yet seems unwilling to recognize the 'fragile underpinnings of the economy' as the product of successive governments, both Labour and Conservative (Wolf 2010a).

Darling's argument gives an account of the context of action which not only conveniently glides over Britain's weaknesses and the government's responsibility for them, but also makes no connection between British finance and the crisis. As it emerges from the PBR, the context of action is that of a global crisis which is not particularly linked to Britain, to past policies pursued in Britain and set in place by previous governments, but is affecting and overwhelming Britain, as a victim of global turmoil. The description of the circumstances can be challenged therefore on account of its rhetorically biased nature: it is not rationally acceptable that the crisis arose as a (quasi-natural) global phenomenon for which no responsibility can be identified. Michael Sandel (2009) has for instance commented on the particularly disingenuous 'tsunami metaphor [which] became part of bailout vernacular' in financial circles in America in 2009. If, he says, bank executives are right that the failure of the banking system was due to larger economic forces, beyond anyone's control, not to their own bad decisions, then this would explain why they were so reluctant to take responsibility and why they continued to insist on the need to reward executives' hard work and talent. But if big systemic economic forces beyond anyone's control can account for the huge losses made by the banks, then most probably they also account for the inordinate profits made in earlier years.

> If the weather is to blame for the bad years, how can it be that the talent, wisdom, and hard work of bankers, traders, and Wall Street executives are responsible for the stupendous returns that occurred when the sun was shining?
>
> (Sandel 2009: 17)

To conclude, then, the context of action is not described in a dialectically acceptable way, but in one which only supports the arguer's rhetorical goals and Labour's more general attempt at self-legitimation.

The goal premise can also be challenged. The goals of action are to 'support the economy', to 'prevent the recession from deepening', to pull the economy 'out of recession', to 'build a stable economy'. These vaguely specified goals say nothing about the character of this future economy, or whether and how it might differ from the pre-crisis economy whose character was arguably a cause of the crisis. What exactly is the nature of this future economy as goal or vision? Is there any reason to believe that it will not be such as to lead to another crisis? Should other possible goals (imaginaries) be examined? In its current vague formulation, the goal premise seems to support a return to 'business as usual', rather than a major rethinking of the economy so as to prevent future crises. It does not invite controversy, yet the questions of what the actual goals of political and economic action ought to be, what kind of national and global economy governments ought to aim for, ought to have been prominent questions in the wake of the financial crisis.

According to the value premise, the government is allegedly committed to acting fairly and responsibly and its main concern is for people's needs, hence government action will be aimed at protecting, supporting and helping people and the economy. These are, implicitly, values that cannot be overridden and that have emerged in a process of deliberation over the appropriate goals of political action and the values that should inform them. The goals (hence, the action) have to be compatible with *all* of these values: a concern for financial responsibility, i.e. for reducing the deficit, will be balanced (or tempered) by a concern for protecting the population, i.e. paying the deficit in a way that does not produce unacceptable costs in terms of well-being. This particular weighing of competing values is different, as we shall see, from the way in which values are weighed in the argument in favour of spending cuts. As far as fairness is concerned, it would seem that *sharing* the losses is fair, with everyone contributing in a way that is proportionate to their income ('the biggest burden will fall on those with the broadest shoulders', according to Darling in the 2009 Budget Report). The presupposition of this notion of fairness seems to be that *everyone* is responsible: consequently, everyone will shoulder the costs, but in different proportions, in relation to their different ability to do so. However, in the wake of the crisis, many people have argued that fairness would require that those agents with primary responsibility for the crisis (e.g. bankers) should suffer most of the losses and that it is in fact unfair to distribute these losses across all sections of society. This raises problems for the acceptability of the value premise that we will address later.

The main claim is that public borrowing should increase: this is 'the right choice for the country'. Darling refers to only one alternative action: 'there is a choice' between his plan and the 'no action plan', which – given the way it is described – amounts to saying there is in fact no choice. The action proposed is implicitly claimed to be necessary to achieve the goals and sufficient to achieve them, though Darling hedges this claim by not simply asserting that it will, but that he is 'confident' that it will. The claim can be challenged on the grounds that, while being presented as the result of deliberation over alternatives, it is clear that many reasonable alternatives have not been considered. Other actions were being proposed by reputable economists at the time, such as nationalizing banks rather than bailing them out with public money, which would have led to less public borrowing. In other words, the action (as means) may not have been necessary, alternatives were available and should have been considered.

How is the Chancellor supporting his argument? Besides the practical argument from goals and circumstances, there is an attempt to rebut the counter-claim, by showing that its consequences will endanger various goals and values that should not be endangered, i.e. publicly recognized, legitimate goals and values. This is intended to strengthen his own argument. However, showing that the opposite of your proposal is not acceptable does not imply that your own proposal is acceptable, unless the two proposals were mutually exclusive (either *a* or *b*, and these are the only alternatives). In spite of the fact that this is how they are represented, as a (rhetorically convenient) choice between *acting* and *not acting*, there may be further options. These are not mentioned, however, and the impression we get is that this is a genuine dilemma, where the only choice is between the consequences of acting and not acting. As the consequences of not acting are said to be worse, the conclusion that the government has to act seems the only reasonable alternative. However, the dilemma is false – there are (or were) several possibilities for action, alternatives that could have been considered.

The claim is also supported by an argument from authority and, more interestingly, by an argument which deals with an anticipated objection, that increasing borrowing is grossly at odds with the Code for Fiscal Responsibility, therefore inconsistent with the government's own rules and past action. The objection is dealt with in the same way as the counter-claim, by pointing to the negative consequences of failing to modify action in response to new circumstances. What seems to be inconsistency is therefore rational behaviour: what would be irrational is to ignore changes in the context of action and to persevere in action which is no longer sensitive to how things turn out. It is important for the Chancellor to anticipate this objection and address it effectively, as accusations of inconsistency are strong dialectical and rhetorical moves: to show that a (political) opponent is inconsistent, that his behaviour is self-contradictory, is to show he is being unreasonable and lacks credibility. Rhetorically, the Chancellor aims to persuade the audience that what could be seen as a weakness (inconsistency) is in fact a virtue. The government can, allegedly, give a satisfactory answer to the implicit 'Feedback' question in the list of possible questions we referred to in Chapter 2. It has not hesitated to modify its course of action in relation to events, which is a mark of reasonableness, rather than an acknowledgement of policy failure. Perceived inconsistency is, allegedly, only *apparent*, not real, as the government is continuing after all its policy of stability, guided by a concern for fairness ('Our objectives are, and remain, to support . . .', 42–43). This can be discussed as argumentation by dissociation between reality and appearance but is not really developed here beyond emphasizing fundamental *continuity*.[3] More obviously, the potential accusation of inconsistency is deflected by appealing to extraordinary circumstances, circumstances beyond the government's control and predictive power. The presumption of reasonableness can be allegedly preserved on the basis of the implicit premise that it is reasonable to change your strategies of action if the context changes. We might, however, want to ask: What is the relationship between the new circumstances and past actions? Is the new context independent from, causally unrelated to past action? Have the circumstances changed *independently* of the government's policies, or is the new context at least partly the outcome of these policies? It can be argued that only in the former context (e.g. natural calamities) can people be exempted from the accusation of self-contradiction when they change course. Dialectically, therefore, Darling's appeal to extraordinary circumstances is dubious and is ultimately not *rationally* persuasive. The government is clearly being inconsistent, and forced to be inconsistent partly by the failure of its own past policies. The fact that it cannot continue along previous lines indicate the underlying fragility of pre-crisis economy, rather than its stability and resilience to shocks.

An argument will be stronger if the arguer can show that he is aware of existing or possible objections, alternative proposals and counter-arguments and can deal with them in a satisfactory way, in other words, if he can show that the argument can withstand a process of critical examination. This is what the Chancellor seems to be doing here. He argues explicitly against the argument which says that *not acting* (which is how he chooses to represent the Conservative's alternative strategy) is the right strategy and attempts to rebut it by saying it will have highly negative consequences in terms of publicly shared goals and values. He also deals with the anticipated objection that he is being inconsistent. But what he does not do *at all* is tell the audience what *negative* consequences *his own proposal* will have and how he can deal with these. No such possible or probable *negative* consequences of action are addressed: nothing is said, for instance, about the future impact of the huge debt incurred. This of course is not surprising: governments are generally reticent about publicly acknowledging the risks of their own policies. It does, however, make his argument dialectically weaker. As we will see, Osborne's strategy on this point is different: by openly acknowledging the negative impact of his proposal, he presumably intends to increase both the dialectical and rhetorical acceptability of his argument, and to come across as a more honest, credible politician.

The fact that the consequences of massive public debt are not addressed at all in this PBR, nor in Darling's following Budget and Pre-Budget speeches is, in our view, a significant failure of the argument from a dialectical perspective, as arguers (normatively speaking) should be concerned not primarily with finding reasons in support of their proposals but reasons *against*. This is what rational decision-making is about: eliminating alternatives through critical examination, weeding out the ones that have undesirable consequences, and adopting the alternative that has, on balance, best survived criticism. Trying to find support, or to justify, can too easily turn into a form of confirmation bias or rationalization. Commenting on Darling's last Budget in office and the Labour government's strategy, Martin Wolf observed that what the Chancellor has offered is a 'barely spelled out' and 'risky' path for fiscal consolidation, full of optimistic predictions whose plausibility is nevertheless highly uncertain, and containing 'very little explanation of how the debt will be repaid and what this will mean for people's living standards'. Failing to spell these implications clearly for the population, who will have to live with the consequences of these decisions, says Wolf, not 'letting the electorate in the know . . . is more than a pity; it is a disgrace' (Wolf 2010a).

Let us now look more closely at how the strategy is actually formulated in the course of the speech, as various (re)formulations are of rhetorical interest. The action is repeatedly described as one that will *protect*, *support* and *help* the economy and the population – this is presumably meant to resonate with the audience's concerns. The main claim (we should increase public borrowing) is represented throughout the speech as *acting, taking action*, and is contrasted to the alleged alternative of the '*no action plan*'. Defining a huge increase in public borrowing as 'taking action' is a rhetorically convenient, persuasive definition of the action, and it is used clearly to legitimize the government's strategy. Can we also say that it is putting an unjustified positive spin on the claim? To answer this question we would have to look at how the definition is used in its argumentative context.

In Chapter 3, we discussed a speech by Blair as an instance of deliberation over alternative options. We said that deliberation can occur both in a multi-agent setting, where several agents deliberate together and engage in face-to-face dialogue, and in a monological process of conductive reasoning, where an agent weighs relevant considerations prior to decision-making. Deliberation undertaken by a single agent mirrors deliberation amongst several agents, i.e. deliberation dialogue. We argued that the structural properties of deliberation, understood as dialogue, an essential element of which is addressing arguments (considerations) that go *against* the proposed thesis, correlate with certain linguistic properties that we can expect to find in any instance of actual deliberation. It is legitimate therefore to expect the counter-argument of the Conservative Party to be represented in Darling's speech in terms which would support *their* conclusion, just as would happen if the dialogue were face-to-face. Instead, however, what we get is a representation of the Conservative argument in terms which *defeat* their own claim: if their alternative is in fact *inaction*, and not doing anything defeats the goals, then it can't be a viable alternative to what the government proposes. Darling's persuasive definition of the Conservative proposal as 'inaction' steers the deliberation towards the Labour government's own alternative, towards their own conclusion, and away from any contrary or alternative proposal. But is it reasonable to represent an opponent's argument in a way which discredits it from the start, without argument? As we saw in Chapters 2 and 3, persuasive definitions are in fact argumentative claims and should therefore be properly argued for. In this particular speech, no adequate justification has been given for why the Conservative position should be dismissed. In fact, it has not been adequately represented at all within the text from the perspective of its proponents; clearly, if it were, it would only involve some *different* type of action (reducing borrowing, cutting government spending), not inaction. The normative structure of deliberation as genre entitles us to expect the presence of *both* arguments, as they would be formulated by their proponents, and a report of some previous process of critical examination of *both* proposals. (In actual deliberation, this would involve the attempt to reject both, by thinking of the strongest possible objections against them, and then tentatively adopting the one that has stood up to criticism better, as a presumptive means towards the goal.) But pointing to probable positive consequences of one's proposal and probable negative consequences of the counter-argument, which is what is happening here, is not sufficient to establish that one's proposal is to be preferred. What is needed is some indication of how one's proposal has survived attempts at refutation more adequately than alternatives. As we have said, no such attempts are made in this text, as no negative consequences of the proposed action are mentioned at all. On the other hand, the counter-argument is represented in a rhetorically convenient way, which steers the arguers' argument towards a foregone conclusion. These rhetorical choices, while possibly enhancing the argument's persuasiveness for some audiences, nevertheless produce a dialectically deficient argument.

Finally, the means–goal premise seems to be stronger than would normally be warranted in a situation of uncertainty and risk. We suggested that, logically speaking, given that alternatives are dismissed and 'confidence', if not complete certainty, is expressed regarding the outcome of the proposed strategy of action, the closest reconstruction of the argument involves a biconditional (if and only if) relation between the means and goal. This is to say that, if we increase borrowing, we will overcome the recession, and we will overcome the recession if we increase borrowing. We will say more about this in our analysis of the June 2010 Budget Report.

Justifying future and past action

So far we have seen how future action is being justified by reasons and how these reasons are supposed to guide future action. Justifying action is different from explaining action, in the same way as arguments are different from explanations. An argument always seeks to establish or challenge a controversial proposition (claim) by providing reasons in its favour or against it. An explanation seeks to account for a proposition which is not controversial, but is taken as a fact (e.g. something that has already happened, or is already the case) by pointing to a possible cause. The explanation (*explanans*) provided may be controversial, but not the fact which it tries to explain (*explanandum*). Seeing people's reasons for action as causes of events is part of an explanation of social reality and can be seen as part of explanatory critique. Assessing how well-grounded people's reasons for action are in relation to a normative framework is part of normative critique.

We can also distinguish between two ways in which people justify action: by constructing an argument for a *future* course of action (which we have illustrated in our analysis so far), or by constructing an argument which attempts to justify *past* action, show that it was the right action. The former argument proceeds from goals and circumstances to a presumptive claim having to do with the future. The latter is developed in relation to a counter-argument, whose claim was that the action should not be performed, because it would lead to negative effects (the goal would no longer be achieved or other important goals would be undermined). To justify his own past action, the arguer could show that the negative consequences that his opponent had predicted, and which would have rebutted his claim, have not materialized. Consequently, the action has stood the test of time and was the right one.

Let us illustrate this type of justification by looking at a few more Budget and Pre-Budget Reports. The 2008 PBR, as we have seen, is concerned with justifying future action. Subsequent Budget and Pre-Budget Reports of the Labour government are more concerned with justifying action that has already been taken and aim to show that 'government action has made a real difference', that there is evidence already that the decisions taken in November 2008 were the right ones. In the April 2009 Budget Report and the December 2009 PBR, the Government's interventionist strategy was defended as a 'choice between two competing visions', with different final outcomes – 'securing recovery or wrecking it' – and different underlying values: 'a choice between ambition driven by the values of fairness and opportunity, or austerity driven by an out-dated dogma', between the project of a 'fair society where all prosper and a divided society that favours the wealthy few'. The government's deliberate choice of action over inaction was the right one, Darling argued, not only because it was in accordance with widely shared values, but also *demonstrably* right, because it has already produced beneficial effects: 'global confidence is returning', the housing market is stabilizing, the crisis has not worsened, etc. Events therefore have *demonstrated* that 'you can grow your way out of recession' but 'you cannot cut your way out': positive feedback, and the absence of negative feedback indicate that the decision taken in November 2008 was right. The same justification was reiterated in the March 2010 Budget speech (the last one delivered by Darling as Chancellor):

> The record shows the right calls were made. Global recession has not turned into depression. Unemployment here in the UK has not risen as much as was feared. (. . .) Not everyone here supported the action taken. But with hindsight, it is even clearer that the right calls were made. Economic disaster was averted. Growth has begun to return across the major world economies. The prospects for the global economy are much

more positive than a year ago. (. . .) The choice before the country now is whether to support those whose policies will suffocate our recovery and put our future at risk. Or support a Government which has been right about the recession, right about the recovery, and is right about supporting the people and business of this country to build a prosperous future.

The government's strategy has, in other words, stood the test of time and attempts to discredit it have been demonstrably wrong. Arguments such as these are used to legitimize the government's political position: the government's strategy is legitimate because it is demonstrably in accordance with values and concerns that are widely shared, with the government's existing commitments to meet those goals and concerns, and has *actually* led to the realization of the government's stated goals. In the paragraph cited above, it is clear that justification of past action was part of an attempt to win voters' support in the upcoming May election.

Argumentation oriented towards the future starts with a hypothesis for action (doing *A* is the right thing in view of the goals), considers possible consequences and concludes that, if the consequences are likely to go against the goal, the action may not be the right one. In situations in which the action has already been undertaken and negative consequences have already emerged and have undermined the goal, then the argument is conclusively rebutted (refuted or falsified). In all other cases, where negative consequences are merely probable, unless the probability is really very high, the argument from negative consequences can only *attempt* to rebut the claim. It is after all perfectly possible that a strategy which could in principle (or even quite probably) fail to achieve the goals might still successfully achieve them. Argumentation that attempts to justify past action will try to show that negative consequences that were predicted to occur have not materialized. In fact, the intended goals of action have been achieved: the hypothesis that the action was right has thus stood the test of time and it is reasonable to continue acting along the original lines.

The argument for cutting public spending

A few weeks after taking office, the new Coalition government produced an Emergency Budget, and a few months later a Spending Review, which put a stop to many of Labour's policies and set out to drastically cut the budget deficit and the public debt. We will first present the content of Chancellor Osborne's June 2010 Budget speech, with the help of relevant quotes and summaries, then we will discuss the structure of the overall argument.

1 Mr Deputy Speaker, This emergency Budget deals decisively with our country's record
2 debts. It pays for the past. And it plans for the future. It supports a strong enterprise-led
3 recovery. It rewards work. And it protects the most vulnerable in our society. Yes it is
4 tough; but it is also fair.
5   This is an emergency Budget, so let me speak plainly about the emergency that we
6 face. The coalition Government has inherited from its predecessor the largest budget
7 deficit of any economy in Europe with the single exception of Ireland. One pound in
8 every four we spend is being borrowed. What we have not inherited from our predeces-
9 sor is a credible plan to reduce their record deficit. This at the very moment when fear
10 about the sustainability of sovereign debt is the greatest risk to the recovery of European
11 economies. Questions that were asked about the liquidity and solvency of banking sys-
12 tems are now being asked of the liquidity and solvency of some of the governments that
13 stand behind those banks. I do not want those questions ever to be asked of this country.

14   That is why we have set a brisk pace since taking office. In the last seven weeks:
15   We have announced, conducted and completed a review of this current year's spend-
16   ing and identified six billion pounds of savings. (. . .) This early, determined action has
17   earned us credibility in international markets. It has meant that our promise to deal
18   decisively with the deficit has been listened to. Market interest rates for Britain have
19   fallen over the last seven weeks, while those of many of our European neighbours have
20   risen. Those lower market interest rates are already supporting our recovery. But unless
21   we now deliver on that promise of action with concrete measures, that credibility – so
22   hard won in recent weeks – will be lost. The consequence for Britain would be severe.
23   Higher interest rates, more business failures, sharper rises in unemployment, and poten-
24   tially even a catastrophic loss of confidence and the end of the recovery.
25   We cannot let that happen. This Budget is needed to deal with our country's debts.
26   This Budget is needed to give confidence to our economy. This is the unavoidable
27   Budget. (. . .)
28   Our policy is to raise from the ruins of an economy built on debt a new, balanced
29   economy where we save, invest and export. An economy where the state does not take
30   almost half of all our national income, crowding out private endeavour. An economy
31   not overly reliant on the success of one industry, financial services – important as they
32   are – but where all industries grow. An economy where prosperity is shared among all
33   sections of society and all parts of the country. In this Budget everyone will be asked to
34   contribute. But in return we make this commitment. Everyone will share in the rewards
35   when we succeed. When we say that we are all in this together, we mean it.
36   Mr Deputy Speaker, the first challenge for this Budget is to set the fiscal mandate –
37   or in other words, our overall objective for the public finances. (. . .) I now turn to what
38   that fiscal mandate will be. The view of the international community was clearly
39   expressed at the latest G20 meeting . . . (. . .) [T]he international community believes
40   countries with high fiscal deficits need to accelerate the pace of fiscal consolidation.
41   That is precisely what we now propose to do. The formal mandate we set is that the
42   structural current deficit should be in balance in the final year of the five-year forecast
43   period, which is 2015–16 in this Budget. (. . .)
44   In order to place our fiscal credibility beyond doubt, this mandate will be supple-
45   mented by a fixed target for debt, which in this Parliament is to ensure that debt is fall-
46   ing as a share of GDP by 2015–16. I can confirm that, on the basis of the measures to
47   be announced in this Budget, the judgement of the Office for Budget Responsibility
48   published today is that we are on track to meet these goals. Indeed, I can tell the House
49   that because we have taken a cautious approach, we are set to meet them one year ear-
50   lier – in 2014–15. Or to put it another way, we are on track to have debt falling and a
51   balanced structural current budget by the end of this Parliament. (. . .)
52   Some have suggested that there is a choice between dealing with our debts and going
53   for growth. That is a false choice. The crisis in the Eurozone shows that unless we deal
54   with our debts there will be no growth. And these forecasts demonstrate that a credible
55   plan to cut our budget deficit goes hand in hand with a steady and sustained economic
56   recovery, with low inflation and falling unemployment. What is more the forecast shows
57   a gradual rebalancing of the economy, with business investment and exports playing a
58   greater role and government spending and debt-fuelled consumption a smaller role. A
59   sustainable private sector recovery built on a new model of economic growth, instead of
60   pumping the debt bubble back up. (. . .)
61   Mr Deputy Speaker, let me now turn to the measures in the Budget designed to
62   deliver this accelerated reduction in the structural deficit. The coalition Government

63   believes that the bulk of the reduction must come from lower spending rather than
64   higher taxes. The country has overspent; it has not been under-taxed. Our approach is
65   supported by the international evidence, compiled by the Organisation for Economic
66   Cooperation and Development, the International Monetary Fund and others, which
67   found that consolidations delivered through lower spending are more effective at cor-
68   recting deficits and boosting growth than consolidations delivered through tax increases.
69   This is the origin of our 80:20 rule of thumb – roughly 80 per cent through lower spend-
70   ing and 20 per cent through higher taxes. (. . .) My measures today mean that 77 per
71   cent of the total consolidation will be achieved through spending reductions and 23
72   per cent through tax increases. I believe this gets the balance right.

At this point in the Budget speech, the Chancellor turns to the Office for Budget
Responsibility's fiscal forecasts. He announces that, as a result of the measures he is about to
announce, public sector net borrowing will be £149 billion in 2010, will fall to £116 billion
in 2011, £89 billion in 2012–13 and £60 billion in 2013–14. By 2014–15 borrowing will
reach £37 billion, 'exactly half the amount forecast in the March Budget' by ex-Chancellor
Darling. In 2015–16, borrowing will decrease further to £20 billion. As to public spending,
Osborne says, all parties 'now accept that spending needs to be cut': 'the state today
accounts for almost half of all national income' and that is 'completely unsustainable'.
Having asserted that 'the bulk of the reduction must come from lower spending rather than
higher taxes', he now turns to a separate justification of the specific proportion between cuts
and tax rises. This is a sub-argument which says that, 'given that the country has overspent'
and 'has not been under-taxed', and also given that there is 'international evidence, compiled by the Organisation for Economic Cooperation and Development, the International
Monetary Fund and others' showing that 'consolidations delivered through lower spending
are more effective at correcting deficits and boosting growth than consolidations delivered
through tax increases', the 4:1 proportion between cuts in spending and higher taxes (actually 77:23) is the right proportion ('gets the balance right'). This claim is therefore supported
both by an argument from the authority of the OECD and IMF, and by a practical argument from circumstances ('the country has over-spent . . .') and the goal of reducing the
deficit and the debt.

The plans for public investment inherited from the previous government, Osborne says,
already provided for 'a steep drop from £69 billion last year to £46 billion in 2014–15' and,
beyond this reduction, there will be no further cuts. But careful choices will need to be made
about how this capital is spent: 'the absolute priority will be projects with a significant economic return to the country'. The Government will also speed privatization in certain areas.
In addition to plans to cut departmental budgets by £44 billion a year by 2014–15 laid out
by the previous Government, there will be further reductions in departmental spending of
£17 billion by 2014–15. With the exception of public health, most other departments will
face an average real cut of around 25 per cent over four years. Public sector pay and pensions will also be restrained. The need to do this is justified in two ways: by invoking negative
consequences (given that 'the country was living beyond its means when the recession came',
if high pay and pensions are not cut or frozen, 'more jobs will be lost') and by invoking fairness ('the culture of excessive pay at the very top of the public sector simply has to end').
However, Osborne says, the lowest paid will be protected (the two-year freeze will not affect
the 1.7 million public servants who earn less than £21,000, who make up 28 per cent of all
state employees).

The 'largest bill in government', however, Osborne says, is the 'welfare bill'. The government intends to put the welfare system on 'more sustainable and affordable footing'.

Governments in the past have failed to reform the welfare system and to 'reward work'. This government, he says, will effectively save the country £11 billion by 2014–15 by succeeding where others have failed. The section on welfare reform concludes the first half of the speech, where Osborne talks about 'paying the bills for the past'. We will look at this section in detail further on.

The Budget, Osborne says, 'is also about planning for the future'. The next section therefore aims to address plans for the future of Britain and is based on a 'deeply held belief that a genuine and long-lasting economic recovery must have its foundations in the private sector'. The Government will facilitate business activity in the private sector by making it cheaper for companies to employ people and by cutting corporation tax (by 1 per cent every year, so that it will go down from the current 28 per cent to 24 per cent in four years). This will be the lowest and most attractive rate of any major western economy and will act as an 'advert' for the country: 'I want', Osborne says, 'a sign to go up, over the British economy, that says "Open for Business"': this will attract investment and create jobs. This comprehensive reform of the corporate tax regime will offer a much-needed 'platform for a private sector recovery', in accordance with the 'unequivocal' message the business community is sending: 'they want certainty and stability from the government', so that they can rebuild their businesses. The banking sector, whose failure 'imposed a huge cost on the rest of society', will have to contribute a 'fair' share. From January 2011, the Government will introduce a bank levy, expected to generate an annual revenue of over £2 billion, and is also exploring the 'costs and benefits' of a tax on financial activities. Other measures aimed at 'boosting growth' have to do with 'rebalancing our economy' in terms of regional development, thus creating jobs in the North and the Midlands, Wales and Scotland. Many infrastructure projects in the domain of public transport will go ahead, as well as a green investment bank and new developments in digital infrastructure, with tax facilities for all businesses in these regions. The government will also speed privatization by disposing of 'assets which should rightly be in private ownership' (the Royal Mail, the 'student loan book', the air traffic control service).

Most of the second half of the speech deals not with future plans for improving business but with future plans for increasing revenue. As announced at the beginning of the speech, the Government will adhere to a 4:1 balance between spending cuts and taxation in order to reduce the deficit. Over and above the previous Government's plans, Osborne says, a 'further fiscal tightening of £40 billion a year by the end of this Parliament' is required, which means that further tax rises will be necessary. There will be an increase in VAT from 17.5 to 20 per cent after January 2011, expected to generate over £13 billion a year of extra revenues, justified by saying that 'the years of debt and spending make this unavoidable', as well as an increase in capital gains tax to make the system fairer. As for income tax, this budget, 'where we are asking so much from so many' aims to help people by lifting more low-paid people out of the income tax system, while not giving more tax breaks to the very rich. The Government will increase the personal allowance by a thousand pounds to £7,475 (this will take 880,000 people out of the tax system altogether). All these measures, Osborne says, 'demonstrate that this coalition Government puts fairness first'. In the concluding sections of his speech, which we quote below in full, Osborne emphasizes the Government's efforts to be fair and protect the poor, and that this 'unavoidable' budget is 'progressive' and 'in the national interest':

73   Mr Deputy Speaker, I do not disguise from this House that the combined impact of the
74   tax and benefit changes we make today are tough for people. That is unavoidable given

75 the scale of the debts our country faces, and the catastrophe that would ensue if we failed
76 to deal with them. My priority in putting together this Budget has been to make sure
77 that the measures are fair. That all sections of society contribute, but that the richest pay
78 more than the poorest. Not just in terms of cash, but as a proportion of income as well.
79   That is far from straightforward when the deficit is this high and when the burden of
80 reduction must rightly fall on government spending. Too often when countries under-
81 take major consolidations of this kind, it is the poorest – those who had least to do with
82 the cause of the economic misfortunes – who are hit hardest. Perhaps that has been a
83 mistake that our country has made in the past. This Coalition Government will be dif-
84 ferent. We are a progressive alliance governing in the national interest. (...)
85   Overall, everyone will pay something, but the people at the bottom of the income
86 scale will pay proportionally less than the people at the top. It is a progressive Budget.
87
88 Mr Deputy Speaker ... Today we take decisive action to deal with the debts we inherited
89 and confront the greatest economic risk facing our country. We've been tough but we've
90 also been fair. We have set the course for a balanced budget and falling national debt by
91 the end of this Parliament. We have insisted that four pounds of every five needed to
92 reduce our deficit will be found from government spending. We have protected capital
93 investment from additional cuts and got to grips with the soaring costs of welfare. We
94 have provided the foundations for economic recovery in all parts of our nation and given
95 our country some of the most competitive business taxes in the world. (. . .)
96   Sadly, with this unavoidable budget we've had to increase taxes. We've had to pay
97 the bills of past irresponsibility. We've had to relearn the virtue of financial prudence.
98 But in doing so we have ensured that the burden is fairly shared. Today we have paid
99 the debts of a failed past. And laid the foundations for a more prosperous future. The
100 richest paying the most and the vulnerable protected. That is our approach. Prosperity
101 for all. That is our goal. And I commend this Budget to the House.

Argument reconstruction

Let us try to identify the main claims that are made in this speech and the premises that support them. The Chancellor is presenting and justifying a strategy of action that the government
has decided to embark on. The government has decided to 'deal decisively with our country's
debts', later expressed as 'delivering an accelerated reduction' of the deficit. In the opening sentences there are several alternative representations of the goals of action (and of the Budget): it
is intended to 'pay for the past' and 'plan for the future'. Some of these goals ('reward work',
'protect the most vulnerable') are explicitly informed by the main value premise: the action will
be fair. From the very beginning, the main values, and more precisely the conflict of values
underlying the strategy, are stated clearly: admittedly, the action will be 'tough; but it is also
fair'. The government, in other words, is committed *both* to being effective in reducing the deficit *and* to doing so in a way that is fair to the population. It is committed to delivering the financial objectives but also undertakes to do so in a way that does not compromise fairness; the
former seems to be its primary commitment, but a simultaneous commitment to fairness is
recognized as a constraint on action. Later on, the former value commitment will be expressed
in terms of financial sustainability and financial responsibility.

A complete argumentative reconstruction of the whole text is in principle perfectly possible. Because the Budget speech outlines a strategy of action, it can be expected that there

will be distinct arguments in favour of distinct elements of this strategy. There is an argument in favour of spending cuts, as well as an argument focusing on growth measures. Spending cuts will affect different areas, so there will be separate arguments dealing with all these. We can expect other types of arguments, not just practical arguments, to support the claims for action, for instance arguments from authority. A complete argumentative reconstruction would identify all of these, in their relation to each other, and in relation to the non-argumentative parts of the text (narrative, explanation). To illustrate how that might be done, let us focus on the introductory paragraphs of the text, lines 1–72 in our extract and identify the main claim and how it is supported. At the end of his speech, Osborne also talks about the negative impact of his proposal (see lines 73–86 above) and, to give a more complete picture of his overall argument, we also include this argument in the reconstruction we suggest below:

Claim (what needs to be done)	The government needs to 'deal decisively' with the deficit and debt, it must 'deliver [an] accelerated reduction in the structural deficit'. More specifically, 'the bulk of the reduction must come from lower spending rather than higher taxes', '77 per cent of the total consolidation will be achieved through spending reductions and 23 per cent through tax increases'.
Circumstances	We are facing an 'emergency': 'The coalition Government has inherited from its predecessor the largest budget deficit of any economy in Europe with the single exception of Ireland . . . Questions that were asked about the liquidity and solvency of banking systems are now being asked of the liquidity and solvency of some of the governments that stand behind those banks'. [The current state of the economy is described as] 'the ruins of an economy built on debt', based on 'debt-fuelled consumption' and 'pumping [up] the debt bubble'.
Goals	[Fulfil 'fiscal mandate', i.e. 'our overall objective for the public finances'] 'The formal mandate we set is that the structural current deficit should be in balance in the final year of the five-year forecast period, which is 2015-16 in this Budget.'; 'this mandate will be supplemented by a fixed target for debt, which in this Parliament is to ensure that debt is falling as a share of GDP by 2015-16'. [Our goals are] 'to have debt falling and a balanced structural current budget by the end of this Parliament.' [Achieve long-term goal of a balanced economy] 'Our policy is to raise from the ruins of an economy built on debt a new, balanced economy where we save, invest and export . . . An economy . . . where all industries grow . . . An economy where prosperity is shared among all sections of society and all parts of the country'. [Our goal is] 'a sustainable private sector recovery built on a new model of economic growth.'
Means–goal	[The strategy is sufficient in view of the goals]: 'a credible plan to cut our budget deficit goes hand in hand with a steady and sustained economic recovery, with low inflation and falling unemployment'. [The strategy is necessary in view of the goal]: 'this is the unavoidable Budget'.
Values	[Fairness, financial responsibility/sustainability, the national interest] (The Budget) 'is tough; but it is also fair'; 'In this Budget everyone will be asked to contribute. But . . . everyone will share in the rewards when we succeed'; 'we are all in this together'; 'we are a progressive alliance governing in the national interest'.

(continued)

(Continued)

Counter-argument and alternative proposal	[The government should not deal decisively with debt, but should encourage growth, as cuts will endanger recovery]: 'Some have suggested that there is a choice between dealing with our debts and going for growth'.
Dealing with counter-argument and alternative: negative consequences of both	[If the government does not act as proposed, the goals will not be achieved; negative consequences will compromise the goals]: 'But unless we now deliver on that promise of action with concrete measures, that credibility – so hard won in recent weeks – will be lost. The consequence for Britain would be severe. Higher interest rates, more business failures, sharper rises in unemployment, and potentially even a catastrophic loss of confidence and the end of the recovery.' [Alternative strategies will not deliver the goals]: alternatives are 'a false choice', 'unless we deal with our debts there will be no growth'.
Argument from authority (1)	'The view of the international community was clearly expressed at the latest G20 meeting . . . (. . .) [T]he international community believes countries with high fiscal deficits need to accelerate the pace of fiscal consolidation'.
Argument from authority (2)	'Our approach is supported by the international evidence, compiled by the Organisation for Economic Cooperation and Development, the International Monetary Fund and others, which found that consolidations delivered through lower spending are more effective at correcting deficits and boosting growth than consolidations delivered through tax increases'.
Argument from authority (3)	'The judgement of the Office for Budget Responsibility . . . is that we are on track to meet these goals.' '. . . Forecasts [by the OBR] demonstrate [that it is possible to attain our goals]'. [Forecasts are taken to show that it is possible to attain goals by following proposed action.]
Emerging positive consequences of action already taken	'This early, determined action has earned us credibility in international markets. It has meant that our promise to deal decisively with the deficit has been listened to. Market interest rates for Britain have fallen over the last seven weeks, while those of many of our European neighbours have risen'. [These consequences are taken to confirm the rightness of the action.]
Dealing with anticipated negative consequences of proposed action	' . . . the combined impact of the tax and benefit changes we make today are tough for people. That is unavoidable given the scale of the debts our country faces, and the catastrophe that would ensue if we failed to deal with them. My priority in putting together this Budget has been to make sure that the measures are fair. That all sections of society contribute, but that the richest pay more than the poorest . . .'; 'Too often . . . it is the poorest – those who had least to do with the cause of the economic misfortunes – who are hit hardest . . .'. (. . .) [Costs will not outweigh the benefits; they are necessary to avoid higher costs; costs are fairly shared; they are mitigated by a concern for fairness and for not repeating the mistakes of the past.]

The way in which these elements of the argument are related is shown in Figure 4.3. Notice that a *concern* for fairness, financial sustainability (responsibility) or the national interest is part of the value premise informing the goal, in the sense that the government has to internalize these concerns in order to act in a way that achieves the goal in accordance with

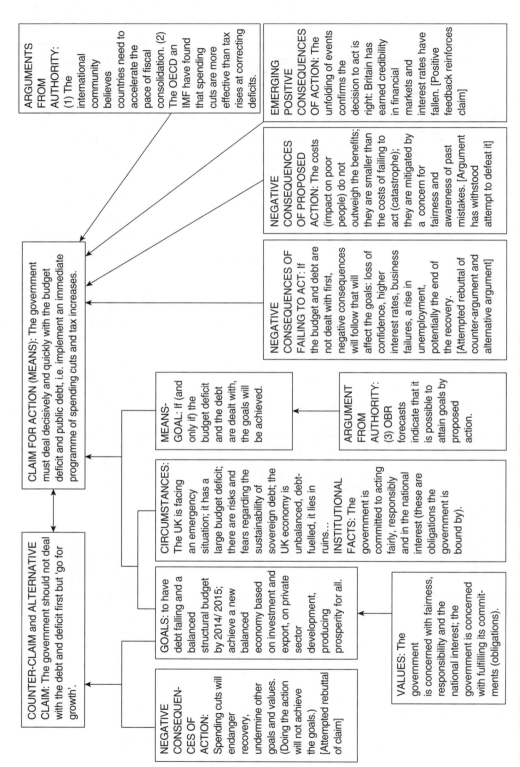

ARGUMENTS FROM AUTHORITY: (1) The international community believes countries need to accelerate the pace of fiscal consolidation. (2) The OECD an IMF have found that spending cuts are more effective than tax rises at correcting deficits.

EMERGING POSITIVE CONSEQUENCES OF ACTION: The unfolding of events confirms the decision to act is right: Britain has earned credibility in financial markets and interest rates have fallen. [Positive feedback reinforces claim]

NEGATIVE CONSEQUENCES OF PROPOSED ACTION: The costs do not outweigh the benefits; they are smaller than the costs of failing to act (catastrophe); they are mitigated by a concern for fairness and awareness of past mistakes. [Argument has withstood attempt to defeat it]

CLAIM FOR ACTION (MEANS): The government must deal decisively and quickly with the budget deficit and public debt, i.e. implement an immediate programme of spending cuts and tax increases.

NEGATIVE CONSEQUENCES OF FAILING TO ACT: If the budget and debt are not dealt with first, negative consequences will follow that will affect the goals: loss of confidence, higher interest rates, business failures, a rise in unemployment, potentially the end of the recovery. [Attempted rebuttal of counter-argument and alternative argument]

COUNTER-CLAIM and ALTERNATIVE CLAIM: The government should not deal with the debt and deficit first but 'go for growth'.

MEANS-GOAL: If (and only if) the budget deficit and the debt are dealt with, the goals will be achieved.

ARGUMENT FROM AUTHORITY: (3) OBR forecasts indicate that it is possible to attain goals by proposed action.

CIRCUMSTANCES: The UK is facing an emergency situation; it has a large budget deficit; there are risks and fears regarding the sustainability of sovereign debt; the UK economy is unbalanced, debt-fuelled, it lies in ruins… INSTITUTIONAL FACTS: The government is committed to acting fairly, responsibly and in the national interest (these are obligations the government is bound by).

GOALS: to have debt falling and a balanced structural budget by 2014/2015; achieve a new balanced economy based on investment and export, on private sector development, producing prosperity for all.

NEGATIVE CONSEQUEN-CES OF ACTION: Spending cuts will endanger recovery, undermine other goals and values. (Doing the action will not achieve the goals.) [Attempted rebuttal of claim]

VALUES: The government is concerned with fairness, responsibility and the national interest; the government is concerned with fulfilling its commit-ments (obligations).

Figure 4.3 Deliberation over alternatives in Chancellor Osborne's 2010 Emergency Budget Report.

the stated values. However, like any similar external reason (obligation, duty, promise), a *commitment* to fairness or other values is at the same time an institutional *fact*: a democratic government is bound by an obligation to act fairly towards citizens, constrained by it, regardless of whether they want to act fairly or not, and can therefore be held responsible if they do not. Invoking such reasons repeatedly as both concerns *and* commitments (for instance as commissive speech acts) functions as an element of ethical appeal (*ethos*): the government is both making public its concern for the impact of the crisis on the population and its desire and intention to be fair, *and* showing that it is aware of its responsibilities and will fulfil them.

Circumstantial premises: the context of action

The context of action, according to the Chancellor, is one of 'emergency': it is one in which the government 'has inherited from its predecessor' one of the largest budget deficits in Europe. The context is also one of risk and fear, 'fear about the sustainability of sovereign debt', about the 'liquidity and solvency' of some European governments. Further specification of the context of action comes at various points in the text and is often in the form of figures ('the Office for Budget Responsibility has revealed the size of the structural deficit to be even larger than we feared, £12 billion larger next year') or other empirical assertions: 'over the past decade the British economy has become deeply unbalanced'; 'nowhere are these disparities as marked as between the different regions of Britain'; 'the country was living beyond its means when the recession came'.

Goal premises: short-, medium- and long-term goals of action

Having defined the context, the Chancellor proceeds to defend a certain strategy of action. The reason why we can speak of a strategy, not merely of an isolated action, is that there is an identifiable relation of coordination between distinct actions aimed at the same goal, and a sequential relation between various means, goals and further goals, where goals, once attained, become the means to further goals, or create the context (circumstances) for their achievement. What the Chancellor sets out to outline is, in his own words, a 'credible approach', a 'credible plan', based on a 'promise to deal decisively with the deficit'. (The claim for action is expressed here as a decision and commitment to act so as to deal with the deficit.)

The long-term goal of this strategy is 'to raise from the ruins of an economy built on debt a new, balanced economy where we save, invest and export', 'an economy where the state does not take almost half of all our national income, crowding out private endeavour', one that is 'not overly reliant on the success of one industry, financial services – important as they are – but where all industries grow', a future Britain 'where prosperity is shared among all sections of society and all parts of the country'. The action is therefore intended to take Britain from the current circumstances (a debt-fuelled economy in ruins, with an overly dominant financial sector, an oversized state sector, etc.) to a future situation (imaginary, vision) based on sustainable private sector development, not on 'pumping the debt bubble back up', and so on. In the shorter term, the Government is setting itself the following 'overall objective for the public finances': to fulfil their 'fiscal mandate' by 2015–16, i.e. 'to have debt falling and a balanced structural current budget by the end of this Parliament'. A future situation where debt has fallen as a share of GDP and the structural budget has been brought into balance is therefore the goal of current action. Once achieved, this goal will create a new context for further action towards further goals or become a means towards further goals.

The claim for action: what the government must do, or the means that will realize the goals

In order to achieve these goals, Britain must *deal decisively with its debts and reduce the deficit*, alternatively expressed as 'accelerate the pace of fiscal consolidation', etc. This is the main action that is being advocated in view of the goals, and its rightness is supported with evidence, in terms of positive and negative consequences (costs and benefits) of proposed and alternative actions, as well as by arguments from the authority of the international community. As we argued in Chapters 2 and 3, goals are states of affairs, imaginaries. This is why the vision of a new balanced economy and of a country where there is prosperity for all are goals, while dealing with debt, or reducing the deficit are actions (means) that can presumably deliver the goals. But reducing the deficit, understood as a *situation* in which the deficit has been successfully reduced (we need to do *A in order to* reduce the deficit), can also be taken as a goal of present action, and this illustrates how the goals of one action, once achieved, become either the means of further action, or create a new context for further action. (Action *A* is necessary in order to reduce the deficit, as goal, and reducing the deficit, as action, is necessary in view of the goal of a balanced economy.)

In terms of how exactly the deficit and the debt will be dealt with, Osborne turns to a list of measures (specific actions). They involve cuts in government spending and tax increases, with the bulk of the money coming from cuts in government spending. Together with measures aimed at boosting growth in the private sector, spending cuts are part of a strategy of action that will deliver not only immediate goals (a reduction in debt and deficit) but also the long-term goals of a more balanced economy and prosperity for all. The actions that will deliver growth are not specified in detail in the Budget, beyond measures to cut corporation tax and create a more favourable business environment. The Chancellor announces that there will be a White Paper that will address measures for growth.

Among the specific measures announced are the following: further reductions in departmental spending; restraining public sector pay; freezing pay and pensions for two years (while 'protecting the lowest paid'); reforming the welfare system; supporting the private sector through tax cuts and other supportive legislation; making banks contribute to the general effort; helping regional development; maintaining existing infrastructure projects in transport; increasing VAT to 20 per cent; increasing the personal tax-free allowance; helping pensioners by linking the state pensions to earnings; increasing the child element of the child tax credit to help poor families.

The means–goal premise

In practical arguments, the means–goal premise usually says that the proposed action is necessary *or* sufficient to achieve the goal. An action may help achieve an aim without being strictly speaking necessary and an action may be necessary but not in itself sufficient to realize the goal. The Chancellor insists that the Budget is 'unavoidable', both at the beginning and end of his speech ('This is the unavoidable Budget'; 'Sadly, with this unavoidable budget we've had to increase taxes'); it is unavoidable given the need to avoid dire consequences and given the context of action ('given the scale of the debts our country faces, and the catastrophe that would ensue if we failed to deal with them'). The claim for action is therefore supported strongly both by an analysis of the circumstances and of the consequences of action, as well as in view of the goals pursued (if Britain adopts the government's strategy of action, we are told repeatedly, then it will be possible to attain these long-term goals). Additional support is provided for this claim, from the authority of the Office for Budget Responsibility, which has allegedly examined the strategy and concluded that it is possible to attain the goals simultaneously with making spending cuts, in other words that it is possible to have an expansionary fiscal contraction. How strong can we assume this means–goal (conditional) relation to be?

On the one hand, the Chancellor is no doubt saying that, if Britain adopts this strategy, the goals will be attained. If we abbreviate the goal as R (Recovery) and the means as A (Strategy of Action), one thing he is saying is 'if A, then R', which means that the actions proposed are a sufficient condition for recovery. However, to say that A is sufficient for R does not preclude the possibility that something else than A might also lead to R: there may be other means, other strategies of action that will also lead to recovery. This, however, is clearly what Osborne would deny. In saying that the budget is *unavoidable*, he is saying that it is necessary, therefore 'if R, then A', i.e. for recovery to be attained, then these actions are necessary. He is therefore saying that the strategy he is proposing is both necessary *and* sufficient to deliver recovery. So, from a logical point of view, what he is saying is in fact this: *if and only if* Britain adopts the strategy of action advocated by the government, will recovery be possible. This relation is much stronger than either of the two relations above, in fact it is a conjunction of both, a biconditional relation: 'R if and only if A' is equivalent to saying: '(if R then A) and (if A then R)', or 'for recovery to occur, this strategy of action must be pursued *and* if this strategy of action is pursued, then recovery will occur'. This means that, in his view, no alternative means would equally deliver the goal, and the strategy will indeed deliver the goal. As we will see later, critics of Osborne's austerity budget have repeatedly denied both of these claims, both that there is no alternative and that the proposed plan will actually deliver the goals. The means–goal premise in the Budget speech seems to be put forward as a very strong relationship but it is a highly contentious issue that the relationship is in fact as strong as the Chancellor claims it to be.

Consequences of action

Shortly after announcing the overall goals of the government the Chancellor deals with an alternative argument for action and an implicit counter-argument, presumably coming from the Labour party: Britain should not try to deal with the deficit first (implicit counter-argument, whose claim negates the government's claim) but ought to 'go for growth' first (an alternative claim for action). The counter-argument and the alternative argument are logically distinct: we can claim that someone shouldn't do what he proposes to do *without* being able to suggest an alternative, and the existence of alternatives does not show that the action we first contemplated is wrong. These arguments are dealt with in the same way. Both failing to act as planned and adopting Labour's alternative will have negative consequences that will compromise the goals: potentially, this could mean the 'end of the recovery'; 'unless we deal with our debts there will be no growth'. Other possible negative consequences are mentioned later: 'if we don't tackle pay and pensions, more jobs will be lost', etc.

The same type of argument from negative consequences was used by Darling in his own Budget and Pre-Budget speeches, to claim exactly the reverse. What is new in Osborne's speech is an explicit acknowledgement of the inevitable negative consequences of *his own* proposed strategy: 'I do not disguise from this House', he argues, 'that the combined impact of the tax and benefit changes we make today are tough for people. That is unavoidable given the scale of the debts our country faces, and the catastrophe that would ensue if we failed to deal with them.' Negative effects are thus acknowledged as unavoidable (in contrast with Darling's speech), but they are not taken to be serious enough to undermine the goals and therefore throw the claim into doubt. The costs are presumably outweighed by the even greater costs of failing to act accordingly ('catastrophe') and also by the eventual benefits of the proposed action. This cost–benefit analysis is used to justify the rightness of the government's strategy, and there is an account of how the 'tough impact' of the action will be dealt with: the costs will be mitigated by a concern for fairness (the rich will pay more than the poor). At least from Osborne's perspective, his claim cannot be rebutted by invoking probable negative consequences because these consequences are not likely to compromise highly ranked goals and values (the action is *not* unfair, and *will* lead to economic recovery). Implicitly, the government has already examined the probable impact of the strategy on *other* legitimate goals and values and has designed its strategy in such a way that these legitimate concerns are taken care of, i.e. the action will fulfil its main objectives without compromising these other goals and values. There has, in other words, been a process of deliberation over which goals should be simultaneously pursued, not just an instrumental assessment of which means will most efficiently fulfil the main financial objectives.

Alleged positive consequences are also used to strengthen the claim. Osborne claims that, since Britain has announced its intention to deal with its deficit, its 'credibility in international markets' has risen, and 'interest rates for Britain have fallen', unlike those of other European countries. Positive consequences have already emerged, in the form of positive feedback, and are thus reinforcing the claim.

Values guiding goals and action

Fairness is the guiding value of this budget. Its rhetorical potential is exploited to the full, including by appeals to *ethos* and *pathos*. Osborne acknowledges 'mistakes' that were made in the past, when it was 'the poorest – those who had least to do with the cause of the economic misfortunes – who [were] hit hardest'. This Government, he says, is 'different' from previous governments, it is a 'progressive alliance governing in the national interest' whose 'priority has been to make sure that the measures are fair', that 'the burden is fairly shared', 'that all sections of society contribute, but that the richest pay more than the poorest'. Fairness is also prominent at the beginning of the speech, when the Chancellor claims that 'when we say that we are all in this together, we mean it', and makes an explicit 'commitment' to fairness: 'everyone will share in the rewards when we succeed'. It is also present throughout, as an implicit or explicit premise in the various sub-arguments in favour of reform and spending cuts ('it is fair and it is right that in future banks should make a more appropriate contribution'; '[increasing the personal allowance] demonstrates that this coalition Government puts fairness first').

Fairness is presented both as an active concern on behalf of the government but also as a public commitment to fairness (the government has a duty to be fair). This existing commitment to fairness, as a fact, is part of the circumstantial premises of action (an institutional fact) and is independent of whether the government actually wants to act fairly or not. This is how we have represented it in Figures 4.2 and 4.3. The distinction between a *concern* for fairness (a desire-dependent reason) and a *commitment* or *obligation* to be fair (a desire-independent reason) underlies the arguments developed in all of these government reports, although it sometimes remains implicit. It is precisely because the government, or politicians, are bound by such institutional facts as reasons, whether they want to act in accordance with them or not, that they can be held responsible when they fail to do so. (We will come back to this discussion in Chapters 5 and 6.)

Other values are also invoked: fiscal prudence ('We've had to relearn the virtue of financial prudence'), and (financial) responsibility ('Past prudence was an excuse for future irresponsibility'). There is also a repeated invocation of sincerity, or truthfulness ('I am not going to hide hard choices from the British people, ... You're going to hear them straight from me'). These values are effectively used to increase both the rhetorical and the dialectical acceptability of the argument. Fairness, sincerity, responsibility not only have a strong rhetorical appeal as values which enjoy wide support, but they are also values which underlie a dialectically optimal process of practical reasoning and decision-making, one in which there has been an impartial weighing of alternatives and there has been no attempt to deceive the public.

Reforming welfare

Let us now look in more detail at the section on welfare reform:

> Mr Deputy Speaker, let me now address the largest bill in government – the welfare bill. It is simply not possible to deal with a budget deficit of this size without undertaking lasting reform of welfare. It has been a key component of most successful fiscal consolidations elsewhere in the world. And around Europe, countries are now tackling their benefits bill. Germany has already announced 30 billion euros worth of cuts to welfare spending. And others are taking similar steps. Here in Britain, the explosion in welfare costs contributed to the growing structural budget deficit in the middle part of this decade. Total welfare spending has increased from £132 billion ten years ago to £192 billion today. That represents a real terms increase of a staggering 45 per cent. It's one reason why there is no money left. It has also left an increasing number of our fellow citizens trapped on out-of-work benefits for the whole of their lives. A greater proportion of our children grow up in workless households than any other country in Europe. We are wasting the talent of millions, and spending billions on it in the process. So we will increase the incentives to work, and reduce the incentives to stay out of work. We will focus our benefits more towards those in need. And we will end some one-off payments that the country cannot afford anymore. First, we need to put the whole welfare system on a more sustainable and affordable footing. (. . .)

How does the Chancellor justify the need to reform the welfare system? Let us try to identify the premises and the claim. The claim is that Britain must reform the welfare system ('must undertake lasting reform of welfare'). There are two practical arguments (see Figure 4.4). According to the first, the government's goal is to deal with the deficit, and the implicit means–goal premise says that only if the government reforms the welfare system will it be possible to 'deal with a deficit of this size'. Given the circumstances ('the welfare bill is the

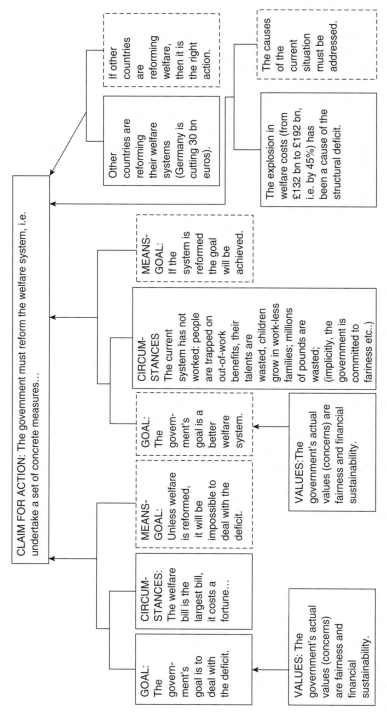

Figure 4.4 Chancellor Osborne's argument for welfare reform in the 2010 Emergency Budget Report.

largest bill in government') and the goal, a set of measures (as specific actions) is proposed, detailing what reforming the system means. Among these, the government will reform housing benefits, will remove various benefits and tax credits which 'sadly . . . the country cannot afford' and means-test others. In arguing for these measures, two concerns are mentioned repeatedly: the government wants to put the welfare system on a *sustainable (affordable)* footing and do so in a way that is *fair*. These two concerns (sustainability, or affordability, on the one hand, and fairness, on the other) make up the value premise and inform the goals and therefore the action. In order to achieve the goal, the government will take action in order to 'increase the incentives to work' and 'reduce the incentives to stay out of work', it 'will focus . . . benefits more towards those in need' and 'will end some one-off payments that the country cannot afford anymore'. These can be taken as partial or intermediate goals in a strategy aimed at achieving a comprehensive reform of the welfare system, itself a component of the broader strategy aimed at reducing the deficit. (Goals, once achieved, become means or circumstances towards further goals.) This strategy will effectively save the country £11 billion by 2014–15, Osborne claims, and will succeed where previous governments have failed. The second practical argument takes a range of problems caused by the current welfare system as premises (people are trapped on benefits, children grow in families where no one works, money is being wasted) and an implicit goal premise referring to the need for a better system, where these problems have been dealt with.

The claim is also justified by an argument based on what other countries have already decided to do: everywhere in Europe, 'countries are now tackling their benefits bill', and viewing this as a 'key component of fiscal consolidation'. For example, 'Germany has already announced 30 billion euros worth of cuts to welfare spending'. This can be taken as a version of an *ad populum* argument, either based on expert opinion or on deliberation (Walton *et al.* 2008: 312), which has produced a considered, well-grounded decision that it would be reasonable for Britain to follow. Finally, there is an argument from the need to reform the welfare system as one of the causes of the current structural deficit; an explanation is embedded in the argument at this point and partly attributes the cause of the deficit to excessive welfare spending in the past (this 'is one reason why there is no money left').

The argument is represented in Figure 4.4.

One justification of the claim (the first practical argument) is in view of what the situation is and what the government wants to achieve. Cuts must be made because money needs to be saved. But cuts, apparently, also need to be made for other reasons. The second practical argument, which takes as circumstances the negative effects the current system has, allegedly, already had on people, supports the claim for action on account of considerations that are not purely or primarily financial. The fact that billions of pounds are spent on welfare benefits is in itself only a reason because this money is 'wasted', because it does not produce the positive consequences it is expected to produce. Instead, the welfare system is said to have a damaging effect, which implies it would be in need of reform *whether there was a budget deficit to deal with or not*. There are therefore other legitimate reasons for demanding reform: the system is not only financially inefficient but has negative effects on people's well-being: it wastes people's talents, deprives them of freedom and choice (people are 'trapped') and harms their children. As the argument develops, the section on reforming housing benefits also adds another negative effect in terms of fairness: it is unfair (as well as financially unsustainable) that some people should receive enormous sums in benefits, as these come from the taxes paid by working people. To sum up, the explicit goal of action has to do with deficit reduction, but not all the arguments that are used invoke financial considerations. A variety of

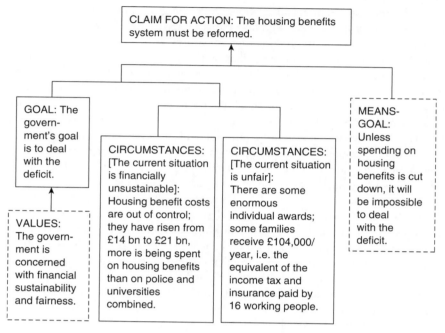

Figure 4.5 Osborne's argument for reforming housing benefits in the 2010 Emergency Budget Report.

moral concerns are used as premises, and these seem to correspond to another goal of action, which is, however, left implicit.

The structure of the argument shows that the government's agenda involves more than making savings. The second practical argument amounts to an implicit critique of the welfare state and this critique is logically independent of the particular context of action which requires savings: whatever the financial situation, the welfare state would be in need of radical reform. Many critics of the current government's strategy have in fact argued that, regardless of the austerity agenda, motivated by the crisis, the government's goal is to roll back the state and this, the argument goes, is an ideologically driven mission, not merely one imposed by necessity. There is therefore *another*, largely unacknowledged goal of action, which can be occasionally glimpsed when Osborne talks about his vision for the future of Britain as 'an economy where the state does not take almost half of our national income, crowding out private endeavour', or claims (without justifying why) that it is 'unsustainable' that 'the state today accounts for almost half of all national income'. The goal of this second argument is not explicit, and this is rhetorically significant and effective, as this does not create disagreement on an additional issue.

Embedded within this main argument are sub-arguments that deal with the various areas in need of reform. Logically, since reform of welfare means (a) reforming the housing benefits system; (b) reforming the system of tax credits; (c) reforming disability allowance, etc., each of these areas involves its own claim and its own set of supporting premises. These sub-claims make more specific what the main claim is: the government needs to reform welfare, i.e. needs to do (a), (b), (c), etc. There is no space to reconstruct all of these embedded sub-arguments, but such reconstruction should be a simple and straightforward matter. Let us just illustrate it by the argument in favour of reforming housing benefits:

> Mr Deputy Speaker, spending on housing benefit has risen from £14 billion ten years ago to £21 billion today. That is close to a 50 per cent increase over and above inflation. Costs are completely out of control. We now spend more on housing benefit than we do on the police and on universities combined. And among these enormous numbers for total spending there are some equally enormous individual awards. Today there are some families receiving £104,000 a year in housing benefit. The cost of that single award is equivalent to the total income tax and national insurance paid by 16 working people on median incomes. It is clear that the system of housing benefit is in dire need for reform.

The argument above is a practical argument, from circumstances, goals and values. There are two sets of circumstantial premises: briefly, (1) the current situation is financially unsustainable and (2) the current situation is unfair. This division corresponds to the two main concerns expressed in the value premise, a concern for financial sustainability and a concern for fairness. As we said in Chapter 2, facts (circumstances) are selected as relevant premises in arguments in light of particular concerns (in other words, there is no fact/value distinction). Although the value premise is implicit in this particular section of the text (as it has been formulated elsewhere), its content is not hard to retrieve from the way in which the circumstantial premises have been formulated. Seeing current costs as 'out of control' can only function as a premise in a practical argument (and constitute a 'problem') if financial sustainability is a concern motivating action. Similarly, the enormous housing benefits awarded to some people but not others would not be seen as a 'problem' in the absence of a concern for fairness. In addition, the fact that fairness and sustainability *are* the value premises is independently confirmed by the presence, in the October Spending Review, of an almost identical version of this paragraph, containing the sentence 'This is totally unsustainable and unfair' exactly at this point in the argument, to refer to the situation in which 16 working families pay tax to support the housing benefits of one.

This argument is represented in Figure 4.5.

Developing the argument for austerity. The Spending Review

On 20 October 2010, in the Spending Review statement, Chancellor Osborne reasserted the same policy lines and made various points more specific. We are just going to indicate what exactly was new or reformulated in a clearer and more precise form in the Spending Review, by comparison with the Emergency Budget speech, to give a better view of the government's overall strategy.

The inevitability of the government's decision is emphasized in similar terms ('tackling this budget deficit is unavoidable'), but the government's choice of action is redefined in more constructive terms. The government has not merely chosen to pay 'the bills of past failure' but has chosen the path of 'investment in the future' and in the country's most important priorities (health, education, security and infrastructure), while 'cutting waste' and reforming a 'welfare system that our country can no longer afford'. The context of action is re-described succinctly with clear figures: 'We have, at £109 billion pounds, the largest structural budget deficit in Europe . . .. We are paying, at a rate of £120 million a day, £43 billion a year in debt interest'. Last year, the IMF warned this country to accelerate the reduction in the deficit and, since May, this has led to decisive action that 'has taken Britain out of the financial danger zone'. The Government's plan of action amounts to 'taking our country back from the brink of bankruptcy' and 'bringing sanity to our public finances and stability to our economy'.

Besides adding considerably more quantitative information, the Spending Review clarifies the three principles (values or concerns) that have underlain the Government's decisions: *reform*, *fairness* and *growth*. There is also further justification why these principles have been chosen to guide government action. The need for reforming all public services is justified by an appeal to evidence from the past. The last decade, Osborne argues, has shown that 'more money without reform was a recipe for failure'; however, 'less money without reform would be worse'. As the previous government's policies, of excessive regulations, targets and assessments have proved to be inefficient, this government, Osborne says, 'will completely reverse' these policies and has 'begun by squeezing every last penny . . . out of waste and administration costs'.

Fairness means that 'we are all in this together and all must make a contribution', but 'those with the broadest shoulders should bear the greatest burden', including the banks. It also 'means creating a welfare system that helps the vulnerable', makes sure that 'it will always pay to work' and that 'those who work will be better off than those who don't', and is 'also affordable for the working families who pay for it from their taxes'. There is a lot more emphasis on fairness in the Spending Review, and it goes beyond saying that the rich are expected to contribute more than the poor. The government's overall strategy is described as fair and that of the previous government as unfair: 'Let's be clear', Osborne says, 'there is nothing fair about running huge budget deficits, and burdening future generations with the debts we ourselves are not prepared to pay'. 'A fair government deals with the deficit decisively', so that the poor and future generations do not have to bear the burden of unsustainable public finances. The way in which the previous government has 'flunked' the reform of the welfare system is also said to be unfair. It is not fair that several working families should support the benefits bills of a family whose members do not work, and it is not fair that the welfare system does not make work pay. Nor is it fair that some people get away with tax evasion and fraud. In the welfare system alone, an estimated £5 billion is lost every year through fraud, i.e. '£5 billion that others have to work long hours to pay in their taxes'. This is why the government will both 'step up the fight to catch benefit cheats' and decisively address tax evasion. Saving in welfare costs, Osborne says, is also fair because these savings will be used to shield other areas form cuts. This decision was supported by 'massive consultations' with the public, which have shown 'the British people think it is fair to reform welfare bills in order to protect important public services', particularly the NHS ('the embodiment of a fair society'), but also education, which has been relatively protected at the expense of bigger cuts in other departments.

Finally, the government is concerned with promoting growth and private sector recovery. Through its actions, the government has already restored stability and certainty to business, Osborne says, and, by cutting taxes, is 'giving business the freedom to compete'. To encourage growth means that 'when money is short we should ruthlessly prioritise those areas of public spending which are most likely to support economic growth': investments in transport and green energy infrastructure, in education and science. The Spending Review is more detailed than the Emergency Budget in presenting and justifying measures for growth.

The premises of action and the claim are not very different from those in the Emergency Budget. Overall, the Spending Review clarifies the government's strategy as involving measures aimed at saving money and measures aimed at achieving economic growth. It also focuses more extensively on fairness. There is also more emphasis on the responsibility

involved in making difficult but carefully considered and 'tough' choices, and on the unavailability of alternatives. There are also several representations of the government's strategy of
action as one which has 'taken our country back from the brink of bankruptcy' and ushered
in a period of sustainable recovery, leading to 'a stronger Britain'.

Evaluation of the argument

We now turn to a critical evaluation of the government's pro-austerity argument, by drawing on the public debate on the government's strategy of action, as it has unfolded in the
media and other institutional contexts, since May 2010. We want to show that, often quite
explicitly, this debate has been carried out by challenging the elements of a practical argument: the goals, the values, the action, the definition of the context of action, the means–
goal premise, the relations between them, and particularly by pointing to the likely negative
and positive consequences of action. We suggest that any analysis of political discourse, to
the extent it focuses on arguments for action, needs to address these elements and use a normative framework for argument evaluation in order to take a non-arbitrary critical stance.

The debate between supporters and critics of austerity has opposed Labour to
Conservative politicians, but has also involved academics, economists and economics editors
of major newspapers, such as Robert Skidelsky, David Blanchflower, Martin Wolf, Larry
Elliott, Paul Krugman, on the side of the critics of austerity and mainly taking their inspiration from Keynes, to Niall Fergusson, Jeffrey Sachs, Jean-Claude Trichet and others, as
advocates of austerity. According to Martin Wolf, the debate is one between the 'cutters'
and the 'postponers': both camps agree that the fiscal deficit must be reduced but they disagree over many things, particularly over the pace of fiscal tightening, as well as on who
should bear the main burden. The 'cutters' argue that huge fiscal deficits endanger long-
term fiscal credibility and can lead to a downgrade of Britain's credit rating, hence to spiral-
ling borrowing costs and a fall in investor and private confidence and spending. They argue
that it was right to stimulate the economy in 2008 and 2009, but the time has now come for
fiscal retrenchment. The 'postponers' agree that spending must be reduced in the long run;
however, given the fragility of the recovery, fiscal consolidation should be put off until
growth resumes (Wolf 2010b).

In January 2011, the Keynesian economist David Blanchflower (economics editor at the
New Statesman and Professor at Dartmouth College, New Hampshire) published a point-by-
point rebuttal of the government's strategy, as summarized informally in David Cameron's
New Year message, in which he contradicted Cameron's description of the context of
action (according to Cameron, 'every sensible person knows' that 'we have been living seriously beyond our means'), his solution to the problem, the 'essential' character of austerity
measures and the likelihood that they will achieve the government's aims. In his New Year
message, Cameron claimed that 'the actions we are taking are essential, because they are
putting our economy and our country on the right path' and making 2011 'the year that
Britain gets back on its feet' (i.e. the actions are necessary and sufficient in view of the
goals). On the contrary, Blanchflower replies, they are certainly not 'essential' (i.e. not necessary, as there are alternatives) and 'there is a significant chance that this is the wrong
path': for many people, it is already clear that '2011 is going to be a year when they are
knocked off their feet' (i.e. the action is not sufficient either, it will not lead to the goals,
and its negative consequences may conclusively rebut the claim). 'Only time will tell',
Blanchflower observes, whether austerity will deliver the goals, but, 'judging by historical

precedent, there is a non-negligible probability that these policies will turn out to be a disaster' (i.e. their negative consequences will compromise the goals). Cameron claims that the government has inherited 'an economy in deep trouble' from the previous government, who is responsible for the 'biggest budget deficit in our peacetime history' (as circumstances of action). In response, Blanchflower observes that the explanation for the deficit is the crisis itself, and that the action taken by Labour at the time successfully prevented another Great Depression (i.e. alternative representations of the context of action and causal explanations are supporting different strategies). To Cameron's insistence that 'We are all in this together', Blanchflower replies: 'No we aren't. VAT is a regressive tax. The millionaires in cabinet will not become homeless or become depressed because of worries about paying the bills.' It is the poor and the young people who are going to pay the price for the coalition's 'doctrinaire attack' on them. According to Cameron, (a concern for) the national interest 'dictates' that the government should act decisively and without delay. Blanchflower disagrees once again: it is perhaps more 'plausible that the national interest is best served by delaying paying off the deficit, in order to stimulate growth'. In other words, the government's stated values or concerns might require alternative actions: austerity is not compatible with the either fairness or the national interest, such arguments are rationalizations. To Cameron's confident claim that 'we have a credible plan for restoring confidence in our economy' and 'we have to see it through', Blanchflower replies that, 'judging by the evidence up to this point, you don't', as 'confidence has collapsed and unemployment is rising' (i.e. emerging negative feedback should prompt a reconsideration of the strategy). The government's plan does not seem to be realistic in fact, he argues, 'as it is based on an assumption the private sector will step in, in a way it has never done before' (their argument is based on false premises). Consequently, Blanchflower urges, Cameron had better have a Plan B ready and be prepared for a major policy U-turn (Blanchflower 2011a).

In Chapter 2, we said that a practical argument is a presumptive argument that assigns a burden of proof not only to the arguer but also to the critics to come up with considerations that would defeat the argument or rebut its claim. This is the source of the inherent legitimacy of a critical approach to practical argumentation: due to human fallibility, no practical argument (and no practical claim) can be accepted as reasonable unless it has withstood systematic critical examination. A version of Walton's set of critical questions attached to the practical reasoning schema can provide an exhaustive examination of the argument. In the case of the government's argument for austerity, most of the questions in the list have in fact been asked (and also answered) by the government's critics, and we will include a review of this debate in the following sections.

In light of our framework in Chapter 2, we will look at criticism of the government's claim for action, as well as criticism of the premises on which the claim is based and of the relationship between premises and claim. Criticizing the premises means primarily examining them in the light of their rational acceptability (or truth). Criticizing the argument means attempting to defeat it, by showing that there are additional considerations, which can be added as premises, in view of which the claim no longer follows (the argument is invalid). For example, there are other means that can deliver the goal more efficiently. Or the goal is achieved, but the action has other effects as well, on other goals that the agent is also pursuing. But one can also attempt to reject the argument's conclusion by showing that the negative consequences it will generate as side-effects will undermine the goal itself or other goals which should not be compromised. We can formulate this alternatively in terms of a normative framework for deliberation. Choosing one proposal for action over others presupposes that, in a process of deliberation, the proposal in question has best stood up to criticism, while alternatives have been critically examined and found wanting.

Let us examine the government's argument for action from this three-fold perspective: (a) criticism of the conclusion, i.e. the attempted rebuttal of the practical claim; (b) criticism of the validity of the argument (attempted defeat); (c) criticism of the rational acceptability of its premises. Opponents of the government's strategy who take the first line have explored the probable (or already evident consequences of action) in their relation to the stated goals and values and have rejected the government's claim for action by showing that it either risks compromising those goals and values or has already done so. They have also criticized the government's failure to revise its strategy in light of emerging evidence indicating that the strategy is mistaken. Those who take the second line of criticism have argued that there are alternatives, better strategies of action that would also deliver the goals; or they have suggested alternative goals. Criticism along the third line has attempted to challenge the rational acceptability or truth of the premises of the government's argument, e.g. the representation of the context of action, designed to serve a particular rhetorical goal. Challenging the truth or acceptability of individual premises comes closest to what CDA practitioners, in the absence of a framework for analysing arguments, would normally do: suggest that the representation of the context of action is biased and serves a particular (power) interest. We suggest that viewing such representations as premises in practical arguments, i.e. as *reasons for action*, provides a better understanding of the interaction between agency and structures and of the relation between language and power.

Challenging the practical claim: has the claim stood up to criticism in light of its probable consequences?

A proposal for action is rationally acceptable if it has emerged from a process of deliberation in which it was subjected to rigorous and systematic criticism. Deliberation may involve considering reasons in favour of a proposal but essentially it should involve thinking of reasons *against* it. Minimally, arguers should consider what reasons, if any, support *not doing* the action (i.e. they should be looking at counter-arguments). Deliberation may involve examining several alternative proposals, in order to choose the one that is comparatively better. Criticizing a proposal amounts to showing that, if adopted, its implementation would either not lead to the intended goal (it would compromise the goal), or that, in the process of leading to the goal, it would undermine other highly important and non-overridable goals. Given that agents have different hierarchies of goals and values, and that some goals and values override others, a claim will stand up to criticism if the arguer can show that no goals or values that should not be overridden are being sacrificed, or – if sacrificing some goals and values is unavoidable – that the decision to do so can be justified. Almost any action will incur costs of some kind. The question is, are the costs acceptable in view of goals and values that cannot be overridden? Could there be a reasonable trade-off between these costs and the benefits that are likely to be obtained?

In relation to the evaluation of practical claims in light of their consequences, we make the following theoretical proposal. Questions such as the above amount to saying that a purely instrumental rationality will not suffice: agents always ought to consider *other goals*, not just try to find the most efficient means–end relation in view of one given goal. Instrumental rationality might turn out to be narrow-minded or morally questionable if, in fulfilling some stated goal of action, the action ends up negatively affecting other legitimate concerns (of the agent or of other agents), concerns which the agent ought to have considered before acting. Briefly, if the action has consequences that *undermine the stated goal of action*, then the action displays a failure of rationality in the *instrumental* sense: the means that were supposed to achieve the goal did not achieve it. This would indicate that *deliberation over means* was not sufficient: if it had been, it would have become apparent that the costs of the proposed action would outweigh its benefits, and that it would not be efficient in delivering the goal, while other means would perhaps be. If the action has negative consequences that *undermine other legitimate goals*, goals that should be not overridden, then it displays a failure of rationality which is *more-than-instrumental*. It indicates that *deliberation over goals* would have been necessary but was not sufficiently (if at all) carried out: agents ought to have considered which other goals should not be compromised in the realization of their stated goal. Both of these situations are, in our view, the strongest type of challenge that can be aimed at a practical argument, as they can refute the argument's *conclusion*, not merely show that there are problems with some premise or with the validity of the *argument*.

In July 2010, the *Financial Times* hosted a debate on austerity, which benefited from the participation of many economists. Defenders of austerity supported the government's strategy by pointing to the likely catastrophic consequences of failing to deal with debt (a possible downgrade of Britain's credit rating, loss of business confidence, an increase in debt through added debt interest), while opponents of austerity pointed to the similarly catastrophic consequences of premature fiscal tightening (e.g. massive unemployment, leading to more welfare spending and eventually to more, not less borrowing; a fall in living standards with consequences for human wellbeing; the possibility of a double-dip recession). In both camps' arguments, the opponents' strategy was implicitly said to incur costs that would either damage the intended goal of action or other legitimate goals (and associated values) that should not be endangered.

Historian Niall Ferguson (2010), a staunch defender of 'austerity now', argued that supersized deficits are affecting business confidence, because they raise the spectre of much higher future taxes to pay off higher borrowing costs. Real dangers arise, in his view, from perceptions of a country as potentially capable of defaulting on its debts: 'Bond market sell-offs', he observes, 'are seldom gradual. All it takes is one piece of bad news – a credit rating downgrade, for example – to trigger a sell-off.' The remedy to the recession, he claimed, lies in policies of the type that the Thatcher and Reagan governments successfully implemented 30 years ago. 'Then, as today, the choice was not between stimulus and austerity. It was between policies that boost private-sector confidence and those that kill it.' Several other economists in the same debate advocated fiscal conservatism rather than further stimulus, as a way to ensure confidence among the banking and business environment. Some acknowledged that a slide back into recession following fiscal tightening was probable but claimed that 'a double dip is a price worth paying' and countries ought to accept 'that bitter medicine in order to get on the right longer term path' (Feldstein 2010). Other advocates of austerity praised the Coalition for understanding that the 'ever-expanding state was no longer the solution to economic lethargy, but the cause for endemic underperformance' and, while acknowledging the salutary role of Keynesian interventionism at the beginning of the crisis, they argued that the time has come to 'throw out the Keynesian rule book' (Monson and Subramaniam 2010).

Not everyone is defending 'austerity now'. Martin Wolf, the *Financial Times* economics editor, has repeatedly warned that concerted austerity measures across Europe will tip the world into recession again. While admitting that 'we cannot be sure who is right', and that only time will tell whether the government's strategy was right or wrong, Wolf has advocated the case of the 'postponers', finding Labour's critique of the government basically correct and warning that politicians must have alternative plans ready in case they are proved wrong (Wolf 2010b, 2010c). The biggest risk of austerity, Wolf has argued, involves the prospects for growth: 'a rapid withdrawal of fiscal support would reduce not just actual GDP, but prospective growth, via its negative impact on investment in physical and human capital'. How is the economy supposed to grow, then, is the fundamental question, to which, Wolf argues, Labour has so far had better answers: the deficit and the national debt must be reduced, but only once growth is fully secured and over a significantly longer period of time than envisaged by the government. As for the alleged risks associated with perceptions of potential insolvency, 'we are terrified of a confidence bogey who is asleep' (Wolf 2010c).

Another fierce opponent of austerity is the Nobel-winning American economist Paul Krugman (2010a). In an article in the *New York Times*, entitled 'Myths of austerity', Krugman argued that there is no evidence for the belief that fiscal contraction improves confidence and is therefore actually expansionary. This belief is based on a mythical belief in the 'invisible bond vigilante and the confidence fairy' – the belief that investors will shun America if the government is incurring more debt and reward her if austerity measures are adopted. Fiscal austerity has suddenly become 'fashionable', he argues, and is decidedly a bold strategy, 'but it boldly goes in exactly the wrong direction': it creates massive unemployment at a time when the private sector is not capable of providing jobs, and reduces demand which will only further depress the private sector (Krugman 2010b).

Along similar lines, Robert Skidelsky (Professor at Warwick University) and Michael Kennedy (former economic advisor at the Treasury), citing Keynes – who (in 1937) wrote 'The boom, not the slump, is the right time for austerity at the Treasury' – claimed that 'austerity now' is the worst possible solution. 'Future generations will curse us for cutting in a slump', Skidelsky and Kennedy (2010) said in the *Financial Times* austerity debate. Contrary to the belief that increased public spending will impose a burden on future generations, they argued that the burden on present and future generations will be much heavier if the public deficit is cut now. As income, profits and tax receipts will fall, investment projects in infrastructure will be cancelled or postponed, 'with the result that future generations will be worse off, having been deprived of assets they might otherwise have had'. The solution they suggest is to increase capital spending to renew the country's infrastructure: a modern transport system, energy-efficient housing, new power-plants, new schools. Labour, they observe, had already taken steps in that direction, and those projects were unwisely scrapped by the current government.

Skidelsky (who is also the biographer of John Maynard Keynes) has argued repeatedly that the new government's strategy is misguided and risks triggering off a double-dip recession. In an article in the *New Statesman*, in May 2010, he observed that government spending in a period of recession is not *at the expense of* private spending, but compensates for its absence. If the government were to cut spending at the same time as the private sector was spending less, and if everyone was saving rather than spending, the recession would only deepen. This, Skidelsky says, is what Keynes called the 'paradox of thrift'. In Britain, where, unfortunately, the injection of money into the economy had a positive effect on the financial sector, but little effect on the real economy, government spending needs to be the main agent of recovery. Chancellor Osborne would therefore be well-advised to disregard fearmongering pundits who agitate the non-existent risk of sovereign debt default and 'continue to pump money into the economy, counting on this advantage: that the markets do not expect the UK government to go bankrupt'. In doing so, the Chancellor would show that he understands that

we cannot continue to run an economic system in which there is such a large gap
between the beliefs of ordinary people and the beliefs of the business and financial worlds
about the properties of the economy and the requirements of a decent economic life

and an awareness that he is ultimately responsible to the people (Skidelsky 2010).

In October 2010, in an article on the UK government's new economic strategy, David
Blanchflower was reporting the astonishment of a number of economists and policy-makers
worldwide at the 'biggest macroeconomic experiment in an advanced country' in recent
decades, which they reportedly saw as a 'wildly unnecessary, misguided, doctrinaire and
potentially dangerous' spending cuts programme, taking 'unnecessary risks with the well-
being of the nation', and the equivalent of 'jumping off a cliff' (Blanchflower 2010b). (Let us
note that this is exactly the opposite of Osborne's characterization of government action, as
taking Britain back from the brink of disaster.) Blanchflower has repeatedly described the
public spending cuts as the 'greatest macro-economic mistake in a century'. One of his main
concerns is youth unemployment, as an unacceptable cost of the cuts and a 'timebomb' that
carries with it the risk of a lost generation (Blanchflower 2011b; see also 2011c). In June
2010, Blanchflower was already voicing his doubt at the optimistic unemployment forecasts
issued by the Office for Budget responsibility, according to which unemployment would fall
steadily each year from 2010, as the private sector would be stepping in to create approximately 2.5 million jobs during 2010–14. These predictions, Blanchflower argued, are 'completely implausible' in the current circumstances. Between 2000 and 2008, over nine years
when the economy was booming, the private sector created no more than 1.6 million jobs,
mainly in the financial and construction sectors, so where exactly 2.5 million jobs are to
come from, over the next five years, is a question that the government has failed to answer
(Blanchflower 2010a).

In spite of the government's insistence on the catastrophic consequences that would ensue
if Britain should continue the policy of fiscal stimulus, Keynesian economists have argued
that there are no real dangers that would be averted at present by a policy of retrenchment
and austerity. The negative impact of this policy, however, is significant and highly probable.
Britain risks a double-dip recession and can expect massive unemployment and a considerable fall in living standards. The evidence on which the Keynesians are basing these predictions includes economic theory but also past mistakes made by governments in the 1930s,
lessons from Japan's history of stagnation, as well as emerging empirical evidence that the
government's policy is misconceived (which we will discuss separately).

The government's strategy has nevertheless found support among business circles. The
Daily Telegraph published an open letter signed by 35 business leaders, expressing their support for immediate spending cuts and opposing Labour's original plan to spread the deficit
reduction over more than one parliament, though some have since retracted. 'The cost of
delay is enormous, and would result in almost £100bn of additional national debt by the
end of this parliament alone', the letter said. Commenting on this perception of the alleged
consequences of postponing spending cuts, Blanchflower has characterized it as a 'terrible
mistake', demonstrating a grievous misunderstanding of the economic issues at stake, and
argued that, on the contrary, 'the sensible thing to do is to spread [the cuts] over a long
time'. Clearly, the deficit has to be addressed, he said, but over a longer time frame and in a
way that is sensitive to observed effects: 'You have to be mindful of the data and if the data
turns down, which it has, you have to adapt' (Kollewe 2010).

Economics editors of major newspapers have used an argument from consequences
to support either the pro-austerity view or its opposite. From the considerable risk of a

double-dip recession and projected massive unemployment, Larry Elliott, writing for *The Guardian*, concludes that the government's policy is irrational ('the lunatics are back in charge of the asylum') (Elliott 2010c). By contrast, Jeff Randall and Jeremy Warner, in *The Daily Telegraph*, think that Osborne is finally attempting to 'restore sanity to the Treasury madhouse' and ought to turn a deaf ear to the 'screeching', 'hysterical voices from the Opposition benches', whose arguments have the 'credibility of the Flat Earth Society' but none of its charm (Randall 2010b, 2010c). In their view, the 'let's spend until we're broke' brigade are clearly wrong and should admit defeat (Warner 2010).

Is the action being revised in the light of feedback and empirical evidence?

In January 2011, UK gross domestic product for the fourth quarter of 2010 fell by 0.5 per cent from the previous quarter, after four quarters of slow but steady growth under the Labour government. (Previously, growth had been 0.7 per cent and 1.1 per cent.) This news came as a shock to the government and to the media. *The Guardian*'s economics editor commented: 'The coalition government has killed the economy stone dead. Trashed it. Pushed it to the brink of a double-dip recession' (Elliott, in Elliott *et al.* 2011). Other economists also issued warnings. In the *Financial Times*, Martin Wolf asked 'Where now is the robust recovery that justified the government's rapid fiscal retrenchment?' The government seems to have been optimistic in its forecasts and in its faith that the British economy could withstand the fiscal contraction, but, 'if any such overconfidence existed before these latest numbers, it should now have gone'. In such circumstances, 'just hoping for the best is simply irrational' and 'the chancellor should plan for the worst, right now' (Wolf 2011a).

At the end of January 2011, at the World Economic Forum in Davos, in Switzerland, George Soros, the international financier, warned David Cameron that the government might push the British economy back into recession unless it altered its austerity package. Soros said that the combination of tax increases and spending cuts was, in his view, unsustainable, and that Britain needed a Plan B (Elliott 2011b). Meanwhile, the Labour opposition produced a similar argument: factual evidence was now showing that the government's strategy was not working. Alan Johnson (Labour's Shadow Chancellor at the time) declared in an interview: 'This is such a huge gamble. It had better work because there doesn't appear to be a Plan B.'

As the metaphor of the 'Plan B' gripped the media in the early months of 2011, neither the Prime Minister nor the Chancellor showed any willingness to consider alternative plans because, they said, it would alarm the financial markets. The fall in output was attributed to the exceptionally cold weather, an explanation which only exposed the government to ridicule: 'Please sir, the weather shrank my economy', a City analyst reportedly sneered. The Prime Minister said it was not a surprise that the recovery would be difficult but the worst thing the coalition could do would be to ditch their plans on the basis of one quarter's figures – the situation will improve if there is clarity of purpose and a strong determination to see the strategy through. Economic analysts were not impressed by this demonstration of consistency. Elliott pointed out that the fall in output came *before* the planned cuts and VAT increase and said: 'Ministers should now admit their mistakes and put growth before deficit reduction. But they won't because they are clowns. Incompetent clowns' (Elliott *et al.* 2011).

Failure to modify a plan of action in the light of either probable negative consequences or empirical evidence is a serious objection against the rationality of action. As we have explained, this only applies to cases where the action is seen not to lead to but actually endanger the intended goal or other goals that should not be compromised. Of course, which goals are expendable is a judgement that might vary from person to person, depending on how goals and values are hierarchically ordered for different agents; deliberation takes place in contexts of fundamental differences in values and interests. Successive British governments and other agents (trade unions, etc.) have for instance taken different stances to the question 'is unemployment a price worth paying?', in exchange for low inflation or other goals. The current government's unwillingness to modify its strategy, as negative consequences that allegedly undermine a variety of important goals have begun to emerge, has offered its critics a powerful attack strategy, but whether the critics are right or not can only be determined over a longer time period.

Opponents of austerity have nevertheless tried to argue that there is in fact *already* sufficient evidence that the government's approach is wrong. The solutions being proposed are neoliberal in nature, yet 'the obsession with market fundamentalism' has obviously by now been 'tested to destruction' by the crisis itself. For decades, 'privatisation, deregulation and labour market flexibility have run their course without producing stable growth or full employment' and without successfully dealing with poverty. Instead, 'the grotesque ballooning of inequality' has generated an unprecedented recession. The 'neoliberal system is clearly broken', yet the solutions to the crisis are along neoliberal lines, the Labour MP Michael Meacher has argued in his blog, in *The Guardian* and, in identical terms, in his interventions in Parliament (2010c). In other words, the system has *already* produced catastrophic consequences, yet the government's solutions are persistently trying to restore the same system. As we have seen, criticism that appeals to negative consequences that have already arisen (as opposed to probable consequences) is very strong, as it can conclusively falsify a claim.

Will the government's strategy actually deliver the goals?
Is it sufficient in view of the goals?

Advocates of austerity have often emphasized the need to combine spending cuts with measures that boost growth. Austerity, in other words, is by itself insufficient in view of the goals. In the *Financial Times* debate on austerity we referred to earlier, Jean-Claude Trichet, President of the European Central Bank, argued that there should be no more fiscal stimulus and that the time has come for all European countries to start reducing their deficits. However, he said, 'adjustment on the spending side' needs to be 'accompanied by structural reforms to promote long-term growth' (Trichet 2010). Similarly, while believing that the UK government is on the right track, Jeffrey Sachs (Director of the Earth Institute, Columbia University, New York) emphasizes that cuts need to be accompanied by forward-looking investments in education, science, technology and infrastructure. The new watchword, according to Sachs, must be investment rather than stimulus, i.e. there must be a combination of austerity and growth-boosting measures (Sachs 2010).

A critical view of the government's growth strategy was expressed in January 2010 by Sir Richard Lambert, outgoing director general of the Confederation of British Industry, who used his last major speech in office to warn against (what he saw as) the government's unsatisfactory growth strategy. Lambert said that the government's single-mindedness in pursuing spending cuts was clearly not matched by an equal determination to support growth. 'It's not enough just to slam on the spending brakes. Measures that cut spending but killed demand would actually make matters worse', he said, and he challenged the government to devise policies that helped the private sector to expand and create jobs (Elliott 2011a).

Criticism along these lines does not deny that austerity is necessary, but warns that it will not be sufficient to achieve economic recovery. It amounts to saying that the means are not sufficient in view of attaining the goals. Let us observe that this is different from warning against negative consequences that will make the goal impossible to achieve. Pointing to negative consequences may rebut the claim and thus indicate that the opposite of the claim is the right action to take. Pointing out that the means are insufficient (or as we shall see below, not necessary) may defeat the argument in the sense of showing that it is invalid, but does not suggest that the opposite of the claim should be adopted.

Is the government's strategy necessary in view of the goals? What alternative means should be considered?

To suggest that there are alternatives is to suggest that the action is not strictly speaking necessary. Other actions could lead to the goal, maybe even more efficiently or more in accordance with the argument's stated values. Many critics of the government have challenged the alleged unavoidability of austerity. Why is the UK's austerity plan deemed necessary, asks Martin Wolf in the *Financial Times*. Is austerity justified by the size of the deficit? At first sight, he says, we might say yes: in 2010, UK borrowing was the third highest among western countries, after the USA and Ireland, which is why the chancellor presented his exceptionally tough fiscal plans as 'unavoidable'. However, Wolf argues, 'this is not so'. The government *did* have alternatives. First, 'it could have decided to leave public spending permanently higher' (Wolf 2011b). Second, 'the government made a deliberate choice to concentrate most of the fiscal adjustment on spending'. This choice was not necessary either: 'reasonable people can differ . . . over how much of the deficit reduction should come from tax rises, instead of spending cuts'. Third, the chancellor's claim that, without fiscal consolidation, Britain would become bankrupt is not very convincing, as 'the UK government was never Greece or Ireland'. If, Wolf argues, the government could not borrow, there would indeed be no alternative. But it *can* go on borrowing, so there *is* an alternative, and Labour's original strategy might have worked better than that of the current government (Wolf 2010c).

Various critics of the government have proposed alternative means to tackle the deficit and encourage growth. Caroline Lucas, Green MP for Brighton, has called for a new taxation system and structural economic reform, involving a major government-led programme of investment in green industries (in Elliott *et al.* 2011). Michael Meacher (2010a) has argued repeatedly in his blog, as well as in his interventions in Parliament, that the deficit should be reduced not by spending cuts but by job creation. Cutting public spending, 'whether drastically or sensitively and straightaway or a bit later' (Meacher 2010c), is the wrong policy, which both parties seem to support, 'unsurprisingly, since both New Labour and the Tories have basically the same Thatcherite ideology'. The right response would be an increase in public sector investment to compensate for the collapse of private investment, e.g. in house-building, infrastructure and the green economy. Why does the government refuse to go for the alternative of 'public sector reflation'? The answer, according to Meacher, is a persistent commitment to market fundamentalism, which rejects any beneficial role for the state. The government is thus pursuing the wrong strategy of action, when better alternatives are available. 'First they focused exclusively on spending cuts rather than a growth and jobs programme as the most efficient means to cut the deficit.' Second, 'they decided that three-quarters of the deficit reduction should come from cutting public expenditure rather than increasing taxes on the rich'. Third, 'they have taken no significant measures to reform the banks or to prevent another financial crash'. Finally, they are expecting the population to accept job losses and a fall in living standards while 'the rich get off virtually scot-free'. He claims that 'the richest 1,000 people in the UK, a minuscule 0.001% of the population, whose wealth . . . quadrupled since 1997 to £370bn, could pay off the entire deficit of £150bn themselves alone and still be £220bn better off'. Yet, proportionally to their vast fortunes, they are being required to pay virtually nothing.

The wrong solutions were adopted from the start, according to many of the government's critics. Instead of spending £680bn of taxpayers' money increasing the national debt to 'protect the banks from their own extreme folly', Meacher says, the government could have, at a fraction of the costs, taken over the banking system. It is incredible, Meacher has argued in Parliament, in *The Guardian* and in his blog, that 'such an obvious common-sense solution is derailed because of extreme ideological aversion to even the faintest whiff of public owner-ship' and at such huge cost to the economy and the population. Failure to adopt this alterna-tive is revelatory, in his view, of 'how deeply embedded in the minds of the political and economic leadership (of both main parties) is the market fundamentalism which is the defining element of the neoliberal era' (Meacher 2009). The wrong means are therefore persistently chosen because of ideological adherence to a questionable goal.

Larry Elliott, *The Guardian*'s economics editor, is one of many commentators who have criticized the 'soft-touch approach to the City', as manifested in the Coalition's first Budget. 'The increase in capital gains tax was smaller than expected and the £2bn bank levy was hardly suitable punishment given the role of the financial sector in Britain's most grievous post-war recession'. Osborne seems to ignore the alternative advocated by the campaigners for a so-called Robin Hood tax, who argue that the Treasury could raise £20bn through a financial transaction tax, which would be more than enough to pay for the £12bn he is planning to raise from increasing VAT to 20 per cent (Elliott 2010d). Similarly, in a recent article in *The Guardian*, Seumas Milne talks about the 'Tory-led gov-ernment's resolute refusal to bring to heel the banks that delivered the economic melt-down'. The government, he says, have made this clear in their unwillingness to force banks to give up bonuses, to tax the banking sector properly and in their haste to cut Labour's bank levy (Milne 2011). The alternative to the spending cuts that will affect so many people who are in no way responsible for the crisis would be therefore to resolutely pursue tax avoidance and to properly tax the City.

To what extent have any alternatives been considered in prior deliberation leading to the Coalition's decision is hard to tell, but the way in which alternatives are addressed in the two texts that we have discussed is in line with the familiar 'There-is-no-alternative' (or 'TINA') principle: spending cuts are unavoidable. The government's critics seem to have produced alternative solutions that would apparently be more efficient in solving the problems and achieving the goals, and also more in accordance with the stated value of fairness. The gov-ernment's argument has not adequately shown that it has considered any of these or that its preferred choice can withstand critical examination. It has not shown that it can give a satis-factory answer to questions such as: (a) Which alternative actions that might also bring about the goal has the government considered? (b) Among possible alternatives, is the govern-ment's proposal the most acceptable in light of considerations of efficiency *and* probable con-sequences *and* in light of the government's stated value commitments? In other words, it has failed to convince that its own alternative is *necessary* in view of the goal, that it is a compara-tively better alternative, and that it is really underlain by a concern for fairness, as claimed.

Once such considerations are brought to bear on the argument – the existence of other means, more compatible with the stated goals and values, as well as the incompatibility between the stated premises and the conclusion they are supposed to support – the argument is considerably weakened. Assuming that we were ready to presumptively accept that, given the government's premises for action, the proposed strategy is the right one, once all these further considerations, as the product of further public deliberation, are taken into account, the claim no longer follows (the argument is defeated). If there are indeed better means that have not yet been considered, then maybe the government ought to revise its strategy of action.

Evaluation of the argument by invoking other means is nevertheless not as straightforward as it might seem. Various journalists have rallied behind the Coalition government and defended austerity *precisely* because it is necessary in view of shared goals and values. Spending cuts are absolutely necessary, argues Jeff Randall (economics editor at the *Daily Telegraph* and presenter of *Randall at 7.00* on Sky News) and there is indeed no alternative. The statistics on the 'welfare indulgence' promoted by Labour as part of their 'failed social experiments', Randall says, are outrageous. For example, about 100,000 households receive benefits and tax credits worth more than the average wage (£23,244); and there are at least 250,000 households where no one has ever worked (Randall 2010d). This is not always due to unavailability of jobs but is more to do with the 'state's disgraceful indulgence of welfare-guzzling layabouts' (Randall 2010b). Cuts are therefore necessary in view of shared goals and also on account of fairness. Without cuts, the goals cannot be achieved. If the Chancellor should merely set out to achieve the goal set out by Alistair Darling, i.e. *halving* the UK's annual £155 billion deficit by the end of this Parliament, rather than eliminating it, the total amount the UK would owe would double to £1.4 trillion, and this would carry interest charges of about £70 billion a year. More substantial fiscal tightening is therefore needed in order to prevent the outstanding debt from becoming completely unmanageable (Randall 2010b). Austerity is absolutely necessary for a return to sustained economic growth, argues Jeremy Warner, another *Daily Telegraph* journalist, and is not 'unnecessary masochism'. Self-imposed fiscal austerity is far preferable to the austerity likely to be imposed by others – markets and the IMF – if the right action is persistently deferred (Warner 2011b). The cuts, in other words, are necessary in view of the goal; without them, the goal will not be achieved.

Are the goals of action rationally acceptable? What other goals have been considered?

Let us now briefly look at the argument's goal premise. It does not follow that an agent ought to do an action *A* in order to realize a goal unless the action will not damage that goal or other goals that should not be compromised, or unless the action does not have unacceptable costs that outweigh its benefits, and these 'costs' should be understood not only in material terms, but in terms of human wellbeing, or as moral costs. The question of which other goals the agent should consider can not only defeat the argument's validity but also rebut the argument's claim, by indicating that the agent should not engage in action that compromises other goals that is committed to (or, from the perspective of his critics, goals that he should be committed to, such as other agents' legitimate goals). We have already discussed this by referring to the debate on the consequences of action.

We have seen how the goals of action are formulated in Osborne's two speeches. The stated goals of the Budget have to do with reducing the size of the deficit and of the debt and the rebalancing of the economy, with a view of creating a future Britain in which there is prosperity for all. It would be hard to deny that these are desirable goals that can reasonably ground political action. However, the vision that is proposed is fairly vague and in need of further specification, particularly in terms of the concrete actions or strategies that can turn it into reality. In the same speech we referred to earlier, the CBI Director General Sir Richard Lambert claimed that the government has 'failed so far to articulate in big picture terms its vision of what the UK economy might become under its stewardship'. When it comes to concrete policies for growth, rather than spending cuts and reducing the size of the state, the Coalition's vision has been in fact found wanting by more than one commentator. To what extent the government has a realistic strategy for achieving its vision of a future Britain, based on a new model of economic growth, starting from the current circumstances and by engaging in the type of action it has adopted, is a controversial issue. As we have seen already, a strong objection is that the combination of spending cuts and growth-friendly measures it proposes is unsustainable and cannot realistically lead to the goals. This line of criticism says that the government's strategy is unreasonable in the instrumental sense: it is designed to achieve a set of goals but it will not achieve them.

Another important question that has been asked refers to the sincerity of the government's commitment to the stated goals. In other words, is it true that the government is committed to these goals and not to others? Critics of the Coalition have argued that the austerity programme is in fact ideology-driven, and that the stated goals are merely window-dressing for an ideological agenda: the deficit is used as an excuse to roll back the state. According to Larry Elliott (2010b), among many others, Osborne's Budget shows that the 'real agenda is to complete the demolition job on welfare states that was started in the 1980s'. Paul Krugman also asks: Why is Britain embarking on an austerity programme? His answer is that 'the real reason has to do a lot with ideology: the Tories are using the deficit as an excuse to downsize the welfare state' while using the 'the official rationale' that 'there is no alternative' (Krugman 2010b). Labour politicians (Alan Johnson, Alistair Darling) have also declared in interviews that the Conservatives are dressing up their ideology as necessity, that the cuts are ideological rather than necessary and inevitable. We have cited Michael Meacher, the Labour MP, as saying that the wrong solutions have been adopted from the start for ideological reasons. The right solutions, based (in his view) on an increased role of the state in the process of recovery, are not likely to succeed because 'the neoliberal agenda – that private markets must be the exclusive mechanism for economic activity – remains dominant in both the main political parties' (Meacher 2010c, 2010d).

Critics of the government have also observed that what lies behind the government's stated goals seems to be a determination to return to business-as-usual, not to restructure the economic system so that similar crises might be prevented from happening in the future. In the wake of the crisis of 2008, talk about the collapse of capitalism and about the need for systemic changes, radical transformation and new goals for action, seems to have given way to resignation. There has been a swift return of business-as-usual, with banks resuming the same practices that led to the crisis (as recently noted by Mervyn King, the Governor of the Bank of England himself), and a particular type of left-wing criticism that seemed vindicated by the unfolding of events in 2008 now seems increasingly marginal. In the political arena, paradoxically, left-wing parties seem to be losing elections rather than winning them as might have been expected. The main challenge that Osborne's argument would have to answer, regarding the goals of action, would therefore be: how is this future Britain that he envisages to be different in the sense of not making a return to business-as-usual, to the same practices that have led to financial meltdown, possible? So far, the 'soft-touch approach to the City' (Elliott 2010c) has failed to convince that the government has seriously considered any radical transformation at the level of goals. It is therefore all the more disingenuous and ironic that the 'debt-fuelled' economic model, in which consumption based on private debt is encouraged and can pass for wealth creation and growth, is being publicly denounced by Osborne in his Budget speech, given that it is an intrinsic element of neoliberal economics, supported by the financial sector and (at least until the crisis emerged) by the Conservative opposition as well as the Labour governments of Blair and Brown.

Some politicians and journalists have called for a fundamental redefinition of the goals of action, for a new political vision. Caroline Lucas, the Green MP, for example, has argued that, instead of 'slashing public spending in the hope of resuming business as usual', the government should 'seize this opportunity to reconfigure the deeply unsustainable economic system which has helped push us towards financial meltdown, a climate crisis and increasing energy insecurity' (Elliott *et al.* 2011). A few days before the G20 meeting in March 2009, Larry Elliott was suggesting five big areas that the summit should concentrate on. First, the G20 ought to 'accept that this is the time for a new economics': both the financial crisis and the environmental crisis are 'crises of excess' and recovery is not possible without the recognition that 'the world needs to slow down a bit'. His other proposals referred to a green new deal, radical reform of the IMF, radical reform of the global financial system and tougher global regulation (Elliott 2009).

For Paul Mason (the economics editor of the BBC programme *Newsnight*), the ideology of neoliberalism is now dead and lies shattered alongside that of Stalinist Marxism (Mason 2010: 172). So far, he says, politicians have been just tinkering with its broken mechanisms. While the government is outlining an improbable shift from an economy based on credit, consumption and government spending to one based on exports and private sector business investment, they are neglecting the crucially important structural reform of the banking system, so that no bank should ever be too big to fail and key functions of banking should be separated. Fairly radical solutions proposed by post-war economists, such as Minsky (e.g. Minsky 1986), would be appropriate in the current context, in his view: nationalizing banks and the insurance system, placing strict limits on speculative finance, changing the tax structure to decrease inequality, limiting the power of large-scale enterprises (Mason 2010: 159). In *The Guardian*, Seumas Milne (2011) also noted that, 'as elsewhere, there is a determined attempt in Britain to restore the economic model so comprehensively discredited in the crash of 2008'. The government, he says, seems 'determined to reinstate a neoliberal order that is beyond repair', rather than reforming the economic model that was 'broken by its own excesses'.

The texts we have looked at do not suggest that the government intends to substantially reform the system, which is why the accusation that it merely intends a return to business-as-usual seems to be justified. Claims to action based on an insufficient critical examination of the appropriate goals of action are not well supported and should be rightly challenged. Reasonable deliberation should be more than instrumental. It should not merely try to find the most efficient means in view of given goals, but should also question the goals and consider the possibility of alternative goals. It should not merely ask 'what should we do in order to reach the goal?' but also 'what goals should we pursue?' and 'are taken-for-granted goals reasonable or justified?' Critics of the government who have pointed to alternative goals that have not been considered are implicitly challenging the rationality of action in a non-instrumental sense. The action may achieve its stated financial objectives (although this is also in doubt) but these objectives themselves are in need of examination and there has apparently been no adequate deliberation in government (let alone democratic deliberation) over the kind of future that Britain should be moving towards.

Is the value premise rationally acceptable? Does it actually support the goal and the action?

A recent study by the Social Policy Association (Yeates *et al.* 2011) identifies 'fairness' as a 'feature of the rhetoric' used by the government to promote their austerity programme. The authors argue that there is no coherent understanding of fairness behind the government's policies. They identify at least five senses of fairness: a concern with intergenerational justice, a concern with social mobility, fairness as a principle of universal but progressive contributions, fairness as just deserts and as the protection of the worst-off. All of these senses of fairness seem to appear in Osborne's 2010 Budget and Spending Review. He insists for instance that it is unfair to saddle future generations with massive debt, that the welfare system should protect the vulnerable, that those who work should be better off than those who don't, and most notably he emphasizes togetherness and solidarity: everyone will be asked to contribute, 'we are all in this together and all must make a contribution'. The authors of the study cite independent research by the Institute of Fiscal Studies that demonstrates the poor will pay a proportionately larger fraction of their income than the rich and will be hit hardest by the spending cuts. They conclude that, in spite of the rhetoric of fairness, the Coalition's policies will most probably widen inequality in Britain in the coming years.

The views of the Institute for Fiscal Studies on the fairness of the Coalition 2010 Budget have been echoed by various media commentators. In *The Guardian*, Milne has argued that Osborne's claims of fairness in the June Budget were fraudulent and cited statistics from the IFS showing that the impact of the Budget on the worst-off tenth of the population will be five times the impact on the richest by 2015. Far from being progressive, as claimed, the Budget is regressive according to the IFS, and will hit the poorest hardest. Or, as Milne comments, it is the poor and disabled who will 'pay the price of the bankers' recession'. By increasing VAT and cutting a wide range of benefits, while cutting corporation tax and letting banks off with a 'levy that is dwarfed by swelling bonuses', Osborne 'has turned his and Cameron's boast of social togetherness into a sour joke' (Milne 2010).

Appeals to fairness are likely to increase the rhetorical and dialectical acceptability of arguments. Fairness, as a publicly shared value, enjoys unquestionable legitimacy. It is not as much the rational acceptability of the value premise that can be challenged here but the relationship between it and the goal premise and, indirectly, the action, as well as the sincerity of the government' commitment to it. Is the goal of a 'fairer Britain', 'where prosperity is shared among all sections of society and all parts of the country' compatible with the value of fairness? Self-evidently, yes. But is the goal of a 'fairer Britain' compatible with the action being proposed? Is the government's action *actually* motivated by a concern for and commitment to fairness? Yes, according to the Chancellor and supporters of the government, and no, according to the Institute for Fiscal Studies and other critics of the government. According to the critics, an appeal to fairness while at the same time defending huge spending cuts and failing to penalize the banks, is just rhetorical window-dressing.

The public debate on fairness is extremely complex. People who do not otherwise support the government's programme of cuts would not necessarily disagree that the welfare system is in need of reform. They would agree, for instance, that it is not fair that taxes paid by working families who commute to work should be used to pay for housing and unemployment benefits for families who live in central London. Osborne skilfully exploits the public's sensitivity to this perceived unfairness in his speech: people should get what they deserve, those who work should be rewarded, and those who choose not to work should no longer be better off than those who do. He is of course choosing not to address any of the thorny issues behind this argument (the causes of unemployment, such as the unavailability of jobs in many areas; the exorbitant prices of houses and rents). By appealing to people's sense of fairness in the sense of 'just deserts' he is presumably trying to advance his other more contentious claim to fairness: that sharing the pain of the cuts amongst the population is also fair. Regarding the latter issue, the obvious critical question that he would have to answer would be: To what extent is it compatible with fairness as desert to force the population to pay for a crisis which they did not cause, while asking for so little from the banks and bankers that caused the crisis and who should, therefore, *by the same logic of fairness as desert*, pay for the damages? To what extent, that is, is the strategy advocated compatible with the value that allegedly informs it?

In Chapter 3, we showed how arguments can be criticized as rationalizations. In rationalizations, the premises that are invoked in support of the claim are not the real premises, from the arguer's perspective. We said that it is hard to find evidence for the arguer's insincerity, for his deceptive intention. However, what we can say on the basis of evidence is that, in Osborne's arguments, there does not seem to be a compatibility between the value premise, the goal premise and the action, as one would expect. This fact can be obscured by the way in which fairness is defined in these texts. In addition to insisting that the rich will pay more than the poor, Osborne is careful to emphasize fairness in the sense of giving people what they deserve: people who work deserve rewards that idle people don't. By the same logic, however, he would also have to address the question: Why do bankers *deserve* to receive bonuses, while the population has to pay for their excesses? This question, which we also address in the next chapter, has not been publicly dealt with in a remotely acceptable way, which is why the government's appeals to fairness ring hollow. As we show in Chapter 5, there has been a prudential public argument in favour of rescuing banks and bankers (they are too big to fail, they would leave the country, the system would collapse), but no adequate moral argument, and it is in moral terms (fairness, desert) that the discussion is cast here.

Arguably, alternative strategies of action, such as defended by the Coalition's critics, are more compatible with fairness: a job-creation programme, or a public sector-driven programme of building affordable housing, or a higher bank levy. These actions would fit in better with the goal of a fairer Britain. Given the value of fairness and the goal of a fairer Britain, the government ought, for instance, to go for a Robin Hood tax on financial transactions and create jobs for people. A *different* set of claims would therefore follow from a genuine concern for fairness. To preserve the claim for action unchanged, the value premise ought to be altered. Either way, the inferential link between the argument's stated premises and its stated claim is defeated by the argument's failure to provide a satisfactory answer to the question about the compatibility between stated values, goals and action. The conclusion in favour of spending cuts does not follow from a commitment to fairness. Moreover, what follows from a commitment to fairness is that the government ought *not* to share the burden of the cuts across society, as this punishes the innocent and fails to penalize those responsible for the crisis.

We have said that fairness is a rationally acceptable value, but questioned to what extent it actually informs action. Fairness is invoked because it is an acceptable, legitimate value, one which enjoys public recognition as an external constraint on government action. The government is committed to fairness whatever other reasons it might have and it is a rhetorically effective move (part of an appeal to *ethos*) to emphasize this commitment as a reason for action. We can nevertheless challenge the implicit definition of fairness, as sharing the burden in accordance with differential ability, with its highly questionable presupposition that everyone is equally responsible, though not everyone is equally able to contribute, as well as the inconsistent application of the logic of just deserts. We can also challenge the value premise by observing that, while being a rationally acceptable concern, fairness displaces other possible values. There is no talk of equality or justice in Osborne's speeches. As Meacher observes, politicians, both Conservative and New Labour, have eventually succeeded in pushing equality off the agenda altogether, and Peter Mandelson's declaration that 'New Labour is supremely relaxed about people becoming filthy rich' has summed up this tendency. The rich are now indeed filthy rich, thanks to New Labour, says Meacher (2010b), and inequalities in income and wealth in Britain are so staggering that no amount of personal effort, education or training can close the gap. After 13 years of New Labour, 70 per cent of the population (the 'squeezed middle') are earning between £12,000 and £30,000 a year, while a chief executive at a major bank has an income of £1.2 million, escalating to £5–10 million a year when bonuses and other benefits are added.

On the whole, the government's arguments are proceeding from a stated commitment to (and alleged actual concern for) *both* fairness and responsibility, and the latter is primarily understood in financial terms (financial sustainability). Constant invocation of this double commitment (and double concern) implies that alternative courses of action and alternative goals have been considered and that the action and goal that were eventually chosen are compatible with (and informed by) *both* these sources of normativity. Briefly, given that these are the guiding values and commitments, the government's argument implies that deliberation has not been a merely instrumental business of matching means to financial objectives (ends), but has involved consideration of several, competing ends of political action, informed by justifiable values, i.e. the goal of a fairer and more prosperous Britain, *simultaneously* with the goal of a Britain in which there is a balanced economy and the deficit has been successfully reduced. It has balanced together a goal defined primarily in terms of human well-being and one defined in terms of financial sustainability. The fact that both fairness and sustainability/responsibility are constantly mentioned together already gives an indication of the difficulty involved in balancing competing considerations and making a choice. Such formulations are presumably meant to indicate that at some point, in the process of balancing competing values and goals, something will need to be sacrificed, and that this should not be taken to mean that an unreasonable decision will emerge. In other words, that the austerity strategy cannot be easily challenged even when it seems to go against (what most people would see as) fairness, as the government (in Osborne's view) has to balance the equally legitimate commitments to financial responsibility, to the national interest, and short-term and long-term perspectives, and so on. For instance, actions which may not be in the interests of individual agents (and unfair on them) might be nevertheless reasonable because they are in the national interest, or in the interests of financial sustainability, and so on. This is to say that there has to be a reasonable compromise among conflicting and equally legitimate concerns and commitments.

To sum up, evaluating a political argument from the perspective of the value premise involves asking whether the values that ostensibly underlie the argument are acceptable from a dialectical point of view, i.e. whether they are rationally defensible, whether (for example) people would agree, at the end of a process of critical discussion, that they are conducive to human well-being; moreover, whether they would agree, given competing values, which values (hence which goals) should have normative priority, or which cannot be overridden. But if the values are found acceptable, the question still remains whether the goals and actions are really based on the stated values, and on a reasonable balancing of competing and equally legitimate values, as they claim to be; in other words, whether the argument is rather a rationalization, based on covert concerns, which merely appeals to legitimate values for rhetorical reasons.

Is the context of action defined in a rationally persuasive way?

In practical arguments, the circumstances of action are defined in a way that supports the conclusion and in accordance with a range of values or concerns. It serves the Chancellor's rhetorical goals to describe the context as one in which the government faces an 'emergency' and one for which the previous Labour government is responsible: 'the country was living beyond its means when the recession came'. Labour's responsibility for the state of public finances has been rejected by many commentators who have instead pointed to the responsibility of the banks in triggering the financial meltdown.

Labour is also blamed for failing to reform the welfare system. We have already looked at the argument in favour of welfare reform in the Emergency Budget. In the Spending Review, the argument is developed along similar lines:

> But the truth – as everyone knows – is that the welfare system is failing many millions of our fellow citizens. People find themselves trapped in an incomprehensible out-of-work benefit system for their entire lifetimes, because it simply does not pay to work. This robs them of their aspirations and opportunities . . ..

Clearly, the representation of the circumstances is rhetorically motivated, in the sense that it supports the proposal that the Chancellor is advocating and could not conceivably support any alternative strategy. The way in which the circumstances are described directs the argument towards one possible conclusion, by using evaluative terms and persuasive ways of defining or presenting the situation that preclude any other conclusion from being arrived at. This is done in a very subtle way in both the Budget and the Spending Review. Osborne is steering clear of the style of various right-wing newspapers writing about 'scroungers' and 'spongers' on benefits, and 'benefit cheats', and is not repeating his own mistake (earlier in September 2010) of castigating benefit claimants for making a 'lifestyle choice'. Instead, he is choosing to refer to people living on benefits as the victims of an inefficient and unfair system. As for what type of actions will solve these problems, these are not presented as simply removing benefits from people, but mostly as concrete steps in a reform plan designed to 'increase the incentives to work and reduce the incentives to stay out of work', a plan that is fair not only to welfare recipients but also to the working people whose taxes pay for the welfare system.

By making these choices, Osborne is arguably increasing the rhetorical appeal of his argument, adapting to the concerns of several audiences, but also, apparently, trying to maximize the argument's dialectical acceptability. He is apparently trying to be fair, unprejudiced, and see the issue from several perspectives. But from the point of view of a welfare recipient the argument is perverse: cutting welfare will not solve people's problems unless jobs that pay are really available. People are robbed of life chances not by the welfare system but by the lack of suitable employment. As press commentators have pointed out, 'maths doesn't seem to be the coalition's strong point' if they think that 2.4 million people can be squeezed into 459,000 vacancies, at a time when the big cuts have not even started (Hasan 2010). The argument is not dialectically acceptable if it is based on an incorrect diagnosis of the problem. In a context of few available jobs and rising unemployment, cutting welfare is not likely to improve the situation or make it less unfair.

In various other ways, critics of austerity have challenged the government's description of the context of action in order to support fiscal austerity and have argued that none of the circumstances that would normally require austerity measures is present in Britain at the moment. To that extent, those who are calling for immediate fiscal consolidation are misdescribing or misinterpreting the context: the relevant comparison, according to these critics, is with the USA in 1937, when early fiscal tightening drove it back into recession. Various critics of the government have also argued that there is no real evidence to suggest that bond markets are really concerned about budget deficits in the USA, UK or Germany, and therefore the government's description of the context of action as one of national emergency is false and misleading (Elliott 2010c).

Most commentators would nevertheless agree with the Chancellor that the UK economy has become 'deeply unbalanced', with the financial sector disproportionately large compared to manufacturing. Some circumstantial premises seem to be beyond dispute. But Osborne's analysis of the situation often seems to conflict with public opinion and documented facts. For example, he says: 'this country has over-spent, it has not been under-taxed'. Yet, as Toynbee and Walker (2008) among many others have convincingly argued, Britain is notorious for allowing the rich to be under-taxed and for failing to pursue tax avoidance and tax evasion.

Is the action represented in a rationally persuasive way?

Both in the Budget speech and in the Spending Review, the government's action is described in terms that aim to ensure its rhetorical success: it is 'tough but fair', it pays 'the bills of past irresponsibility', the 'debts of a failed past', and it also lays the 'foundations for a more prosperous future'. Crucially, it enables Britain to 'step back from the brink' and ensures that 'the financial catastrophe that happened under the previous Government' will never happen again. These are ways of describing the current and previous government's action, what it amounts to, in terms which direct the audience towards the arguer's conclusion, namely that the current government's action is the right action, while condemning the alternative strategy of the previous government.

Let us look at the opening lines of the Spending Review:

> Mr Speaker. Today's the day when Britain steps back from the brink. When we confront the bills from a decade of debt. A day of rebuilding when we set out a four-year plan to put our public services and welfare state on a sustainable footing . . . (. . .) It is a hard road, but it leads to a better future. We are going to bring the years of ever-rising borrowing to an end. We are going to ensure, like every solvent household in the country: that what we buy, we can afford; that the bills we incur, we have the income to meet; and that we do not saddle our children with the interest on the interest on the interest of the debts we were not ourselves prepared to pay.

How is the government's action represented? Or, to use Lakoff's (2002) term, how is it 'framed'? As saving Britain, as pulling the country back from the brink of disaster, as ushering in an age of reconstruction and strength, as the beginning of a difficult journey, yet one with a happy ending. The end of the speech also represents government action as restoring 'sanity' and 'stability' to public finances and the economy. The analogy between a country's finances and those of a household is also particularly significant and designed to increase the persuasiveness of the broader argument. We would not disagree that a household needs to be solvent, therefore we should presumably accept the Chancellor's strategy designed to ensure that Britain becomes solvent. The acceptability of this latter claim depends on whether the analogy itself is acceptable and, on this point, economists would disagree that the analogy holds. For a family or an individual business, it makes sense to cut costs, but if the world economy or the economy of a country tries to cut costs, this will shrink demand. In other words, 'an individual may not spend all his income. But the world must do so' (Wolf 2008).

All these are metaphorical re-descriptions or re-definitions of the government's strategy of action. The strategy (involving spending cuts and measures aimed at private-sector led growth, etc.) amounts to pulling Britain back from the brink of bankruptcy, saving the country, etc. We have seen how this strategy is defended argumentatively, in terms of the goals it will achieve starting from the current undesirable circumstances. But these representations of the action, although not, strictly speaking, part of any argument, also serve to justify the strategy. They do so by presenting it in a way that makes all argumentative support superfluous: there is no real need for defending an action if that action is represented in evaluative terms which strongly and exclusively recommend it. If the action is really equivalent to pulling Britain from the brink of disaster, the claim that the action should be performed, which will be made later on, does not really need defending. But is the rightness of the action so beyond doubt or is the arguer merely cleverly evading the burden of proof by presenting it in this way? In light of everything we have said, the latter seems to be the case. The representations in question have a clear rhetorical function, and may be quite effective from this point of view, but are not dialectically acceptable. For a strategy of action that has given rise to such controversy and therefore requires substantial defence, to be presented as *self-evidently* the one strategy that will save the country (and restore sanity, etc.) involves an unacceptable evasion of the responsibility to defend a highly controversial claim.

Most of the definitions above happen to involve metaphors and they are used to describe the action. Given that analyses of discourse in terms of metaphors, based on Lakoff's original cognitive theory of metaphor (Lakoff and Johnson 1980, 1981, Lakoff 1987, Lakoff and Turner 1989, Lakoff 2002) are an extremely productive area of language analysis (see for instance, most notably, Semino 2008), we would like to suggest how analysis of metaphor can be integrated with analysis of argumentation. The advantage of integrating analysis of metaphor with analysis of argument would be a clearer view of how the use of metaphor connects with human action, and what the (insufficiently defined) process of 'framing' actually amounts to.

There is no space to develop these suggestions in detail here, but here is the gist of our proposal. We suggest that metaphor is a persuasive definition and that it should be seen as part of argumentation by definition or by analogy, as a premise of the form '$a = b$', purporting to *describe* some aspect of reality or a future state of affairs. This description of reality can be part of a practical argument's circumstantial or goal premises and will support a claim which is consistent with the way in which that aspect has been described ('framed') in the premise in question. Seeing metaphor as part of an argument's premises thus explains how 'framing' works: to say that a discussion is 'framed' in a certain way is to acknowledge that the linguistic formulation of certain statements (premises) *favours* or *entails* certain other statements (conclusions) and not others. Thus, seeing the country in terms of a household will support certain claims and actions related to finance management and debt better than others. Of course, the cogency of such arguments depends on whether the equivalence or analogy that underlies them is defensible or not. As we said in Chapter 2, persuasive definitions (metaphor included) used as premises stand themselves in need of justification, and should be seen as claims of previous arguments. It is not often understood, or deliberately ignored, by arguers or audiences, that the equivalence (conceptual transfer, framing) that metaphors propose should not be taken for granted but should be critically examined, and these equivalences are often presented as objective, neutral descriptions of what the world is like.

Are the causes of the crisis represented in a rationally persuasive way?

Representations of the context of action (but also of other premises as well) are significant not only in relation to the argument being made, but also in relation to an explanation of the causes of the current situation. Explanations of why the situation is as it is, or why certain events have occurred are often embedded in arguments for action and are linked to the circumstantial premises. For example, the government has to cut spending (claim) because the country is running a huge deficit and owes over £170 bn (circumstances, facts) and these facts are the result of the previous government's policies (explanation). Strictly speaking, the fact expressed in the circumstantial premise is an *explanandum* to the *explanans* element of the explanation, namely the statement identifying the alleged cause of the debt and deficit. Understanding (or trying to accredit a version of) why the crisis happened will contribute to an argument about what action needs to be taken. The same is true for the function of narrative in relation to argument: the way the story is told produces alternative 'facts' (circumstantial premises) that can be used in alternative arguments for what should be done. Re-writing history serves political ends.

Explanations are relevant to analysis of argument and therefore to normative critique. The reason, we suggest, is that explanations can be embedded in an implicit argument of legitimation: to attribute responsibility to another party means that you are not to blame, and this can serve a legitimation strategy. The Coalition government has exploited and reinforced the public perception of the previous government as being responsible for the crisis and for the spending cuts, in order to legitimize their own position and delegitimize that of the opposition.

The past and current governments have been for some time now engaged in a 'blame game', with public opinion and economic and political commentators taking sides with either camp. In an article in *The Guardian*, Jonathan Freedland (2010) suggested the following explanation for the British population's apparent passivity in the face of cuts: 'right now, even those people who fear and loathe the government's cuts don't blame the government', but believe that, 'however painful the government's actions, they are merely the unavoidable consequence of Labour recklessness'. The case against the cuts won't be made convincingly until Labour manages to win the blame game and explode the 'myth . . . . that Brown, not bankers, caused our economic woes'. Paul Mason has also repeatedly emphasized that the causes of the crisis must not be forgotten: the current crisis is 'the product of giant hubris and the untrammelled power of a financial elite' (Mason 2010: 173).

Labour politicians have also tried to convince the public of the same view. In his recent Bloomberg lecture (August 2010), Ed Balls declared that 'it is a question of fact that we entered this financial crisis with low inflation, low interest rates, low unemployment and the lowest net debt of any large G7 country'. It was not a mistake to rescue the banking system and increase borrowing. This is not to say that Labour has not made mistakes. At a time when the Conservatives were clamouring for less regulation of the City, Labour 'should have ignored Tory and City claims that we were being too tough on financial regulation and been much tougher still' (Balls 2010). A similar account, including an acknowledgement of Labour's 'serious mistakes' – the Iraq war, but also its failure to regulate banks and its neglect of Britain's manufacturing base – was made by Ed Milliband, the Labour leader, in a recent speech (Milliband 2011). (For an analysis of 'Labour's mistakes', see Elliott 2010b.)

By contrast, according to Jeff Randall, from *The Daily Telegraph*, Labour leaders need to be constantly reminded where the deficit came from. It came from excessive spending and from running an ever-increasing and unjustified deficit in good years, from 'jet-hosing public services with taxpayers' money'. In Britain, he says, 'living on borrowed money', 'excessive consumption and 'irresponsible state spending' have been for too long mistaken for normal behaviour (Randall 2010e). In Randall's words, New Labour's success over the last decades was 'a sham, based on a simple formula: spend more than we earn; pass off consumption as investment; wallow in self congratulation' (Randall 2010a). Labour should put a stop to its 'revisionist' attempt to deny they are to blame, says Jeremy Warner, also of *The Daily Telegraph*. For decades, Labour and the banks were locked in a 'Faustian pact': as long as the banks continued to produce tax revenues for Labour's political projects, they could do what they wanted. But neither can the Conservatives claim they were not 'complicit', as they opposed all Labour's attempts to tighten financial regulation, and thus lamentably failed to oppose the more fundamental 'mischief' that was going on under the Labour government: the 'ruinous credit expansion' that underlay Labour's alleged economic success (Warner 2011a).

Conclusion

In this chapter we have tried to give an overview of the two main arguments for action that have been advanced by the previous Labour government and the current Coalition government, and of the way the debate between the supporters and opponents of austerity has unfolded in the British press and other institutional settings. We have analysed the arguments in terms of the structure of practical reasoning we are proposing in this book and we have tried to suggest how they may be evaluated in terms of our dialectical framework. We have also selectively drawn on the wider public debate in which these strategies have been continuously evaluated. We have juxtaposed our own analytical normativity to the normativity invoked by various participants in the debate over these strategies, and tried to view their arguments in terms of our own analytical framework. This, in our view, confirms the interpretive and explanatory validity of our framework for analysing and evaluating practical reasoning. There is, in other words, empirical confirmation that people's conception of what would constitute a reasonable practical argument is not essentially different from the analytical and normative model we suggest.

We quoted Martin Wolf as saying that only time will tell whether the current government's strategy will achieve the desired effects. The test for the government's strategy lies in the consequences it will produce as it unfolds. Already, the negative impact on employment and living standards seems to be considerable and does not justify the chosen policy unless it is really the case that all alternatives have been exhausted. Emerging data for growth in the spring of 2011 seem to reinforce the view that, in Wolf's words, 'fiscal contraction is unlikely to prove expansionary', consequently that the UK is headed for 'economic stagnation, or worse' and 'it is optimistic to expect very much better than that'. Britain's fiscal policy at the moment is 'a huge gamble'. On the contrary, there is evidence that the strategy is not working (this is not surprising, critics observe, as 'expansionary austerity' has not worked in the past either): real incomes have significantly fallen, consumer spending has slumped, inflation is much higher than predicted and unemployment is growing. The private sector has not yet surged to fill the gaps created by public sector cuts, desirable export-led growth is less vigorous than hoped due to depressed markets in the EU, the level of aggregate demand in the economy is low, banks are not lending and big companies are not borrowing, while forecasts regarding deficit reduction have already been revised. As we have seen, reasonable alternatives have been proposed, yet the government has decided that there is no alternative. It is, on the other hand, impossible to know how Labour's strategy would have panned out, as 'the alternative is the road not taken' (Wolf 2011d). As for the government's growth strategy, while 'its broad directions are sensible', how much difference it will actually make is uncertain, given what the facts are, after decades of 'unsustainable' development 'driven by market forces' irresponsibly encouraged by *both* political parties: the 'grim reality' is that there is no 'growth fairy' and Britain 'faces a hard slog' (Wolf 2011c).

In the arguments for and against austerity, we have found that critics of austerity challenged (implicitly) both the validity of the argument (e.g. the necessary or sufficient character of the means advocated) and the rational acceptability of the claim, by showing that probable or actual negative consequences are casting strong doubt on this claim and indicating that the government should *not* go ahead with its strategy. Regarding the former type of challenge, involving an attempt to *defeat* the argument, critics have for instance pointed to other desirable goals, e.g. a new restructured economic system (rather than returning to business-as-usual), and to alternative action that would deliver economic recovery more efficiently: massive public investment in infrastructure and green energy sources, a job-creation programme rather than spending cuts. To the extent that these are rationally acceptable alternatives, and also better alternatives, failure to show that other goals and other means have been properly considered defeats the government's argument for action. The latter type of challenge, the attempt to *rebut* the claim (and thus support the counter-argument), appeals to highly probable consequences and can be particularly strong when actually emerging negative consequences can be invoked, as these can conclusively falsify the claim. The rational acceptability of the premises has also been challenged, particularly of the representation of the context of action, as well as the relation between premises, e.g. between values and goals, as well as between values and action.

However, just as the previous government, the current government is engaged in an attempt to legitimize a strategy of action in terms of shared and publicly justifiable values. Decisions for action are shown to have emerged from a process of deliberation, of considering and weighing appropriate goals for action and the values that should inform them. Appeals to fairness are meant to show that deliberation was not purely instrumental, but involved a more-than-instrumental rationality in which moral considerations were taken into account, including existing political commitments recognized as binding and other considerations of the effect of action on human well-being. It is not only financial sustainability that is an overriding concern, in other words, but fairness as well, and these conflicting demands have been adequately balanced together, so that political action might be compatible with and informed by both. This is precisely what the government's critics would challenge, in observing that there has been no deliberation on goals, on the ends of political action, and no real concern for fairness. Not only is the government's argument a purely instrumental attempt to match means to a pre-defined end, an end which they refuse to question even in the face of competing alternatives, but it also tries to rationalize the pursuit of an ideological goal as involving a concern for fairness, and thus to disguise the real ideological or self-interested reasons for action.

To conclude, the government's vision for the future of Britain, as well as the strategy designed to achieve it, have not been found rationally persuasive by the government's critics:

other political goals ought to be considered, and have not been; there are reasonable alternatives that should be considered but have not been. There is a strong probability that the strategy will misfire and fail to achieve its stated goals, and will end up sacrificing goals that should not be sacrificed. Even in the case of those directions of policy that seem highly desirable (a balanced economy, based on a strong manufacturing sector), how these goals may be achieved is not yet clear on the basis of current circumstances and proposed actions. Overall, the combination of goals, values, circumstances and presumptive means seems insufficient to make the claim rationally persuasive, given the existence of alternatives and goals that have not been properly explored, stated value concerns that do not seem to fit in with the actual action, and the high risk of negative consequences affecting living standards, life chances, and other legitimate concerns that should not be overridden.

5 Values as premises in the public debate over bankers' bonuses

In *The Idea of Justice*, Amartya Sen (2009: 12–15) imagines a situation in which a decision has to be made as to which of three children ought to receive a particular gift, a flute. One child argues that she ought to receive it because she is the only one that can play it. Another child says the flute should be given to him because he is poor and has no toys to play with. The third child claims she deserves to get the flute because she has actually made it. How is one to decide between these three legitimate claims, between these three reasonable arguments? As Sen argues, there is no one institutional arrangement that will help us resolve this dispute in a universally accepted manner, no unique impartial resolution. The choice an agent might eventually make will depend on the relative value he or she attaches to the fulfilment of human virtue, the fight against poverty or inequality and the entitlement to enjoy the results of one's labour. It will depend on that agent's actual values or concerns, and on which value or concern, i.e. which particular conception of justice should take precedence over others in his or her view. Giving priority to one or another of these three rival conceptions of justice will result in radically different future outcomes. Yet all three particular *conceptions* make a claim to impartiality and are all ultimately non-arbitrary and reasonable. As we will argue later, they all embody a *concept* of justice.

In this chapter[1] we will look more closely at values as premises in practical arguments. As the above example shows, our values (and our actual concerns to fulfil them) underlie our goals, the futures we imagine and try to bring about, and thereby the actions we undertake. In Chapter 2, we said that the value premise specifies the particular source of normativity that underlies the goal premise and that we can imagine goals in relation to what we actually desire but also in relation to moral values and other external reasons (duties, commitments). Honesty, for instance, is a socially recognized, legitimate value that can motivate action: an actual concern for honesty will make an agent act in a certain way. But even when the agent is not concerned to act honestly, and therefore does not, there is still a sense in which it can be claimed that he *had a reason to be honest* and he therefore ought to have acted honestly. In our view, moral values, as well as duties, obligations, commitments can appear in arguments as (social, institutional) facts, in factual (circumstantial) premises, or as actual concerns, in motivational premises, or as both. We will illustrate our view of how values enter as premises in arguments by analysing a fragment of the wide-ranging public debate (in the UK) on whether or not bankers should continue to receive bonuses. We will focus on the government's perceived *commitment to justice* as a reason that the government can be said to have regardless of whether it is actually concerned to act accordingly or not. We will therefore distinguish between reasons for action having to do with what agents *want to do* (their actual concerns) and reasons having to do with what they are *bound to do* in light of existing institutional or moral orders which they are part of. This corresponds to the distinction drawn by philosophers between internal and external reasons, or desire-dependent and desire-independent reasons. We will continue this discussion in the last section of Chapter 6, where we illustrate how *political promises* function as (external, desire-independent) reasons for action by examining widespread public criticism of Liberal-Democratic Party over their breaking of the electoral promise not to increase tuition fees.

Moral values, duties and commitments as external reasons for action: justice and the 'social contract'

The main argument we develop in this chapter can be summed up as follows. A *concern* to act in accordance with some (moral–political) value or in accordance with a commitment or obligation is part of the value premise of the argument (in other words, the value premise that underlies the goal is a motivational premise). For example, the government may be actually concerned with achieving fairness and this is why it may act in certain ways and not others. But the socially recognized *obligation* to act in accordance with such values (e.g. the government's *duty* to act justly) or the *promises* and *commitments* that agents (politicians, the government, citizens) are bound by, as *facts*, are part of the circumstantial premise. They are *institutional facts*, created by people themselves in accepting various institutional roles, and are part of a *social contract* between citizens, and between citizens and the state. They are *legitimate*, publicly recognized values, duties and commitments, part of the normative fabric of society. In a modern democratic state, for example, people expect politicians to be bound by the promises they make and expect the institutions of the state to act justly and treat them as equals. Action based on such reasons is legitimate both because a concern with doing one's duty or fulfilling one's obligations enjoys public recognition, but also because such reasons can be argumentatively and publicly justified as institutional facts, regardless of whether agents (the government, politicians) *want* to act in accordance with them or not. It is in fact on this basis that actions which violate such values, duties and commitments can be criticized. Nick Clegg, the Liberal-Democrat leader, has not been publicly reviled for no longer being *concerned* with fulfilling his electoral promises: it is not the absence of relevant *desire* that is important here, but the perceived infringement of a desire-independent obligation incurred as part of a previous *contract* with the citizens.

Moral–political values and institutional facts appear in two ways in practical arguments in our view: in the circumstantial premise – as they are socially constructed, epistemically objective *facts* – and in the value premise, as actual *concerns* that the agent has or is motivated by. Briefly, if I have made a promise, that promise is a fact that cannot be undone; I may be concerned with its realization and thus act accordingly, or I may not, in which case I will not act to fulfil it. In the latter case, the fact of the promise will remain an (uninternalized) external reason and, in this sense, I will continue to have it as a reason. It is therefore reasonable for others to hold me responsible for breaking my promise.

A comment made by Vince Cable (2009) on the crisis raises the question of values in a way that is strikingly compatible with our view:

> The problems faced by some countries, especially Britain and the USA, are nor just technical and economic, but represent a blow to the *underlying value system, the social contract*. Most people's sense of fairness and equity had already been assaulted by widening extremes of wealth and income. By 2007, (. . .) [t]he income of the world's richest 500 billionaires exceeded that of the world's poorest 420 million people. However, widening

inequality (. . .) has been tolerated and politically endorsed, because it appeared to be a consequence of economic progress. A rising tide lifted all boats, it was argued, even if the biggest boats derived the biggest benefits. The rich should get richer, because they were seen to be applying entrepreneurial talents that, apparently, benefited the common good – even if some of them were rogues. (. . .) That now has changed. A lot of people are getting hurt: hard-working, thrifty, law-abiding people. Many are losing their jobs, their homes and businesses. (. . .) Yet the losers can see that some of those who made a fortune in bonuses brought their banks to their knees, and that those banks are now being rescued by the taxpayer. The reckless and incompetent are being rewarded, the prudent and socially responsible punished. Therein lies a great sense of unfairness . . . .

(Cable 2009: 127–128, our italics)

Moral–political values such as justice are part of the modern social arrangement, of the modern *social contract* between state and citizens, and their objectivity and binding nature cannot be ignored. Yet, as Cable observes, the crisis and its aftermath have violated taken for granted commitments of the state towards its citizens. Citizens are therefore justified in thinking that the state is being unjust in making the population pay for a crisis they did not cause, while failing to punish the banks and fundamentally reform the economic system.

This chapter will look at some of the ways in which ordinary citizens, in comments threads or discussion forums, have expressed their own views about who is responsible and therefore should pay for the crisis, how the crisis has been handled by the state and how this has violated citizens' legitimate expectations of justice. As we will see, ordinary people's arguments invoke publicly shared, legitimate values as objective, external constraints on action that the state ought not to ignore.

A prudential argument for inequality: inequality is in the general interest

Let us draw a distinction between two types of concerns that motivate action, corresponding to a distinction made in philosophy between two types of practical reasoning, 'prudential' and 'moral' (Gauthier 1963). Prudential arguments take the agent's desires (wants), needs or interests as premises: if the agent desires a certain outcome (or thinks that outcome is in his interest), then a certain course of action is recommended; if he doesn't desire the outcome (or thinks the outcome is not in his interest), then he has no reason to do the action. Moral arguments do not seem to have this conditional (hypothetical) structure, they present an action as necessary in itself, regardless of the agent's desires or interests, simply because it is the right thing to do. Prudential reasoning (in Gauthier's view) corresponds to Kant's hypothetical imperative, while moral reasoning corresponds to his categorical imperative.

In this and the following sections we are going to look at practical arguments over bankers' bonuses: arguments in favour and against the view that banks should continue to pay bonuses to bank employees in the aftermath of the financial crisis. We will first look at a debate organized by St Paul's Institute and hosted by St Paul's Cathedral (2009, 20 October) in London,[2] which focused on the responsibility of banks in the current crisis and the broader issue of 'markets and morality'. We will examine some of the arguments made by the panellists: Vince Cable, then Liberal-Democrat Deputy Leader (currently Business Secretary in the Coalition government); (Lord) Brian Griffith, Vice-Chairman of Goldman Sachs

International, and (Lord) Adair Turner, then Chair of the Financial Services Authority, in response to one of the questions asked by the audience: 'Should bankers be made to pay for the bailout, rather than keeping their profits and bonuses?' Then, we will consider how a section of the general public seems to perceive the question of bonuses by analysing *The Guardian*'s comments thread in response to the brief report of this debate on 21 October 2009.[3]

The first question addressed to the panelists was 'What good does the City do?', and the speakers expressed a relative consensus on the fact that the free market, including the complex financial system that is central to it, performs valuable and economically useful functions and is the best mechanism for delivering prosperity to billions of people across the world. All speakers agreed that, in the words of Adam Smith, 'good results can derive from self-interested actions'. But, as Adair Turner observed, trading and financial activities can grow beyond their economically useful size. In Britain, he said, the financial sector has attracted to itself revenue and profit beyond those required to provide economically useful functions and this was essentially a 'transfer of income from the rest of the economy to the financial services sector'. This is why, in his view, a convincing argument can be made for an increased role of regulation and taxation to counter that income transfer effect and ensure that 'the useful activities predominate over the useless'. Brian Griffith expressed his reservations regarding Turner's idea that more regulation can prevent crises from happening. Instead, he pointed to the 'culture of banks and of financial institutions' – a culture of excessive risk and social irresponsibility – and to the 'failed moral compass of bankers' as the main culprits for the crisis: this is what needs reforming, in his view. In one of his interventions, Vince Cable pointed out that seemingly unchallengeable economic assumptions have been proved wrong in the aftermath of the crisis and that, in addition to market failures, there have been serious failures by regulators and governments. Consequently, not everything can be laid at the door of banks. But the moral issue Cable chose to address was that of the extraordinary payments that are still being made in the City:

> On the issue of rewards, realism . . . tells me that people are very angry. Of course, they are also angry with politicians but I think particularly angry at the gross inequality of rewards in society. . . . There have been rewards for failure; the RBS management is completely inexcusable. There have been rewards for excessive risk taking . . .. But there is an additional problem we're now seeing, of banks, which are basically dependent on tax-payers support, paying out very large rewards to their executives and others. I think this is something that the public find impossible to understand. If this was a purely competitive market, people were operating as entrepreneurs who are likely to fail and go down with their ship as necessary, that's one thing. But when you have banks that are underwritten by the state it is not acceptable to have the kind of reward structures that operate at present. (. . .) I don't think we can tolerate a system where the British government, the tax-payer, acts as guarantor of last resort to banks that are trying to operate on a global scale, often in very risky operations. I think we have not yet bitten the bullet of deciding that some of these institutions are going to have to be broken up.

Another question was: 'Who should pay when the markets get it wrong and why?', in response to which Turner reiterated the need for tougher bank regulation, while Cable emphasized the need for a fair and efficient taxation system and voiced his concern that people who have no responsibility for the crisis are in fact being made to pay for it:

I just wanted to focus on this question about who pays, because this is becoming a very big public concern. A lot of people are paying a heavy price for this crisis, and it's people who are completely unconnected with it. The government's paying, and eventually you will all have to pay in reduced services or higher taxes. A lot of young graduates are leaving universities without jobs. The pain is being felt by people who didn't cause the crisis in any meaningful sense. So, we are then faced with the question of how you make the people pay who caused the problem? That's, I think, what people are groping for. How do you do it in a rational way? We have now got this big cry going out for a windfall tax as a way of getting the guilty to pay . . . (. . .) If we are trying to get a just settlement, some kind of reparations for this crisis, it has to be resolved through some form of progressive taxation . . .. Very high earners will pay more. The problem is, under our system, there are so many loop-holes through lower rates of capital gains tax, and in other ways, that very often they don't and it is the responsibility of government to make sure that happens . . ..

This is how Brian Griffiths, Vice-Chairman of Goldman Sachs, addressed the question about who should pay for the crisis:

When it comes to the question of bankers paying for the bailout, I think at a personal level some have paid very expensively . . .. But I come back to one point I was trying to make earlier, and it particularly applies to compensation and it applies to the common good . . . I think it is very easy to construct a short-term perception of what the common good is. Let's assume, for example, we all said we're not going to have big bonuses, they're going to be even the same as – let's say – last year. I believe you would then find that leading City firms could easily hive off operations to Switzerland, to the Far East. Never forget that the UK economy, that London as a financial centre, is very different from somewhere like New York or Tokyo. In London, we have – in the UK – a relatively small economy and a large financial sector. In New York, they have a large financial sector but based on a very large economy – in Tokyo, the same. I believe that we should be thinking about the medium term common good, not the short-term common good, and in thinking about the medium-term common good we should be making sure that, going forward, at least one cluster of industries we have is the financial sector. We should be proud of that in London, and we should not therefore be ashamed of offering compensation in an internationally competitive market which ensures the business is here and employs British people.

He developed this argument further in his final intervention, which concluded the evening:

The first and I think the most serious issue at present is the issue of social cohesion. I grew up in Wales, in a mining community, and both my grandfathers were injured underground. I think I can honestly understand, I can say I really understand inequality personally.

If I felt that the present situation of rising unemployment, of high youth unemployment, of almost despair in some ways – and then the City on the other hand – was a permanent feature of our society, frankly I would find it very difficult to defend the City. But what I've tried to say is I'm not a person of despair, I'm a person of hope, and I think that we have to tolerate the inequality as a way to achieving greater prosperity and opportunity for all. That's the only way I can reconcile the two issues [markets and morality].

Secondly, I think we all have to ask ourselves – in whatever institution we work – what is your moral compass and what is my moral compass? There will always come a time when you and I will have to stand up and be counted, and sometimes that is very difficult, can be very embarrassing and can be very painful – but I think that is what we have to do, and this evening has confirmed for me the need to examine my own moral compass more and more.

The event was widely reported in the press the following day. However, only the last intervention, by Griffith, was mentioned in any detail, and headlines everywhere quoted his view that people should 'learn to tolerate inequality' as a way to greater prosperity for all of us. *The Daily Telegraph* headline was: *Goldman Sachs vice-chairman says: 'Learn to tolerate inequality'*, and the journalists went on to say that 'One of Goldman Sachs's senior advisers in London has said that British taxpayers should "tolerate the inequality" stemming from the investment bank's plans to dole out a record $22bn (£13.4bn) in pay and bonuses this year for the sake of the "common good"' (Quinn and Hall 2009). Also in *The Daily Telegraph*, Jonathan Russell (2009) asked: *Has Goldman Sachs's Lord Griffiths been reading George Orwell . . . before he offered the world his thoughts on bankers' bonuses?* and quoted from Orwell:

> In chapter three of *Animal Farm*, Squealer told the animals: 'The whole management and organization of this farm depend on us. Day and night we are watching over your welfare. It is for your sake that we drink that milk and eat those apples.'

The *Guardian* headline said: *Public must learn to 'tolerate the inequality' of bonuses, says Goldman Sachs vice-chairman*, and continued as follows: 'Bankers' soaring pay is an investment in the economy, Lord Griffiths tells public meeting on City morality . . . One of the City's leading figures has suggested that inequality created by bankers' huge salaries is a price worth paying for greater prosperity' (Hopkins 2009). The *Guardian* article provided several quotations from Griffith's interventions and added the information that Goldman Sachs was 'on track to pay the biggest ever bonuses to its 31,700 employees after raking in profits at a rate of $35m (£21m) a day', which means that 'City bonuses could soar to £6bn this year'. It also mentioned Lord Turner's reiterated support for a global tax on financial transactions and his insistence on the need for stricter bank regulation.

This news item was subsequently picked up widely by the UK and international press and received a lot of commentary in discussions forum, blogs, etc. Within a couple of days, there were 313 comments on *The Guardian*'s website following Hopkins' report, with a record of 48 comments deleted by moderators for unacceptably offensive language. Apparently, *Guardian* readers were almost unanimously outraged at Griffith's views. The discussion on the forum was carried explicitly in terms of justice and injustice, and people were revolted at what they saw as 'blackmail': if we don't get our bonuses, we will move abroad. Many commentators urged each other to 'call the bankers' bluff', encourage them to leave, and offered to provide travel expenses, ships, submarines and torpedoes. There was also a lot of talk of revolution and a call for hanging the bankers.

As we have seen, Griffith's argument was in favour of tolerating inequality (i.e. tolerating bonuses and high pay for bankers) in view of the goal of prosperity and opportunity for all and of a concern for the ('medium-term', not 'short-term') common good. The argument was thus a *prudential* justification of inequality: people should tolerate it because it is

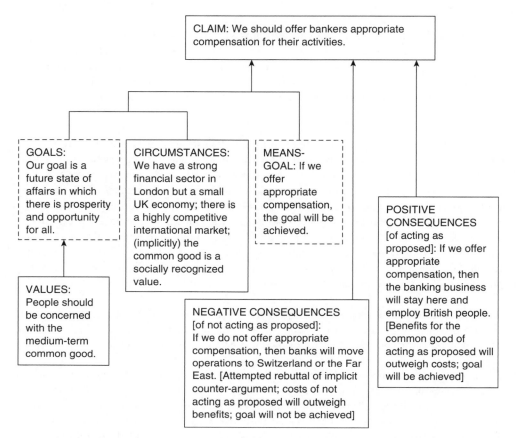

Figure 5.1 Goldman Sachs Vice-Chairman's prudential argument in favour of bankers' bonuses.

eventually in everyone's interest. In other words, people may think that inequality should not be tolerated, but this would correspond to a short-sighted perception of their interests. What *really is* in their interests, and in everyone's interest, and can deliver a future of prosperity and opportunity for all, is inequality. The argument was made in two stages (see the two passages we quoted above, from the middle of the debate and the very end) and, in its first formulation, can be represented as in Figure 5.1.

The argument attempts to justify allowing appropriate 'compensation' for bankers, from a desirable concern for the 'medium-term common good' and the implicit goal of a future of general prosperity in which this medium-term common good is served, as well as from the circumstances of the UK having a strong financial sector that is operating in a highly competitive international market (as well as a comparatively small economy). The claim is also supported by invoking the negative consequences that would ensue if bankers were not remunerated properly (the banks might 'hive off' operations to Switzerland or the Far East) and the positive consequences of acting as proposed (they will stay here and employ British people). Implicitly, therefore, the argument is the outcome a previous deliberative process, in which the counter-argument has been considered, and the benefits and costs of each of the two options have been weighed against each other. The claim has implicitly emerged as

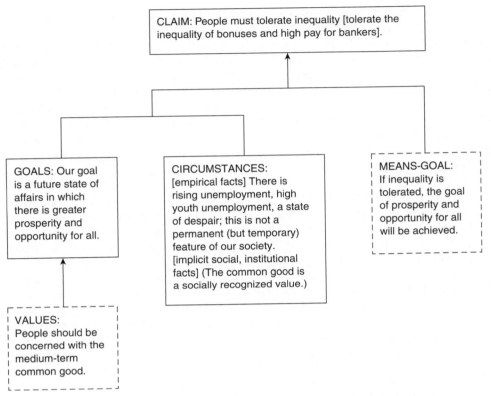

Figure 5.2 Goldman Sachs Vice-Chairman's prudential argument for tolerating inequality.

comparatively better: the costs of *not* offering bankers appropriate compensation would be higher, and the benefits for the common good of acting as proposed would be considerable (the financial sector will stay in Britain and employ British people). Moreover, in Griffith's view, such prudential considerations should outweigh any moral discomfort: we should pay bankers properly and *not be ashamed of doing so* either. Implicitly, the moral costs of the proposal are less significant than the material advantages obtained.

The second formulation (Figure 5.2) restates the claim as saying that people ought to tolerate the inequality of bankers' pay and bonuses. The claim is based on the goal of a future of prosperity and opportunity for all and on current circumstances having to do with 'rising unemployment' and 'despair'. There is no explicit value premise in this second formulation, but we can assume that there is an underlying concern for everyone's prosperity and opportunity, equivalent to a concern for the common good, as in the previous formulation.

Argument evaluation: the 'trickle-down' defence of inequality as blackmail

This section and the next are concerned with the way in which *Guardian* readers evaluated Griffith's argument in favour of inequality in the comments thread following Hopkins's

(2009) article.[4] Several people identified Griffith's argument as a defence of 'trickle-down' economics and rejected it on the basis of empirical evidence: people have always 'tolerated inequality' for the sake of an increase in general prosperity (or economic growth), yet this has now resulted in worldwide recession and a dramatic decrease in prosperity. In other words, the actual consequences of pursuing a form of 'trickle-down' economics over several decades have invalidated the argument that could be made in favour of it (more precisely, they have conclusively rebutted the claim that inequality ought to be tolerated). The 'trickle-down' conception is therefore false, and so is the claim that inequality ought to be tolerated: tolerating inequality has not led to an increase in prosperity for all but has in fact undermined that goal. Some comments also questioned the possibility and desirability of 'infinite growth', or challenged it as spurious notion, by pointing out that it has been fuelled by debt and house price inflation:

> *MichaelZ* 21 Oct 2009, 3:45PM. So hold on a minute, we have a recession that completely discredits 'trickle-down' economics, and is only averted from getting even worse by granting tax payers' money to the very institutions that caused the crash – and Griffith argues for more 'trickle-down' economics. Just how out-of-touch with reality are these people? . . .. We've 'tolerated' inequality for a good few decades now, and is Britain any more prosperous? . . .. The working people saw 'wealth' built on debt (effectively Monopoly money) and an utterly insane period of house price inflation . . ..
>
> *Zerozero* 22 Oct 2009, 12:37PM. (. . .) What this man says is stupendously and obviously wrong – the wealth was not created but squandered and used selfishly and we are all left impoverished by these people, who now get bigger bonuses!!!! There is no 'trickle down', there is a 'trickle up' definitely.
>
> *BuddyBaker* 21 Oct 2009, 2:26PM. Don't these people ever ask themselves why we need our economies to keep growing? I suppose they think in phrases like 'a rising tide lifts all boats' and 'trickle-down' economics. But after all these years of GDP growth, is the average person in Britain really much better off than 30 years ago? I say thee nay. Instead we've just seen rising inequality, and a few people have become stupidly rich . . .. You can't have infinite growth. I don't even understand why you'd want infinite growth.

Some readers equated 'trickle-down' economics with a 'scam', a 'Ponzi scheme'. This amounts to saying that the argument in favour of inequality is in fact a rationalization: the real reasons are not the overt reasons. The way in which the entire banking system works is in fact a scam and a confidence trick, some people said, and what is happening has to do more with the 'middle ages', rather than with a modern society. Comments along these lines introduce a moral factor (as well as an allusion to the modern 'social contract', which requires justice and equality): what bankers have done involves massive deceit, and they themselves do not believe that the reasons they publicly offer in defence of an unequal system are genuine reasons:

> *MorrisZap* 21 Oct 2009, 2:18PM. Griffiths said the British public should 'tolerate the inequality as a way to achieve greater prosperity for all'. 'Trickle-down' never worked. It was always a scam for a bunch of (. . .) greedy, incompetent, lying bastards, to justify their outrageous salaries which they try to avoid paying tax on in any case . . .. If Lord Griffiths went back to his childhood mining town and attempted to justify his claim, he'd be shoved down a mineshaft (. . .). I think Griffiths will find that we have reached the end of our tolerance.

teganjovanka 21 Oct 2009, 4:58PM. 'Trickle up' economics actually. As in all the wealth of society trickles up to a tiny minority of thieving kleptocrats at the top of society, pulling their complex banking Ponzi scheme on us yet again. And we never ever learn, do we? We actually fall for the idea we somehow need these people to be prosperous, when the exact opposite is the truth.

AlsoRan 21 Oct 2009, 2:40PM. What prosperity is that then, the prosperity enjoyed by him and his greedy self-serving bastard banker mates? Not the rest of us, obviously, especially those who have been flung out of their jobs as a consequence of his trade? We've discovered that claims of the bankers are nothing more than lies, and their vaunted 'prosperity' is nothing more than an illusion and a scam on the rest of us. No surprise that we're angry.

SeanThorp 21 Oct 2009, 2:55PM. Every time I hear the banksters have something to say I think of this: the fractional reserve banking system allows these people to create up to ten times more debt money than the amount of actual real money that they hold. That means when anybody goes for a mortgage the money, or rather the debt, is created out of thin air. Now on top of this money that the banksters did not have in the first place the mortgage holder must also pay a huge amount of interest that is often greater than the debt itself. Of course the money paid to service the debt and the interest is not made up out of the air, it is real. What I'd like to know is how this scam from the middle ages is still legal in the modern era? Unwarranted bonuses seem to pale in comparison to the continued legality of this confidence trick.

Aleksandrow 21 Oct 2009, 8:51PM. (. . ..) It is quite clear that the lords of the middle ages – aggressive, violent, ignorant and without any kind of moral values – live on today. Griffiths said the British public should 'tolerate the inequality as a way to achieve greater prosperity for all'. (. . .) Greater prosperity for all??!! All who??!!

Another substantial set of comments address Griffith's argument in explicit moral terms. Quite a few readers were outraged at what they perceived as blackmail in Griffith's warning that bankers might move their operations to other countries if not rewarded properly. Some of these responses challenged the truth of the presumptive negative consequences. Will these consequences really occur? And if they did, will they really be significantly negative? And is it really plausible that bankers will leave if they lost their bonuses? Others were indignant at the idea that bankers are allowed to make such threats and hold the country to ransom:

Ebert 21 Oct 2009, 2:24PM. Griffiths said that many banks would relocate abroad if the government cracked down on bonus culture . . ... The morality of the blackmailer – so let's call his bluff.

salofinkelstein 21 Oct 2009, 2:38PM. What Griffiths is saying amounts to making a direct threat. Just shows you who runs the country doesn't it? Spot on, Ebert, let's call the bankers' bluff. That's what should have happened in the first place: protect people's savings but let the banks collapse.

FranchiseThis 21 Oct 2009, 2:28PM. . . ... So is he trying to say that the entire home-grown financial services sector with their mansions in Gerrards Cross and Chelsea season tickets will decamp en masse with their privately educated children to Lausanne, or Hong Kong? Do me a favour.

sproutboy 21 Oct 2009, 2:21PM. I would gladly chip in for the airfare for these human parasites to be shipped off to Switzerland and the Far East. We will not miss them. If a less-well off but fairer Britain is the price for getting shot of them, it's a price worth paying.

> *Alebob* 21 Oct 2009, 2:17PM . . .. Let him relocate abroad. In fact let's charter a ship and get rid of them all.

> *Goto100* 21 Oct 2009, 2:39PM . . .. You organize the ship. I'll organize the submarine and the torpedo.

Let us now look more closely at what 'trickle-down' economics says. One of the readers ('pminwaiting', 21 Oct 2009, 3:18PM) defines it, quoting Galbraith, as 'the less than elegant metaphor that if one feeds the horse enough oats, some will pass through to the road for the sparrows'. According to political philosophers, the 'trickle-down' conception says that 'inequality is justified because it promotes economic growth, thereby benefiting even the poorest members of society'. Given that people are motivated by economic incentives, trying to equalize and excessively redistribute resources will cause the most hard-working people to lose the incentives to produce as much as they might if they were allowed to keep the results of their labour. A better way of helping the poor is then to promote economic growth. 'Even if their share of the overall pie remains the same, perhaps even if it gets smaller, the pie will be growing at such a rate that the absolute size of their piece will be growing'. Instead of 'minding the gap' between the rich and the poor (relative inequality), we should be concerned with improving the position of the worst-off members of society in absolute terms. We should therefore be concerned with growth, not (re)distribution, and growth is made possible by *in*equality (Swift 2006: 110).

Guardian readers, as we have seen, rejected Griffith's argument and identified it with blackmail. On this point, political philosophers would agree. Swift (2006) also discusses 'trickle-down' as essentially blackmail. People who defend it, he shows, are saying something along the following lines: unless some people are paid more than others, people will have no incentive to do certain jobs that benefit all of us; these jobs are essential for growth and a bigger pie will increase the size of everybody's slice; if some people are not paid more, the system will collapse; so inequality actually helps everyone, including the worst-off members of society. But this, he shows, already presupposes that people's motivations have to do with selfish interest for economic advantage and not with a desire to maximize benefits for others or the common good. Swift argues that 'trickle-down' might make sense as a realistic *description* of how people would behave if incentives were removed and everyone were paid the same, but it cannot provide a coherent *justification* of inequality. Yet this is how its advocates want to use it, to justify inequality in terms of benefits for everyone. The double motivation (self-interest or other people's interest?) makes 'trickle-down' economics ultimately incoherent. Demanding incentive payments in order to do a job that will benefit the others amounts to holding people to ransom. I can be perfectly justified in paying a lot of money to those who are holding my child hostage, but it does not mean that the final distribution of money, after I've paid them off, is justified or fair (Swift 2006: 125–127). We may say that a good prudential argument (based on everyone's interests and on a cost-benefit analysis) is not necessarily a good moral argument as well: it is not fair that the blackmailers should get the money.

It is much easier to understand why, as Swift suggests, the 'trickle-down' argument is 'incoherent' and cannot actually *justify* inequality if we translate it into a practical argument and identify its premises. The goal of prosperity for all, and an alleged underlying concern for the common good, including the worst-off, are used by defenders of inequality, we suggest, as overt *goal* and *value* premises. On this basis, we could say, therefore, that the need to tolerate inequality is *motivated* by a concern for the common good and a future of prosperity for all. However, the argument, thus formulated, seems to be a rationalization. In its standard form, the 'trickle-down' argument starts from an open acknowledgment of man's self-interested nature (people's actual motivations are selfish, this is why an egalitarian system, we are told, would not work). The real underlying value (as a motivating premise) therefore has to do with a concern for self-interest. But if the common good is not a motivating (value) premise, how does it enter the argument, what type of premise is it? We think that, logically, the alleged concern for everyone's interest can only belong to a premise that specifies some (alleged) *positive consequences of tolerating inequality*. In other words, the 'trickle-down' argument overtly cites the alleged positive consequences (benefits) of the action (i.e. of tolerating inequality) as if they were a value premise, while concealing the actual value premise (i.e. a concern for self- or group-interest). The common good or general interest enters the argument as a result of a *cost–benefit* analysis of tolerating versus refusing to tolerate inequality. Overtly, the argument says: given the goal of prosperity or growth, motivated by a concern for everyone's interest or the common good (value premise), inequality should be tolerated. But the underlying argument is in fact the following: given the goal of prosperity or growth, motivated by a concern for self-interest or group-interest (value premise), and given that, in the process of serving self- or group- interest, some positive *side-effects* will 'trickle down' for everyone as *by-products* of the logic of perpetual growth (alternatively, given the high costs for the common good of refusing to tolerate inequality), inequality ought to be tolerated. The argument is a prudential one analogous to saying: it is in your interest (because of the potential costs and benefits) to pay off the blackmailers. If you do, *everyone's* interests will be served (although in different ways). But while the arrangement between the blackmailers and their victim will, in this sense, be mutually beneficial, the mutual benefit has been obtained through extortion, by artificially creating a context of risk (of potential costs) for one party which that party would pay to avoid; as for the 'common good', there is no 'common good' or value that both parties genuinely share. You should pay the blackmailers not because the action contributes to the fulfilment of some shared goal and value, but because it is the reasonable thing to do, given a cost–benefit analysis. It is therefore possible to justify inequality (inequality is functionally necessary, it may be a necessary evil, the lesser evil, etc.), but its best approximation is the argument from blackmail, which is how many *Guardian* readers insightfully interpreted it.

To sum up, what the argument says in fact is not that inequality is *designed* to promote everyone's goals but that it is *designed* to promote some people's goals and that, as a *side-effect*, it manages to serve to some extent or at least not undermine the goals of other agents. If it were overtly formulated in these terms, with self-interest as the motivating (value) premise, the argument would not be easy to accept because of the strong resemblance to blackmail. It would be clear that one is invited to choose the less bad alternative of two bad alternatives (i.e. inequality may have its disadvantages but an egalitarian system would be even worse). This is why the argument has to disguise the real motivation of action as a concern for the general interest. Notice, however, that the prudential defence of inequality is only reasonable if indeed *it is true* that an egalitarian arrangement would lead to poverty for all, or that inequality promotes growth and prosperity for all. As we have seen, however, the truth of these premises is precisely what some *Guardian* readers have challenged: tolerating inequality and decades of 'trickle-down' economics have failed to deliver the promised goods. The terms of an implicit social contract have thus been broken.

Various comments challenged the logical soundness of the 'trickle-down' argument (e.g. the truth of the premises). The rationality of the British population's own behavior was also questioned: persistently, people seem to fail to draw the logical conclusion from the evidence at their disposal. Both throwing money at the banks and passively tolerating the consequences of the crisis are irrational responses:

> *almart000* 21 Oct 2009, 3:02PM. He gambles. He loses. We bail him out. He gambles. He loses. We bail him out. Do we deserve to be laughed at? You bet.
>
> *Cheylore* 21 Oct 2009, 2:50PM. (. . .) Does this man think we are completely stupid? Perhaps he has grounds to. We have been robbed and we continue to be robbed. Instead of rioting on the streets, lynching bankers, . . ., we blog and whine. And yes, annoyingly, at this precise moment this includes me.
>
> *Donald2000* 21 Oct 2009, 2:29PM. Let's get this right; the banks caused the recession and now the Chairperson of an investment bank says that prosperity would arrive and that bankers' bonuses would be just part of the price to pay for that prosperity. I think that these people need to sign on for a psychiatric evaluation; their logical faculties are broken beyond redemption.

What was suggested instead, in response to the bankers' perceived blackmail, was a revolution, a fundamental change of the economic system, with capital punishment for those responsible for the crisis:

> *TopMarx* 21 Oct 2009, 3:00PM. Maybe this is the spark we have been waiting for! Maybe it's just worth getting the machine gun out and giving it a polish. If you haven't got one, there's always a pitch fork. I've got a few bags of barricade bricks. Let's get the bastards this time! (. . .)
>
> *Self* 21 Oct 2009, 2:22PM. These people are evil, pure evil. Get them out of the country *now*. We don't want them and the recessions and misery they cause. Just get them out, at gunpoint.
>
> *floptastic* 21 Oct 2009, 2:56PM . . .. [G]reedy bankers will be among the first in front of a firing squad come the revolution – after greedy politicians . . ..
>
> *usasoneiaswe* 21 Oct 2009, 2:19PM. Let *us* bring the whole of the banking sector to heel. Tear down the structure and stuff all the weasels who work within it solely for their own self interested greed with poverty: *tear it down!* Build from us, the people, up. *Do it.* When are we going to stop the suffering? When we cease to see apathy as a virtue, that's when: *act!* Take your money *out* of the (. . .) money machines and put it in a bank that banks, not one that takes, rip-offs, hoards . . . (. . .) *Act!* Tell your family, friends and colleagues to do the same. Let's destroy them as they so readily do us and through our actions create a morally secure society, free from their greed and abuse.
>
> *vaughanie* 21 Oct 2009, 10:33PM. The actions of bankers in causing the damage and largest budget deficit in living history is tantamount to one and one thing only . . . (. . .) *High treason!* 'Trickle-down' economics and free market principles as espoused by Milton Friedman and the Chicago Group are nothing more than a grab of tax payers money, weaken government and plunge the world into poverty. *Charge them now!*

The analogy with the French Revolution was humorously used by several people to suggest a similar fate for British bankers:

> *2LSE* 22 Oct 2009, 9:22AM. Err . . . didn't the French aristocracy also think that the peasants should tolerate inequality???

WWIT 21 Oct 2009, 5:10PM. The peasants must learn to tolerate inequality, said the French in 1788.

AlsoRan 21 Oct 2009, 2:40PM (. . .) Is this the bankers' 'let them eat cake' moment? Here's hoping.

A moral argument against inequality: the state is committed to justice, therefore inequality should not be tolerated

We have argued that Lord Griffith's argument is not in fact underlain by a concern for the common good, in spite of its overt form. Its underlying value premise is self-interest and its best approximation is to a prudential argument in favour of paying off the blackmailers in order to avoid higher costs. A large proportion of the comments thread, however, involved genuine moral argumentation. People did not argue from their own interests or desires, or from the desirability of politicians manifesting a concern with justice or fairness, but from moral–political values they thought everyone ought to be concerned with because, implicitly, they are part of an institutional arrangement, as fact, regardless of whether anyone wants to act accordingly or not. Justice was understood in two main ways, in relation to what people deserve, and in relation to equality, as fairness. Let us look at these arguments in turn.

Many comments focused on the idea that bankers do not *deserve* the high pay they get: it is unjust that they should get these rewards, as they do not produce anything useful, their so-called talents are worthless and they are being rewarded for failure. This is one possible understanding of justice, as just deserts:

> *LeavesNoWitnesses* 21 Oct 2009, 2:38PM. What an arrogant swine! Can he please explain how do banks serve the economy by sucking money out of it when most of the economy is in ruins? Why should we reward these idiots in charge of financial institutions that *do not produce anything of value* to the society? I'm really lost here. Furious, just furious.
>
> *AlanMoore* 21 Oct 2009, 2:16PM. Idiot. It might be considered an investment *to the general good if these bastards actually generated* any wealth – or did *anything* useful. But they don't, all they do is distort markets for short-term benefit . . ..
>
> *Somebodysaid* 21 Oct 2009, 2:15PM. I've always rather liked the way they term it 'compensation' . . . for what exactly? Long hours? Sipping an espresso in a shiny office whilst looking at a few screens of shifting numbers and getting a bit het up when they go red? . . ..
>
> *Zerosum* 22 Oct 2009, 4:47AM. (. . .) Just how does Goldman Sachs contribute to the 'greater prosperity of all'? (. . .) There have been articles in the US press lately about these firms generating huge profits using super-fast computers to carry out so-called 'flash' trading, which is utterly devoid of any social utility. Much of the wealth generated by GS is not real; they specialize in the invention of bogus financial instruments to generate huge profits and then flip the risk onto other investors. Most of this 'financial' activity is nothing but parasitism on a economic system whose rules they have helped write via their oversized legislative influence. Half of Obama's economic policy people are in bed with Goldman. We're being suckered by these vampires into thinking they're indispensable to the greater good when in fact they benefit no one but themselves. The whole business is deeply unethical; why are they allowed to get away with it?

A frequent comment was that bailing out the banks with taxpayers' money, as well as the entire bonus culture, amount to rewarding people who have failed in their job, while punishing hard-working and productive people:

> *Samboy* 21 Oct 2009, 2:21PM. What these greedy snout-in-the-trough bankers utterly fail to grasp is that the obscene bonus culture which was in place before the collapse of the financial sector rewarded long term *failure* not success. Where's my f*cking bonus for being part of the investment group which provided 1 trillion pounds worth of capital to ensure that Goldman Sachs could continue to trade?
>
> *HeroicLife* 21 Oct 2009, 10:03PM. . . . The problem is that the money these companies are getting . . . is keeping unproductive, financially irresponsible companies afloat. By virtue of being bankrupt in the first place, these companies have demonstrated that they are consuming more resources than they are creating – and ought to be bankrupt. What we should really be angry about is that the political class is punishing success and rewarding failure by taking money from productive people and businesses and giving it to unproductive ones.
>
> *farandolae* 21 Oct 2009, 2:38PM. Unbelievable, I'm not surprised that there is a long list of offensive comments which have been moderated. I'm not against bonus payments for jobs well done, even for bankers.. . . however this is against a background of enormous failure. The British population will be paying for this failure for a long time to come yet for the bankers it is business as usual . . ..

Justice was also defended in the sense of fairness and equal treatment of people and of similar situations. If the bankers want to keep the profits, they must swallow up the losses and repay their debts first, they must face up to the consequences of their actions. It is not fair to receive bonuses while taxpayers, who have rescued the system, lose their jobs and businesses struggle to stay afloat with no help from the state. In other words you cannot demand one rule for yourself and another one for everyone else.

> *farandolae* 21 Oct 2009, 2:38PM. . . . so we face unemployment, massively reduced pensions, big cuts in public services and some of the people who put us in this mess get an average of GBP 450,000 + on top of their salary. Seems fair.
>
> *Peter4321* 21 Oct 2009, 2:26PM. Frankly, the pay of bankers used not to be any of my business. I didn't own shares in investment banks and if they decided to pay stupid wages to a few choice individuals, that was up to them as private companies. *But* – the moment they come arrogantly demanding bail-outs is the moment it does become my business. These people run a casino – except who ever heard of a casino being so badly run that it crashed? If they want to keep all the profits, they have to swallow down the losses. So, let them keep their bonuses – once they repay the taxpayer in full.
>
> *jacko121* 21 Oct 2009, 11:40PM. . . . if you are not ashamed at paying your staff then you should not be ashamed at repaying your debt to the tax payers first.
>
> *NicolaD* 21 Oct 2009, 3:24PM. . . . I think what the banks need to remember is that it was public funds that were used to keep them open . . . I think this greedy man also needs to remember that the hard-working tax payers bailed them out only to be made redundant as a result of the bankers' greed and ignorance. I don't have a problem with people receiving bonuses but at the end of the day most businesses are struggling to stay open with little or no help from the government so why should the banks get away with it . . .. How can banks that just a few months ago had to be given millions to stay afloat

afford to give bonuses like this??? The ordinary law-abiding tax payer loses *again – as usual!!*

The Paladin 21 Oct 2009, 9:39PM. That's fine. Next time when you collapse we'll let it happen and just force defaults on all of the mortgages you owned. Meaning, you own nothing. Savings get wiped out, so do the mortgages. We wipe out the entire banking system with one fell swoop. If you let one fall, the rest will fall into line. You want to keep paying, I'll let you collapse when you don't bloody listen. Fair dos.

The whole idea of demanding extra payments for a job well done was dismissed as a case of special pleading, by observing that 'no one ever makes that argument for any profession other than bankers and chief executives' (*daytimeTV* 21 Oct 2009, 2:31PM) and in no other jobs do people receive or expect bonuses for doing what they are supposed to do, however hard they work (*henchard1* 21 Oct 2009, 2:45PM).

The claim that people should tolerate inequality is transformed into a claim about what bankers should themselves tolerate, according to an implicit principle of fairness or reciprocity:

> *SimonBarSinister* 21 Oct 2009, 2:18PM. Yes, and bankers need to learn to tolerate being strung up from lamp-posts by the heels, and machine-gunned to ribbons. Because it's gonna happen. Yes it is.
>
> *FilkaMorozov* 21 Oct 2009, 2:26PM. Bankers must learn to tolerate prison food when they're found guilty of fraud.
>
> *patelvijay* 21 Oct 2009, 2:14PM. Banks must learn to 'tolerate the fairness' of collapse when they mess up.

Besides justice, people also appealed to equality and some quoted Wilkinson and Pickett's critique of inequality in their 2009 book, *The Spirit Level.*

> *deano30* 21 Oct 2009, 2:36PM. Foolish tosser – a society is never the richer if its good fortune is based on rampant inequality. It is a flawed and fractured place which is just about to fall apart at the seams.
>
> *Harrymanback* 21 Oct 2009, 2:15PM . . .. [O]ne rather large hole in his argument . . . is the mountain of evidence that shows that happy societies are those that have low inequality, not those that are rich.
>
> *LesterJones* 21 Oct 2009, 2:35PM The public should tolerate the inequality . . . really? . . . then explain this: http://www.equalitytrust.org.uk/about
> . . . inequality is the very thing we can never tolerate . . ..

The government's solution of rescuing the banks was also challenged as fundamentally unjust by several *Guardian* readers and a concept of inter-generational justice was implicitly invoked in arguing that, due to the government's ill-advised rescue of the banks, future generations will have to pay for the crisis. The alleged negative consequence of failing to rescue the banks were also challenged, and the consequences of having rescued them, moreover without public consultation, were said to be far worse:

> *salofinkelstein* 21 Oct 2009, 2:38PM. As Mervyn King has pointed out, the government has lumped future generations with the burden of paying bankers' bonuses. Along with all the other shit we've dumped on our children to deal with.

> *Peter4321* 21 Oct 2009, 2:26PM. (. . .) All these scare stories about how the economy would have disappeared if the bankers hadn't been given vast sums of money – would it have been any worse than massive black holes in public finance that we have now? Couldn't we have a referendum as to which gamble the general public would like to take?

There were also one or two comments that defend Griffith's claim, and these gave rise to heated exchanges. One poster claimed that Goldman Sachs people are 'normal, hardworking folks' who 'do tend to earn a good deal but that shouldn't be a crime'. Most people on the comments thread, he said, are 'just a bunch of jealous crybabies who love to talk a tough guy revolutionary game but don't take their bluster more than three feet away from their computer screen' (*martis1* 21 Oct 2009, 8:18PM). In response, it was pointed out to him that he fails to understand people's entirely justified anger at having been swindled:

> *expury* 21 Oct 2009, 8:49PM. Credit people with some intelligence, it is not jealousy. People just don't want to be royally shafted i.e. their tax money used to underwrite the risk taking of banks who can 'invent' markets that bear little reality to real economies, and actually end up damaging them. It is the relationship between the state and the banks that people are rightfully pissed off about . . .. When people are losing their jobs, houses, pensions, businesses as a result of the credit crunch and then the bonus culture is not curtailed then you can see why people are pissed off . . ..

Political values as desire-independent, external reasons for action

As comments formulated in terms of justice and equality make up a significant proportion of this thread, let us say a few words about these values from the point of view of political philosophy. Our discussion of justice below follows Swift's (2006) account and will be relevant in choosing an adequate representation of the arguments from justice.

Together with liberty, justice and equality are fundamental moral–political values. For some philosophers, such as Rawls, justice is the primary political value, the first virtue of social institutions. Justice is closely connected to rights: the state treats citizens justly in respecting their rights; similarly, citizens behave in a way that is just towards each other in respecting each other's rights. Justice is also tied to duty, to what is morally *required* that we do to and for one another. The state is justified in making sure that people carry out their duties to one another, and this includes using its coercive power to force people to do what they might not want to do, or what is not desirable from their own point of view. Swift suggests drawing a distinction between the *concept* of justice and various *conceptions* of what justice is. The basic concept of justice (its basic grammar or logic) seems to be that it is about 'giving people what is due to them, and not giving them what is not due to them'. Giving them what is due is not the same with what it would be desirable or polite or good for them to have: punishing criminals is a way of giving them what is due to them, without being what they desire. While people and philosophers alike seem to agree on this basic understanding of the concept of justice, there are still various particular *conceptions* of justice, different ways of fleshing out the logic of the term. The most influential conceptions are Rawls's (1971, 1993, 2001) conception of justice-as-fairness, Nozick's (1974) conception of justice-as-entitlement and the popular conception of justice-as-desert. Most people, Swift argues, endorse elements of all three, often in ways that, upon closer inspection, are not really coherent (Swift 2006: 11–13).

According to the popular conception of justice-as-desert, giving people what is due to them means rewarding work, talent, success. Talented and hard-working individuals deserve to get more than untalented and idle ones. Some philosophers disagree with the popular conception by pointing out that people's talent or success is often a result of luck and other factors beyond their control. They also point out that which talents and abilities societies happen to value at any given time is also an arbitrary matter, so people don't, strictly speaking, deserve to earn more. Other philosophers believe that, on the contrary, people own their talents and are entitled to do whatever they like with what is theirs (their body, their property). And talented individuals (artists, sportsmen) may end up being very rich because a lot of people have *freely* chosen to pay to see them exercise their talents; nothing objectionable has taken place in this case. The question of desert, however, is irrelevant; rather, on this view, justice should be understood as *entitlement*. Regardless of the philosophical controversy, the popular view remains a strong one: talented and hard-working people may be just lucky, but they deserve to earn more.

The conception of justice-as-fairness is associated with John Rawls. As is well known, his argument is that, in the 'original position', under the 'veil of ignorance', people would choose principles that are fair and do not privilege anyone over anyone else. They would thus presumably choose:

1   The principle of equal basic liberties: each person is to have an equal right to the most extensive total system of basic liberties compatible with a similar system of liberty for all.
2   The difference principle and the principle of fair equality of opportunity. Social and economic inequalities are to be arranged so that they are both (a) to the greatest benefit of the least advantaged, and (b) attached to offices and positions open to all under conditions of fair equality of opportunity.

According to Rawls, people would choose *equality* of distribution, rather than unequal arrangements. The only departures from equality that would be fair are those distributions that also raise the standard of the worst-off. So, the fairest *unequal* distribution would be one that maximizes the position of the worst-off, one that leaves the most disadvantaged members of society better off than they would have been under an egalitarian arrangement.

The 'original position' and the 'veil of ignorance' are devices of representation that model the sense in which people are conceived as free and equal. If people were deprived of all particular knowledge about their social position, race, gender, ethnicity, their natural talents, their conception of the good, if they were therefore wholly free of personal interest, not knowing anything personal about themselves, and not knowing how the principles they are about to agree on will affect them personally, they would agree on fair principles of cooperation and distribution, principles that do not privilege anyone over anyone else. These principles would be the content of a hypothetical contract that people would arrive at if they were free and equal. If you don't already know that you are going to get the biggest piece of the cake anyway, you are more likely to cut it fairly, because you might end up getting the smallest piece (Swift 2006: 21–29).

A just society, therefore, will give all its citizens the same set of basic liberties and rights. Then, if there are social and economic inequalities, it will ensure that all its citizens enjoy equality of opportunity, i.e. have the same chances to achieve those positions which are unequally rewarded, and finally, it will only allow such inequalities if they are geared towards *maximizing* the position of the worst-off members of society. Rawls therefore does accept inequality: without it, people will have no incentive to do certain jobs that benefit everyone else. But inequalities are justified if they serve to maximize the position of the most disadvantaged members of society. (Notice that, unlike the 'trickle-down' conception, the difference principle can constitute a moral justification of inequality. This is, in our view, because a concern for serving the interests of the worst-off is genuinely a value premise.)

The political value of equality is closely related to justice. Equality in the sense that all citizens have an equal right to be treated with concern and respect by the state (and by each other) is usually not contested. This conception of equality is about equality of status and recognition, the equal worth of all human beings, and equal social relations, and is reflected in equality before the law and equality of citizenship. What is nevertheless often contested by political philosophers, politicians and ordinary people alike is the understanding of equality as a distributive ideal, as having to do with equalizing outcomes.

In this comments thread, people argued from a conception of justice which rules out privileging certain people at the expense of others, or treating people in arbitrary ways, in ways that are not related to their actions, or not giving them what is due to them. People argued against Griffith's prudential argument by constructing their own moral arguments, with different underlying values and goals. Instead of the goal of growth and material prosperity, people argued from the normative goal of a just or fair society, as the goal that the state or politicians implicitly *ought* to pursue (in Swift's terms, from a *concept* of justice, as a state of affairs in which everyone gets what is due to them, whether according to desert or a more egalitarian conception, such as Rawls's justice-as-fairness). As we have seen, the popular conception of justice-as-desert, for example, says that talented, hard-working or successful individuals deserve more rewards than untalented, idle or unsuccessful ones. We can represent the typical argument from justice-as-desert as in Figure 5.3.

Given that, in fact, bankers have failed in their jobs, have caused the crisis with all its negative effects on people, and do not have any genuine talent or social usefulness, and given a legitimate concern for justice that the state is bound by and is expected to act upon, bankers should not continue to receive bonuses. They should not receive them because the state's goal should be a state of affairs that is just, in which people get what is due to them, and do not get what is not due to them, i.e. are not unjustly punished or rewarded, but justly so. Implicit in people's arguments was the premise that the state is *morally required* to act justly, that there is a *commitment* to justice that the state is bound by. This corresponds to what Vince Cable, in the passage we quoted at the beginning of this chapter, called the *social contract* between the state and its citizens. In failing to act justly, in punishing the innocent and rewarding the guilty, the state is violating the terms of this contract and breaking its implicit commitment to justice. The claim that the inequality of bankers' bonuses should not be tolerated refers to what the *government* ought to do: the government is expected to act out of a concern for justice (a desire-dependent reason), based on recognizing an existing commitment to justice, *as an institutional fact or norm* (a desire-independent reason), in order to put an end to an unjust situation.

The arguments from a conception of justice-as-fairness have a similar structure. Let us take the example of those arguments from the empirical circumstances that 'trickle-down' economics has, over decades, not contributed to general prosperity but has resulted in an unprecedented economic collapse. Such arguments are denying that the neoliberal economic model has genuinely benefited the worst-off members of society. According to Rawls's justice-as-fairness conception, inequalities would be allowed if they maximized the position of the worst-off, if they left those people better off than they would have been under an egalitarian arrangement. A whole range of comments that we have looked at deny that this has been the case. We represent this argument in Figure 5.4.

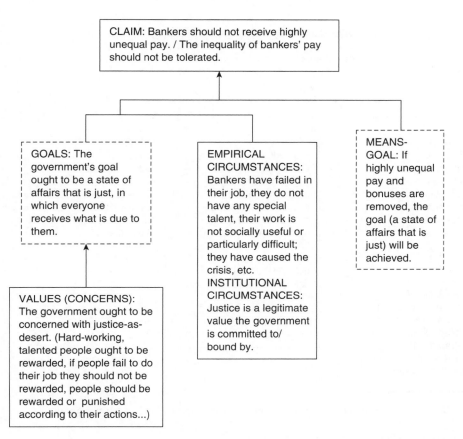

Figure 5.3 Guardian readers' moral argument against inequality from the value of justice-as-desert.

Again, there is an implicit appeal to an existing commitment that the state has to justice, part of the social contract. This is quite clear in various comments in which people express their disapproval or anger at what the government has actually done (rescued the banks by taking money from taxpayers) or failed to do (regulate the banking sector, protect the population, make sure bail-out money would be repaid), at the complicity between the government and the banking sector (which they see as a cause for the unwillingness to find adequate solutions) and at the population's apparent inability to force politicians to act according to the public interest. What people should do, these comments say, is force the government to act *as it ought to*, in view of its existing commitments, i.e. serve the public interest:

> *vaughanie* 21 Oct 2009, 10:33PM. (. . .) *Our* government should be smashing *any* organisation or industry that has the ability to destroy *our* country as has happened. It should be protecting us from the near collapse of our society as a duty to its citizens, taking bankers out of the city and charging them with *high treason!!*
>
> *losmarcos* 21 Oct 2009, 3:09PM. (. . .) The only way for democracy to function, is that the people (us) puts pressure on politicians to do their job: create regulations on a sector

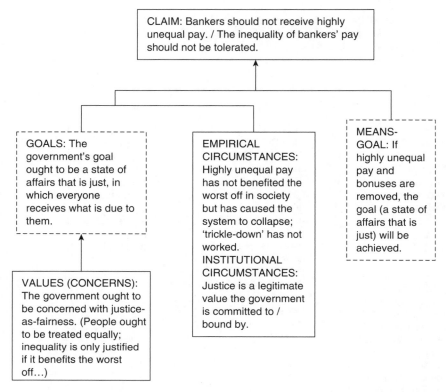

Figure 5.4 Guardian readers' moral argument against inequality from the value of justice-as-fairness.

which has proven to have one objective: their own interest, and put them back in their real role . . . so we don't all get dissolved in extreme capitalism as a totalitarianism . . ..

jacko121 21 Oct 2009, 11:40PM. To our governments I would say, I thought the point of the EEC is there should be some cohesive strategies between countries. If not it's about time you got a grip and ensured that these companies who threaten to move from one country to another are told in no uncertain [terms] that the rules are the same where ever they go . . . (. . .) The other great shame is that we do not have any Outstanding Statesmen in any of our political parties who have the clout to get to grips with these issues. (. . .) Someone needs to start putting Britain and its people first. Do we have any politicians with the balls to do it ???

nicholson 22 Oct 2009, 11:30AM. (. . .) It seems to me [that bankers are] still living in a bubble because the government is allowing them to do so. If the government initiated an action to claim banking profits for the people by taxing their profits as part of the recompense for the damage made by the overall financial sector to society – you may well see a global trend where other countries follow suit and bankers would once again become integrated into social responsibility . . .

coachway 21 Oct 2009, 4:08PM. Whilst all the 'bloggers' here are rightly outraged at bankers' pay and bonuses, it is a sad fact that most of the population accept the present status as something that they cannot do anything about. If people really cared they would force politicians to act . . ..

reactual 21 Oct 2009, 4:16PM. (. . .) Griffiths has shown us that these people have utter contempt for us. The politicians don't care either because all of the parties are in thrall to the banking industry.

Blither 22 Oct 2009, 7:20AM. The banks should never have been bailed out before signing an agreement not to claim bonuses for the next 5 years – they could have chosen at that point whether to relocate or not.

Kaks 21 Oct 2009, 4:51PM. Don't expect any changes anytime soon. The banks and the government are one big organisation that look after each other's interests . .

flamingrrose 21 Oct 2009, 2:20PM. (. . .) There is one thing he is right about: The banking elite in the UK is controlling the government to such an extent that it can do practically anything it wants.

The *Guardian* comments thread also includes a few sporadic references to another conception of justice, justice-as-entitlement. As a few readers observe, bankers feel *entitled* to their bonuses and in a sense they are, because the bonus culture is part of a system of rules they have themselves written. However, these rules themselves are wrong and need changing (*Zerosum* 22 Oct 2009, 4:47AM; *cassey* 21 Oct 2009, 3:22PM). Sadly, under the current rules, 'the banks are doing nothing that they are not allowed to do', and 'if we want to change the system we need to change the politicians and the regulations governing the operation of the financial system that these same politicians have instituted' (*Ocala* 21 Oct 2009, 8:05PM). To sum up, bankers may be entitled to their rewards if these are the result of rules that are in place. It does not, however, follow that such rewards are fair or deserved, nor that the rules are just.

Conclusion

In this chapter we have suggested our own view of the structure of the prudential and moral arguments in favour of or against the inequality of bankers' pay by analysing a particular public debate. The prudential argument for inequality takes people's interests (or desires) as premises: given what is in people's interests, or given that people want prosperity for all, inequality ought to be tolerated. The argument, we said, amounts to a form of blackmail: the alternative, of not tolerating inequality, is said to involve high costs, costs that are allegedly avoided by tolerating inequality. This is how the public spontaneously interpreted it, and this is how the 'trickle-down' defence of inequality is discussed by political philosophers. In its most characteristic form, we suggested, the defence of inequality by appealing to the alleged general interest is rationalization, as it disguises a concern for self-interest as a concern for the common good. We have proposed our own view, in terms of our analytical framework, of why the prudential argument in favour of inequality is an unreasonable argument and suggested that it attempts to pass off a particularly self-interested calculation of the *costs and benefits* of alternative actions for a genuine concern for the common good, i.e. for a genuine *value* (motivating) premise.

We have drawn on political philosophy, on a distinction between a concept of justice and particular conceptions of justice, to represent the moral argument against inequality. We have looked at two such arguments, based on the value of justice-as-fairness and justice-as-desert. These arguments, we said, start from circumstantial premises of two sorts: premises stating the empirical facts that bankers have in fact failed or that 'trickle-down' economics has not worked, but primarily from premises referring to the institutional, desire-independent *fact* of the state's socially recognized, normatively binding commitment to justice, as well as from the desire-independent goal of a *just* state of affairs, as something that the state (politicians) ought to be concerned with. The moral argument does not therefore proceed from what is in the agent's interests or what the agent desires. It proceeds primarily from a desire-independent reason, from a normatively binding commitment to justice on the part of the state, part of a contract with the citizens. This is a factual, circumstantial premise, an external reason that politicians and the state are expected to act upon even in those cases when there seems to be little political will to do so. The goal premise is also different in such arguments. The goal is not a state of affairs that some people happen to desire because it satisfies their own concerns, but a just society that gives everyone what is due to them and in which nobody's particular desires or concerns are arbitrarily privileged over anyone else's.

The distinction between a concept of justice and particular conceptions of justice confirms our suggestion, in Chapter 2, that the goal premise should be detached from any intrinsic connection with what agents want, and should be viewed instead as a (possible, future) state of affairs which the agent *may or may not desire*. Goals can be normative states of affairs that we, as agents, ought to bring about even if we don't particularly desire them, and *a just arrangement, as a normative goal, may be one that some people will not like or desire*. We argued that goals are often generated by reasons independent of the agent's desires, 'external' reasons such as duties, obligations, moral values, norms, which act as external constraints on action, and often go against the agent's wishes. This way of seeing goals is compatible with Searle's account of institutional reality and the priority he gives to external reasons, originating in institutional reality. Whether or not people act in accordance with such reasons, these reasons *are objectively there* (in the sense that they are epistemically objective) and people can be said to have them, even when they disregard them. On the other hand, recognition of such reasons can lead people to internalize them as motivations to act. Values therefore enter as premises in practical arguments either as agents' concerns (their desires, their interests) or as external reasons, as social or institutional facts. A socially recognized duty, obligation or commitment is a reason for action whether or not the agent will internalize it as a concern. But agents can also be concerned to fulfil their duties and commitments, to act morally, in which case the value or duty in question will turn into an internal *motive* for action.

In the arguments we looked at, from political values such as justice, people argued from the government's implicit commitment to justice, from an implicit 'social contract', whose objective binding nature ought (in their view) to be recognized and internalized as motivation by politicians and by the state in deciding on a course of action. Underlying these arguments is a belief that, even when politicians apparently fail to care about this social contract and thus fail to act from a commitment to justice, they *ought to* do so: they *have a reason* to do so, in fact one that they have themselves created by accepting a mandate of political representation. External reasons that ought to motivate but fail to do so (e.g. social contracts that are broken, publicly recognized values and norms that are disregarded) are a good starting point for social critique. Recognizing the specificity of the social world as a world of man-made institutions (commitments, contracts, laws, norms) that one is bound by even when one chooses to act otherwise underlies in fact the very possibility of normative critique.

In our view, the specificity of moral reasoning (including moral–political argumentation) derives from the recognition of external, desire-independent reasons for action as basic. External reasons in the political field vary from promises made by politicians in electoral campaigns, which they are then expected to act upon, to moral–political values (justice, equality, freedom) recognized as legitimate and binding and enshrined in laws. Because they are collectively recognized or accepted as legitimate reasons, they can shape human action without any recourse to coercion or force. Not all external reasons are moral: agents often act prudentially in respecting the authority of the law in order to avoid undesirable consequences. The system of deontic powers of the state is in fact always backed by the possibility of using coercion to make agents comply with collectively recognized norms when such compliance is not voluntary. Such external reasons lie at the interface between agents and structures and show how agency and structure interact and shape each other. We have suggested placing such reasons in the circumstantial premise: they are *facts* that speakers argue from in saying that agents ought to be concerned with their realization. In the case of promises or norms and laws, the fact that the agent made a promise or is bound by a norm or law typically override any other possible consideration of what the context is or might require. When we say, for instance that, regardless of any other circumstances, and whether he wants to or not, the agent ought to do what he promised, we regard the fact that the agent made a promise as a reason for action that cannot be overridden. More generally, when the public argues that, regardless of any other circumstances and regardless of their actual inclinations, interests and concerns, politicians ought to do their duty, act justly and serve the public interest, they implicitly regard the social contract between the state and citizens, and the mutual obligations that ensue thereof, as the most relevant reason, a reason that cannot be overridden.

In this chapter, we have seen citizens challenging government policy, as well as the actions of private entities (banks), in virtue of their formally recognized (and here, taken-for-granted) *rights* as citizens of a modern democratic state. We have seen them arguing that the government and politicians are violating commitments to justice that they *ought to* be concerned with, precisely because these commitments are part of their *obligations*, part of a contract between the state and the citizens. One of the ways in which the government is violating this commitment to justice (and ignoring the legitimate character of justice as a publicly justified political value) is by failing to punish the guilty and instead punishing the population for a crisis the latter did not cause. As we said in Chapter 2, in our discussion of Searle's conception of institutional reality, *status functions* (here, being a citizen, or being an elected politician in a democratic state) carry deontic powers, i.e. rights, obligations, and so on, and are therefore the vehicles of power in society, the channels through which political power circulates. Citizens are here exerting their power in criticizing government (although, as they themselves note, with self-irony, they only use it very weakly, and merely talk tough without moving on to action), while politicians are exerting their own power to ignore dissent, under an institutional framework that is set in such a way so as to allow them, to some extent, the freedom to do so, and acting under the pressure of economic reasons and private interests that effectively override reasons which should not, in the public's opinion, be easily overridden.

6 Deliberation as genre in the parliamentary debate on university tuition fees

In this chapter we want to illustrate deliberation in a multi-agent context where a political decision has to be arrived at. We will focus on the debate in the House of Commons of 9 December 2010, on the government's proposal to raise university tuition fees from roughly £3,300 to a maximum of £9,000 per year, which ended in a vote.[1] We will reconstruct this debate as critical discussion, along pragma-dialectical lines, and also discuss institutional constraints on argumentation in a parliamentary debate. We will also identify the structure of the arguments advanced by the participants, according to the structure of practical reasoning we are suggesting in this book. We will focus in particular on the way in which participants are evaluating each other's arguments and on the quality of the deliberative process, but we will also suggest an evaluation in terms of a normative external perspective.

In the final section of this chapter we will address a particular argument developed by a participant in the tuition fees debate, which invokes the Liberal Democrats' promise (during the electoral campaign of 2010) not to raise fees. We discuss this promise as a reason for action – an external reason that ought to have acted as a constraint on the Liberal Democrats' action in government, but was nevertheless disregarded – and we look at some of the criticism that the Liberal Democrats, and Nick Clegg in particular, have received over this broken commitment.

Debate and deliberation in institutional contexts

In Chapter 2, following van Eemeren (2010) we distinguished between genres, activity types (as specific genres) and speech events. Concrete speech events draw upon or implement activity types (specific genres), which themselves draw upon or implement genres – deliberation, adjudication, mediation, negotiation. Activity types can draw upon a combination of genres, and speech events can draw upon a combination of activity types. We adopt van Eemeren's (2010: 142–143) distinction between deliberation and debate as analytical categories placed at different levels of analysis: *deliberation is a genre*, while *debates are activity types*. Parliamentary debates are therefore activity types which draw on the genre of deliberation and our analysis will show that this view of the relationship between deliberation and debate is correct.[2]

We also agree with van Eemeren (2009a, 2010) that argumentative genres of communicative activity, such as deliberation, can be reconstructed as *critical discussion*, i.e. as a procedure aimed at disagreement resolution in a reasonable way, or 'on the merits'. Critical discussion is a general procedure which takes different forms, or is contextualized in different ways in particular empirical institutional settings, depending upon their particular logic. Institutional contexts provide pre-conditions for argumentative discourse, in the form of constraints or opportunities (rules of procedure specifying what is allowed or acceptable, what the initial situation or the final outcome is, etc.) which differ from one activity type to another. We will try to identify some of the specific features of parliamentary debate that arise from the institutional context in which it occurs.[3]

Starting from the above view on the distinction between deliberation and debate, and the relationship between critical discussion (as an abstract normative model) and deliberation and debate as respectively genre and activity type, we suggest the following development of these conceptual distinctions. First, in our view, not all debates draw on the genre of deliberation because not all debates focus on a normative proposition: some focus on epistemic claims. To put it differently, people can debate both over matters of truth (e.g. the causes of global warming) *and* normative or practical issues (what should be done about global warming), but they can only deliberate over normative–practical issues, over what to do. Hence, only debates that focus on normative–practical issues can be deliberative.

Second, for any individual agent, deliberation results in a *normative judgement* (a normative proposition about what one ought to do or what it would be good to do): this is the outcome that all actual instances of deliberation are normatively oriented to, although sometimes people fail to arrive at it in a reasonable way (even after deliberation, they may still not come to a conclusion about what they should do and might adopt some arbitrary solution). This cognitive outcome can be followed by an *intention* to act, a *decision* to act and by the *action* itself, but does not need to: people may think they ought to do *A* but still not do it, nor decide or intend to do it (Audi 2006: 87). Similarly, multi-agent debates, such as the public debate over the fairness of bankers' bonuses that we analysed in Chapter 5, while essentially deliberative, may not result in any palpable decision or action, whether individual or collective, but only in a normative judgements (e.g. it is unfair that bankers should continue to receive bonuses, the government ought to put a stop to these practices, bankers should be put in prison, etc.). This does not mean that such debates are not ideally oriented towards a decision and towards action, but only that – given the absence of an institutional context and the dispersed, disorganized nature of the deliberating public – decision and action cannot be realistically arrived at. For a debate to instantiate the genre of deliberation, in our view, a minimum requirement is that it should focus on a normative proposition that can (but does not have to) ground a collective decision for action and (as we have already argued in other chapters) that it should weigh reasons in favour of an action (e.g. how the action might help fulfil the agent's goals) against reasons that may count against it, such as the consequences of doing the action. Some debates, we suggest, and parliamentary debates are a case in point, require more than the minimal outcome of a practical judgement. It is part of their underlying institutional rationale or point that they should lead to a decision for action; this decision may not be in agreement with the normative judgement arrived at by *all* participants who have deliberated together.

Third, in parliamentary debates, disagreements are not resolved in the sense that agreement among *all* participants is actually reached, so the outcome that can be reasonably expected is different from the one that can be expected in other contexts. As we will argue later, what is reasonably expected is a collective decision on a common course of action, not unanimity of views. Participants in such a debate still aim to persuade each other, but the particular genre (interaction) that they are engaged in does not require that they all become persuaded of the same view, only that they share some procedural commitments – in particular, that they acknowledge the binding nature of the decision to be arrived at by voting. Deliberation offers a means for dealing with disagreements in a cooperative (and peaceful, non-violent) way without necessarily removing them or resolving them. This is, we argue, because the outcome of deliberation is a *collective decision* that can ground action, and not a *shared belief* that *A* is the right course of action.

Fourth, individual deliberation is different from multi-agent deliberation in one important non-obvious way. An agent deliberating alone will weigh reasons in favour of doing *A* and against doing *A* and arrive at a practical judgement about what he ought to do. It is, however, irrational for him to believe that *A* is the right course of action but do the opposite of *A*, when doing the opposite of *A* goes against his beliefs and his goals. Multi-agent deliberation seems to be different. Parliamentary debates lead each and every participant to a normative judgement, which is typically followed by a collective decision (which can subsequently be turned into government action), but it is not irrational for the decision to go against the goals and the beliefs of some of the agents involved. In fact, overriding the concerns of some of the deliberators is the only reasonable thing to do, as – in conditions of persistent and often fundamentally irreducible disagreement – no decision can be made that fully satisfies the concerns of *all* participants. We will develop all of these suggestions in the course of this chapter.

A detailed analytical framework, involving eight stages or moves (*Open, Inform, Propose, Consider, Revise, Recommend, Confirm, Close*) is proposed by Hitchcock *et al.* (2001) and McBurney *et al.* (2007) for reconstructing actual instances of 'deliberative dialogue' (by which we understand deliberation as genre). These stages, we think, can be seen as more specific formulations of the pragma-dialectical stages. We suggest that the *opening* stage correlates with the *Inform* move, the *argumentation* stage correlates with *Consider*, the *closing* stage correlates with *Recommend, Confirm* and *Close*. The *Propose* move defines the *confrontation*: it is the stage at which it a standpoint (a proposal for action in this case) is advanced and questioned, and a difference of opinion is identified. If the proposal is revised (at the *Revise* stage) – and this often happens in parliamentary debates, when amendments are proposed – then the argumentation returns to the *confrontation* stage (over the revised standpoint). Actual instances of deliberation, such as those occurring in parliamentary debates, can therefore be reconstructed both as critical discussion and, more specifically, as instantiating the genre of deliberation, defined in terms of these eight stages.[4]

In this eight-stage model for deliberation dialogue, the starting point is an *open question* that expresses a problem to be solved (e.g. How should we deal with global warming? How should we mitigate the impact of the financial crisis?). There is no initial commitment to a particular standpoint by any of the participants. This is followed by a discussion of what goals should be pursued, what constraints on action there might be and what perspectives might be used to evaluate proposals. In our framework, evaluation of a proposal is in terms of its *consequences* or impact on value and goals. These consequences may be very different – there may be financial costs or costs in terms of human wellbeing, so there are indeed different 'perspectives' (e.g. financial vs. moral) from which an action may be assessed. Then various proposals and counter-proposals are made, are jointly discussed and evaluated, then accepted, rejected or revised. Finally, an option is recommended and either accepted or rejected by each participant, and the deliberation dialogue is finally closed.

In actual deliberative interactions, the order of some of these stages can change to some extent and some stages can recur. We take the following sequence, proposed by McBurney *et al.*, to define deliberation as genre:

> *Open.* Opening of the deliberation dialogue and the raising of a governing question about what is to be done.

Inform. Discussion of: (a) the governing question, (b) desirable goals; (c) any constraints on the possible action which may be considered; (d) perspectives by which proposals may be evaluated; and (e) any premises (facts) relevant to this evaluation.

Propose. Suggesting possible action-options appropriate to the governing question.

Consider. Commenting on proposals from various perspectives.

Revise. Revising of: (a) the governing question; (b) goals, (c) constraints, (d) perspectives, and/or (e) action-options in the light of the comments presented; and the undertaking of any information-gathering or fact-checking required for resolution.

Recommend. Recommending an option for action, and acceptance or non-acceptance of this recommendation by each participant.

Confirm. Confirming acceptance of a recommended option by each participant. (All participants must confirm their acceptance of a recommended option for normal termination.)

Close. Closing of the deliberation dialogue.

(McBurney *et al.* 2007: 6)

In our view, this model defines a normative model of deliberation, with respect to which various activity types and concrete speech events will vary more or less significantly. The stage of *Revise*, for example, may be absent in certain activity types and concrete events. Or, as we show below, parliamentary debates (both as activity types and speech events) do not have an *Open* stage in the sense of starting from an open question, but begin directly with the *Propose* stage at which only one proposal is submitted. More interestingly still, while parliamentary debates have a highly specific *Confirm* and *Close* stage (which we take to include the actual vote by each MP, followed by a declaration of the outcome of the vote), other debates, such as the public debate on bankers' bonuses that we analysed in Chapter 5, do not have specific *Confirm* and *Close* stages. In fact they seem to be open-ended, without clear time boundaries, and to close arbitrarily in one location only to be reopened in another, while the individual confirmation of participants' adherence to one or another of the views that are being debated never seems to lead to the collective adoption of one particular proposal for action, let alone count as a decision for action. However, we think, in spite of these peculiarities, which (we suggest) characterize them at a normative level as activity types (not just at the empirical level of events), and are partly due to differences in institutional context and pragmatic purpose, the normative ideal orientation of these debates as instances of deliberation is still towards arriving at a proposal for action, at a collective decision that can ground action.

Having looked at the features of deliberation as genre, let us now look at parliamentary debate, as an activity type that implements the genre of deliberation. Our proposal is the following. Parliamentary debate typically involves a critical examination of a specific proposal for action that has been put forward (a 'motion'). This involves primarily deriving the implications or consequences of the action and assessing its likely impact on various publicly shared, legitimate goals and values; pointing to negative consequences will support the counter-claim (action *A* should not be performed). Parliamentary debate ends in a normative judgement (proposal *x* ought to be accepted or proposal *x* ought not to be accepted) *and* a decision for collective action, which can ground subsequent action (by the government and other executive bodies). The outcome of a *collective decision* is intrinsic to parliamentary debate (and to deliberation in this particular institutional context): MPs *vote* at the end of the debate and their vote effectively decides which action is taken. Whether the proposal is adopted or not as a basis for government action is *decided* by this democratic vote, but not all participants will also *agree* that the outcome is the best way forward.

The proposal that is the object of deliberation in parliament is itself the outcome of a previous process of deliberation within government. In this new round of deliberation in parliament, deliberation is no longer over several distinct proposals (and therefore no longer starts with an open question), but involves a critical examination of the proposal previously arrived at, ideally aiming to provide participants with all the relevant information they need in order to make a considered decision, i.e. *to deliberate as individuals* and then cast their vote; the result of this vote will embody their collective will. The critical examination of the proposal, done collectively, is used in a process of *deliberation by each and every participant*, prior to voting. Deliberation is *collective* and *collaborative* in that participants exchange information and come up with reasons (arguments) in favour or against the action that, *weighed together*, might enable participants to construct a rationally persuasive argument in favour or against the action. This is something that agents might not be able to do by themselves, before deliberation has started, before information has been pooled together and reasons exchanged and critically examined. Political theorists refer to this as the *epistemic* value of deliberation. At the same time, the final outcome (the decision) is the result of an *individual* deliberative process. Having heard the case both for and against the proposal, and having often actually contributed to the debate by giving reasons for or against, each participant will weigh all these reasons together and arrive at *his own* normative judgement. MPs will not all vote in the same way, and will vote as individuals, not as a collective, unanimous entity.

Parliamentary debates are therefore fundamentally deliberative in nature. The extended critical examination of a specific proposal which makes up most of the actual debate can be viewed as a stage within a wider deliberation process over what means (action, solution) are appropriate in order to deal with a practical problem. This deliberative process starts in government, continues in parliament and possibly extends afterwards as well, as it is government that finally takes the decision on whether to actually act in accordance with the outcome of the parliament vote, in the light not only of the vote in the House of Commons but also in the House of Lords. It is part of the institutional logic of these democratic institutions that the original deliberation in government, while now closed in its previous context, cannot effectively lead to a legitimate decision until after the debate in Parliament has taken place. Both in government and in parliament, all actual 'debate' that takes place is embedded in deliberation and eventually feeds into a decision-making process. If we take this view, then most of what goes on in a 'parliamentary debate' is in fact an extended *Consider* stage of a process of deliberation which begins with an open question asked in government and ends with a decision arrived at by voting in parliament. While, of course, in reality, MPs' final vote may completely disregard the quality of the arguments that have been expressed, the normative orientation of the practice (as distinct from what may happen in reality) is towards reasonable persuasion, persuasion by the force of the better argument.

Persuasion is, in our view, central to deliberation, as it is to all argumentative genres. This is not often clearly understood. Walton, for instance, argues that persuasion is not central to deliberation and that it is not the mechanism that drives deliberative dialogue forward (Walton 2007a: 68–69). This claim is presumably based on the empirical observation that agents deliberating together (such as MPs in Parliament) will arrive at a common decision without *all of them* agreeing (having been persuaded) that the action is the most reasonable action. In order for deliberation to close, therefore, not all participants need to have been persuaded *of the same view*. This, however, does not mean that persuasion is not central to deliberation. Agents involved in deliberation ending in a vote are engaged in an attempt to persuade as many of the other participants as possible of the acceptability of their own standpoint. This is precisely because the deliberation is to end by voting and the majority will carry the day, so it is important to *create* a majority by changing other participants' beliefs. Persuasion seems, in a sense, to be therefore essential for the desired outcome but, in another sense, is not necessary for a legitimate outcome. How can this be explained?

The distinction we mentioned earlier between four different types of responses to a practical problem, and therefore between *normative judgement* and *decision* as distinct outcomes of deliberation, is relevant here and will hopefully enable us to clarify this puzzle. Participants in parliamentary debate may not arrive at the same normative judgement about what would be good to do (i.e. there may be no *shared* cognitive outcome of deliberation) but will nevertheless arrive, by voting, at a *collective* decisional outcome, which will moreover ground a *common* course of action by relevant agents. In multi-agent deliberation, such as parliamentary debate, as we have suggested, the outcome of the practice (or genre) includes the outcome of a shared and collectively binding decision. Unlike single-agent deliberation, we suggest, multi-agent deliberation is incomplete unless a decision is arrived at, not just a normative judgement. This is precisely because there are several agents involved and they might come to *different* normative judgements, and this multiplicity cannot close the deliberation. The fact that multi-agent deliberation can close without everyone having been persuaded of the same view does not mean that persuasion is not essential, but that the required outcome is not (only) *cognitive* but *decisional*, and the decision will be based on the judgement of a majority. It is in this sense that democratic deliberation is a mechanism for dealing with disagreement. In parliamentary debates, although some MPs will continue to believe that the decision was not the best one, they will be bound by it if it has emerged from a collective democratic vote. While for an individual it may be irrational to think that *A* is the best course of action and then decide to do the opposite of *A*, multi-agent deliberation legitimizes and makes rational a decision which runs against the beliefs and goals of some of the deliberators. Persuasion *is* therefore a central goal in deliberation: participants are trying to influence the *decisional* outcome of deliberation (which will be based on the number of votes) by attempting to persuade the other participants of the reasonableness of the practical judgement they support. The only way to change the decision is by changing beliefs, by succeeding in changing the *cognitive* outcome.

An obvious objection to this view is that MPs hardly ever vote except along party lines, in accordance with the party whip, and that they are rarely persuaded to take a different position during parliamentary debates and as a result of them. Like other objections to analysing political discourse as argumentation, this objection conflates the normative and empirical levels of analysis. It is of course true that MPs normally vote in accordance with the party line and sometimes against their better judgement. However, the normative orientation of parliamentary debate as an activity type is towards persuading the other party and resolving disagreements by reasonable means, and towards *rational* decision-making. If persuasion (changing belief) were not the goal of the activity type, then parliamentary debate would lose its institutional rationale, its purpose. There would be no point in having debates at all, as all outcomes would be predetermined by the majority that happened to prevail in the last elections. MPs that choose to vote against the party whip are certainly doing something unusual and with possible repercussions, but whatever consequences they suffer, *these consequences do not follow from rules of procedure that define the practice*: there are *no* rules that say that MPs *have to* vote according to the party whip. The particular debate we are looking at, in which several MPs voted against the view of their own party, as well as the numerous pleas made, during the debate, by MPs to their fellow-MPs to 'listen to their conscience' and vote against the motion, are an empirical confirmation of the fact that participants orient to an implicit normative model of parliamentary debate which allows for reasonable disagreement resolution *through and as a consequence of* argumentation. To say that parliamentary debate involves deliberation does not mean that the reasons entering individual deliberation will all be 'good' reasons, that the decision will be necessarily taken on the strength of the better argument. As we said, sometimes MPs simply follow the party line, and considerations having to do with power *are also a reason* in support of a certain conclusion. Whatever the quality of the reasons, however, the process of arriving at an individual judgement and collective decision by discussion, by giving reasons, is fundamentally argumentative and deliberative in nature. In reality, not all decisions are made on the strength of the better argument, but the normative orientation of the practice is towards rational decision-making, and this normative orientation should not be confused with what may happen in actual argumentative practice.

We have said that the purpose of deliberation is to arrive at a shared decision on a course of action, in spite of persistent disagreement. Deliberation that ends in voting can provide a legitimate outcome, one that is at least procedurally legitimate. But deliberation, if accompanied by sufficiently extended and reasonable debate, has a chance of delivering an outcome that is also substantively legitimate, a *good* decision (at least comparatively speaking), not merely one that has happened to obtain a majority of votes. This insight, which underlies a political conception of the virtues of deliberative democracy, is also one of the fundamental insights of pragma-dialectics. When free from moves that hinder the resolution of differences of opinion, argumentation can deliver a reasonable standpoint. We understand this as saying that adherence to a reasonable, *dialectical* procedure, a reasonable code of argumentative dialogue (as embodied by the pragma-dialectical rules), can deliver a standpoint which is reasonable in the substantive sense as well, in the sense that – *having withstood systematic criticism* – can be provisionally accepted as the right course of action. This standpoint is *reasonable* precisely *because* it has emerged from extensive critical discussion, from following a dialectical *procedure*. In other words, the right procedure, critical discussion, yields a standpoint (in this case, a normative judgement and decision) that is worthy of being accepted by the participants. A reasonable standpoint (descriptive or normative) is worthy of belief or acceptance pending to the emergence of further considerations that may count against it; there is no guarantee that the standpoint is a true proposition or the 'best' action, only that there are no good reasons to reject it.

The provisional nature of the outcome is a particularly sensitive issue in the case of political deliberation. Given inevitable time constraints, incomplete information, human fallibility, but also considerations having to do with power (e.g. who is the majority party), political decisions may not always be the most reasonable decisions. There are institutional constraints on what participants can do, argumentatively speaking: the debate cannot extend indefinitely and the result of a vote which is perhaps premature will have to suffice as a legitimate basis for action. We shall illustrate participants' awareness of this particular problem in our analysis, by referring to interventions from various MPs in which they were asking for more time, for delaying the vote, until all the implications are properly understood, and all MPs can make a better informed decision. The normative orientation of deliberation is nevertheless (ideally) towards disagreement resolution: given sufficient time and information, more participants might become persuaded that a certain standpoint, having emerged from systematic critical examination, has a chance of embodying a comparatively more rational decision. If the debate on the Iraq war had included more information, for example, and if reasons having to do with power had not prevailed, then the outcome might have been different.

Finally, let us note that, in spite of the fundamentally collaborative nature of deliberative practice, parliamentary debates have a highly adversarial, antagonistic nature, given fundamental differences in values, goals and beliefs. This does not hinder but facilitates the goal of arriving at the 'best' decision. It is only by thinking of the strongest attacks and defences of the standpoints that are at stake that the debate will have a chance of producing an outcome that is epistemically superior to one that is produced by participants simply aggregating their individual options by voting *without* debate or after insufficient debate. The latter situations might result in a decision that is based on a superficial and biased consideration of all the relevant aspects of the situation, simply because people have not been given the chance to engage in sufficient debate and get a clear sense of what is at stake and of the merits and shortcomings of each position. People's tendency to find confirmation for their own views, their unwillingness to subject their own views to systematic criticism are counterbalanced in multi-agent contexts by the physical presence of other participants, who will actively think of counter-arguments and objections to the others' arguments.

The parliamentary debate on tuition fees as critical discussion: the confrontation and opening stage

The tuition fees debate is mainly a critical examination of a proposal for action and can be analysed in pragma-dialectical terms as involving four stages: confrontation, opening, argumentation and closing. The debate begins with the *confrontation* stage (corresponding to the *Propose* stage of deliberation as genre), at which a difference of opinion is identified and submitted for discussion by the proponent, the Business Secretary, Vince Cable (who 'begs to move', i.e. proposes for discussion in parliament that tuition fees should be increased) and by the Deputy Speaker, in his role as moderator of the debate:

> *The Secretary of State for Business, Innovation and Skills (Vince Cable)*: I beg to move,
>   That, for the purpose of section 24 of the Higher Education Act 2004, the higher amount should be increased to £9,000, and to £4,500 in the cases described in regulation 5 of the draft regulations (. . .), and that the increase should take effect from 1 September 2012.
>   *Mr Deputy Speaker*: With this we shall discuss the following motion on education:
>   That the draft Higher Education (Basic Amount) (England) Regulations 2010, which were laid before this House on 29 November, be approved. (6–13)[5]

This is the standpoint that is advanced and will be immediately called into doubt by other MPs who will register their intention to speak and call on Vince Cable to 'give way', i.e. to allow to be interrupted. The existence of disagreement, hence the need for debate, is acknowledged from the start both by the Speaker of the House ('There are strong opinions on this matter, and passions are aroused', 32) and by the proponent (the House should 'entertain debate on the wider issues involved, because they arouse very strong feelings inside and outside' parliament, 15–16). This takes the debate into the *opening* stage, where, following the identification of a disagreement, participants typically decide (implicitly or explicitly) to have a regulated argumentative discussion with a view to resolving the disagreement. The pragma-dialectical model assigns an exploration of participants' shared common ground, of what they *do not* disagree on, to the *opening* stage. This involves agreement on both substantive and procedural matters and is often implicit, as the relevant common ground is assumed to exist: there is no need, therefore, for example to remind participants that there is a budget deficit and that the government intends to reduce it at great speed. However, some clear procedural points are made explicitly, both by Vince Cable and by the Deputy Speaker, at the *opening* stage of the debate, and are prompted by an interruption from a Labour MP, followed by more interruptions (marked as such in the *Hansard* transcript):

> *Kevin Brennan (Labour, Cardiff West)*: Will the Secretary of State give way?
>
> *Vince Cable*: I will take interventions later. You have asked, Mr Speaker, that both Front Benchers should keep their introductions brief. [Interruption.] As hon. Members know, I am very happy to take interventions, but I will take them when I have developed an argument. [Interruption.]
>
> *Mr Speaker*: Order. The Secretary of State should resume his seat for a moment, and I apologize for having to interrupt him. There are strong opinions on this matter, and passions are aroused. That is understood and accepted. What is not accepted by any democrat is that the Secretary of State should not receive a fair hearing. The right hon. Gentleman will be heard, and if Members are making a noise and then expecting to be called, I fear that is a triumph of optimism over reality. (25–35)

These procedural matters are made explicit precisely because, while normally being part of a taken for granted common normative framework (which includes all rules of procedures that define parliamentary debate, e.g. that debate will end in voting and the result of the vote will decide, etc.), they have been temporarily ignored by some of the participants, who apparently need to be reminded of them. Namely, the proponent will receive a fair hearing; interventions will be brief; no interruptions will be accepted before the proponent's case has been heard; the proponent will respond to interventions only after being allowed to develop his argument. These (and all other reminders about proper procedure throughout the debate) are part of the *opening* stage.

From the beginning, the proponent (Vince Cable) announces the goals of the higher education motion: it is 'a central part of a policy that is designed to maintain high-quality universities in the long term, that tackles the fiscal deficit and that provides a more progressive system of graduate contributions based on people's ability to pay' (17–19). This already belongs to the argumentation stage (the action is justified in terms of its goals) but the *argumentation* stage is more fully developed later on. Next, the proponent informs the parliamentary assembly of certain relevant facts (of the 'sequence of events that has led to this debate'), referring to the Browne review of higher education, commissioned by the previous government, whose task was to 'make the existing system of graduate payments more progressive and more related to future graduates' ability to pay', and 'look thoroughly at the alternatives, and particularly at the alternative of a graduate tax'. The Labour proposal of a graduate tax, the Business Secretary says, initially seemed a promising alternative but the Browne report, after careful consideration, had found it has many disadvantages. The government, the proponent says, has considered many options for funding universities while having to cut their budget, but most of these had serious drawbacks. The solution to increase tuition fees, while making graduates pay later, when they are in employment, has emerged as the only 'practical alternative'.

This is a report of a previous process of collective deliberation, within government, over what action would best serve the goals. All of the stages of deliberation (the specific framework suggested by McBurney *et al.* 2007) can be reconstructed from this report, from the *opening governing question* (How can we solve the problem, i.e. make cuts so as to deal with the deficit but also ensure universities have adequate funding?), to the final recommendation for action, and passing through the *Propose* and *Consider* stage (references to various proposals that had been advanced and discussed, and to how most of them had been discarded on account of negative consequences) and the *Revise* stage (an account of how the current proposal has itself been revised in order to mitigate its potential negative impact – e.g. no fees will be paid up-front, loans will be repaid only when earnings exceed £21,000, etc.). Implicitly, there was also *Confirmation* of acceptance by all participants and a provisional *Closing* of the deliberation dialogue, as it had taken place in government. However, having the proposal accepted within government is not enough, as it has to be submitted to Parliament for debate and confirmation. It is Parliament, through debate followed by voting, that can turn the outcome of the deliberation within government into a legitimate decision (if the motion also passes in the House of Lords).

In the parliamentary debate, this report of the deliberation that has already occurred in government takes place at the *Inform* stage. Let us look at some relevant sections of the report of the original deliberation process, particularly those that corresponds to the *Propose*, *Consider*, *Revise* and *Recommend* stages of that deliberation. In the *Hansard* transcript, the paragraphs quoted below occur between lines 150 and 354 and are interspersed with several interventions from several MPs (not included here). Notice that the first paragraph, while beginning to report on the choices that were proposed and considered, also refers to the *Open* stage, the asking of the governing question, in one of its formulations (What options do we have, faced, as we are, with the task of making cuts of about 25 per cent?):

> *Vince Cable (The Secretary of State for Business, Innovation and Skills)*: What were the options for a Department facing 25% cuts of the kind that [Labour was also] going to introduce? Some 70% of all spending in the Department is on universities. [Labour] could – and I could – have chosen to make the cuts elsewhere, the largest category would have been in further education. We could have made the choice to cut apprenticeships and skill-level training by a modest amount, but we need to deal with the problem we have inherited of 6 million adults in this country without the basic literacy of a 12-year-old. We could have cut that, but we chose not to. So we were left with the question of how to make cuts in the university budget of about 25%. There were various options – [Interruption] (150–160).
>
> There were various options for cutting the university budget. We could have reduced radically the number of university students by 200,000, but all the evidence suggests, as the previous Government used to argue, that increasing university participation is the best avenue to social mobility. We therefore rejected that option and did not cut large numbers of university students. We could have made a decision radically to reduce student maintenance, which would have been easier, less visible and less provocative in the short run. We could have done that, but the effect of that would have been to reduce the support that low-income students receive when they are at university now. We rejected that option. We could have taken what I would call the Scottish option. We could have cut funding to universities without giving them the means to raise additional income through a graduate contribution. The certain consequence of that would have been that in five to ten years, the great English universities – Manchester, Birmingham, Bristol and the rest – would still be great, world-class universities, whereas universities such as Glasgow, . . ., and Edinburgh would be in a state of decline. We rejected – and rejected consciously – all those unacceptable options . . .. (163–177)
>
> We have eliminated, I think, most of the other alternatives to raising funding for universities. I hope that nobody on the Opposition Benches is seriously arguing that we should drastically reduce the number of students, that we should drastically reduce

maintenance or that we should simply withdraw funding from universities. The only practical alternative was to retrieve income for universities from high-earning graduates once they have left. That is the policy that we are pursuing . . .. (240–246)

Opposition Members who follow these arguments closely have often made the following argument. 'We acknowledge', they say, 'that universities will continue to have high levels of income, but you're replacing public funding with private funding, and this is – in some sense – ideological'. [Hon. Members: 'It is!'] That is a debating point, and I am happy to take it on. At present, roughly 60% of the income of universities comes from the public sector, through different funding streams. The rest comes from private sources – something that the previous Government were trying to encourage. That will be reversed: in future, roughly 40% of university funding will come from the public sector and 60% will come from the private sector. I am keen to encourage more private funding of universities, which is why I have spoken to the director general of the CBI. (. . .) I hope that not too many Opposition Members would regard additional funding from employers as somehow ideologically contaminated, because we will need more resources going into universities, not less, and that is what we are doing. (248–265)

Let me proceed. Of course increasing the graduate contribution is bound to have an effect – it is an additional cost – to graduates. I therefore want to summarise the steps we are taking to make sure that this happens in a fair and equitable way. First of all, no full-time students will pay upfront tuition fees and part-time students doing their first degree will for the first time – unlike under the last Government – have the opportunity to obtain concessional finance under the student loan scheme arrangements. (. . .) (291–301)

Third, we will introduce a threshold for graduate repayment of a £21,000 salary – a significantly higher level than before – and it will be uprated annually in line with earnings. It is important to emphasise that point because under the Labour Government, there was a threshold of £15,000, but it was never uprated on any basis whatever. (. . .) Those existing students whom the last Government did absolutely nothing to protect will have inflation-proofing in future. (303–310)

Furthermore, we are introducing variable interest rates so that those on high incomes pay relatively more to ensure the progressivity of the scheme, as a result of which a £30,000 salary will carry a monthly payment of approximately £68, which is far lower, incidentally, than it would be under a graduate tax system. Under that system, people would have to start paying much earlier and at much lower levels of income. (314–318)

(. . .) In addition, universities wishing to move to a higher threshold will have demanding tests applied to their offer requirements in respect of access. It is worth recalling the situation that we have inherited. There are a lot of crocodile tears from Labour Members, so let me remind them that social mobility, judged by the number of people from disadvantaged backgrounds getting into Russell group universities, has deteriorated over the last decade. (. . .) That is a shameful inheritance from people who claim to be concerned about disadvantaged backgrounds – and we intend to rectify it. (323–334)

Let me conclude in this way. I do not pretend – none of us pretends – that this is an easy subject. Of course it is not. We have had to make very difficult choices. [Interruption] Yes, we have. We could have taken easier options, but we were insistent that at the end, we would make a substantial . . . [Interruption] . . . I now wish to summarize where we are. As I was saying, there have been difficult choices to make. We could have made a decision drastically to cut the number of university students; we could have cut student maintenance; we could have cut the funding to universities, without replacing it. Instead, we have opted for a set of policies that provides a strong base for university funding and makes a major contribution to reducing the deficit, while introducing a significantly more progressive system of graduate payments than we inherited. I am proud to put forward that measure to this House. (335–354)

Part of the first paragraph above and the whole of the second is a report of the alternatives the government looked at and of the reasons why they were rejected (the *Propose* and *Consider* stages). The alternatives of reducing the number of students, or reducing student maintenance grants, or simply cutting funding without setting up a system of graduate contributions would have entailed unacceptable costs or negative consequences, and would have compromised goals and concerns that the government is committed to (social mobility, support for low-income families, standards of quality). The alternative of cutting from other education areas, for instance from further education, would have worsened the already serious situation that the government has inherited, of having millions of people in the UK without basic literacy. Consequently, in the third paragraph, the Business Secretary concludes that, having 'eliminated' all these unacceptable alternatives (by considering what consequences they were likely to have), 'the only practical alternative was to retrieve income for universities from high-earning graduates once they have left' (the *Recommend* stage of the previous deliberation). The proposal to increase fees has thus emerged after careful consideration of all possible alternatives and their probable consequences, and from an effort to balance all relevant considerations, and particularly several potentially conflicting goals and values: the goal of saving money *and* of ensuring fairness *and* of not compromising quality.

Next, the proponent addresses a challenge that has been made against his proposal (and is in fact made again, just as he speaks): allegedly, the proposal is 'ideological', as it replaces public funding by private funding. He claims he is happy to discuss this objection, but he defends his proposal by saying that more funding will be needed in future from private sources and by implying that to regard such extra funding as 'ideologically contaminated' is an unreasonable view. This objection challenges the goals of action themselves, not just the means, and we will discuss its significance later.

From this point onward (paragraphs 5–8), Vince Cable details a number of measures that the government has agreed on in order to make sure that the increase in tuition fees is 'fair and equitable', and 'progressive', i.e. in accordance with the government's stated values: no full-time student will pay upfront tuition fees, student loans will only be repaid once graduates start earning more than £21,000 per year, there will be variable interest rates and grant provisions for low-income families, and universities wanting to charge the maximum fee (£9,000) will be subjected to strict conditions. These measures were implicitly developed in response to (real or anticipated) objections at the *Revise* stage of the previous deliberation, and this section of Cable's speech reports on how the original proposal has been revised in government, how it has been fine-tuned so as to be as fair as possible and have as little negative impact as possible. All of these measures will ensure fairness and increase social mobility; the latter has decreased, Cable says, under the Labour government. In other words, Labour's education policies have not fulfilled Labour's stated goals, whereas the current government's proposal will. The government intends to 'rectify' Labour's 'shameful inheritance' in respect of social mobility and deliver the goals that Labour failed to deliver. This is part of a comparison with, and a negative evaluation of, Labour's previous education policies, based on a contradiction between action and stated goals (and values). In the final paragraph quoted above, the Business Secretary summarizes the alternatives and the decision-making process and recommends the government's choice, as one which can provide a strong basis for university funding, contributes to reducing the deficit and introduces a far more progressive system of graduate payments than proposed by Labour. The argument in favour of increasing fees has implicitly withstood critical questioning in government. The proposal has emerged as being, allegedly, necessary and sufficient in view of the goals: there are no better alternatives, and the goals will be achieved. All alternatives that have been examined have been found wanting, and as for possible negative consequences that may undermine the goal, they too have been examined on the basis of past evidence, and have been found to be improbable.

Briefly, the deliberation in government that is being reported here started with an open question: How do we achieve the *goal* of making cuts of 25 per cent in a way that does not have unacceptable negative consequences, comparatively speaking, and is also compatible with certain values or concerns? (*Open* stage of deliberation). After considering all relevant information (*Inform*), several alternatives were proposed and examined (*Propose, Consider*) and all but one were rejected. The alternative that emerged as comparatively better is that of cutting state funding for universities and allowing them to increase tuition fees to compensate for these cuts. After suitable revision and refinement, this proposal was recommended for adoption and was approved in government (*Recommend, Revise, Confirm, Close*). In the new round of deliberation, this proposal is now submitted for debate in parliament. Like the procedural points we mentioned earlier, Vince Cable's report of the previous deliberation is part of the *opening* stage of the parliament debate, viewed as critical discussion, and makes explicit the background information (shared substantive commitments) that MPs are expected to start from in developing their arguments. As we will see, subsequent argumentation will in some cases challenge these starting points as well: in particular, the allegedly shared goal of making 25 per cent cuts in the education department budget, as a something that uncontroversially needs doing, will be called into question.

The way in which the stages of this particular parliamentary debate correspond to those of the *previous* debate in government and to the stages of the critical discussion model can be summed up as in Table 6.1.

The *Inform* stage of parliamentary debate may include, as here, a report on some or all the stages of the previous debate in government. Let us note that parliamentary debate does not start with an open question (there is no *Open* stage) but with a specific proposal and there is no *Revise* stage within this type of debate, although, as in the particular case we are looking at, there are references, by some participants, to unsuccessful attempts to propose amendments *prior* to the start of the debate. The purpose of this activity type is not to revise the proposal but to discuss it and vote on it; revisions are possible but are part of another activity type. Similarly, alternative proposals can be aired, but cannot be discussed and voted on: only the motion is subject to debate and voting. We should also note that the *Consider* stage of parliamentary debate does not consider several alternatives, but only critically examines one specific proposal, although there are references to the existence of alternatives; these, however, cannot form the object of a decision within the same debate. Crucially, the institutional context requires that deliberation in parliament should end in a decision for action, not just in a normative judgement that action *A* is the right or wrong action. The *Confirm* stage is highly specific in parliamentary debate as activity type and involves voting; the result of the vote counts as a decision for action (it is not parliament that will act, but government, based on the decision that has been legitimately, democratically arrived at in parliament). This, again, is part of the institutional logic of executive and legislative power in a democratic society. The institutional context thus determines what participants may or may not

Table 6.1 Stages of deliberation in government and parliamentary debates

Stages of deliberation in government	Stages of deliberation in parliament	Deliberation in parliament reconstructed as critical discussion
	Propose the motion (result of previous deliberation in government)	Confrontation stage
Open (asking of open question)	*Inform* participants of relevant facts (may include report of previous deliberation in government)	Opening stage (shared substantive and procedural commitments)
Inform participants of relevant facts		
Propose alternatives		
Consider alternatives and eliminate alternatives that are comparatively worse		
Recommend alternative that has best withstood critical examination		
Revise chosen alternative to mitigate negative impact		
Confirm acceptance or rejection by all participants		
Close deliberation	*Consider* (or critically examine) the motion	Argumentation stage
	Recommend motion for acceptance or rejection by all participants	Closing stage
	Confirm acceptance or rejection by all participants (voting)	
	Close deliberation	

do, or can reasonably be expected to do, argumentatively speaking, and what counts as a reasonable outcome: in this case, not a shared belief but a collective decision. It also imposes time constraints, temporal boundaries beyond which the debate (and each individual speech) may not continue, as well as other procedural constraints.

The eight-stage ideal model of deliberation as genre we referred to earlier is thus *contextualized* in various ways in different *institutional* contexts. The deliberative activity type that takes place in government is different in structure from the one that takes place in parliament. The former seems to correspond more closely to the eight-stage model, the latter less so. Both of these (as normative models defining the activity type that draw in different ways on the normative model of deliberation as genre, placed at a higher level of abstraction) are implemented in concrete events, which can also differ more or less from the model of the activity type. In particular parliamentary debates, such as the tuition fees one, the *Consider*, *Inform* and *Recommend* stages recur a great many times, as there are very many speeches by MPs who all examine the motion, bring arguments for or against it, inform other participants of relevant facts they should take into account, and recommend it for adoption or rejection.

The argumentation stage: a critical examination of the proposal to increase tuition fees

The argumentation stage of the parliamentary debate starts shortly after the Business Secretary begins his report of the previous deliberation in government, and takes the form of critical challenges addressed by other MPs, to which the proponent responds, by agreeing to 'give way' (interrupt his account) and take these interventions. (In the eight-stage model of deliberation, the *argumentation* stage corresponds mainly to *Considering* the proposal and its implications.) The MPs are questioning the rightness of the government's proposal by arguing, variously, that: the extent of the cuts in higher education, particularly cutting the teaching grant by 80 per cent, is excessive and disproportionate in relation to the cuts made in other departments (86–94; 136–142); trebling tuition fees will have a disastrous impact on Scottish universities and Scotland's devolved government (180–183); by increasing fees, participation among lower and middle-income students will decrease (187–192); the proposal will not be fair to families across the UK, as Scotland and Wales will not demand fees (200–204); it is likely that all universities will charge the maximum amount, £9,000, not just £6,000 or less (266–271). Most of these interventions challenge the proponent to indicate what 'assurances' and 'guarantees' he can provide that the negative effects outlined in the interventions will be dealt with, and show how the government intends to 'mitigate' those effects, how it will closely 'monitor' the situation in order to take 'corrective action', should the proposal have an adverse impact. As we have seen, such critical challenges are typical for practical reasoning, as the emergence of negative consequences, as well as agents' failure to correct a decision in view of emerging negative feedback, indicate a failure of rationality and undermine the claim.

While arguing against the proposal, some participants also suggest a clearer definition of what is at stake, a re-definition of the confrontation. Very early on, Jack Straw (Labour MP for Blackburn and former Home Secretary) (87–94) claims that 'the central issue is the fact that the teaching grant is to be cut by 80 per cent, the burden of which is to be transferred to students'. Jack Straw's point is developed more clearly a little later by John Denham (Labour MP for Southampton, Itchen), the Labour Shadow Secretary for Education and spokesman on the issue of tuition fees (lines 373 onwards), who makes his own speech after Cable has finished. Here are some extracts from his speech:

Mr John Denham (Labour/Southampton, Itchen): (. . .) There are millions of parents and millions of current and future students who do not care about the Liberal Democrats, but who do care about the huge fee increase that we are being asked to decide today. Today's decision must be taken on the facts and on the merits. If this Tory measure goes through with the support or abstention of Liberal Democrats, that party will forfeit the right to call itself a progressive political party. The House can stop that decision today. (. . .) Let me set out why Members should vote against, or vote for a delay and a rethink, rather than abstaining. (383–397)

As you said last night, Mr Speaker, today's vote is on a narrow issue – the fee cap. Behind that, however, is the most profound change in university funding since the University Grants Committee was set up in the 1920s. It is the ending of funding for most university degrees. It is a huge burden of debt on graduates. It is an untried, untested and unstable market for students. Although there is always room for improvement, England enjoys a world-class university system: world-class in research, with a disproportionate number of the best research universities; and a richness and diversity of higher education to compare with the best. The risks are so high, and the consequences so unclear, that no sane person would rush the proposal through without proper debate or discussion. (. . .) (410–420)

(. . .) As a result of these Tory policies, this country will stand alone with Romania as the only OECD countries cutting investment in higher education. (. . .) The fee increases are not designed to raise extra money for universities. That was Labour's scheme – we took the difficult decision to introduce top-up fees, to add to record university income, and to enable more students to go to better-funded universities. The Prime Minister's plan, put forward by the Business Secretary, is totally different. Fees are being trebled simply to reduce the 80% cut in the funding of university teaching, not to raise extra money. Most graduates will be asked not to pay something towards their university education, but to pay the entire cost of their university education. Universities will have to charge £7,000 to £8,000 simply to replace the money they lose, and many universities will lose 90% of their public funding. That is what is at stake today. If the House passes the fee increase, English students and graduates will face the highest fees of any public university system anywhere in the developed world: higher than France, higher than Germany, and higher – yes – than the United States of America. (476–490)

(. . .) Most graduates will be paying off their debts for 30 years. Under the current scheme, the average is 11 years. The children of those graduates will have started university before they have paid their own fees. As I will show, the payment system is not fair. (. . .)

We certainly need to sustain investment in higher education, but . . . it is not necessary to adopt our macro-economic policies to know that the Government could have made a different choice. No other country in the world is taking the step we are taking, and no other country in the world can understand why we are taking it. As always, rather than defending their position, the Government give the pathetic answer, 'We had no choice'. But they did have a choice. Everyone knows they had a choice. (510–517)

We in the Labour party would take a more measured and responsible approach to deficit reduction, but even on its own terms, if the coalition had cut higher education in line with the rest of public services, we would have been looking at fee increases of a few hundred pounds. The Business Secretary has told us that the figure should be not 10%, but 20%. That would mean fee increases of not much over £4,000, rather than the £6,000 to £9,000 for which the House is being asked to vote today. (518–523)

Let me explain . . . .. There are two stages in this process. The first is deciding how much public funding there will be and how much money needs to come from graduates. The second is deciding how the graduates are to make their contributions. The first stage is the critical one to consider today, because it is the 80% cut in university education that is forcing the graduate contributions so high . . .. (528–533)

First John Denham makes an appeal to reasonableness ('today's decision must be taken on the facts and on the merits') and reminds Liberal Democrats, as coalition partners, of the values they are supposed to uphold: they are a 'progressive' party (their underlying values, that is, can only lead them to support one type of action, not other). Then he begins to make an attempt to persuade MPs of his standpoint, by setting out the reasons 'why Members should vote against, or vote for a delay and a rethink'. In the second and third paragraphs he redefines the confrontation: what is at stake is not just the fee cap, which is a narrow issue, but a radical change in the system of university funding: practically, this means ending university funding by the state and transferring this burden almost entirely onto the students (410–414). The consequences of this change risk being disastrous (e.g. Britain will ruin its world-class universities), which is why 'no sane person would rush the proposal through without proper debate or discussion' (another invocation of norms of reasonableness). If the motion is adopted, UK students will face some of the highest fees in the world and will incur enormous debts, which they will still be paying long after their own children have started university. Universities will not enjoy more funding but will struggle to replace the funds that are being cut. Having outlined why the proposal should be rejected on account of its negative consequences, the Shadow Secretary talks about alternatives (paragraphs 5–7). The government claims it had no choice, but 'everyone knows they had a choice': fees could have been increased by hundreds of pounds, to £4,000, as the Labour government was going to do, not trebled. Denham distinguishes once again between two issues: the question of *how much* of the education budget has to come from the students is one thing, while *how* graduates are to make their contribution (the repayment scheme) is another (529–533). He suggests that the former issue is critical, and this is what the disagreement is really about, as students are being asked to practically replace the state budget from their own resources. This is part of the redefinition of the confrontation suggested by other MPs as well: the main disagreement is about the *new balance* in funding between state and students, which means that possible agreement on the progressive character of the repayment scheme should not obscure the more fundamental difference of opinion on this more important issue. Finally (last paragraph), Denham outlines the likely negative consequences of the proposal in financial terms: the proposal will backfire, it will cost more than it will save. He brings evidence from various reliable sources estimating that the government will have to write off a lot of the debts which it will not be able to collect ('every year they will borrow £10 billion to fund student loans, and every year they will write off £3 billion of the £10 billion that they have just borrowed because they cannot collect the loans'). This is to say that, rather than achieving the goal of saving money, the proposal will compromise that goal too, along with other goals and values that should not be compromised, as all parties concerned (students, universities and taxpayers) will be worse off.

One of the goals that risk being compromised is social mobility, underlain by the value of fairness. As the Shadow Secretary says earlier in his speech (lines 650–651; 696–704), fairness must be measured both by how much graduates have to pay and 'by the chance of becoming a graduate at all'. The prospect of huge debt will discourage people coming from low-income backgrounds from going to university and will effectively freeze social mobility. John Denham's speech also includes a lengthy demonstration why the government's repayment scheme is not in fact fair, particularly on graduates of average earnings. He acknowledges that low-earning graduates might end up not having to repay much of their debt, but he argues that 'nothing about the tiny benefit for the lowest-income graduates justifies doubling or trebling the debt of the vast majority of graduates' (610–611): such a huge rise in fees and in debt cannot be but unfair.

The issue of social mobility is taken up by several MPs in their interventions and it is one of the major arguments against the government's proposal. David Blunkett (former Secretary of State for Education and Skills and Labour MP for Sheffield, Brightside and Hillsborough) argues, in his own intervention (889–959), that the government's proposal to introduce a £9,000 a year fee 'on top of cuts in youth and careers services across the country is a deliberate, consistent and unfair attack on young people in our country and their future'. This is the main reason 'why it should be rejected', as 'it is not fair to young people and their families, it is not fair to universities, and it is not fair to our country and the future of Britain'. The proposal will have a devastating impact on social mobility, as children from disadvantaged backgrounds will no longer be able to go to university at all. In addition to this 'perverse' impact on goals and values, the proposal will also fail to achieve its financial purposes. As the Office for Budget Responsibility has already said, 'the borrowing that will be required to fund the loans in the first place will actually outstrip any gain that might have been made': from £4.1 billion this year, borrowing will increase to £10.7 billion in 2015–16, which means, Blunkett says, that 'we are making the deficit worse in the period when we are supposed to be reducing it'. If the economy recovers, he argues, the government will be fully capable of sustaining the £3 billion that is now being removed from higher education teaching. Blunkett's argument attacks the proposal on account of negative consequences that will compromise goals and values (social mobility and fairness, on the one hand, and the goal of saving money on the other), and also by showing that the action is not necessary, on the normal assumption that the economy will eventually recover. This is to say that the proposed means is neither necessary nor sufficient in view of the goals. There are alternatives, but they are not considered because, he says, the proposal 'is designed to change the architecture of higher education in this country' in accordance with an *ideological* vision ('it is ideologically based, not logically based'), and this is why the government is pressing for its adoption as the only reasonable choice. There are covert or ideological reasons involved, and to that extent, he seems to be implying, the argument is a rationalization and attempts to deceive and manipulate.

As we have seen, both Jack Straw and John Denham are attempting to redefine the confrontation, or redefine what the disagreement is really about. Similar attempts are made later by other MPs, who argue that what is at stake is a 'huge transfer of responsibility and cost from the state to the individual', and that reducing the teaching grant by 80 per cent is huge by comparison with the small reduction of 1.6 per cent announced in Labour's last budget (2690–2704). Also, that the *essence* of the debate is that 'we are breaking the partnership between student, state, and university' and 'saying that the state can step out of this arrangement, and that the arrangement should be entirely between the student and the university' (1632–1635).

There is no space here to go through the entire of range of arguments used by opponents and supporters of the government's proposal at the argumentation stage. There is, for instance, an argument made by David Lammy (Labour MP for Tottenham and former

Higher Education Minister), saying that what students are being asked to contribute is excessive given what they are likely to receive in exchange. There are too few contact hours and students will be justified in asking 'What do we get for that £9,000?' (1644–1655). Typically, opponents try to rebut the claim by invoking the highly probable *negative consequences* of its adoption, particularly on social mobility. Supporters, on the other hand, deny that these negative consequences will occur (on the contrary, they argue that social mobility will increase and the quality of education will rise) and point to the proposal's alleged progressiveness by comparison with alternatives, particularly by comparison with Labour's graduate tax scheme, which is said to be both unfair and to generate adverse effects (faced with higher taxes, graduates will move abroad). Several interventions focus not on consequences but on *alternatives* for action. Pointing out that an action is not necessary because better alternatives exist is an attempt to defeat the argument. The first intervention below points to the alternative of making bankers pay more, rather than cutting the budget for education; the second supports a business education tax on the biggest companies that benefit directly from graduates; the third focuses on taxing the wealthy and pursuing tax evasion. Choosing any of these alternative proposals would mean that the education budget would not have to be cut at all, hence tuition fees would not need to go up, or could even be dispensed with:

> *Geraint Davies (Labour / Co-op, Swansea West)*: Does my right hon. Friend accept that reducing access and increasing relative price to our competitors will reduce the productivity and tax receipts of future generations and undermine economic growth? What we should be doing is making the bankers pay the levy rather than giving it back in corporation tax, and investing that money in higher education and the future productivity and economic growth of this country. (1504–1509)
>
> *Caroline Lucas (Green, Brighton)*: The hon. Gentleman rightly spoke about the importance of employers paying their contribution towards higher education. Does he therefore support the University and College Union's proposal for a business education tax that would essentially be a corporation tax on the 4% biggest companies that benefit directly from graduates? That would generate £3.9 billion for higher education and would mean that we could scrap tuition fees altogether. (1108–1011)
>
> *Jeremy Corbyn (Labour, Islington North)*: By this vote today, we are destroying the opportunities, hopes and life chances of a whole generation. (. . .) We need to tax the wealthy. We do not need a graduate tax or an increase in income tax to pay for it. Some £6 billion has not been collected from Vodafone thanks to a cosy deal with Her Majesty's Revenue and Customs. That is actually more than the total amount paid through tuition fees over the past year. (2551–2555)

What these MPs are doing is challenging the goals of action, previously presented by the Business Secretary as shared starting points. They are therefore trying to broaden the scope of the debate to include deliberation about goals, not only about means. The question therefore should not be whether increasing tuition fees is the best way to meet the demand for cutting the education budget but whether the education budget should be cut at all. We will return to this discussion later.

The government's proposal is also vigorously defended in several interventions. The Conservative MP for Reading West, Alok Sharma, answers the Opposition's three main challenges (related to consequences on numbers of students, on social mobility and its alleged unfairness) and claims that the negative consequences being predicted will not occur (in fact, contrary, positive effects will occur – i.e. making universities more accountable to students as customers), all the goals will be achieved and the underlying values will not be affected, as the proposal is fair (it is in fact fairer than Labour's proposal). It is fair not only to graduates and their families, but also to non-graduate taxpayers, whose taxes should not be spent on financing the university education of others (this argument is also made by another MP, in lines 940–943). He also reminds the audience of why the increase in fees is necessary: to deal with the 'shocking state' of public finances inherited from Labour. This particular definition of the circumstances of action appears several times in the debate (e.g. 804, 1461, 3381) and leads to additional disagreement, with Labour MPs denying that the increase in fees is can be justified in terms of a situation which they are responsible for, pointing to the banks as the real culprits and suggesting (as David Blunkett above) that there are other reasons for the rise in fees. As one MP asks rhetorically, if the rise in fees is necessary to help reduce the deficit, will the government guarantee that 'in four years' time – when they intend to have paid off the deficit – these proposals will be reversed and the money will go back into the higher education sector?' (1946–1954).

There are on the whole many appeals to honesty, many challenges in terms of alleged hypocrisy and many suggestions that the reasons being given are not the real reasons, i.e. that the decision is political and not economic (2023–2125), that it is ideological (as David Blunkett says, raising tuition fees is an 'ideological issue', not having to do with deficit-reduction, 971–972), hence, the proponents' argument is a *rationalization*, whose real goal is to change the system of education in accordance with an ideological agenda. Conservative MPs also claim that it is hypocritical of Labour to oppose the motion by invoking the dangers of personal indebtedness, given the debt incurred on behalf of every individual by the government's massive borrowing. Labour's arguments 'would carry a little more weight if they had not left every man, woman and child in this country with a debt of £22,000' (3180–3182). Similarly, it is hypocritical for Labour MPs to say that the government is 'pulling the away' from poorer students, when their own 'policies in government were pulling the ladder away from the whole country' (2028–2031).

The arguments for and against are summed up at the end of the debate by two Front Benchers, Gareth Thomas (Labour MP for Harrow West) and the Minister for Universities and Science, David Willetts. Thomas emphasizes that the government could have chosen differently and could have raised the fees by a few hundred pounds, not thousands. Second, that what is at stake is a radical change in the balance of funding between the government and graduates, which 'might have been a reasonable line if a slight shift was involved, but the Government have thrown away the scales and are loading the whole cost – not a bigger part, but the whole cost – of university education on to the graduate'. Third, that the fees increase will have a severe impact on social mobility and will particularly deter students from lower-income families. Again, a negative comparison is made with Romania, as the only other OECD country that has cut the higher education budget. Thomas ends his speech by an appeal to the interests and values of 'ordinary working people' and of 'all those who are outraged by this attack on the ambitions and aspirations of the brightest and best of Britain's next generation'. He warns that 'an abstention is not enough' and recommends the rejection of the proposal ('I urge the House to reject these proposals').

In his own summing up, David Willetts begins by observing that 'all three parties, when in government and confronted by the challenge of how to finance higher education in our country, have reached the same conclusion', that the solution is tuition fees, paid for by loans from the taxpayer and then repaid by graduates. Moreover, what the government is proposing to do is not very different from what Labour was proposing, but the government's solution is actually more progressive than the graduate tax. There would appear to be no fundamental disagreement, hence (implicitly) no real reason for the Opposition to vote against the proposal. Experience has shown, he says, that fees do not deter poor students from going to university. In fact, the proposal will improve social mobility, it is progressive and will give universities a sound financial backing, including substantial increases in funding 'in accordance with student choice'. The Opposition, according to Willetts, has only offered delay but no constructive alternative. In spite of the Opposition's complaints about the lack of time, Willetts says, the proposal has been carefully considered, has emerged from the Browne review, and is therefore 'not rushed'. The government has no choice but to act as proposed, given the context of action (the 'mess' bequeathed by Labour) and the goal of dealing with it in a fair way and avoiding further negative consequences (an increase in government borrowing which will affect the younger generation). Faced with the 'challenge of how to deliver progressive policies in a time of austerity', the government has made the best decision. This is an abridged version of his speech:

> *The Minister for Universities and Science (Mr David Willetts)*: We have indeed had a passionate and robust debate, and I am sorry that there will not be time for me to respond to all the points that have been made. The reason for the passion is that all of us care about the future of our universities, and about how we discharge our obligations to the younger generation. It has to be said that all three parties, when in government and confronted by the challenge of how to finance higher education in our country, have reached the same conclusion. All have concluded that the way forward is fees, paid for by loans from the taxpayer and repaid by graduates. (. . .)
>
> I was explaining to the House how all three parties have reached the same conclusion, albeit by a rather circuitous route. (. . .) We have now seen the evidence, however, and it shows that, since fees came in – and because there were loans as well – the proportion of people going to university from the poorest backgrounds in England has actually gone up. (. . .) That is why my party has concluded that fees supported by loans do not deter poor students from going to university.
>
> The Liberal Democrat party and my right hon. Friend the Secretary of State for Business, Innovation and Skills, when confronted with the challenge of how to deliver progressive policies in a time of austerity, have rightly concluded that this is what we have to do. (. . .)
>
> We have improved on the policies that we inherited from the previous Government. They had a threshold of £15,000 and we are increasing that to £21,000, which is why the poorest quarter of graduates will be better off under our proposals than on the scheme we inherited. (. . .)
>
> The Government are committed to explaining how our proposals are progressive, how they will improve social mobility and how they will give our universities secure financial backing for the future. (. . .)
>
> We often hear Opposition Members talk about the loss of teaching grant, but they do not talk about the other side of the proposal – the extra money that can come to universities through the choices of students. We trust students. Taxpayers will provide students with the money to pay the fees. That will ensure that universities can continue to enjoy the levels of income that they enjoy at the moment. That money will not be handed out from Whitehall; it will come from the choices of students. (. . . .) Our proposals are equitable, and we believe that they will ensure that students can choose the courses that they wish. (. . .)

We believe that the proposals are the right way forward for our universities. All the Opposition can offer is delay. They did not even dare propose their graduate tax today. (. . .) Labour left a mess in the public finances, and the Government must tackle it. If we do not tackle it in the way we propose, and if we go for the delay that the Opposition advocate, it will simply mean less funding for universities or more Government borrowing. Who pays the Government debt? It is the younger generation whom the Opposition claim to care about.

That is why the Government commend the motions to the House. We believe that we have tackled the challenge – in a time of austerity – of proposing a policy that is fair and progressive, and one that puts power in the hands of students and universities on a solid financial footing for the future. (3261–3390)

Willetts's speech attempts to downplay or minimize the disagreement: as he says, all parties *agree* on the need for fees, hence of loans funded by the taxpayer, and the government's proposal is actually an improvement on Labour's previous plans. He says nothing about the huge difference, in absolute terms, between the budget cuts and fee increases proposed by the current and previous government. Nor does he address at all the broader issues behind the rise in fees, suggested by the opponents, namely that the government is in fact aiming to radically reorganize higher education in accordance with an ideological vision, and break up the partnership between the students and the state as far as the burden of funding is concerned. In so doing, the Minister is defining the confrontation in a rhetorically convenient way. Briefly, he seems to imply, the confrontation is minimal, as it is underlain by a very broad zone of agreement, and there is no good reason why the Opposition should reject the proposal, hence by implication, no need for him to defend it. Similarly, his choice to refer to the debate in conciliatory and positive terms, as having been 'passionate and robust' and motivated by a *common* concern for the future of universities and for the young generation, is meant to smooth out antagonism and suggest a commonality of purpose that, once again, can only presumably lead to the Opposition agreeing with the proposal. Willetts not only implies that there is little reason for disagreement, hence no real need for defence, but also suggests that Labour politicians are inconsistent in arguing against it: if they care about the younger generation, as they claim, they should support the proposal, otherwise state borrowing will only increase, which will affect the chances of the younger generation. This implies, once again, that their position is indefensible, being self-contradictory.

Willetts also downplays the negative consequences and focuses instead on the advantages the government's proposal will bring, not only in terms of securing funding for universities, but in enabling students to have more 'power' and a greater stake in their own education. There are implicit references to a desirable reorganization of universities according to market principles (the money will not come from the government, but from students, in relation to where and what students *choose* to study; students can be trusted to make the best choices, etc.), but the challenges addressed by the government's critics in connection with what is seen as a final and radical stage in the reorganization of universities as private markets (see 885, 2162, 2551, 2951) are not at all really developed in his intervention and more generally in this debate.

Willetts' speech ends the debate and is followed by the vote (the *Confirm* and *Close* stages). The result of the vote on 9 December 2010 was: 323 votes in favour of the proposal and 302 against, with several Liberal Democrats and Conservative MPs voting against the party whip, against the government's motion.

Reasonable debate under time constraints

A noticeable feature of this debate is an emphasis on time constraints. Several interventions and speeches (by the opponents of the government's proposal) contain explicit pleas for more time, for delaying the decision so as to enable MPs to make a better-informed decision. The underlying presupposition of these pleas is that extended discussion will persuade more MPs of the reasonableness of rejecting the motion. In pragma-dialectical terms, we suggest, appeals for more time and a more extensive discussion invoke the Freedom Rule (Rule 1): participants must have the freedom to advance and cast doubt on any standpoint. Preventing them from doing so, such as by imposing a temporal closure on the debate before all relevant views have been considered, is a violation of their freedom and obstructs the resolution of the disagreement. As one MP complains at the end, 'the guillotine that was imposed [i.e. a four-minute speaking limit] was unjustified' and has 'denied Back Benchers the right to speak' (3153–3154).

Parliamentary debate does not end in the resolution of disagreement (consensus) amongst *all* participants and the difference of opinion is finally settled by voting. It is thus not reasonable to expect consensus as an outcome. Nevertheless, as we have said, disagreement resolution by reasonable persuasion is a central goal of such deliberative debate and is the normative orientation of participants' argumentation. Let us look at a speech whose main focus is on time constraints, hence information constraints, as obstacles to reasonable disagreement resolution. The Liberal Democrat MP for Leeds North-West, Greg Mulholland argues that a 'mere five-hour debate' only a month since the Government first announced their proposals on higher education is not enough. 'Rushing things through . . . without proper parliamentary scrutiny' and 'without considering the other proposals' will end in a bad policy being adopted. Mulholland argues that the government must accept 'they have not won the argument' and still need to persuade people of their case (1041–1046). We can reformulate this as saying that moving to the closing stage of the critical discussion is premature; the discussion cannot be closed until parties to the disagreement have been given a proper chance to systematically examine and remove doubt regarding the proposals in question. To prevent them is a violation of the freedom rule. Here is an extract from Greg Mulholland's speech (977–1003; 1029–1046; 1064–1073):

> *Greg Mulholland (Liberal Democrat MP for Leeds North West)*: I rise to speak in a debate in which I do not want to speak. I do not believe that this debate should be happening today, and I do not believe that it should be happening in the way that it is. It is only seven months since the general election and the Government were formed; it is less than two months since we saw the Browne report for the first time, and it is a month – a month – since the Government announced their proposals on higher education. Yet, today, we are being forced to hold the significant vote, without considering the other proposals, with a mere five-hour debate.
>
> I make it clear that I am a Government Back Bencher. I support the coalition Government and I support what they are doing. I also support, understand and accept that both parties and MPs in the coalition have to compromise, but let me tell you, Mr Speaker, being asked to vote to increase fees up to £9,000 is not a compromise. It is not something that Liberal Democrat Back Benchers or even many Conservative Back Benchers should have been asked to consider.
>
> As you and the House will know, Mr Speaker, I tabled an amendment, which unfortunately was not successful. (. . .) That was the final attempt to get the Government to

listen, because the simple reality is that, even if their proposals are the best way forward for higher education, and I do not believe that they are, the Government have to accept that they simply have not convinced people of that, not only on the Liberal Democrat Benches, but far more importantly among the wider public and, crucially, future students and their families. (. . .)

[S]ometimes Governments are wrong, and sometimes one needs to have the courage to say so. I am doing that today.

(. . .) On the current proposals, I have said all along, . . ., that there are indeed many progressive things in the proposals. The levels at which graduates will have to make a contribution, the measures for part-time students and the £21,000 threshold are very welcome.

I fully acknowledge all those things, but we need to debunk a myth. All those positive things, which are in the proposals and are progressive in terms of the graduate contribution, do not need to be tied to a huge increase in fees. That is simply a non sequitur. It is simply not true to say, 'You cannot have one without the other', and that is the crucial flaw in the Government's argument today. (. . .)

The Secretary of State knows, and we all know, that there is much confusion about the proposals, but is that not another reason to have more time for the Government to try to convince people? He and all Ministers who support the proposals today have to accept that they have not won the argument, and rushing things through, given the concern and anxiety about how it has been done without proper parliamentary scrutiny, is simply a recipe for bad policy.

So, I say one last time, having done so over the past week, that it is not too late. There needs to be a re-think and a proper review of how we come up with the best system for higher and, indeed, all post-18 education. That should be done properly. It should not be rushed through; it should be done with proper parliamentary scrutiny. I say to this House and I say to colleagues, for the sake of the Liberal Democrats, for the sake of this Government, for the sake of Parliament, please vote against these proposals tonight.

According to the Liberal Democrat MP for Leeds, the house is 'being forced' to vote on a significant issue without sufficient debate (we have referred above to closure as a violation of freedom, and this formulation suggests this clearly). He mentions that he has, without success, tried to table an amendment (this corresponds to the *Revise* stage of deliberation as genre) in order to cause a rethinking of the proposal. While agreeing with the progressive measures in the proposal, he thinks that the goal of a progressive solution does not entail a huge increase in fees. The question of *how much* students will have to pay is a different issue from the question of a progressive repayment scheme. It is false that you cannot have one without the other, he says, and the government's argument is fallacious. The intuition behind claiming that the argument is fallacious is similar to John's Denham's earlier distinction between two issues that are at stake and should not be conflated: the progressiveness of the repayment scheme, on which there may be little or even no disagreement, and the actual balance between what the state will pay and what individuals will pay for education. This is to say that agreement on the former issue should not obscure the need to critically examine the latter, more controversial issue, and the same repayment scheme could be applied to much smaller tuition fees. The proponents 'simply have not convinced people' of their case. Reasonable persuasion, in other words, is the aim of the debate, and this is clearly recognized by participants. There is also an interesting reference to another genre, negotiation.

Having to vote for such a huge increase in fees, the MP says, is not the kind of reasonable 'compromise' that MPs should expect to have to settle for. It is not an issue that can be the object of a negotiation, and MPs should not have been asked to consider it. This suggests that the considerations involved are non-negotiable and cannot be overridden, that there are principles at stake that cannot be ignored. We will come back to this discussion in the last section of this chapter, where we discuss external reasons for action.

A similar case for more time, for delaying the closure of the debate until all alternatives and implications have been properly considered, is made by a Conservative MP (for Brigg and Goole), Andrew Percy. In his view, the Government 'have not made their case' for trebling tuition fees, and there has not been enough debate, enough consideration of all possible alternatives. On the other hand, the Opposition has not produced a 'credible alternative' either (1407–1409, 1426–1436). In pragma-dialectical terms, this can be reformulated as saying that the government have not discharged their burden of proof in a satisfactory way: they have not dealt with criticism and objections in a satisfactory way, and they have not found the most persuasive arguments in support of their claim. On the other hand, the Opposition's critical questioning has merely raised doubt, but has not produced a plausible alternative claim for action. John Pugh, the Liberal Democrat MP for Southport, sums up the situation very effectively: Vince Cable, as proponent, 'though very wise, does not know for certain that he is right', while John Denham, the main opponent, 'though equally wise, does not know for certain that he is right', which is why the House should be given the opportunity to consider more carefully rather than rush into an irreversible decision (1004–1009). In other words, reasonable discussion has not yet produced a clarification of the entire range of arguments in favour of each view, not all objections have been properly answered, neither of the two parties has managed to make a thoroughly convincing case. Critical questioning has not convincingly defeated the argument, nor rebutted the claim, but the proponent has not answered these challenges in a satisfactory way either. Neither party has had enough time and information at their disposal to make a rationally persuasive case, a case that is capable of satisfying its critics, one that is both rhetorically and dialectically acceptable. Moreover, further opportunities to extend the discussion by addressing amendments formally advanced by Opposition members have been prevented. Consequently, the debate cannot support a well-grounded, reasonable practical decision. As one MP observes, 'policy made speedily and on the hoof is not good policy' (1102) and more extended debate is needed to 'get the balance right' between what the state, employers and students should contribute (1090). Of course, decisions can be legitimate in the procedural sense even if no debate at all has occurred. But what participants are aiming for here is a decision that is also legitimate in a more substantive sense, a decision that has emerged from considered deliberation, not merely from voting.

Let us now look at other obstacles to reasonable decision-making besides time constraints.

Evading the burden of proof

In making a claim (a proposal), arguers incur a burden of proof. In a dialectical framework, the burden of proof rests initially with the proponent, to the extent that his proposal goes against a prevailing *status quo* (by making a substantial change to the existing situation) and thus stands in need of defence, but is then shifted to the opponent, whose task is to come up with reasons why the proposal should not be accepted.[6] In the tuition fees debate, this initial burden of proof is undertaken by the main proponent (Vince Cable), who justifies the proposal as one which has emerged from careful deliberation within government, and can – as far as the original deliberators can see – adequately meet the goals and solve the problem in accordance with the government's values and commitments. But the logic of the democratic institutions involved requires that the argument must answer a new round of critical questioning in a new institutional setting, and the burden of proof is now shifted to the opponents of the proposal in parliament. If the opponents should fail to come up with criticism, then there is no reason why the claim should not stand.

Plenty of such critical challenges are advanced by the opponents in this case: highly probable negative consequences, better alternatives, critical questioning of the alleged fairness of the proposal, critical questioning of the sincerity of the proponents' commitment to the claim on the basis of overt reasons, and of the sincerity of their commitment to fairness, given perceived inconsistencies or contradictions in behaviour. As one MP says, it will be 'impossible to explain to students . . . that the proposals are fair when the Government are rowing back on the bankers' levy'; the government's attitude towards banks shows clearly 'what their priorities are for this country', in spite of their professed commitments to fairness (3198–3201). There is also criticism of the actual truth (rational acceptability) of some of the premises, for instance of the description of the context of action (circumstantial premise): it is not Labour's fault that there is such a huge budget deficit, but the fault of the banks. In response, supporters of the proposal address the opponents' challenges and attempt to show that their claim can still be maintained. Most MPs seem to agree that the repayment scheme is more progressive than a graduate tax, and that increasing the repayment threshold, the maintenance support for low-income students, and extending loans to part-time students under the same terms are indeed progressive measures. It is not on the details of the repayment scheme that the main disagreement seems to focus, but on the wider issue of the state's role in funding higher education and the transfer of *most* of the financial burden onto individuals, on the *sheer size* of the debt incurred and its likely implications.

The debate involves a single difference of opinion (over the increase in tuition fees as the right means to achieve the goals), but there is a persistent attempt, coming from one of the parties, to redefine and expand the confrontation. As Shadow Secretary John Denham, as well as other MPs argue, there is more at stake than a rise in tuition fees, the disagreement is also over how far the state should withdraw from the funding of higher education, how much of the burden can be legitimately transferred onto the students. These, the opponents implicitly suggest, are alternative formulations of the means: increasing tuition fees is *equivalent* to an almost complete withdrawal of the state from funding higher education. This is what the debate is about, in their view, and this is what MPs should understand before they vote. However, this (repeatedly suggested) redefinition of the confrontation, as a more profound political and ideological (not merely technical or quantitative) issue, is nevertheless not properly addressed or argued against by the proponents, who evade part of the burden of proof that this challenge should prompt them to assume. A similar evasion occurs in the case of the objection that what the government is doing is related to *other goals* than the overt ones (a fundamentally restructured higher education system, no longer publicly but privately funded), i.e. that the government's argument is a rationalization. This critical challenge, raised by Labour MPs, is dismissed early on, in Vince Cable's speech (248–259) and a few times later on (e.g. in an intervention that stresses the purely 'economic', not 'political' nature of the decision and claims that the need to overcome the deficit is the real and only reason, 2020–2028), but no proper response is offered to the questions why no alternative (such as those actually suggested by various MPs – making the banks and businesses contribute more, pursuing tax avoidance, etc.) has been considered and why this shift in the funding balance should be so radical, or why it should be made definitive, rather than temporary, until the deficit is paid.

The very need to make extensive cuts is questioned. Challenging the government's stated goal of making 25 per cent cuts (which in this debate has been presented as a shared, uncontroversial goal of action, something that needs doing) is a more radical move than challenging the increase in tuition fees as means to this goal. It is meant to provoke deliberation about goals, not only about means, and thus raises doubt about previous arguments for action (or previous deliberation), made in other settings, in a temporal sequence of arguments making up the government's current strategy for action. It is not only the argument in favour of increasing fees that is thrown into doubt, but other (previous) arguments that *concluded* in the need to make radical cuts in response to the crisis (as recommended action or means). The conclusions of those previous arguments are providing the current argument with one of its goals (the need to make cuts is no longer argued for here but taken for granted), but this goal – as the MPs we quoted above imply – is not uncontroversial. There is no good reason why cuts should be so drastic when other reasonable and better alternatives exist (taxing the banks and businesses, properly taxing the wealthy, pursuing tax evasion) and have not been considered. Choosing any of these alternatives would easily enable the government to raise the money that is being cut from education. Finally, the means–goal premise of the argument is challenged. Increasing fees is not necessary, as better (fairer, less costly to the population) options are available, and will adversely affect the government's other stated goals (that of a fair education system).

To sum up, the confrontation, narrowly defined, is one about means, under a specific formulation of the means (about whether or not to increase tuition fees, as a means to certain taken-for-granted goals), but the wider confrontation, as suggested repeatedly by Labour politicians, is one over a more encompassing definition of what the proposed action (means) actually amounts to, as well as over what goals are being pursued. This means that, instead of asking 'Should we increase tuition fees or not?', MPs should ask 'Should we allow the state to withdraw from education?', 'Should we transfer the cost of education onto the students?', 'Should we privatize higher education, and allow the market to take over?', 'Should we change the system'?, 'What political goals or vision should we pursue?' This deliberation over the *ends* of political action, and on the connection between the proposed action and goals that may be radically different from currently taken-for-granted ones, and should be therefore critically examined, is not one that actually occurs within the timeframe of this particular parliament debate. Technically, it cannot occur within this debate *as deliberation* (as it would return the argumentation to the confrontation stage over a new standpoint) but is repeatedly suggested by the government's opponents, in challenging the goals of the proposed action, as a discussion that would be desirable to have because it involves *what is really at stake* in this confrontation (i.e. *a potentially fundamental alteration of the system, not just a minor change within the same system*). Independently of what can or cannot be done, or of time constraints, there is a persistent avoidance of this particular discussion of goals, formulated in these terms, coming from the government's supporters. They manage to avoid pertinent critical questioning (e.g. about the allegedly *ideological* nature of their proposal, their actual commitment to fairness, about unexplored alternatives in relation to other goals) and the obligation to respond to such questioning, and this is perceived by the opponents as obstructing the clarification of the matters under discussion.

As we have said, there are repeated attempts to widen the scope of the debate along these lines, but they are relatively unsuccessful, not in the sense that these arguments are not clearly formulated by the opponents, as indeed they are, but in the sense that they are not properly addressed by the proponents. David Willetts's speech, for instance, focuses extensively on defending the fairness of the scheme and denying the negative consequences, while defending its advantages, but ignores the issue of the radical shift in the balance of funding and the size of the debt to be incurred, in absolute terms, which have been, throughout the debate, a major focus in Labour interventions. He downplays the disagreement, chooses not to address the really contentious issues and suggests there is no reason why the disagreement should not be resolved in the proponents' favour. To that extent, we can say that the proponents' burden of proof is not, on the whole, properly assumed, and their arguments choose to focus excessively only on some issues which can be more easily defended and to ignore others. Their arguments are relevant only to some of their critics' objections and to a narrow definition of the difference of opinion, but not to the wider confrontation, as it is being redefined by the opponents, and not to the objections that arise from that redefinition. In evading the burden of proof that relates to the wider argument, as it is being redefined, the proponents are obstructing, not helping, the resolution of the difference of opinion, and are failing to address the fundamental bone of contention between the government and its critics. This rhetorical strategy (involving which particular issues to address and which to ignore) is of course designed to further the proponents' own rhetorical goals and arrive at a decision that is best *in their view*, but this is done at the expense of dialectical reasonableness, by obstructing the goal of arriving at a decision on the merits, in an truly impartial way.[7]

Structure of the argumentation in the tuition fees debate

What are the main arguments put forward in this debate and how are the two parties dealing with their own burden of proof? The government, as proponent, is making the following argument. Tuition fees should be increased (Means/Action) in order to deal with the budget deficit (which requires an average of 25 per cent cuts across all departments) and at the same time ensure a financially sustainable higher education system, one that provides high-quality standards of performance and is based on a progressive system of graduate contributions (these are the stated goals of action, the 'vision'), in a context of lack of funds (circumstances – these are further explained as having been caused by Labour) and in accordance with certain values or concerns (fairness, a concern for quality, financial sustainability). The argument has been already critically examined and it has been established that there will be no negative consequences, as prospective students will not be deterred from attending university, and there will be positive consequences (more financial accountability, higher quality, more choice, etc.), in addition to the positive consequences of achieving the goals. There are no better alternatives in view of the goals (the action is necessary) and the action will deliver those goals (it is sufficient in view of the goals). The proposal has been revised in government so as to adequately balance various potentially conflicting goals and values that are being simultaneously pursued.

In response, the government's opponents are arguing that increasing tuition fees is wrong, or tuition fees should not be increased (counter-argument). The negative consequences of the government's proposal will outweigh the benefits and will affect goals and values that should not be overridden (the goal of a high-quality education system that provides fair opportunities for all). The government's stated goals and values are in fact incompatible with the proposed action, as the action will undermine them, and this includes the goal of dealing with the deficit, as the proposal will not save any money in the end. Moreover, the argument in favour of raising tuition fees is a rationalization, based on the covert ideological goal of fundamentally restructuring higher education and shifting the funding balance between the state and graduates, and on covert ideological values (*not* on a concern with fairness). The counter-argument challenges therefore both the goal and value premises of the proponent's argument and its means–goal premise. In addition, there is a practical argument that supports the counter-claim, which says that, given the (implicit) normative vision of an ever better and more progressive higher education system, i.e. based on developing, not on radically changing the existing one, and given that, if fees are increased, the quality and progressiveness of the current system will be seriously damaged, tuition fees should not be increased. Last but not least, there is an argument against increasing fees from the institutional and non-overridable fact of the promise made by the Liberal Democrats before they were in government. The counter-claim is thus multiply supported, by practical arguments from goals and circumstances, from negative consequences, and other types of argument. All of these challenges are ultimately aimed at rebutting the proponent argument's claim (this is how we have represented them, although, strictly speaking, some can only defeat the validity of that argument). In a simplified form, the argument and counter-argument are represented in Figure 6.1.

Political promises as reasons for action

As is well known, the Liberal Democrats' promise to abolish tuition fees was one of the cornerstones of their 2010 electoral campaign. Both Nick Clegg, the Liberal Democrat leader, and Vince Cable, together with over 50 other Liberal Democrat politicians, signed the NUS pledge to oppose raising the cap on tuition fees and also promised to get rid of fees altogether. This promise won them many seats, particularly in university towns, including Sheffield, Nick Clegg's own constituency. Below is one of the many similar declarations made by Nick Clegg during the electoral campaign. This one was made to students at Oxford University on 28 April 2010:

> Despite the huge financial strain fees already place on Britain's young people, it is clear both Labour and the Conservatives want to lift the cap on fees. If fees rise to £7,000 a year, as many rumours suggest they would, within five years some students will be leaving university up to £44,000 in debt. That would be a disaster. If we have learnt one thing from the economic crisis, it is that you can't build a future on debt.
>
> The Liberal Democrats are different. Not only will we oppose any raising of the cap, we will scrap tuition fees for good, including for part-time students. (. . .) Students can make the difference in countless seats in this election. Use your vote to block unfair tuition fees and get them scrapped once and for all.[8]

Once in government, however, Nick Clegg came round to the view that tuition fees could not be scrapped and went along with the Tory proposal to raise the cap to £9,000. Consequently, as many people have argued, the Liberal Democrats have done themselves damage from which they may never recover and have forfeited any chance to count as a political force in British politics in the foreseeable future. Nick Clegg's going back on the promise not to raise tuition fees, after signing the NUS pledge, has been seen as an unforgivable betrayal of the pact between a politician and the citizens who vote for him and it can be expected that the electorate will penalize this betrayal at the next elections.

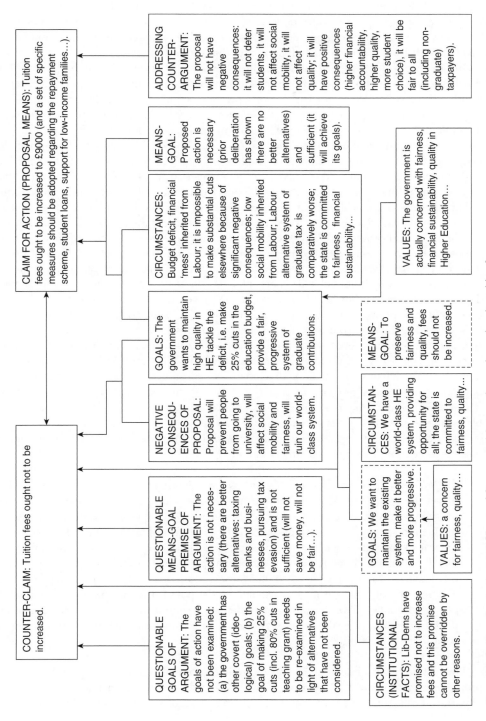

Figure 6.1 Deliberation in the 2010 House of Commons debate on increasing university tuition fees.

In Nick Clegg's defence, some media commentators have argued that, realistically, political promises are made to be broken, especially in a coalition government whose fundamental principle is compromise. In an article in *The Guardian*, Simon Jenkins argued that, in an electoral campaign, 'promises are mere expressions of intent, feel-good phrases', and Clegg's promise was not hypocritical, but merely 'reckless', and he should have known it could never be fulfilled. It is thus 'ridiculous' to hold him to that promise (Jenkins 2010).

In response to Jenkins' view, in the online comments to his article, *Guardian* readers predominantly took the line that 'a promise is a promise is a promise' and argued that people rightly feel betrayed. When a clear electoral promise is 'put in writing and every single one of your candidates sign that promise, the electorate has the right to expect it to be kept'. The tuition fees promise was a 'signed pledge' (not only an electoral manifesto promise), an 'oath', and 'even in coalitions there are lines that should *not* be crossed'. 'Only unprincipled people go back on such commitments and pledges', and if they are consequently vilified for 'dishonourable behaviour', 'they have only themselves to blame'. The promise on tuition fees was one of the main reasons why the Liberal Democrats obtained as many seats as they did and became a political force at all. That people who wished to oppose the Tories ended up unwittingly contributing to a Tory-led majority, on the basis of this false promise, was 'the ultimate insult to voters'. The Lib Dems 'bought' the students' vote and then betrayed them. As someone pointed out, 'this was a specific promise, to a specific group of people (who don't normally turn out to vote in large numbers), in specific constituencies' and the Lib Dems effectively 'manipulated a particular section of the population for electoral gain'. They have committed 'an act of gross deception', given that 'people voted for them to do precisely the opposite' of what they eventually did. It is right, *Guardian* readers argued, 'to hold Governments to account for lies and broken promises'. To claim otherwise (as Jenkins suggests) is a cynical view that 'rubbishes democracy' because it implies that 'a vote for something you believe in no longer means anything'. While 'hardened' and 'cynical' commentators like Jenkins may believe that politicians' promises mean nothing and incur no obligation, one reader argued, 'there are still some of us who believe that if a politician makes a clear commitment and gains votes because of it then they should be held accountable for it, and not just 5 years later'.[9]

The issue of Nick Clegg's broken promise is also addressed in the parliamentary debate on tuition fees, particularly in one intervention:

> *Emily Thornberry (Labour MP for Islington South and Finsbury)*: . . . As soon as he got into power, the right hon. Member for Sheffield Hallam dumped his principles and pushed his Ministers into a new policy of tripling fees. (. . .) The Lib Dem leadership has double-crossed the electorate and is not fit for office. The question for Back-Bench Liberal Democrats is whether they have the backbone to vote against the policy. Do they have the backbone to vote for their principles? Never mind pledges and promises, the debate is about principles. As politicians, we cannot say, 'I've got a principle. I keep it in my pocket. I take it out occasionally and I polish it before putting it back in my pocket.' Equally, if we get into government, we cannot take the principle out of our pocket and chuck it in the gutter. We have to apply our principles to power and do the right thing. (1463–1492)

Both Thornberry's intervention and the online comments above clearly regard political promises, and more widely, political principles as reasons for action that cannot be used opportunistically, but should constrain action regardless of what other goals and circumstances happen to prevail. As one *Guardian* reader ironically commented, Nick Clegg seems to have invented a 'situational pledge', a type of pledge that can change according to which group of the electorate he is trying to win favour with. Similarly, the Labour MP for Islington and Finsbury's comment amounts to saying that politicians cannot use their principles when and where it is convenient, and cannot abandon their principles once they are in power. On the contrary, politicians have to 'apply principles to power and do the right thing'. She invokes an implicit pact between politicians and the voters: people voted for what the Liberal Democrats said they stood for, yet the Lib Dems have 'double-crossed' the electorate by going back on their pledges and 'dumping' their principles.

We have argued that reasons such as promises, pledges and principles, as well as duties, obligations and moral values are *external reasons* for action, of the sort theorized by Searle (2010), who used *promise* as a paradigmatic example. These reasons are 'desire-independent': once you make a promise, you have a reason to act accordingly, whatever your desires. In the previous chapter we suggested that such external reasons belong to the circumstantial premise. They are *facts* (institutional facts) that speakers argue from in saying that agents ought to be concerned with their realization. In the case of promises or norms and laws, the fact that the agent made a promise or is bound by a law or moral norm typically overrides any other possible consideration of what the context is or what the agent might want to achieve. Regardless of circumstances and regardless of his desires, an agent who is bound by such a reason ought to act accordingly. There are of course exceptions, of the sort that are usually discussed in connection with Kant's too stringent categorical imperative. But this should not obscure the fact that, in signing a pledge or making a promise, or in entering any contractual agreement, people create for themselves reasons for action that can be expected to constrain their future action.

Such reasons can constrain action because, in the act of their creation as reasons, by declarative speech acts, certain well-defined deontic powers are conferred on the people involved. In signing the pledge, Nick Clegg has incurred obligations towards the students he made the pledge to, in exchange for their electoral support. More generally, in running for political office, politicians undertake to democratically represent the citizens and incur obligations towards the electorate who, in turn, give them the power to represent their interests. If this pact or contract is broken, politicians are 'not fit for office', as Thornberry says, and the electorate is justified in penalizing such behaviour. As we argued in Chapter 5, such external reasons for action are regarded as fundamental in politics, as part of a social contract that cannot be broken except at a cost. In the representation of the argument (Figure 6.1), this promise enters as an independent argument in favour of the counter-claim. For many people, regardless of any other reasons (such as the negative consequences of increasing fees), this reason (as an overriding, institutional fact that Liberal Democrat politicians have themselves created and are consequently bound by) is sufficient in itself to support the claim that fees should not be increased. This representation also matches, we think, the non-instrumental character that philosophers assign to arguments of this type. Doing your duty, acting morally are not means towards the satisfaction of goals (desires, interests): the fact that you are bound by duties or norms is a sufficient reason regardless of what goals you happen to have.

Conclusion

In this chapter we have tried to analyse the parliamentary debate on tuition fees as a concrete speech event that draws on parliamentary debate as an activity type; this activity type in turn draws on or implements the genre of deliberation. There is considerable confusion in the literature over the status of deliberation and debate – Are they both genres? What are their distinctive features? – and not enough work has been done to clarify these questions. Starting from van Eemeren's (2010) convincing suggestion that deliberation is a genre and debate an activity type, we have proposed an original account of parliamentary debate, partly along pragma-dialectical lines, partly along the lines pursued in the other chapters of this book, i.e. in terms of the structure of practical arguments and deliberation. We have tried to illustrate the way in which genres are contextualized in institutional settings, again along pragma-dialectical lines, by looking at how the specific activity type of parliamentary debate implements the genre of deliberation, and we suggested features of this activity type that arise from the institutional context. At the same time, we have illustrated how the abstract model of critical discussion is contextualized in the institutional context of parliament. Mainly, we think, the outcome that can be reasonably expected at the concluding stage is not a resolution of the original disagreement in the sense that all participants adopt the same view, but a *decisional* outcome based on a majority vote, while disagreement will persist.

We have briefly reconstructed this particular debate as critical discussion and identified its several stages. We have identified the arguments advanced at the argumentation stage, in terms of the schema for practical reasoning that we have suggested in this book and related them to the goal of disagreement resolution, seeing them as argumentative moves (made by two parties) in a process of critical examination of a normative proposition. We have also focused on the proponents' persistent avoidance of the burden of proof associated with a reasonable redefinition of the confrontation by the opponents. We claimed that various attempts, made throughout the debate, to refocus the disagreement on the radical shift in the balance of funding (and its alleged ideological underpinnings), as well as on any alternatives, fail to really redirect the discussion, as the proponents tend to evade the burden of proof associated with this wider confrontation and only choose to address those issues that can be more easily defended. Although the need for deliberation over the goals of political action (not only over means) is strongly suggested by some of the participants, this suggestion is successfully avoided by the proponents and the debate remains focused on the narrower issue of whether or not to adopt the proposed means in view of goals which remain relatively unchallenged. This narrow focus is not unexpected, and in principle not illegitimate, given that the debate is not *supposed* to be about goals but about means, about whether increasing fees will deliver taken-for-granted goals. But what the government's opponents are trying to clarify is the exact nature of the goals and they are suggesting that the government is being dishonest about the goals they really pursue. In failing to question these goals, MPs may in fact vote for action which promotes covert goals which they may not want to endorse, such as a privatized, market-driven higher education system, from which the state has entirely withdrawn, accessible only to the rich. Clarification of goals, seeing through the reasons that are being offered as goals, is thus relevant for this debate because of what this will entail for the choice of action.

We have suggested a new view of the way in which parliamentary debate draws on the genre of deliberation. Parliamentary debate is essentially deliberative in nature, given that argumentation in favour and against the proposal feeds into an individual deliberation process that is finalized in an individual vote that will ground a collective democratic decision. A distinctive feature of parliamentary debates as a form of deliberation is that they address a 'motion' in favour of one practical proposal, which is itself the outcome of prior deliberation within the government. Unlike deliberation as genre, therefore, parliamentary debate as deliberative activity type does not start from an open question over what to do in response to a problem, but with a specific proposal. It is structured as speeches for and against the proposed motion, in which the government's arguments for the motion are critically evaluated, particularly by invoking negative consequences on shared goals, and thus developing counter-arguments (for rejecting the motion). In the course of the debate, other proposals may also be put forward (but cannot themselves be the subject of deliberation and decision) and amendments or revisions to the motion may be suggested (but have to be submitted independently, before the actual debate).

The main distinctive feature, in our view, has to do with the nature of the closure procedure, which involves a decision arrived at by voting. Not all deliberative activity types have to involve decision: both single-agent and multi-agent deliberation can end on a normative judgement (agents might come to a conclusion that *A* is the right way forward without deciding to do anything). Decision-making as part of the normal closure of parliamentary debate comes in our view from the nature and rationale of the institution, which has to find a way of acting in conditions of persistent disagreement. To put it differently, the minimal outcome of a normative judgement is not enough for closing deliberation in parliamentary debates, as the multiplicity of views belonging to all the participants cannot ground a common course of action, which is the institutional rationale of such debates.

The theoretical discussion we have proposed is in agreement with the view of politics we advanced in Chapter 1. There, we cited views of democracy as a mechanism for dealing with disagreement in a reasonable way and for using competition for a cooperative end. While *normatively* oriented to disagreement resolution and to persuasion by reasonable means, in terms of what each participant is trying to do, parliamentary debate does not *actually* end in the resolution of disagreement amongst *all* participants, nor can it be reasonably expected to do so, and voting effectively settles the issue without really resolving it. This, as we argued in Chapter 2, is not a relativist view. It is part of the institutional pre-conditions of parliamentary debate as activity type that the closure procedure does not require all participants to have been persuaded of the *same* view. What is required, we have suggested, is not a *shared cognitive* outcome (shared belief) but a *shared decisional* outcome that all participants regard as binding even if they disagree. Parliamentary debates (unlike many deliberative interactions) also have clear rules of procedure and time constraints. These impose a temporal and epistemic closure which can be an obstacle to the dialectical goals of the debate. In spite of these constraints, parliamentary debate delivers an outcome which is procedurally legitimate and can ground political action, although it may not embody the most reasonable decision. In other words, the decision may not be the right decision, but has been arrived at in the right way.

We have acknowledged that MPs may vote for other reasons than their beliefs, or for reasons that have nothing to do with the quality of the arguments that have been put forward, but we argued that the fundamental normative orientation of participants' argumentation is towards changing or reinforcing belief by reasonable means and of coordinating action on that basis. Persuasion is crucial precisely because of the need (which at the same time is an opportunity to be taken advantage of) to create a majority of votes on any given issue. Persuasion is also central in securing the support of all those on whom the eventual success of any policy depends, who are a third party non-interactive audience in this case (e.g. students, parents, university teachers, banks in this case), of all those on whom the legitimacy of the political system depends. This normative orientation finds empirical support in the interventions of those MPs who demanded more time, a more extensive discussion that might enable all parties to make a more convincing case, leading to a more reasonable outcome, as well as in the fact that, on this particular occasion, many MPs voted against the party whip and on the strength of (what they presumably perceived as) the better argument.

Finally, in accordance with our suggestions in Chapter 5, we have discussed political promises and principles (values) as external reasons for action, as commitments which are binding on politicians regardless of their other reasons and therefore should override other reasons. 'Putting power over principles', as the Liberal Democrats have been accused of doing in going back on the promise not to raise tuition fees has been widely regarded as a breach of the implicit contract between government and citizens.

Conclusion

In this final chapter we shall summarize what we have tried to achieve in the book and then identify what we think are the main contributions that we have made to argumentation theory and analysis, to critical discourse analysis (CDA) and to political discourse analysis in social and political science.

Summary of chapters: our main arguments

In the Introduction, we set out the aims and objectives of the book, gave a brief account of the financial and economic crisis and of various political responses to it, and sought to preempt possible misunderstandings of our position. Our main aim has been to present a new approach to analysing political discourse, which we see as a contribution to the development of critical discourse analysis, based upon a view of political discourse as primarily argumentative and deliberative. We tried to clarify a number of potential confusions, arising from a misunderstanding of what argumentation and deliberation are, and from conflating descriptive and normative levels of analysis. In particular, we argued against the misconceived objection that politics has little to do with argumentation or deliberation, as it is primarily about power. As we argued throughout the book, the fact that argumentation and deliberation in politics may not always be reasonable does not mean that political discourse is not fundamentally argumentative or deliberative in nature, but only that bad arguments and bad reasons sometimes prevail. One such bad reason can of course be power itself, when decisions are taken on the basis of power interests and not on the strength of the better argument. However, power considerations themselves are reasons in agents' practical reasoning. The alleged opposition between argumentation and power is meaningless; only distinguishing between reasonable ('good') arguments and unreasonable ('bad') arguments, or between acceptable and unacceptable claims, makes sense.

In Chapter 1, we briefly discussed two current approaches in political discourse analysis (those of Chilton and Wodak) in order to put our own approach into perspective within the field of political discourse analysis and to justify the need for a new approach. We argued that analysis of political discourse should proceed from a coherent view of politics, i.e. from a view of the nature of politics developed in political theory. In contemporary political theory, but also in Aristotle, politics is defined in terms of such concepts as deliberation, decision and action, and the context in which politics operates is said to be one of disagreement (including irreducible conflicts of values and interests), incomplete information and uncertainty as to what the right course of action might be (hence, risk), urgency, as well as other constraints. It is also a context in which the possibilities for democratic deliberation and political participation are often limited by people's unequal access to resources, by power inequalities and by the institutional complexity of modern societies. It is features such as these, we argued, that should inform a view of the objectives and methods of political discourse analysis. Politics has to do primarily with decisions for action on matters of common concern, and decisions are the outcome of deliberation; not all deliberation is reasonable or democratic, and not all decisions are reasonable decisions. Politics is about arriving cooperatively at decisions about what to do in the context of disagreement, conflict of interests and values, power inequalities, uncertainty, and all these factors can affect the rationality of the decisions that are made.

In Chapter 2, we presented our conception of practical reasoning. We argued that practical arguments have *circumstances* and *goals* as premises, as well as *value* and *means–goal* premises. The action (as means) emerges as a conjecture or hypothesis that it might enable agents to achieve their goals, starting from the circumstances they finds themselves in and in accordance with their values. In acting, agents intend to transform current circumstances into future state of affairs in accordance with the normative source that underlies their goals. In developing this new account of practical reasoning we started from conceptions of its nature in philosophy, and the chapter also included an overview of the main philosophical arguments. In particular, we drew on Audi's and Walton's theories of practical reasoning, Searle's theory of the construction of social reality, as well as on a view of modal (deontic) reasoning in semantics.

We adopted a dialectical approach to the evaluation of practical arguments; logical and rhetorical considerations are integrated within this approach, which we take to be primary. (In so doing, we are drawing on pragma-dialectics and on a version of informal logic, particularly on the work of van Eemeren and Walton.) It is part of the logic of practical arguments that they are only presumptively reasonable and can default. Critical questioning can challenge arguments in terms of the rational acceptability of goals, values and the representation of circumstances, the relation between all these premises and the claim, as well as the likely consequences of proposed actions and existing alternatives. In our view, questions about the consequences of action for goals (and implicitly for values) and their realization are most important from a critical perspective because they can lead to rejecting the proposal for action.

Deliberation, we said, is a genre involving mainly practical argumentation. We suggested that it minimally involves considering a counter-argument, i.e. reasons against doing the action, but usually involves considering reasons in favour and against several possible alternatives. Deliberation can be considered from a purely instrumental point of view, in which the goal is taken as given, and costs and benefits of alternative actions are examined and weighed together in order to choose the 'best' alternative. But it can also display a rationality that is non-instrumental, and involve a comparison among different goals and values, associated with possibly different courses of action, and a choice among such actions depending on which goals and values appear to be more worthy of being pursued, of having normative priority. This may lead to revising a proposed action so that it is compatible not just with one goal but with the realization of several goals that the agent should not (or would not want to) compromise. Deliberation can be (and should be) about goals and values as well, not just about means.

Our approach is underlain by a critical conception of reasonableness (which we take over from pragma-dialectics and critical rationalism). It is a conception in which a reasonable standpoint, either descriptive or normative, and a reasonable decision, are seen as the possible outcome of a dialectical procedure of critical questioning. In this sense, making the 'right' decision is a matter of following the 'right' procedure, a procedure involving systematic criticism, of thinking of reasons *against* a tentative proposal, and not a matter of justifying it by finding reasons that seem to support it. This procedure does not guarantee that the 'best' decision will be arrived at, but its outcome is likely to be, nevertheless, a *reasonable* decision, one that has successfully withstood critical examination. Critical questioning can challenge arguments but in so doing it can lead to the production of stronger arguments; it can lead arguers to revise their claims and replace them with new ones, in the light of the progressive uncovering of considerations that affect their rational acceptability. Regarding reasonableness, we are trying to explore and develop pragma-dialectics' intrinsic connection to critical rationalism. For this purpose, we draw on the version of critical rationalism developed by Miller.

Our main objective in Chapter 3 was to argue that the analysis and evaluation of argumentation can increase the capacity of CDA to pursue normative and explanatory critique. For this purpose, we offered a new analysis of a text originally analysed in an older book, *New Labour, New Language* (Fairclough 2000a), with the objective of showing that analysing it as an practical argument significantly strengthens the original analysis, and that the critical force of the analysis of representations (e.g. the representation of 'change') is substantially increased when we recognize that these representations are in fact constituents of the premises of practical arguments and of an implicit deliberative process which, in this case, is highly questionable from a dialectical point of view. We argued that discourses (such as the discourse of the Third Way) provide arguers with premises in arguments, hence with reasons for action, and that a view of semiotic representations that integrates them within practical arguments as premises is far more capable of showing how discourses can shape reality. More generally, we argued that understanding political discourse as argumentative offers an adequate understanding of the way in which structures interact with agency: *discourses (and orders of discourse, as structures) provide agents with reasons for action.* The same connection between agency and structure is evident, we argue, in the way in which institutional and moral orders (as structures) provide agents with desire-independent (external) reasons for action which constrain or enable their agency.

In the same chapter, we also offered an argumentative definition of other concepts that figure prominently in CDA analyses and in critical social analysis. We suggested that 'imaginaries' are in fact goal (motivational) premises in arguments for action; their performative power can be explained in terms of how they are taken up in arguments as representations of how the world actually is (as alleged circumstances of action), rather than as non-actual states of affairs. We also discussed manipulation, in terms of a violation of the sincerity condition of speech acts, and treated Blair's arguments in favour of the Iraq war as an instance of rationalization. We also showed that legitimacy has not been adequately defined in CDA in terms of a theory of argument, although it is inherently a particular type of justification, and we suggested how this might be done. Finally, we discussed the concept of power, drawing on Lukes and Searle, and related it to agents' reasons for action. We saw that, intrinsically, all political power is deontic power, having to do with what people have a right to do, are obliged to do, authorized, permitted or forbidden to do, in light of an institutional framework which provides them with reasons for action. Not all power is, of course, 'bad' power: the power of the law or of socially accepted moral norms constrains agents to act in ways which conform to legal and moral standards. Reclaiming or 'reinventing' politics, freeing it, for instance, from the distorting effects of economic power, can be understood, we suggest, as being able to collectively ensure that the deontic powers conferred on individuals by institutions (e.g. the power to exert their own rights or to force others to abide by their public commitments or the law) are effectively used and not hindered. It can mean ensuring, for example, that citizens can effectively use their rights to challenge government in a way that leads to changes in government action.

Chapter 4 is our main analytical chapter. We offered an analysis and evaluation of the main arguments for action in response to the crisis, advanced by the British Labour government which was in power when the crisis began to unfold, and the Conservative/Liberal Democrat Coalition government which was formed after the general election of May 2010. We focused on two budget reports delivered to the House of Commons by Labour and Coalition Chancellors of the Exchequer: the November 2008 Pre-Budget Report delivered by Alistair Darling, and the June 2010 Emergency Budget report delivered by George Osborne. We evaluated these arguments in terms of our framework, but also by drawing selectively on the wider public debate in which the two strategies for action have been constantly evaluated by politicians, economists and journalists amongst others. We found, for instance, that critics of the Coalition government's austerity strategy have tried to show that the argument in favour of spending cuts is flawed (actually, invalid), by pointing to other desirable goals, questioning the necessary and sufficient character of the action (as means), and indicating the existence of other, arguably better means that would lead to economic recovery. We also showed that they have tried to reject the proposal by observing that its negative consequences will make various legitimate goals of action impossible to achieve. The action, they said, will have a negative impact on the goals and values that are explicitly being pursued or should be pursued (it will not achieve economic recovery, it will be unfair and detrimental to human well-being) and therefore the government should change its strategy, particularly given that emerging, as well as historical, evidence strongly suggests that the current course of action is unreasonable. We have also looked at how both governments have tried to legitimize their strategies by invoking a deliberative process in which several competing concerns and value commitments have, allegedly, been carefully weighed together in order to arrive at a decision for action that will be compatible with these values as overriding values, i.e. as values that can ground reasonable action because they have emerged from extensive deliberation. We have also indicated in what ways criticism of the current government's action can be interpreted as a challenge to the reasonableness of this implicit deliberative process, as merely disguising – through an appeal to fairness and other moral concerns – a purely instrumental rationality in the service of a taken-for-granted goal. This goal, critics implicitly argue, is exempt from critical examination, and has not emerged from genuine deliberation over the appropriate ends of political action, let alone from genuine democratic, public deliberation over such ends. It is moreover an ideological goal, having to do with the pursuit of particular power interests, and not with a concern for fairness and the common good.

We also distinguished between stronger and weaker forms of critique. A strong challenge to an argument for action is the attempt to reject the claim by pointing to the unacceptable consequences of the action, and this attack indicates that the counter-claim (i.e. not going ahead with the proposed action) is more reasonable. This is the strongest challenge that has been aimed at the current government's crisis strategies: the consequences of (proposed and current) action on human well-being are too serious to justify the proposed action. The primary objects of critique therefore are the claims themselves (the conclusions of arguments), and to a lesser extent the premises and inferences that claim to support them, and this is because a claim can be acceptable even when it is supported by a bad argument. In the case of the government's argument for austerity, criticism based on (emerging or probable) negative consequences also amounts to saying that more deliberation is required on what the goals of action should be, and how action can be devised that adequately meets *other* goals which should not be compromised, not just the goal of deficit reduction.

In Chapter 5 we discussed arguments for and against bankers continuing to receive large bonuses, such as were formulated in a debate organized by St Paul's Institute in October 2009 on the responsibility of banks in the current crisis and the broader issue of 'markets and morality', as well as, subsequently, in public reactions to that debate in a *Guardian* comments thread. We analysed this material in terms of our own view of the distinction between prudential arguments (arguments from what people perceive as their own interests) and moral arguments (arguments from the desire-independent goal of a just society). We suggested that what is distinctive about moral arguments is that they recognize and give normative priority to external reasons for action as overriding reasons. Such reasons range from promises made by politicians during election campaigns to moral–political values (justice, freedom, equality) collectively recognized as legitimate and binding. We argued that external reasons for action are part of the circumstantial premise: these are *facts* that speakers argue from, reasons that they *have* even when they choose to disregard them, or fail to be actually motivated by them. In the comments thread that we analysed, according to the argumentative reconstruction that we proposed, people argued that the state ought to put a stop to the injustice of bonuses for bankers, by invoking the normative goal of a just state of affairs, a set of empirical circumstances and an existing commitment to justice on behalf of the state, part of a social contract or an institutional order. It is therefore on account of this (pre-existing, epistemically objective) commitment, as external, deontic reason, that the state ought to act in a certain way, or ought to be concerned with justice. Even when (political) agents are not actually motivated or concerned to act justly, justice will continue to be a reason for action, a legitimate and publicly recognized value. It is, we said, on the basis of the public recognition of the normative force of such external reasons (as institutional facts) – political values, rights, obligations, commitments – that politicians (or the state, the government) can be held responsible for failing to act in accordance with them. The chapter illustrated our view of the difference between a moral argument based on deontic reasons and a prudential argument grounded in self-interest: only the former appeals to reasons that are collectively recognized as binding and therefore *ought* to motivate action.

Chapter 6 analysed the debate in the House of Commons (in December 2010) on the Coalition government's proposal to raise university tuition fees from roughly £3,000 to £9,000 per year. Following pragma-dialectics, we suggested a view of parliamentary debate as an activity type which draws on the genre of deliberation. We sketched a reconstruction of this debate as critical discussion and outlined the main structure of the overall argument. Parliamentary debate in our view is normatively oriented to disagreement resolution and to persuasion by reasonable means. Persuasion is crucial in order to secure both a majority of votes and the support of people outside Parliament on whom the eventual success of any policy depends. This normative orientation is evident in this case in interventions by MPs to demand more time and a more extended debate so as to enable all parties to make a more convincing case, leading to a more reasonable outcome, and in the fact that many MPs voted 'on conscience' against the party whip, i.e. on the strength of (what they took to be) the better argument. We also noted that the binding nature of political promises was recognized in widespread public criticism of the Liberal Democrats for 'putting power over principles' in going back on their promise not to raise tuition fees. Parliamentary debate does not actually end in the resolution of disagreement, in the sense of consensus, nor does it need to, and voting effectively settles the issue without really resolving it, and delivers an outcome which is procedurally legitimate and can ground political action. It is part of the institutional rationale of parliamentary debate as activity type that the reasonable outcome that is required is not a shared normative *judgement* (a consensus of views) but a collective *decision* that can legitimately ground action, and this latter outcome is obtained by a democratic vote and is reasonable even in the absence of disagreement resolution amongst all participants.

Main contributions of this book

We think that this book has made a number of substantive contributions: to argumentation theory, to CDA and, potentially, to social and political theory to the extent that it is interested in discourse. The book also intends to make a methodological contribution, in presenting a framework for analysing and evaluating argumentative discourse in politics in a clear and explicit way, which should make it practically useable for researchers and students. We shall take these in turn and summarize the main contributions in each case.

Contributions to argumentation theory

We argue that it is important to correct the relative neglect of practical argumentation in argumentation theory (Walton's approach is the main and most systematic contribution) and we suggest a suitable starting point for its theorization in philosophical approaches to practical reasoning, particularly in moral philosophy and philosophy of action (including a theory of speech acts). We give an original account of the *structure of practical argumentation*, involving a new conception of what the main premises of practical arguments are and how they should be defined. The action is intended to connect the present state of affairs to a future state of affairs (transform the present, solve the problem) in accordance with the agent's values or concerns. The value premise, we propose, specifies the particular *normative source* that underlies the goals, and the goals are to be understood as *future states of affairs* which agents imagine in accordance with their values (concerns) and try to bring about by means of action. Circumstances are said to include empirical aspects of the context of action but also *institutional or social facts* (external reasons). Agents may be actually concerned to act in accordance with such external reasons or they may disregard them, but it is possible to say that they ought to have acted in accordance with those reasons, e.g. that they had a reason to act morally even when (being free) they chose not to do so. Not only agents' goals but also their representations of the circumstances of action (the 'problems' they see) are informed by their concerns, by what they value, so a simple fact/value distinction makes no sense. In developing this account we have also tried to reformulate and interpret a wider philosophical debate on the nature of practical reasoning in terms of a theory of argument and suggested our own view of how philosophical discussions (on internalism vs. externalism, instrumentalism vs. non-instrumentalism, a Humean vs. a Kantian perspective on practical reasoning, facts vs. values) can be related to a view of argument.

We also aim to make a contribution to a dialectical theory of argument evaluation. Here, we start from existing proposals in pragma-dialectics and informal logic, according to which systematic critical questioning of arguments and claims, embodied in analytical normative frameworks, can deliver a standpoint that is reasonable, a standpoint that has emerged from systematic criticism (i.e. from the 'right' *procedure*, or from following the 'right' *method*) and can therefore be tentatively accepted. We develop the notion of *critical questioning* used in dialectical approaches, in accordance with the structure of practical arguments that we propose, and we suggest that questions that attempt to rebut (falsify) the claim are the most important questions. They appeal to negative consequences of action that compromise its stated goals or other important goals, and thus indicate the existence of a counter-argument, supporting a more rationally acceptable counter-claim (and do not merely question the validity of the original argument). In pointing to negative consequences on *other* legitimate goals, critical questioning indicates the need for *deliberation over ends* (goals), and over which ends should have normative priority, not just *deliberation over means*.

We develop the pragma-dialectical view of *deliberation* as a genre and thus make a contribution to the pragma-dialectical study of argumentation in institutional contexts. Our main insight and theoretical contribution here is that the way in which the logic of political institutions manifests itself as a constraint on argumentation in parliamentary debate is by requiring a shared decisional outcome as a basis for legitimate action, and not a shared cognitive outcome (consensus). This collective decision is a reasonable outcome even if disagreement has not been actually resolved. Our analysis also supports the pragma-dialectical view of the normative orientation of all argumentative discourse: parliamentary debate, we argue, would lose its institutional rationale if what was aimed at every step by participants was *not* disagreement resolution. *Persuading* as many participants as possible of a particular standpoint on an issue is in fact essential in creating a majority. While being a normative aim, such disagreement resolution is hardly ever achieved in practice but, as we argue, the outcome that is *normatively required* in this particular institutional activity type is *decision, not consensus*, and deliberation in parliamentary debate does not thereby fail to meet normative standards if it fails to result in consensus.

Contributions to CDA

The new focus we bring on arguments challenges CDA's primary focus on *representations*, and on *discourses as ways of representing* the (social) world. We view *analysis of action* and of *genres* as having primacy over analysis of representation and discourses. This is because representations are critically significant insofar as they support particular lines of action, by entering as premises in agents' arguments about what to do. Rather than being analysed in isolation, as they often have been in CDA, we propose that *representations should be analysed as constitutive elements of arguments*, and therefore that analysis of discourses should be integrated within analysis of genres – in this case, argumentative genres. One of our main insights here is that *discourses provide agents with reasons for action*, i.e. provide premises in agents' practical arguments. Consequently, it is only by understanding representations as premises in arguments for action that CDA can provide an adequate understanding of the relations between structures (orders of discourse, social and institutional orders) and agency, of the *agency–structure dialectic*.

We view *evaluation of argumentation as an appropriate grounding for normative critique and explanatory critique* (including critique of ideology). We can contribute to explanatory critique in analysing the way in which arguments draw selectively on certain discourses and not others, or the way in which deliberating agents can restrict the range of options that could conceivably be addressed, in accordance with certain power interests. We address normative critique from several angles in this book, corresponding to the Habermasian three-fold distinction between truth, sincerity and normative appropriateness as presuppositions of rational discourse. In analysing arguments, false premises (such as wrong diagnoses of the context of action, or wrong assessments of means–end relations) are seen to lead to unsound and therefore unacceptable arguments: this feeds into normative critique in relation to the first criterion. Arguers can attempt to manipulate audiences, by using rationalizing arguments, arguments which violate the sincerity conditions of speech acts (e.g. by invoking legitimate values as reasons while not being actually motivated by those reasons): this feeds into normative critique in relation to the second criterion. Finally, claims for action that are based on unacceptable goals or values, or on rationally indefensible normative priorities, (i.e. that have not resulted from systematic critical questioning or from adequate deliberation), can be rejected as unacceptable, for instance by pointing to the consequences that the pursuit of those goals and values is likely to have: this feeds into normative critique based on the third criterion. Normative critique can also be grounded in an assessment of the character of public deliberation: Has it been inclusive, free from constraints that might lead to an unreasonable outcome?

We reinterpret various concepts that CDA and critical social science have worked with in terms of a theory of argument. We argue, for instance, that *imaginaries* are discourses that envisage possible future states of affairs and that they feature as *goals* in practical arguments; that they are capable of guiding and motivating action precisely because they constitute reasons for action in arguments. We also associate the performative power of imaginaries with the tendency in politics *to shift them from goal to circumstantial premises*, i.e. to represent what is aimed for and aspired to as an actual fact. We also argue that to assert *power* over an agent is to give him reasons for action, prudential or deontic, which he would otherwise not have, so *power too can be seen as providing agents with reasons* (and as part of a structure–agency dialectic via arguments). Consequently, alleged oppositions between power and argumentation are simplistic and misconceived. We also emphasize the inherently argumentative nature of *legitimation* (a concept which, in our view, is inadequately theorized in discourse analysis). Legitimation, we argue, drawing on political theory, is public justification, an argumentative process in which an action is justified in terms of *reasons which can themselves, in turn, be justified as (worthy of being) collectively accepted or recognized*.

Persistent confusions regarding deliberation and what it is possible to achieve in actual democratic deliberation as distinct from 'deliberative democracy' as a normative ideal, i.e. confusions between a descriptive and normative level of analysis, have tended to lead to various misconceptions in analytical approaches that focus on discourse. These include claims that politics is not about deliberation, argumentation or reasoning, and sometimes even the claim that politics is an irrational activity. We argue that an adequate understanding of the argumentative nature of political discourse, of the nature of practical argumentation and deliberation can help discourse analysts to address political discourse in a better way. On the whole, we attempt to correct CDA's blindness to analysis of argumentation and also to provide a framework that is more systematic and rigorous than those provided by other discourse-analytical approaches, including approaches that list argumentation as one of their concerns (e.g. the Discourse-Historical Approach).

Contributions to analysis of political discourse in social and political science

In this book, we argue that political discourse is primarily argumentative discourse and primarily involves practical argumentation for or against lines of action in response to political problems. Analysis of other features of political discourse, including non-argumentative genres (narrative, explanation) and analysis of representations (including analysis of metaphor, cognitive framing) need to be integrated within analysis of practical argumentation. Some of the contributions we have tried to make to CDA are at the same time contributions to other fields of research in critical social science. They can be seen as bringing some clarification to the concerns with discourse that are manifest in these fields, and particularly to the 'argumentative turn' that has been made in some of them.

We argue that *deliberation* is a particularly important genre in political discourse, given that politics is about arriving at decisions cooperatively in the context of disagreement and conflicting interests and under conditions of uncertainty, risk and urgency. Our analysis of deliberation makes a contribution to both argumentation theory and to political theory of deliberative democracy. It arises from a view of politics and deliberative democracy that is widespread in political theory and shows how the concepts of reasonable and unreasonable disagreement, cooperation and conflict, and legitimate decision-making can be understood from the perspective of a theory of argument.

In our view, adequate understanding of a theory of argumentation can contribute to a better understanding of the nature of *deliberation in political theory*. The nature of argumentation in political deliberation is not always properly understood, and theorists speak of 'discussion', 'arguing', 'reasoning', 'collective decision-making', 'deliberation about goals' and 'deliberation about means' (see for instance the essays collected in Elster 1998b), without being able to integrate them within a coherent structure, i.e. a structure of practical argument and a structure of deliberation as genre. Moreover, it is often observed that deliberation in democratic institutions rarely, if ever, leads to consensus, and this generates confusion over the nature and goal of deliberation: as we have said, from a level of empirical observation, a conclusion is drawn about a normative level of analysis which tends to inadvertently conflate the two. In our view, deliberation, e.g. in parliamentary debate, can be reasonable in spite of not leading to disagreement resolution (in the sense of consensus) amongst all participants, and we suggest this is because, institutionally, the required outcome is a decision, not some shared belief. Its normative orientation (coming from its institutional rationale) is nevertheless towards reasonable persuasion and disagreement resolution. Argumentation theory can also help towards a better theorization of the actual outcomes of political deliberation, which (as we said) often have to do with compromise (negotiation) or mediation, not consensus. In pragma-dialectics, like deliberation, *mediation* and *negotiation* are argumentative genres, and a substantial body of theoretical research has already been undertaken into their structure which political theory might profitably draw on.

We also argue (as we have already indicated) that the concept of *imaginary*, used in Cultural Political Economy (e.g. by Jessop), as well as the performative power of imaginaries, and their ability to motivate action, can be understood more clearly in terms of a theory of practical argument. The performative success of imaginaries, we argue, depends on agents' ability (including power) to *transform them from goals into circumstances* of action, and *gain collective recognition of the deontic system* that imaginaries acquire in the process of being declared facts. We also argue that *political legitimation* is an argumentative process, and that political decisions are legitimate in so far as they are arrived at through a process of deliberation which meets argumentative standards of reasonableness, and in which – crucially – an action is justified in terms of values that are themselves capable of public justification.

We are also trying to clarify what contribution discourse analysis, enhanced by analysis of argumentation, can bring to *normative and explanatory social critique*, and we have briefly given an account of this contribution earlier in this chapter. We have been arguing that analysis and evaluation of argumentation can provide a sound basis for normative and explanatory critique. This does not mean that critique is simply analysis and evaluation of argumentation, but such analysis and evaluation can be integrated within social theorizing that is specific to various fields; it can contribute to a better understanding of agency, of social action, and thus to an explanation (and normative evaluation) of social processes and practices. The external normative perspective we advocate (a critical, dialectical conception of reasonableness) should not be dismissed as utopian (and empirical and normative levels of analysis should not be conflated). As we have indicated, normative models of argumentative practice are used to assess actual practices, occurring within real social and political contexts and, for argumentation to be reasonable *and to achieve its goals*, various *higher-order conditions* would also have to be met; such conditions partly have to do with agents and partly with power. Reasonable argumentation, i.e. argumentation (deliberation) that leads to an outcome 'on the merits' of the case, presupposes freedom and equality, and agents are often not free to challenge arguments, nor in equal positions of power with other arguers. In spite of this, it is only a critical notion of reasonableness as manifested in critical questioning of claims and arguments, and of the institutional, social world they support, that can not only underlie critique but also hold the promise of social change.

An understanding of political discourse as argumentative and of the structure of practical arguments along the lines we have suggested, and particularly our understanding of values and their relationship to the way people formulate goals and represent the circumstances of their action, can (in our view) also make an important contribution to the theorization of *'moral economies'*, as proposed in social science by Sayer. This is a direction we have only suggested in this book and not developed explicitly, and we intend to explore it further in future work.

We have also been trying to provide a better understanding of the *agency–structure* dialectic, as a concept theorized in social science. We see *practical reasoning as the interface between agency and structure:* in reasoning practically, agents draw on discourses which reflect structural, institutional and moral orders, and these orders or structures provide them with reasons for action. Typically, these are external reasons, independent of agents' desires, and act as constraints on action. In order to actually motivate action, they have to be internalized by agents (as concerns) but they need not be (agents are at the same time free to disregard the force of such reasons). In the case of political actors, failing to act in accordance with commitments and norms that are part of the institutional fabric of the political system, and part of an implicit 'contract' with the citizens, leads to the possibility of legitimately challenging political action, as a politician's commitments and obligations derive from his status functions (and are thus constitutive of his role, non-optional).

We have distinguished between *descriptive and normative approaches* and between different *types of normativity*. Besides the distinction between a descriptive and a normative level of analysis, where the normative standpoint is that of the external normativity of the analyst (discourse analyst, argumentation theorist or political theorist), there is also a distinction between analytical normativity and lay normativity, where the latter refers to the norms that participants orient to and against which they constantly evaluate the practices they take part in. Both argumentative practice and political practice are constantly being evaluated both by participants and by analysts; they are both inherently normative activities that can at the same time be evaluated against external analytical standards. Participants' evaluations may or may not be warranted, and it is therefore not enough for analysts to *describe* how people evaluate arguments and to identify the normative standards they apply in doing so. When people accept an argument as a good one or dismiss it as a bad one, analysts also need to ask whether it is reasonable for them to do so, whether they are failing to see flaws in an argument or seeing flaws that do not exist. If the analysts did not do so, they would be failing to adequately describe argumentative practices, for it is a fact about such practices that people do evaluate arguments in unwarranted ways and are persuaded by arguments that should not persuade them. To do this, normative analytical models of argumentation are needed, providing standards for evaluating both arguments and participants' evaluations of arguments. These normative models are derived from the standards which participants apply in evaluating arguments, but they generalize from particular instances and particular contexts of evaluation to identify principles of evaluation which people recognize as reasonable even though they do not always apply them, and they systematize these principles by connecting them with a theory of human rationality. Political discourse analysis needs therefore to incorporate both *descriptive* and *normative* standpoints, and needs a clear view of the relationship between them, as well as of the different types of normativity involved.

Finally, we believe that that practical argumentation for and against particular courses of action is at the heart of current attempts to develop, win acceptance for and impose political strategies for seeking to overcome the economic crisis. We hope that the framework we have set out will provide those researching political responses to the crisis with a much-needed *method for analysing political discourse*. Much academic work on the crisis recognizes that discourse is crucially important, but there have so far been few attempts to actually analyse it, partly because of the unavailability of suitable analytical frameworks that focus on decision and action.

Other methodological contributions

The book aims to offer a *practically useable framework* for those who wish to analyse argumentative texts. It presents a framework for analysing and evaluating argumentation in a sufficiently clear and explicit way for students and researchers to be able to use it as a model for carrying out analysis of argumentation in their own work. We think that the value of the book is increased by the substantial number of *extended examples* that we analyse and their *generic diversity* as *activity types* in the political field, in a variety of *institutional contexts*. We also hope that representing argumentation in the form of *diagrams* is a useful methodological instrument that political discourse analysts will want to adopt and develop. On the whole, we hope to contribute to expanding the interests of CDA practitioners beyond their current concerns (for instance, beyond their traditional concern with systemic-functional linguistics), to give them a motivation to explore powerful argumentation theory paradigms and fundamental work in pragmatics and philosophy of language.

We hope that the book will work well as a course-book on advanced courses in discourse analysis and will be of value in teaching people how to identify, analyse and evaluate arguments. We hope that it will prove helpful for the many students and academics in various areas of the social sciences who wish to analyse texts of various kinds (e.g. policy texts, interviews, media texts) but commonly find it difficult to find appropriate frameworks for analysis. And of course we hope to have communicated to our readers some of our own enthusiasm for developing CDA by integrating it with argumentation theory and thinking about arguments in political discourse.

Notes

1 Political discourse analysis and the nature of politics

1 We would question the suggestion that politics can be viewed as an *irrational* activity, which is made in the book on the basis of referring to theorists who reject rational choice theories (Wodak 2009a: 28, 51). While we agree with the general critique of rational choice in political theory, the alternative of bounded rationality, we would argue, does not entail irrationality, but is perfectly compatible with reasonableness. Deliberating with others is in fact essential in lessening the impact of bounded rationality and in ensuring that a *reasonable*, even if not necessarily the 'best' or the 'right' decision will be taken.

2 Examples of *topoi* include a *topos* of abuse, of advantage or usefulness, of all human beings being equal, of authority, of burdening or weighing down, of comparison, of consequence, of culture, of definition, of example, of finances, of fulfilling duty, of history, of humanitarianism, of ignorance, of justice, of law, of limitation period, of numbers, of reality, of responsibility, of threat or danger, of threat of racism, of time, of uselessness or disadvantage (Reisigl and Wodak 2001); alternatively, a *topos* of authority, *topos* of burden and costs, of challenge, of comparison, of constructing the hero, of definition, of difference, of diversity, of history, of threat, of urgency (Wodak 2009a).

3 It also obscures the fundamental value oppositions which, according to Aristotle, are specific to various types of rhetoric, as *special topoi*: what is good/bad, useful/harmful, just/unjust, worthy/ unworthy, etc.). According to Aristotelian-based contemporary views, *topoi* should be viewed as abstract patterns ('springboards' for thought, Corbett 1971, or 'machines for making arguments', Rubinelli 2009) that warrant the inference from a premises to the conclusion and, being abstract, allow the arguer to develop arguments *on any topic*. *Topoi*, according to Corbett, should be seen as reflecting the way the human mind thinks (by categorizing, comparing, thinking of relations between cause-effect, in the case of the *common* topics) or the basic principles underlying various fields in the case of the *special* topics (e.g. justice). A well-argued critique of the use of *topoi* in DHA has been independently developed by Zagar 2010, 2011).

4 Our view of strategies is partly compatible with the definition suggested by Ricoeur. According to him, *strategies are ordered chains of means towards desired ends* and 'it is this character of desirability that orders, regressively, the series of means envisioned to satisfy it' (Ricoeur 2008: 189). As we argue in Chapter 2, however, goals are not only always states of affairs that the agent desires, but may be states of affairs that he *ought to* bring about. In addition, circumstances are also part of these chains, not just means and ends.

5 The DHA also provides extensive taxonomies of strategies. For instance, 'macro-strategies' include: 'constructive strategies', 'strategies of perpetuation and justification', 'strategies of transformation' and 'de(con)structive strategies'. Sub-strategies include: 'legitimation', 'delegitimation', 'strategy of shifting blame and responsibility', of 'downplaying' or 'trivialization', 'assimilation, inclusion and continuation', 'singularization', 'autonomization', 'heteronomization', 'avoidance', 'positive self-presentation', 'calming down', 'portrayal in black and white', 'continuation', 'defence', 'avoidance', 'devaluation', 'vitalization', etc. (Wodak *et al.* 1999). In Reisigl and Wodak (2001), strategies of 'reference' are said to include: 'collectivization', 'spatialization', 'de-spatialization', 'explicit disassimilation', 'originalization', 'actionalization'/'professionalization', 'somatization', 'culturalization' ('linguistification', 'religionization', 'primitivization'), 'economization' ('professionalization', '(de)-possessivization', 'ideologization'), 'politicization' ('nationalization', 'party political alignment',

'organizationalization', 'professionalization', 'political actionalization', 'granting' or 'deprivation of political rights', 'ascription' or 'denying of political membership', 'temporalization'); 'militarization', 'social problematization' ('criminalization', 'pathologization', 'victimization') (Reisigl and Wodak 2001: 48–52). We have strong reservations about these taxonomia.

2 Practical reasoning: a framework for analysis and evaluation

1 This distinction is worth emphasizing because of the altogether different way in which 'practical reason' is used in sociological literature, as *practical sense*, as an essentially non-discursive (hence non-argumentative), tacit, intuitive 'feel for the game' (Bourdieu 1994, 2000; Sayer 2011).

2 To say that practical reasoning is an inferential process should not be understood as saying that it underlies or precedes every action we engage in. Agents do not usually 'recite' premises to themselves as a preamble to the judgements, intentions or decisions they form, although sometimes they may do. Practical reasoning does not precede actions we perform spontaneously or automatically, and it does not have to precede intentional action either, in spite of the fact that intentional reason is 'action for a reason'. It is not necessarily present in the *genesis* of every intentional action, but for every intentional action there is a *corresponding* practical argument that is *reconstructively* available and can express the structure of motivation and cognition that gave rise to the action. It can explain the action (why it is that the agent did *A* and not something else) and justify the action (Audi 2006: 103–104).

3 Audi's account is Kantian in that practical reasoning can also take *duties*, not only *desires*, as major premises. Both desires (what I want) and imperatives of reason (duties, obligations, etc.) can figure as major premises and can motivate action (as internal reasons) (Audi 2006; see also Audi 2001, 2009).

4 There are various accounts in informal logic that link goals (ends) to desirability, e.g. Bowell and Kemp (2005: 215). Walton draws on earlier work by Atkinson *et al.* (2004) and uses their example of practical reasoning ('Friendship requires that I see John before he leaves London . . .') to show how the goal ('seeing John') is supported by the underlying value of friendship and leads to a claim for action. According to Atkinson *et al.* (cited in Walton 2007a: 34), values are 'social interests that support goals by explaining why goals are desirable'. However, the use of the verb 'requires' ('friendship requires . . .') raises unanswered questions in our view. Friendship would *require* the agent to travel to London *whether or not* he actually *wanted* to do so, and whether or not he actually did choose to go. So, clearly, there is more to goals than *wanting* them to be fulfilled.

5 Some philosophers say that what usually happens when people say 'I (know I) ought to do *x*, but I don't want to do it' is that they do have *some* internal motivation to do it, but not enough as to override other stronger internal motivations not to do it. So the person who says 'I ought to recycle but I just can't be bothered' *does* want to recycle, only doesn't want it strongly enough to override her other desires (Baggini and Fosl 2007: 134–136). This would suggest, contrary to Searle, that the internalist perspective is correct.

6 We are grateful to Alexandra Cornilescu for originally bringing Kratzer's framework to our attention (see also Iețcu 2006a, 2006b).

7 For instance, we suggest, 'given what is morally required', as a normative premise, means 'given a future state of affairs (goal) in which moral requirements (values) have been met or realized'; the goal is thus a future state of affairs 'generated' by a concern for the realization of some value.

8 Because the structure of practical reasoning we propose is different from Walton's, we have not been able to use Araucaria diagrams (Reed and Rowe 2005), but have developed our own view of how practical arguments can be represented graphically.

9 The Popperian perspective on reasoning, including its extension to decision-making (Miller 1994: 39–45, 2006: 119–124), rejects justificationism. The conclusion never *follows*, strictly speaking, from the premises. Hence, it is not arguing from premises towards conclusions that drives intellectual thinking forward and produces new belief. Our hypotheses or conjectures (however well-informed) are ultimately the outcome of imaginative guesswork and never the outcome of an inferential process that starts in facts, observation or experience. Reasoning does not 'drive us forward', from premises to a hopefully well-justified claim, but 'pulls us back' (Miller 2005) from the claims we generate, helps us to criticize them and leads us to try out new hypotheses.

10 The argument from negative consequences (represented on the left side of Figure 2.3) is the *only* type of practical argument that a deductivist, Popperian approach would recognize.

11 An excellent discussion of rational persuasiveness can be found in Bowell and Kemp (2005, Chapter 6).

12 For the ten rules of critical discussion, see van Eemeren and Grootendorst (1992: 208–209, 2004: 190–196), van Eemeren (2010: 7–8).

13 These are: *symptomatic* argumentation, *causal* argumentation and *comparison* argumentation. Each scheme is associated with characteristic questions that are available to the critic in order to test out the tenability of the standpoint. The key critical questions associated with the three argument schemes are: (a) whether what is presented in the premises really is *typical* for what is mentioned in the standpoint, in the case of *symptomatic* argumentation; (b) whether there are really enough *relevant similarities*, or whether the analogies drawn do really hold, in the case of *comparison* argumentation; (c) whether what is presented as a cause *really leads to* the event that is presented as a result, in *causal* argumentation or argumentation from consequence (van Eemeren 2010; van Rees 2009; Garssen 2001).

14 Not all emotional appeals in politics and advertising are fallacious, but only those which are irrelevant or serve to disguise the absence of a really relevant argument (thus avoiding the burden of proof). For example, instead of useful facts and figures, that might enable us to choose a product on its merits, we are often given only an attractive image (Walton 2008a: 108–110).

15 Both Perelman's *New Rhetoric* and Tindale's approach try to avoid relativism by distinguishing a *particular audience* from the *universal audience* constructed from it by the arguer. Tindale develops the rhetorical perspective by incorporating a cognitive notion of relevance (Sperber and Wilson 1986). Good argumentation on the rhetorical perspective is argumentation that aims to persuade an audience in a *reasonable* (not merely effective) way, i.e. by using reasons that are *contextually relevant* (relevant to the audience in its particular context), hence *audience-relevant*, and *acceptable* to that particular audience *and* to the universal audience constructed from it. Tindale thus adds a clear normative perspective to rhetorical argumentation.

16 A similar position is defended by Billig (1996) in his 'rhetorical psychology'. The world of rhetoric, he says, is a world of uncertainty. A rhetorical approach is premised on the two-sidedness of human thinking and the fallibility of human cognitive capacities. The fact that we can argue both sides of an issue in most matters that we are confronted with does not mean that we do not or cannot eventually make choices, on the basis of various practical, moral and other criteria. Yet, the positions we eventually reject are not easily dismissed as illogical, irrational or absurd, and we may still recognize that such positions have a lot in their favour.

17 Berlin claimed that he was a pluralist not a relativist, and that 'all human beings must have some common values or they cease to be human'. One 'can exaggerate the absence of common ground. A great many people believe, roughly speaking, the same sort of thing' and 'accept more common values than is often believed' (Berlin 1998, in Lukes 2005: 135).

18 Not every philosopher is pessimistic about the possibility of resolving even such deep disagreements. According to Popper, in his well-known critique of the 'myth of the framework', the belief that 'a rational and fruitful discussion is impossible unless the participants share a common framework of basic assumptions' (Popper 1994: 34) is a myth: frameworks are not ultimately incommensurable. Given enough time, there is a prospect for the resolution of the most intractable disagreements, as long as one goes about it the right way, not by seeking empirical verification or justification for the alleged axioms of the worldview in question, but by asking: what follows from the acceptance of this or that worldview? What are the consequences of a given hypothesis? Are they acceptable? How do they fit with available evidence? An interesting argument against the multicultural relativist argument is made along Popperian lines by Siegel (1999). See also Feldman (2005) and Fogelin (2005).

19 Audi (2006: 176–177) formulates Ross's list to include the following obligations: justice, non-injury, fidelity, reparation, beneficence, self-improvement, gratitude, liberty, respectfulness. Freeman (2005: 245) organizes it as follows: sympathy (beneficence, non-maleficence, reparation), fairness (equity, reciprocity, impartiality), personal integrity (self-improvement, self-respect), fidelity (keeping promises, not telling lies).

20 Practical reasoning is not specifically addressed in pragma-dialectics as a distinct type of argumentation but some of the examples that are reconstructed as critical discussions are in fact cases of practical reasoning and deliberation. The birthday party conversation in van Eemeren and Grootendorst (2004: 101–122) is a good example of collective practical deliberation over what to do.

21 Let us abbreviate the means as *M*, the goal as *G*. The argument has the form: If *M* then *G*./ *G* is true./ Therefore *M*. But this is the standard form of the fallacy of *affirming the consequent*: If it rains, the streets are wet./ The streets are wet./ Therefore it has rained. Clearly, the conclusion is

false from true premises, as there are other possible causes for the streets being wet than rain. Similarly, economic recovery can result from several 'causes', not just from spending cuts.

22 Aristotle does allow for one particular end which we cannot deliberate upon in any context, or pursue as a means to some further end, and this is *happiness*, well-being or flourishing (*eudaimonia*), which is desired or valued simply for its own sake. For Aristotle, happiness is the ultimate ground of action and our motivationally final end, and even actions that are performed apparently for their own sake (intrinsically motivated, non-instrumental actions), such as listening to music or dancing, are *constitutive* means to happiness. The happy man is not one who pursues a life of hedonistic pleasure, but the man who excels at those activities that constitute human flourishing, those activities that it is *natural* for human beings to excel in. Thus, flourishing or happiness is not only the motivational but also the normative foundation of our actions, our appropriate end (*telos*) as human beings. Action that is contrary to our flourishing (for example, self-destructive behaviour springing from weakness of the will, or *akrasia*) is irrational for Aristotle. In other words, Aristotle does not oppose a moral life to self-interest: to live well is to act virtuously (Audi 2006).

23 As Hume says, 'Tis not contrary to reason to prefer the destruction of the whole world to the scratching of my finger . . .' (Hume 1739, 1967: 416). And if one should prefer to see the whole world destroyed rather than tolerating a minor injury to oneself, the defect would not be one of reason, but one of feeling. The person would show callous indifference to the fate of others, an absence of caring and fellow feeling. But is there a *rational* basis on which we might say that he *ought* to care? For Hume, the answer would be negative, desires are at best natural, not rational (Graham 2004: 107–108).

24 Hypothetical imperatives are grounded in desires that people happen to have or tend to have. The absence of appropriate desire is enough to dispel the force of the normative judgement. Categorical imperatives ('You ought to keep your promise of helping your friend') are special in that they do not rest upon any conditional desire and thus cannot be rejected by pointing to the absence of that desire. Should you say: 'But I don't want to do it', someone could legitimately reply: 'Whether you want to or not, you have to keep your promises.' Categorical imperatives thus transcend or override our desires and inclinations by providing us with rational principles of action, i.e. principles of action grounded in reason (whose rationality can be examined without recourse to experience), which override or take precedence over all other considerations when we decide what to do. In order to test whether what we propose to do is right or wrong, we should ask ourselves whether we could consistently universalize the 'maxim' of our action: could we consistently will that everyone who happened to have the same reasons for action as ourselves should act in that way? Categorical imperatives are grounded in reason because they can be universalized (Graham 2004: 108–111).

25 Blackburn criticizes the Kantian picture of the relationship between reason and desire as being based on a flawed implicit metaphor, that of Reason as Captain of a ship, with our desires, inclinations or passions as the unruly crew members, and the equally implausible picture of the deliberation process. When we deliberate, we do not *survey* our desires, from the vantage point of some 'inner deliberator' (the Kantian Captain), but pay attention to the relevant *features* of the external world. Concerns (desires, values, attitudes) are not the objects of deliberation but *constitutive features of the deliberating agent*, and they determine the selection of features of the situation that are considered relevant (Blackburn 1998: 250–261).

26 There are five classes of speech acts: assertives, directives, commissives, expressive and declarations (Searle 1969). Declarations are Austin's (1962) original *performatives* ('I now pronounce you husband and wife', or 'I declare war on Iraq', said by the right person in the right context) and they require the right institutional context to be felicitously uttered. Declarations are those speech acts that change the world by declaring that a new state of affairs exists and thus bringing that state of affairs into existence. They have a double direction of fit (world to word, and word to world at the same time) and they create the very reality they represent.

27 The view we develop in this section partly draws on Bowell and Kemp (2005: 129–130); Graham (2004: 58–63); Baggini and Fosl (2007: 119–121).

3 Critical discourse analysis and analysis of argumentation

1 Walton discusses persuasive (value-laden) definitions extensively from a dialectical perspective (see Walton 2001b, 2005, 2006: 245–265, 2007a: 275–322; Walton and Macagno 2009, 2010; Macagno and Walton 2008, 2010), drawing on early work on definitions by Stevenson (1944) and others.

Persuasive definitions ('abortion is murder') attempt to redefine the descriptive meaning of a word (while preserving the old emotive meaning) in order to change the extension (reference) of a term in accordance with the purposes of the arguer.

2   An important question from a dialectical perspective is whether all bias is unreasonable. Both Blair (1988) and Walton (1999, 2007a) agree that 'not all bias is bad bias'. In many cases, bias is nothing else than the kind of advocacy that one would expect from the parties involved in persuasion dialogue, where each party is supposed to strongly advocate his own side. Bias is only problematic when accompanied by a dialectical shift from a dialogue which is supposed to be two-sided (persuasion dialogue) to one that is normally expected to be one-sided (eristic). A dialogue that masquerades as a balanced, even-handed critical discussion and in fact is only one-sided advocacy is dialectically defective.

3   From a different perspective, which seems nevertheless compatible with our focus on the argumentative nature of manipulation, given that manipulation is contrasted with 'legitimate persuasion', van Dijk (2006) defines it as being, simultaneously, a form of power abuse or illegitimate domination, of cognitive mind control and of discursive interaction. It is at once a social, cognitive and social-discursive phenomenon. Illustrative examples are also selected from Blair's attempts to legitimize the Iraq war.

4   Jonathan Simons, http://news.bbc.co.uk/1/hi/uk/8487703.stm.

5   There is no distinction in this account between examples of (supposed) 'legitimation' which are arguments and examples which are explanations. This is in spite of the fact that the latter type of examples clearly do not involve answers to the question 'why should we do x'? (van Leeuwen's correct starting point), but to the question 'why did x happen?', or 'why did someone do x?', which is a totally different question. In argumentation theory, the difference between argument and explanation is a very clear one. Clauses of the form 'because y' do appear in both arguments and explanations, yet not any 'because y' signals 'justification' or 'legitimation', simply because *not any 'because y' clause is a premise in an argument*. Some 'because y' clauses are *explanans* clauses in explanations. Explanation can of course raise interesting issues of its own. In saying 'I did this *because I wanted to help you*', the italicized *explanans* may be an insincere statement, might provide a false reason (in the sense of *cause*) for the way I acted, i.e. it might be a rationalization. (Both arguments and explanations can be rationalizations.) Notice that the above explanation can be correlated with a previous argument: 'I want to help you, therefore I will do x', which does attempt to legitimize the action. But it is arguments that can legitimize action, properly speaking, not explanations, unless they report, as here, a previous argument.

6   For Searle, power is always intentional. One cannot talk meaningfully about power unless one is able to say 'who exactly has power over exactly whom to get them to do exactly what' (Searle 2010: 152). In this, he seems to differ from Lukes, for whom the power of systems is unintentional. For Searle, societies and other collectivities can exert power over their members (we can refer to this as social pressure, or the power of conformity) because members of such groups are able to get individuals to behave in certain ways whether those individuals want to or not, or can impose informal sanctions on those who violate the norms, in the knowledge that these sanctions will be supported by others (Searle 2010: 158–159). Searle refers to this type of power as 'Background' power. Also, for him, because the system of status functions requires collective recognition or acceptance, all genuine power, while exercised from above, comes from below (Searle 2010: 164–165).

4 The economic crisis in the UK: strategies and arguments

1   For reasons of space we have abridged the text and created paragraphs out of the original format; in the original format (on the Treasury website), every sentence begins a new paragraph.

2   In Fairclough and Fairclough (2011a) we discussed this in terms of distinct cost–benefit premise. So-called cost–benefit and efficiency premises are suggested by Bowell and Kemp (2005: 203–204) as necessary in order to make the argument valid. The conclusion of a practical argument will follow from the premises if the costs do not outweigh the benefits and if the proposed action is the most economical or efficient way of bringing about the goal. Not all practical arguments can be discussed in such consequentialist, utilitarian terms. In our view, considerations having to do with moral values, duties, rights, obligations, enter the argument as external constraints (institutional facts) and they may override any cost–benefit or efficiency calculation. This is why the framework we present here is different.

3 For argumentation by dissociation, see Perelman and Olbrechts-Tyteca (1969) and particularly van Rees (2009).

5 Values as premises in the public debate over bankers' bonuses

1 This chapter is a revised version of Fairclough and Fairclough (2011b), originally presented at the ISSA Argumentation Conference, Amsterdam, June 2010.
2 A transcript of this debate is available at http://www.stpauls.co.uk/Learning-Education/St-Pauls-Institute/2009-Programme-Money-Integrity-and-Wellbeing.
3 We have also looked at *The Daily Telegraph* comments thread (following the article by Quinn and Hall, 2009), which is fairly similar in terms of the overall views expressed but less extensive (only 12 comments). There is no space to include any discussion of this thread here.
4 We have abridged some of the comments to avoid repetition, corrected various typos and replaced words written in uppercase for emphasis by italicized words.

6 Deliberation as genre in the parliamentary debate on university tuition fees

1 The transcript of the debate is available in *Hansard*, Columns 540–629, at http://www.publications.parliament.uk/pa/cm201011/cmhansrd/cm101209/debtext/101209-0002.htm.
2 Walton's (2007a) view of deliberation and debate is different. For Walton, deliberation is one of six types of *dialogue*, alongside persuasion dialogue, inquiry dialogue, information-seeking dialogue, negotiation and eristic dialogue. More recently, he has added debate to this list as another dialogue type. In his view, debates (such as TV debates or talk-shows) come closest to (but are more regulated than) eristic dialogue (quarrels) (Walton 2008a: 4). This typology does not draw a clear distinction between different levels of analysis: debate and deliberation are placed at the same level and it is not clear whether they correspond to genres or to activity types, or whether they are normative or descriptive concepts. See also van Eemeren's discussion of this typology (2010: 131–138).
3 Ieţcu-Fairclough (2008, 2009) attempts to discuss strategic manoeuvring in the political field, focusing on a particular example of adjudication.
4 Note that the *opening* stage of the argumentation reconstructed as critical discussion is not the same as the *Open* stage of deliberation dialogue (as genre) – these two sequences of stages belong to different theoretical models and have been developed entirely independently, hence the terminological overlap and the possibility of confusion.
5 All references to line numbers in this chapter are to the *Hansard* transcript.
6 We are drawing on a discussion on strategic manoeuvring with the burden of proof, including the notion of a 'pragmatic status quo', in van Eemeren (2010: 213–240). The fallacy of evading the burden of proof is discussed in van Eemeren and Grootendorst (1992, Chapter 10).
7 It is interesting to observe that David Willetts's failure to address the relevant issues is justified (rationalized) in terms of (legitimate) time constraints: he is not avoiding the issue, he merely does not have enough time to address it properly ('I am sorry that there will not be time for me to respond to all the points that have been made').
8 The excerpt comes from Nick Clegg's official website, at http://www.libdems.org.uk/nccom_home.aspx.
9 See the entire comments thread at http://www.guardian.co.uk/commentisfree/2010/nov/16/coalition-poker-clegg-broken-promises?commentpage.

Bibliography

Ackrill, J. (1987) *A New Aristotle Reader*, Princeton, NJ: Princeton University Press.

Anderson, B. (1991) *Imagined Communities: Reflections on the Origin and Spread of Nationalism*, London: Verso.

Atkinson, K., Bench-Capon, T. and McBurney, P. (2004) 'A dialogue game protocol for multi-agent argument over proposals for action', in Rahwan, I., Moraitis, P. and Reed, C. (eds) *Argumentation in Multi-Agent Systems*, Berlin: Springer, 149–161.

Audi, R. (2001) *The Architecture of Reason: The Structure and Substance of Rationality*, New York: Oxford University Press.

Audi, R. (2002) 'Prospects for a naturalization of practical reason: Humean instrumentalism and the normative authority of desire', *International Journal of Philosophical Studies* 10(3): 235–263.

Audi, R. (2006) *Practical Reasoning and Ethical Decision*, London: Routledge.

Audi, R. (2009) *Business Ethics and Ethical Business*, New York: Oxford University Press.

Austin, J. L. (1962) *How to Do Things with Words*, London: Oxford University Press.

Baggini, J. and Fosl, P. S. (2007) *The Ethics Toolkit: A Compendium of Ethical Concepts and Methods*, Oxford: Blackwell.

Balls, E. (2010) 'There is an alternative', Speech at Bloomberg, 27 August, at *Ed Balls – Labour MP Blog*, http://www.edballs4labour.org/blog/?p=907 (accessed 10 October 2010).

Bauman, Z. (1999) *In Search of Politics*, Cambridge: Polity Press.

Beetham, D. (1991) *The Legitimation of Power*, Atlantic Highlands, NJ: International Humanities Press.

Benhabib, S. (1992) 'Models of public space: Hannah Arendt, the liberal tradition, and Jurgen Habermas', in Calhoun, C. (ed.) *Habermas and the Public Sphere*, Boston, MA: MIT Press, 73–98.

Berlin, I. (1990) *The Crooked Timber of Humanity: Chapters in the History of Ideas*, London: John Murray.

Berlin, I. (1998) 'My intellectual path', *New York Review of Books*, 14 May, 57.

Bhaskar, R. (1979) *The Possibility of Naturalism*, Hassocks: Harvester.

Bickenbach, J. E. and Davies, J. (1997) *Good Reasons for Better Arguments*, Ontario: Broadview Press.

Billig, M. (1996) *Arguing and Thinking: A Rhetorical Approach to Social Psychology*, Cambridge: Cambridge University Press.

Blackburn, S. (1998) *Ruling Passions: A Theory of Practical Reason*, Oxford: Clarendon Press.

Blair, A. (1988) 'What is bias?', in Govier, T. (ed.) *Selected Issues in Logic and Communication*, Belmont, CA: Wadsworth, 93–104.

Blair, A. (2003) 'Relationships among logic, dialectic and rhetoric', in Eemeren, F. H. van, Blair, J. A., Willard, A. C. and Snoek-Henkemans, A. F. (eds) *Anyone Who Has a View: Theoretical Constributions to the Study of Argumentation*, Dordrecht: Kluwer Academic, 91–108.

Blanchflower, D. (2010a) 'Job cuts: Slasher Osborne drives us back into recession', *The Guardian*, 30 June, at http://www.guardian.co.uk/commentisfree/2010/jun/30/public-sector-job-cuts-private-sector-growth1 (accessed 15 January 2011).

Blanchflower, D. (2010b) 'We've just jumped off a cliff', *New Statesman*, 21 October, at http://www.newstatesman.com/uk-politics/2010/10/government-spending-labour (accessed 15 January 2011).

Blanchflower, D. (2010c) 'Welcome back to 1930s Britain', *New Statesman*, 28 October, at http://www.newstatesman.com/economy/2010/11/osborne-money-cuts-britain (accessed 15 January 2011).

Blanchflower, D. (2011a) 'Let's hope Cameron is for turning', *New Statesman*, 6 January, at http://www.newstatesman.com/economy/2011/01/ireland-greece-cameron (accessed 30 January 2011).

Blanchflower, D. (2011b) 'Scrapping the EMA and cutting the young adrift', *The Guardian*, 20 January, at http://www.guardian.co.uk/commentisfree/2011/jan/20/ema-deadweight-youth-unemployment-jobs (accessed 30 January 2011).

Blanchflower, D. (2011c) 'The scars of a jobless generation', *New Statesman*, 17 February, at http://www.newstatesman.com/economy/2011/02/youth-unemployment-labour (accessed 20 March 2011).

Bohman, J. (1996) *Public Deliberation: Pluralism, Complexity, and Democracy*, Cambridge, MA: The MIT Press.

Bourdieu, P. (1994) *Practical Reason*, Cambridge: Polity Press.

Bourdieu, P. (2000) *Pascalian Meditations*, Cambridge: Polity Press.

Bourdieu, P. and Wacquant, L. (2001) 'New liberal speak: Notes on the new planetary vulgate', *Radical Philosophy* 105: 2–5.

Bowell, T. and Kemp, G. (2005) *Critical Thinking: A Concise Guide*. London: Routledge.

Brown, K. (2006) (ed.) *Encyclopaedia of Language and Linguistics* vol. 9, 2nd edition, Oxford: Elsevier.

Burke, K. (1973/1941) *The Philosophy of Literary Form*, 3rd edition, Berkeley: University of California Press.

Bybee, J. L., Perkins, R. and Pagliuca, W. (1994) *The Evolution of Grammar: Tense, Aspect and Modality in the Languages of the World*, Chicago: The University of Chicago Press.

Cable, V. (2009) *The Storm: The World Economic Crisis and What It Means*, London: Atlantic Books.

Callinicos, A. (2010) *Bonfire of the Illusions: The Twin Crises of the Liberal World*, Cambridge: Polity Press.

Chilton, P. (2004) *Analysing Political Discourse: Theory and Practice*, London: Routledge.

Chilton, P. (2010) 'The language–ethics interface: reflections on linguistics, discourse analysis and the legacy of Habermas', in de Cillia, R., Gruber, H., Krzyzanowski, M. and Menz, F. (eds) *Discourse–Politics–Identity*, Vienna: Stauffenburg Verlag, 33–43.

Chouliaraki, L. and Fairclough, N. (1999) *Discourse in Late Modernity*, Edinburgh: Edinburgh University Press.

Cillia, R. de, Gruber, H., Krzyzanowski, M. and Menz, F. (eds) (2010) *Discourse–Politics–Identity*, Vienna: Stauffenburg Verlag.

Cohen, J. (1998) 'Democracy and liberty', in Elster, J. (ed.) *Deliberative Democracy*, Cambridge: Cambridge University Press.

Corbett, E. P. J. (1965/1971) *Classical Rhetoric for the Modern Student*, 2nd edition, New York: Oxford University Press.

Cruddas, J. and Nahles, A. (no date) *Building the Good Society: The Project of the Democratic Left*, Compass, leaflet in the 2010 electoral campaign.

Debray, R. (1993) *Prison Writings*, London: Allen Lane.

Dijk, T. A. van (1997a) (ed.) *Discourse as Social Interaction. Discourse Studies 2: A Multidisciplinary Introduction*, London: Sage.

Dijk, T. A. van (1997b) 'What is political discourse analysis?', in Blommaert, J. and Bulcaen, C. (eds) *Political Linguistics*, Amsterdam: Benjamins, 11–52.

Dijk, T. A. van (2006) 'Discourse and manipulation', *Discourse & Society* 17(2): 359–383.

Dryzek, J. (1993) 'Policy analysis and planning: from science to argument', in Fischer, F. and Forester, J. (eds) *The Argumentative Turn in Policy Analysis and Planning*, Durham, NC: Duke University Press, 213–232.

Dryzek, J. (2000) *Deliberative Democracy and Beyond: Liberals, Critics, Contestations*, Oxford: Oxford University Press.

Eemeren, F. H. van (ed.) (2001) *Crucial Concepts in Argumentation Theory*, Amsterdam: Amsterdam University Press.

Eemeren, F. H. van (2005) 'Foreword: Preview by review', in Saussure, L. de and Schulz, P. (eds) *Manipulation and Ideologies in the Twentieth Century*, Amsterdam: John Benjamins, ix–xvii.

Eemeren, F. H. van (2009a) 'Strategic maneuvering: examining argumentation in context', in Eemeren, F. H. van (ed.) *Examining Argumentation in Context: Fifteen Studies on Strategic Maneuvering*, Amsterdam: John Benjamins, 1–24.

Eemeren, F. H. van (2009b) 'Democracy and argumentation', in Williams, D. C. and Young, M. J. (eds) *Discourse, Debate and Democracy*, New York: Idebate Press, 37–54.

Eemeren, F. H. van (ed.) (2009c) *Examining Argumentation in Context: Fifteen Studies on Strategic Maneuvering*, Amsterdam: John Benjamins.

Eemeren, F. H. van (2010) *Strategic Maneuvering in Argumentative Discourse*, Amsterdam: John Benjamins.

Eemeren, F. H. van and Grootendorst, R. (1992) *Argumentation, Communication and Fallacies*, Hillsdale, NJ: Lawrence Erlbaum Associates.

Eemeren, F. H. van and Grootendorst, R. (2004) *A Systematic Theory of Argumentation: The Pragma-Dialectical Approach*, Cambridge: Cambridge University Press.

Eemeren, F. H. van and Houtlosser, P. (2002a) (eds) *Dialectic and Rhetoric: The Warp and Woof of Argumentation Analysis*, Dordrecht: Kluwer Academic Publishers.

Eemeren, F. H. van and Houtlosser, P. (2002b) 'Strategic maneuvering: maintaining a delicate balance', in Eemeren, F. H. van and P. Houtlosser (eds) *Dialectic and Rhetoric: The Warp and Woof of Argumentation Analysis*, Dordrecht: Kluwer Academic Publishers, 131–159.

Eemeren, F. H. van, Grootendorst, R., Jackson, S. and Jacobs, S. (1993) *Reconstructing Argumentative Discourse*, Tuscaloosa, AL: The University of Alabama Press.

Eemeren, F. H. van, Grootendorst, R. and Snoek Henkemans, A. F. (2002) *Argumentation: Analysis, Evaluation, Presentation*, Mahwah, NJ: Lawrence Erlbaum Associates.

Eemeren, F. H. van, Blair, J. A., Willard, A. C. and Snoek-Henkemans, A. F. (2003) (eds) *Anyone Who Has a View: Theoretical Constributions to the Study of Argumentation*, Dordrecht: Kluwer.

Eikmeyer, H. J. and Rieser, H. (1981) (eds) *Words, Worlds, and Contexts: New Approaches in Word Semantics*, Berlin: de Gruyter.

Elliott, L. (2009) 'Time for change: five proposals', *The Guardian*, 22 March, at http://www.guardian.co.uk/business/2009/mar/22/larry-elliott-proposals-for-g20#history-link-box (accessed 20 August 2010).

Elliott, L. (2010a) 'Budget 2010: Labour forgot industry for 13 years', *The Guardian*, 24 March, at http://www.guardian.co.uk/business/2010/mar/24/budget-2010-birmingham-manufacturing-forgotten#history-link-box (accessed 20 August 2010).

Elliott, L. (2010b) 'Labour needs to admit what it got wrong', *The Guardian*, 3 May, at http://www.guardian.co.uk/politics/2010/may/03/labour-should-admit-mistakes-larry-elliott (accessed 20 August 2010).

Elliott, L. (2010c) 'The lunatics are back in charge of the economy and they want cuts, cuts, cuts', *The Guardian*, 14 June, at http://www.guardian.co.uk/business/2010/jun/14/lunatics-economy-cuts-frankin-roosevelt (accessed 20 August 2010).

Elliott, L. (2010d) 'Budget 2010: the axeman cometh', *The Guardian*, 22 June, at http://www.guardian.co.uk/uk/2010/jun/22/budget-2010-the-axeman-cometh-analysis (accessed 20 August 2010).

Elliott, L. (2011a) 'Outgoing CBI chief slams government growth strategy', *The Guardian*, 24 January, at http://www.guardian.co.uk/business/2011/jan/24/cbi-chief-slams-government-growth-strategy (accessed 20 March 2011).

Elliott, L. (2011b) 'George Soros tells David Cameron: change direction or face recession', *The Guardian*, 26 January, at http://www.guardian.co.uk/politics/2011/jan/26/george-soros-david-cameron-recession (accessed 30 January 2011).

Elliott, L., Butler, E., Chakrabortty, A., Parsons, L., Burke, M., Noble, F. and Lucas, C. (2011) 'Britain's shrinking economy: panel verdict', *The Guardian*, 25 January, at http://www.guardian.co.uk/commentisfree/2011/jan/25/gdp-shock-quarter-shrinking-economy (accessed 20 February 2011).

Elster, J. (1998a) 'Introduction', in Elster, J. (ed.) *Deliberative Democracy*, Cambridge: Cambridge University Press, 1–18.

Elster, J. (1998b) (ed.) *Deliberative Democracy*, Cambridge: Cambridge University Press.

Fairclough, N. (1989) *Language and Power*, London: Longman (2nd edition 2001).

Fairclough, N. (1992) *Discourse and Social Change*, Cambridge: Polity Press.

Fairclough, N. (1995) *Critical Discourse Analysis*, London: Longman.

Fairclough, N. (2000a) *New Labour, New Language?* London: Routledge.

Fairclough, N. (2000b) 'Dialogue in the public sphere', in Sarangi, S. and Coulthard, M. (eds) *Discourse and Social Life*, London: Longman.

Fairclough, N. (2001) 'The dialectics of discourse', *Textus* 14: 231–242.

Fairclough, N. (2003) *Analysing Discourse: Textual Analysis for Social Research*, London: Routledge.

Fairclough, N. (2004) 'Critical discourse analysis in researching language in the new capitalism: overdetermination, transdisciplinarity and textual analysis', in Harrison, C. and Young, L. (eds) *Systemic Linguistics and Critical Discourse Analysis*, London: Continuum.

Fairclough, N. (2005) 'Neo-liberalism – a discourse-analytical perspective', in *Proceedings of Conference on British and American Studies*, Braşov: Editura Universităţii Transilvania, 1–18.

Fairclough, N. (2006) *Language and Globalisation*, London: Routledge.

Fairclough, N. (2010) *Critical Discourse Analysis: The Critical Study of Language*, 2nd edition, London: Longman.

Fairclough, N. and Fairclough, I. (2010) 'Argumentation theory in CDA: analyzing practical reasoning in political discourse', in de Cillia, R., Gruber, H., Krzyzanowski, M. and Menz, F. (eds) *Discourse–Politics–Identity*, Vienna: Stauffenburg Verlag, 59–70.

Fairclough, I. and Fairclough, N. (2011a) 'Practical reasoning in political discourse: the UK government's response to the economic crisis in the 2008 Pre-Budget Report', *Discourse & Society* 22(3): 243–268.

Fairclough, I. and Fairclough, N. (2011b) 'Practical reasoning in political discourse: moral and prudential arguments in the debate over bankers' bonuses in the British press', in Eemeren, F. H. van, Garssen, B., Godden, D. and Mitchell, G. (eds) *Proceedings of the Seventh Conference of the International Society for the Study of Argumentation*. Amsterdam: Sic Sat, 434–447.

Fairclough, N. and Graham, P. (2002) 'Marx as critical discourse analyst: the genesis of a critical method and its relevance to the critique of global capital', *Estudios de Sociolinguistica* 3(1): 185–229.

Fairclough, N. and Wodak, R. (1997) 'Critical discourse analysis', in Dijk, T. van (ed.) *Discourse as Social Interaction*, London: Sage, 258–284.

Fairclough, N., Jessop, B. and Sayer, A. (2004) 'Critical realism and semiosis', in Joseph, J. and Roberts, J. (eds) *Realism, Discourse and Deconstruction*, London: Routledge, 23–42.

Fairclough, N., Pardoe, S. and Szerszynski, B. (2006) 'Critical discourse analysis and citizenship', in Hausendorf, H. and Bora, A. (eds) *Analyzing Citizenship Talk*, Amsterdam: John Benjamins, 98–123.

Fearon (1998) 'Deliberation as discussion', in Elster, J. (ed.) *Deliberative Democracy*, Cambridge: Cambridge University Press.

Feldman, R. (2005) 'Deep disagreements, rational resolution, and critical thinking', *Informal Logic*, 25(1): 13–23.

Feldstein, M. (2010) 'A double dip is a price worth paying', *Financial Times*, 22 July, at http://www.ft.com/cms/s/0/2447452e-95af-11df-b5ad-00144feab49a.html#axzz1MXPSpLPd (accessed 15 August 2010).

Ferguson, N. (2010) 'Today's Keynesians have learnt nothing', *Financial Times*, 19 July, at http://www.ft.com/cms/s/0/270e1a6c-9334-11df-96d5-00144feab49a.html#axzz1MXPSpLPd (accessed 15 August 2010).

Financial Times (2009) 'The consequence of bad economics', Editorial, 9 March, at http://www.ft.com/cms/s/0/cbc4cfd8-0ce4-11de-a555-0000779fd2ac.html#axzz1al6RBXMu (accessed 7 December 2010).

Finlayson, A. (2007) 'From beliefs to arguments: interpretative methodology and rhetorical political analysis', *British Journal of Politics and International Relations* 9(4): 545–563.

Fischer, F. and Forester, J. (eds) (1993) *The Argumentative Turn in Policy Analysis and Planning*, Durham, NC: Duke University Press.

Fogelin, R. J. (2005) 'The logic of deep disagreements', *Informal Logic*, 25(1): 3–11.

Foster, J. and Magdoff, F. (2009) *The Great Financial Crisis: Causes and Consequences*, New York: Monthly Review Press.

Fowler, R., Hodge, B., Kress, G. and Trew, T. (1979) *Language and Control*, London: Routledge.

Freedland, J. (2010) 'Osborne will escape public wrath if Labour lets him win the blame game', *The Guardian*, 19 October 2010, at http://www.guardian.co.uk/commentisfree/2010/oct/19/osborne-public-wrath-labour-blame-game (accessed 20 October 2010).

Freeman, J. B. (2005) *Acceptable Premises: An Epistemic Approach to an Informal Logic Problem*, Cambridge: Cambridge University Press.

Furley, D. and Nehamas, A. (1994) (eds) *Aristotle's Rhetoric: Philosophical Essays*, Princeton, NJ: Princeton University Press.

Gamble, A. (2009) *The Spectre at the Feast: Capitalist Crisis and the Politics of Recession*, London: Palgrave Macmillan.

Garner, R. (2009) 'The nature of politics and political analysis', Introduction to Garner, R., Ferdinand, P. and Lawson, S. (eds) *Introduction to Politics*, London: Oxford University Press.

Garner, R., Ferdinand, P. and Lawson, S. (2009) *Introduction to Politics*, London: Oxford University Press.

Garssen, B. (2001) 'Argument schemes', in Eemeren, F. H. van (ed.) *Crucial Concepts in Argumentation Theory*, Amsterdam: Amsterdam University Press, 81–100.

Gaus, G. F. (2003) *Contemporary Theories of Liberalism*, London: Sage.

Gauthier, D. (1963) *Practical Reasoning: The Structure and Foundations of Prudential and Moral Arguments and Their Exemplification in Discourse*, Oxford: Clarendon Press.

Giddens, A. (1984) *The Constitution of Society*, Cambridge: Polity Press.

Giddens, A. (1987) *Social Theory and Modern Sociology*, Cambridge: Polity Press.

Govier, T. (1988) (ed.) *Selected Issues in Logic and Communication*, Belmont, CA: Wadsworth.

Govier, T. (2001) *A Practical Study of Argument*, 5th edition, Belmont, CA: Wadsworth/Thomson Learning.

Graham, G. (2004) *Eight Theories of Ethics*, London: Routledge.

Gray, J. (1989) *Liberalisms: Essays in Political Philosophy*, London: Routledge.

Gray, J. (2000) *Two Faces of Liberalism*, Cambridge: Polity Press.

Gutmann, A. and Thompson, D. (1996) *Democracy and Disagreement*, Cambridge, MA: The Belknap Press of Harvard University Press.

Habermas, J. (1984) *The Theory of Communicative Action. Vol. 1: Reason and the Rationalization of Society*, trans. T. McCarthy, London: Heinemann.

Habermas, J. (1990) *Moral Consciousness and Communicative Action*, trans. C. Lenhardt and S. Weber Nicholsen, Cambridge: Polity Press.

Habermas, J. (1996a) *Between Facts and Norms: Contributions to a Discourse Theory of Law and Democracy*, Cambridge, MA: MIT Press.

Habermas, J. (1996b) 'Discourse ethics', in Outhwaite, W. (ed.) *The Habermas Reader*, Cambridge: Polity Press, 180–192.

Habermas, J. (1996c) 'Legitimation problems in the modern state', in Outhwaite, W. (ed.) *The Habermas Reader*, Cambridge: Polity Press, 248–265.

Halliwell, S. (1994) 'Popular morality, philosophical ethics and the *Rhetoric*', in Furley, D. and Nehamas, D. (eds) *Aristotle's Rhetoric: Philosophical Essays*, Princeton, NJ: Princeton University Press, 211–230.

Hansen, H. V., Tindale, C. W., Blair, J. A. and Johnson, R. H. (2001) (eds) *Argument and Its Applications: Proceedings of the Fourth Biennial Conference of the Ontario Society for the Study of Argumentation (OSSA 2001)*.

Harris, S. (2010) *The Moral Landscape: How Science Can Determine Human Values*, New York: Free Press.

Harrison, C. and Young, L. (2004) (eds) *Systemic Linguistics and Critical Discourse Analysis*, London: Continuum.

Harvey, D. (1996) *Justice, Nature and the Geography of Difference*, Oxford: Blackwell.

Harvey, D. (2010) *The Enigma of Capital and the Crises of Capitalism*, London: Profile Books.

Hasan, M. (2010) 'The war on welfare scroungers part 77', *New Statesman*, Blog, 27 October, at http://www.newstatesman.com/blogs/mehdi-hasan/2010/10/benefit-claimants-work-atos (accessed 15 January 2011).

Hausendorf, H. and Bora, A. (2006) (eds) *Analyzing Citizenship Talk*, Amsterdam: John Benjamins.

Hay, C. (2007) *Why we Hate Politics*, Cambridge: Polity Press.

Hitchcock, D. (2002) 'Pollock on practical reasoning', *Informal Logic* 22(3): 247–256.

Hitchcock, D., McBurney, P. and Parsons, S. (2001) 'A framework for deliberation dialogues', in Hansen, H. V., Tindale, C. W., Blair, J. A. and Johnson, R. H. (eds) *Argument and Its Applications: Proceedings of the Fourth Biennial Conference of the Ontario Society for the Study f Argumentation (OSSA 2001)*.

HM Treasury (1997–2009) 'Pre-Budget Report statement to the House of Commons', delivered by the Chancellor of the Exchequer, available at http://webarchive.nationalarchives.gov.uk/20100407010852/http://www.hm-treasury.gov.uk/bud_bud09_index.htm (accessed 10 October 2010).

HM Treasury (1998–2010) 'Budget Report statement to the House of Commons', delivered by the Chancellor of the Exchequer, available at http://webarchive.nationalarchives.gov.uk/20100407010852/http://www.hm-treasury.gov.uk/bud_bud09_index.htm (accessed 10 October 2010).

HM Treasury (2008) 'Pre-Budget Report statement to the House of Commons', delivered by the Rt Hon Alistair Darling MP, Chancellor of the Exchequer', 24 November, available at http://webarchive.nationalarchives.gov.uk/20100407010852/http://www.hm-treasury.gov.uk/prebud_pbr08_speech.htm (accessed 10 October 2010).

HM Treasury (2010) 'Budget statement by the Chancellor of the Exchequer, the Rt Hon George Osborne MP', 22 June, available at http://www.hm-treasury.gov.uk/junebudget_speech.htm (accessed 25 June 2010).

HM Treasury (2010) 'Spending Review statement' delivered by the Chancellor of the Exchequer, the Rt Hon George Osborne MP, 20 October, available at http://www.hm-treasury.gov.uk/spend_sr2010_speech.htm (accessed 25 October 2010).

Hopkins, K. (2009) 'Public must learn to "tolerate the inequality" of bonuses, says Goldman Sachs vice-chairman', *The Guardian*, 21 October, http://www.guardian.co.uk/business/2009/oct/21/executive-pay-bonuses-goldmansachs (accessed 25 March 2010).

Hume, D. (1739/1967) *A Treatise on Human Nature*, Oxford: Clarendon Press.

Iețcu, I. (2006a) *Dialogue, Argumentation and Ethical Perspective in the Essays of H.-R. Patapievici*, București: Editura Universității din București.

Iețcu, I. (2006b) *Discourse Analysis and Argumentation Theory: Analytical Framework and Applications*, București: Editura Universității din București.

Iețcu, I. (2006c) 'Argumentation, dialogue and conflicting moral economies in post-1989 Romania', *Discourse & Society* 17(5): 627–650.

Iețcu-Fairclough, I. (2008) 'Legitimation and strategic maneuvering in the political field', *Argumentation* 22: 399–417. DOI 10.1007/s10503–008–9088–9.

Iețcu-Fairclough, I. (2009) 'Strategic maneuvering in the political field', in Eemeren, F. H. van (ed.) *Examining Argumentation in Context*, Amsterdam: John Benjamins, 131–151.

Irwin, T. (1999) *Aristotle: Nicomachean Ethics*, Indianapolis, IN: Hackett.

Jenkins, S. (2010) 'In coalition poker, broken promises are small change', *The Guardian*, 16 November, at http://www.guardian.co.uk/commentisfree/2010/nov/16/coalition-poker-clegg-broken-promises (accessed 10 January 2011).

Jessop, B. (2002) *The Future of the Capitalist State*, Cambridge: Polity Press.

Jessop, B. (2004) 'Critical semiotic analysis and cultural political economy', *Critical Discourse Studies* 1–2: 159–174.

Jessop, B. (2008) *State Power*, Cambridge: Polity Press.

Jessop, B. and Sum, N-L. (2001) 'Pre-disciplinary and post-disciplinary perspectives in political economy', *New Political Economy* 6: 89–101.

Jessop, B. and Sum, N. (2012) 'Cultural political economy, strategic essentialism, and neoliberalism', in Mayer, M. and Künkel, J. (eds) *Neoliberal Urbanism and its Contestation: Crossing Theoretical Boundaries*, Basingstoke: Palgrave-Macmillan, 80–96.

Johnson, M. (1981) (ed.) *Philosophical Perspectives on Metaphor*, Minneapolis: University of Minnesota Press.

Johnson, R. H. (2000) *Manifest Rationality: A Pragmatic Theory of Argument*, Mahwah, NJ: Lawrence Erlbaum Associates.

Johnson, R. H. and Blair, J. A. (2006) *Logical Self-Defense*, New York: International Debate Educational Association.

Joseph, J. and Roberts, J. (2004) (eds) *Realism, Discourse and Deconstruction*, London: Routledge.

Kant, I. (1959) *Foundations of the Metaphysics of Morals*, trans. L. White Beck, New York: The Liberal Arts Press.

Kaplan, T. (1993) 'Reading policy narratives: beginnings, middles, and ends', in Fischer, F. and Forester, J. (eds) *The Argumentative Turn in Policy Analysis and Planning*, Durham, NC: Duke University Press, 167–185.

Kennedy, G. (1991) *Aristotle on Rhetoric: A Theory of Civic Discourse*, New York: Oxford University Press.

Kennedy, G. (1994) *A New History of Classical Rhetoric*, Princeton, NJ: Princeton University Press.

Kock, C. (2007) 'Dialectical Obligations in Political Debate', *Informal Logic* 27(3): 233–247.

Kock, C. (2009) 'Choice is Not True or False: The Domain of Rhetorical Argumentation', *Argumentation* (2009) 23: 61–80, DOI 10.1007/s10503–008–9115-x.

Kollewe, J. (2010) 'David Blanchflower: spending cuts could lead to recession', *The Guardian*, 18 October, at http://www.guardian.co.uk/business/2010/oct/18/david-blanchflower-warns-against-spending-cuts (accessed 10 December 2010).

Kratzer, A. (1981) 'The notional category of modality', in Eikmeyer, H. J. and Rieser, H. (eds) *Words, Worlds, and Contexts: New Approaches in Word Semantics*, Berlin: Walter de Gruyter, 38–74.

Kratzer, A. (1991) 'Modality', in von Stechow, A. and Wunderlich, D. (eds) *Semantics: An International Handbook of Contemporary Research*, Berlin: Walter de Gruyter, 639–650.

Krugman, P. (2010a) 'Myths of austerity', *The New York Times*, 2 July 2010, at http://www.nytimes.com/2010/07/02/opinion/02krugman.html (accessed 10 July 2010).

Krugman, P. (2010b) 'British fashion victims', *The New York Times*, 21 October 2010, at http://www.nytimes.com/2010/10/22/opinion/22krugman.html (accessed 25 October 2010).

Lakoff, G. (1987) *Women, Fire, and Dangerous Things: What Categories Reveal About the Mind*, Chicago: University of Chicago Press.

Lakoff, G. (2002) *Moral Politics: How Liberals and Conservatives Think*, Chicago: University of Chicago Press.

Lakoff, G. (2004) *Don't Think of an Elephant: Know Your Values and Frame the Debate*, White River Jct, VT: Chelsea Green Publishing.

Lakoff, G. and Johnson, M. (1980) *Metaphors we Live By*, Chicago: University of Chicago Press.

Lakoff, G. and Johnson, M. (1981) 'Conceptual metaphor in everyday language', in Johnson, M. (ed.) *Philosophical Perspectives on Metaphor*, Minneapolis: University of Minnesota Press.

Lakoff, G. and Turner, M. (1989) *More Than Cool Reason: A Field Guide to Poetic Metaphor*, Chicago: University of Chicago Press.

Lasswell, H. (1958) 'Clarifying value judgment: principles of content and procedure', *Inquiry* 1: 87–98.

Lawson-Tancred, H. (1991) *Aristotle: The Art of Rhetoric*, Harmondsworth: Penguin Books.

Leeuwen, T. van (2007) 'Legitimation in discourse and communication', *Discourse and Communication* 1(1): 91–112.

Leeuwen, T. van and Wodak, R. (1999) 'Legitimizing immigration control: a discourse-historical analysis', *Discourse Studies* 1(1): 83–118.

Lepore, E. (2000) *Meaning and Argument: An Introduction to Logic Through Language*, Oxford: Blackwell.

Lukes, S. (2005) *Power: A Radical View*, London: Palgrave Macmillan.

Lukes, S. (2008) *Moral Relativism*, London: Picador Books.

Macagno, F. and Walton, D. (2008) 'The argumentative structure of persuasive definitions', *Ethical Theory and Moral Practice* 11(5): 545–549.

Macagno, F. and Walton, D. (2010) 'What we hide in words: emotive words and persuasive definitions', *Journal of Pragmatics* 42: 1997–2013.

McBurney, P., Hitchcock, D. and Parsons, S. (2007) 'The eightfold way of deliberation dialogue', *International Journal of Intelligent Systems*, 22(1): 95–132.

Marsden, R. (1999) *The Nature of Capital: Marx After Foucault*, London: Routledge.

Mason, P. (2010) *Meltdown: The End of the Age of Greed*, London: Verso.

Mayer, M. and Künkel, J. (2012) (eds) *Neoliberal Urbanism and its Contestation: Crossing Theoretical Boundaries*, Basingstoke: Palgrave-Macmillan.

Meacher, M. (2009) 'The cost of rejecting public ownership', *The Guardian*, 26 March, at http://www.guardian.co.uk/commentisfree/2009/mar/24/banking-recession (accessed 15 August 2010).

Meacher, M. (2010a) 'Reduce the deficit by job creation not spending cuts', *Left Futures* (weblog), 4 Jan, at http://www.michaelmeacher.info/weblog/2010/01/reduce-the-deficit-by-job-creation-not-spending-cuts/ (accessed 15 August 2010).

Meacher, M. (2010b) 'The rich really are now filthy rich thanks to Mandelson', *Left Futures* (weblog), 27 Jan, at http://www.michaelmeacher.info/weblog/2010/01/the-rich-really-are-now-filthy-rich-thanks-to-mandelson/ (accessed 15 August 2010).

Meacher, M. (2010c) 'The state's role in economic recovery', *The Guardian*, 2 March, at http://www.guardian.co.uk/commentisfree/2010/mar/02/recession-public-sector-investment (accessed 15 August 2010).

Meacher, M. (2010d) 'If neo-liberalism is bust, what next?', *Left Futures* (weblog), 6 March, at http://www.michaelmeacher.info/weblog/2010/03/if-neo-liberalism-is-bust-what-next/ (accessed 15 August 2010).

Miller, D. (1985) (ed.) *Popper Selections*, Princeton, NJ: Princeton University Press.

Miller, D. (1994) *Critical Rationalism: A Restatement and Defence*, Chicago: Open Court.

Miller, D. (2005) 'Do we reason when we think we reason, or do we think?', *Learning for Democracy*, 1(3): 57–71.

Miller, D. (2006) *Out of Error*, Aldershot: Ashgate.

Millgram, E. (2001) (ed.) *Varieties of Practical Reasoning*, Cambridge MA: The MIT Press.

Millgram, E. (2005) *Ethics Done Right: Practical Reasoning as a Foundation for Moral Theory*, Cambridge: Cambridge University Press.

Milliband, E. (2011) 'The challenge for Labour: becoming the standard-bearer of Britain's progressive majority', Speech to the Fabian Society, 15 January, at http://www.fabians.org.uk/events/transcripts/ed-miliband-speech-text (accessed 20 January 2011).

Milne, S. (2010) 'Budget 2010: Osborne's claims of fairness are now exposed as a fraud', *The Guardian*, 23 June, at http://www.guardian.co.uk/commentisfree/2010/jun/23/george-osborne-fairness-claim-fraud (accessed 20 July 2010).

Milne, S. (2011) 'The fallout from the crash of 2008 has only just begun', *The Guardian*, 9 March, at http://www.guardian.co.uk/commentisfree/2011/mar/09/fallout-2008-crash-oil-prices (accessed 10 March 2011).

Minsky, H. P. (1986) *Stabilizing an Unstable Economy*, New York: McGraw-Hill.

Minsky, H. P. (2008) *John Maynard Keynes*, New York: McGraw-Hill.

Monson, G. and Subramaniam, S. (2010) 'Austerity drives can unleash confidence', 27 July, *Financial Times*, at http://www.ft.com/cms/s/0/7a4707f2–98cf-11df-9418–00144feab49a.html#axzz1 MXPSpLPd (accessed August 2010).

Mouffe, C. (2005) *On the Political*, London: Routledge.

Nussbaum, M. (2000) *Women and Human Development: The Capabilities Approach*, Cambridge: Cambridge University Press.

Nussbaum, M. (2006) *Frontiers of Justice: Disability, Nationality, Species Membership*, Cambridge, MA: Harvard University Press, Belknap Press.

Osborne, G. (2010) 'Building the economy of the future', Speech by the Chancellor of the Exchequer, Rt Hon George Osborne MP, at Bloomberg – HM Treasury, 17 August 2010, at http://www.hm-treasury.gov.uk/press_37_10.htm (accessed 10 September 2010).

Outhwaite, W. (1996) (ed.) *The Habermas Reader*, Cambridge: Polity Press.

Parsons, C. (2007) *How To Map Arguments in Political Science*, Oxford: Oxford University Press.

Perelman, C. and Olbrechts-Tyteca, L. (1969) *The New Rhetoric: A Treatise on Argumentation*, Notre Dame, IN: University of Notre Dame Press.

Peter, F. (2008) *Democratic Legitimacy*, New York: Routledge.

Peter, F. (2010) 'Political legitimacy', *The Stanford Encyclopedia of Philosophy (Summer 2010 edition)*, in Zalta, E. N. (ed.), at http://plato.stanford.edu/archives/sum2010/entries/legitimacy/ (accessed October 2010).

Pollock, J. L. (1995) *Cognitive Carpentry*, Cambridge, MA: The MIT Press.

Popper, K. R. (1959/1995) *The Logic of Scientific Discovery*, London: Routledge.

Popper, K. R. (1963) *Conjectures and Refutations: The Growth of Scientific Knowledge*, London: Routledge.

Popper, K. R. (1994) *The Myth of the Framework* (edited by Mark Notturno), London: Routledge.

Quinn, J. and Hall, J. (2009) 'Goldman Sachs vice-chairman says: "Learn to tolerate inequality"', *The Daily Telegraph*, 21 October, at http://www.telegraph.co.uk/finance/recession/6392127/Goldman-Sachs-vice-chairman-says-Learn-to-tolerate-inequality.html (accessed 25 October 2009).

Rahwan, I., Moraitis, P. and Reed, C. (eds) (2004) *Argumentation in Multi-Agent Systems*, Berlin: Springer.

Rancière, J. (1995) *On the Shores of Politics*, London: Verso.

Randall, J. (2010a) 'It will take a long time for the new boys to unravel Gordon Brown's mess', *The Daily Telegraph*, 13 May, at http://www.telegraph.co.uk/finance/comment/jeffrandall/7721082/It-will-take-a-long-time-for-the-new-boys-to-unravel-Gordon-Browns-mess.html (accessed 5 August 2010).

Randall, J. (2010b) 'Budget 2010: The days of spend now and pay back later are over. Later is now', *The Daily Telegraph*, 17 June, at http://www.telegraph.co.uk/finance/budget/7836688/Budget-2010-The-days-of-spend-now-and-pay-back-later-are-over.-Later-is-now.html#disqus_thread (accessed 5 August 2010).

Randall, J. (2010c) 'The cure is painful: work harder, save more – and spend less', *The Daily Telegraph*, 8 July, at http://www.telegraph.co.uk/finance/economics/7880312/The-cure-is-painful-work-harder-save-more-and-spend-less.html#disqus_thread (accessed 5 August 2010).

Randall, J. (2010d) 'Welfare reform: only radical action will save our valleys of despair', *The Daily Telegraph*, 12 August, at http://www.telegraph.co.uk/finance/comment/jeffrandall/7941822/Welfare-reform-only-radical-action-will-save-our-valleys-of-despair.html#disqus_thread (accessed 25 August 2010).

Randall, J. (2010e) 'Spending Review 2010: let's remind Ed Miliband where the deficit came from', *The Daily Telegraph*, 21 October, at http://www.telegraph.co.uk/finance/comment/jeffrandall/8078864/Spending-Review-2010-Lets-remind-Ed-Miliband-where-the-deficit-came-from.html (accessed 15 August 2010).

Rawls, J. (1971) *A Theory of Justice*, Cambridge, MA: Harvard University Press.

Rawls, J. (1993) *Political Liberalism*, New York: Columbia University Press.

Rawls, J. (2001) *Justice as Fairness: A Restatement*, Cambridge MA: Harvard University Press.

Ray, L. and Sayer, A. (1999) (eds) *Culture and Economy After the Cultural Turn*, London: Sage.

Raz, J. (1978) (ed.) *Practical Reasoning*, Oxford: Oxford University Press.

Reed, C. and Rowe, G. (2005) *Araucaria, Version 3*, available free at http://www.computing.dundee.ac.uk/staff/creed/araucaria (accessed 10 October, 2009).

Rees, M. A. van (2005) 'Strategic maneuvering with dissociation', *Argumentation*, 20: 473–487.

Rees, M. A. van (2009) *Dissociation in Argumentative Discussion: A Pragma-Dialectical Perspective*, Dordrecht: Springer.

Rein, M. and Schön, D. (1993) 'Reframing policy discourse', in Fischer, F. and Forester, J. (eds) *The Argumentative Turn in Policy Analysis and Planning*, Durham, NC: Duke University Press, 145–166.

Reisigl, M. (2008) 'Analyzing political rhetoric', in Wodak, R. and Krzyzanowski, M. (eds) *Qualitative Discourse Analysis in the Social Sciences*, London: Palgrave Macmillan.

Reisigl, M. and Wodak, R. (2001) *Discourse and Discrimination*, London: Routledge.

Reisigl, M. and Wodak, R. (2009) 'The discourse historical approach', in Wodak, R. and Meyer, M. (eds) *Methods of Critical Discourse Analysis*, London: Sage.

Rheg, W. (2009) 'The argumentation theorist in deliberative democracy', in Williams, D. C. and Young, M. J. (eds) *Discourse, Debate and Democracy*, New York: Idebate Press, 9–36.

Ricoeur, P. (2008) *From Text to Action*, London: Continuum.

Rose, N. and Miller, R. (1989) 'Rethinking the state: governing economic, social and personal life', manuscript.

Ross, W. D. (1930) *The Right and the Good*, Oxford: The Clarendon Press.

Rubinelli, S. (2009) *Ars topica: The Classical Technique of Constructing Arguments from Aristotle to Cicero*, Dordrecht: Springer.

Russell, J. (2009) 'Has Goldman Sachs's Lord Griffiths been reading George Orwell?', *The Daily Telegraph*, 21 October, at http://www.telegraph.co.uk/finance/comment/citydiary/6396818/Has-Goldman-Sachss-Lord-Griffiths-been-reading-George-Orwell.html (accessed 25 October 2009).

Sachs, J. (2010) 'Sow the seeds of long-term growth', *Financial Times*, 21 July, at http://www.ft.com/cms/s/0/01d88b16–94cd-11df-b90e-00144feab49a.html#axzz1MXPSpLPd (accessed 15 August 2010).

Sandel, M. (2009) *Justice: What is the Right Thing to Do?* London: Allen Lane.

Sarangi, S. and Coulthard, M. (2000) (eds) *Discourse and Social Life*, London: Longman.

Saussure, L. de and Schulz, P. (2005) (eds) *Manipulation and Ideologies in the Twentieth Century*, Amsterdam: John Benjamins.

Sayer, A. (1999) 'Valuing culture and economy', in Ray, L. and Sayer, A. (eds) *Culture and Economy After the Cultural Turn*, London: Sage, 53–75.

Sayer, A. (2000) 'Moral economy and political economy', *Studies in Political Economy*, 61: 79–103.

Sayer, A. (2005) *The Moral Significance of Class*, Cambridge: Cambridge University Press.

Sayer, A. (2007) 'Moral economy as critique, *New Political Economy*, 12(2): 261–270.

Sayer, A. (2011) *Why Things Matter to People: Social Science, Values and Ethical Life*, Cambridge: Cambridge University Press.

Searle, J. R. (1969) *Speech Acts*, Cambridge: Cambridge University Press.

Searle, J. R. (1995) *The Construction of Social Reality*, New York: The Free Press.

Searle, J. R. (2008) *Philosophy in a New Century*, Cambridge: Cambridge University Press.

Searle, J. R. (2010) *Making the Social World: The Structure of Human Civilization*, Oxford: Oxford University Press.

Semino, E. (2008) *Metaphor in Discourse*, Cambridge: Cambridge University Press.

Sen, A. (2009) *The Idea of Justice*, London: Allen Lane.

Siegel, H. (1999) 'Argument quality and cultural difference', *Argumentation*, 13: 183–201.

Skidelsky, R. (2010) 'Deficit disorder: The Keynes solution', *New Statesman*, 17 May 2010, at http://www.newstatesman.com/uk-politics/2010/05/government-spending-money (accessed 20 May 2010).

Skidelsky, R. and Kennedy, M. (2010) 'Future generations will curse us for cutting in a slump', *Financial Times*, 27 July, at http://www.ft.com/cms/s/0/307056f8–99ae-11df-a852–00144feab49a.html#axzz1MXPSpLPd (accessed 1 August 2010).

Skinner, Q. (2002) *Visions of Politics. Vol. 1: Regarding Method*, Cambridge: Cambridge University Press.

Sperber, D. and Wilson, D. (1986) *Relevance: Communication and Cognition*, Cambridge, MA: Harvard University Press.

St Paul's Cathedral/St Paul's Institute (2009) 'Regulation, freedom and human welfare', transcript of public debate, available at http://www.stpauls.co.uk/Learning-Education/St-Pauls-Institute/2009-Programme-Money-Integrity-and-Wellbeing (accessed 15 March 2010).

Stechow, A., von and Wunderlich, D. (1991) (eds) *Semantics: An International Handbook of Contemporary Research*, Berlin: Walter de Gruyter.

Stevenson, C. L. (1944) *Ethics and Language*, New Haven, CT: Yale University Press.

Stokes, S. C. (1998) 'Pathologies of deliberation', in Elster, J. (ed.) *Deliberative Democracy*, Cambridge: Cambridge University Press.

Swales, J. (1990) *Genre Analysis*. Cambridge: Cambridge University Press.

Swift, A. (2006) *Political Philosophy*, Cambridge: Polity Press.

Taleb, N. (2007) *The Black Swan: The Impact of the Highly Improbable*, Harmondsworth: Penguin Books.

Tindale, C. W. (1999) *Acts of Arguing: A Rhetorical Model of Argument*, Albany: State University of New York Press.

Toulmin, S. E. (1958) *The Uses of Argument*, Cambridge: Cambridge University Press.

Trichet, J.-C. (2010) 'Stimulate no more – it is now time for all to tighten', 22 July, *Financial Times*, at http://www.ft.com/cms/s/0/1b3ae97e-95c6–11df-b5ad-00144feab49a.html#axzz1MXPSpLPd (accessed 18 August 2010).

UK Parliament, House of Commons (2010) House of Commons debate on Higher Education Fees, 9 December, transcript available at http://www.publications.parliament.uk/pa/cm201011/cmhansrd/cm101209/debtext/101209–0002.htm (accessed 20 January 2011).

Vogler, C. (2002) *Reasonably Vicious*, Cambridge MA: Harvard University Press.

Walton, D. (1989) *Informal Logic: A Handbook for Critical Argumentation*, Cambridge: Cambridge University Press.

Walton, D. (1990) *Practical Reasoning: Goal-Driven, Knowledge-Based, Action-Guiding Argumentation*, Savage, MD: Rowman & Littlefield.

Walton, D. (1991) 'Rules for plausible reasoning', *Informal Logic* 14: 33–51.

Walton, D. (1992a) *Plausible Argument in Everyday Conversation*, Albany: State University of New York Press.

Walton, D. (1992b) *The Place of Emotion in Argument*, University Park, PA: Pennsylvania State University Press.

Walton, D. (1993) 'The speech act of presumption', *Pragmatics and Cognition*, 1: 125–148.

Walton, D. (1996) *Argumentation Schemes for Presumptive Reasoning*. Mahwah, NJ: Lawrence Erlbaum Associates.

Walton, D. (1999) *One-Sided Arguments: A Dialectical Analysis of Bias*, Albany: State University of New York Press.

Walton, D. (2001a) 'Abductive, presumptive and plausible arguments', *Informal Logic* 21: 141–169.

Walton, D. (2001b) 'Persuasive definitions and public policy arguments', *Argumentation and Advocacy* 37(3): 117–132.

Walton, D. (2005) 'Deceptive arguments containing persuasive language and persuasive definitions', *Argumentation* 19: 159–186.

Walton, D. (2006) *Fundamentals of Critical Argumentation*, New York: Cambridge University Press.

Walton, D. (2007a) *Media Argumentation*, New York: Cambridge University Press.

Walton, D. (2007b) 'Evaluating practical reasoning', *Synthese* 157: 197–240.

Walton, D. (2008a) *Informal Logic: A Pragmatic Approach*, 2nd edition, New York: Cambridge University Press.

Walton, D. (2008b) 'Arguing from definition to verbal classification: the case of redefining "planet" to exclude Pluto', *Informal Logic* 28(2): 129–154.

Walton, D. (2009) 'Dialectical shifts underlying arguments from consequences', *Informal Logic* 29(1): 54–83.

Walton, D. and Macagno, F. (2009) 'Reasoning from classifications and definitions', *Argumentation* 23: 81–107.

Walton, D. and Macagno, F. (2010) 'Defeasible classifications and inferences from definitions', *Informal Logic* 30(1): 34–61.

Walton, D., Reed, C. and Macagno, F. (2008) *Argumentation Schemes*, New York: Cambridge University Press.

Warner, J. (2010) 'Budget 2010: why the "let's spend until we're broke" brigade are wrong', *The Daily Telegraph*, 22 June, at http://www.telegraph.co.uk/finance/budget/7844390/Budget-2010-why-the-lets-spend-until-were-broke-brigade-are-wrong.html (accessed 15 September 2010).

Warner, J. (2011a) 'GDP shock provides a wake-up call for more growth-inducing policies', *The Daily Telegraph*, 25 January, at http://www.telegraph.co.uk/finance/comment/jeremy-warner/8281803/GDP-shock-provides-a-wake-up-call-for-more-growth-inducing-policies.html (accessed 5 February 2011).

Warner, J. (2011b) 'Why George Soros is talking nonsense', *The Daily Telegraph*, 26 January, at http://www.telegraph.co.uk/finance/comment/jeremy-warner/8284569/Why-George-Soros-is-talking-nonsense.html (accessed 5 February 2011).

Weber, M. (1978) *Economy and Society: An Outline of Interpretive Sociology*, vol. 2, Berkeley: University of California Press.

Wilkinson, R. and Pickett, K. (2009) *The Spirit Level*, London: Allen Lane.

Williams, B. (2001) 'Internal and external reasons, with postscript', in Millgram, E. (ed.) *Varieties of Practical Reasoning*, Cambridge MA: The MIT Press, 77–98.

Williams, D. C. and Young, M. J. (2009) (eds) *Discourse, Debate and Democracy*, New York: Idebate Press.

Wintour, P. (2011) 'People do not understand how bad the economy is, warns Cable', *The Guardian*, 21 May.

Wodak, R. (2009a) *The Discourse of Politics in Action*, London: Palgrave Macmillan.

Wodak, R. (2009b) 'Language and politics', in Culpeper, J., Katamba, F., Kerswill, P., Wodak, R. and McEnery, T. (eds) *English Language: Description, Variation and Context*, London: Palgrave Macmillan, 576–593.

Wodak, R. and de Cillia, R. (2006) 'Politics and language: Overview', Brown, K. (ed.) *Encyclopaedia of Language and Linguistics* vol. 9, 2nd edition, Oxford: Elsevier.

Wodak, R. and Meyer, M. (2009) *Methods of Critical Discourse Analysis*, London: Sage.

Wodak, R., de Cillia, R., Reisigl, M. and Liebhart, K. (1999) *The Discursive Construction of Austrian National Identity*, Edinburgh: Edinburgh University Press.

Wolf, M. (2008) 'Keynes offers us the best way to think about the financial crisis', *Financial Times*, 23 December, at http://www.ft.com/cms/s/0/be2dbf2c-d113–11dd-8cc3–000077b07658.html?ftcamp=rss#axzz1MXPSpLPd (accessed 5 February 2011).

Wolf, M. (2009) 'Why Britain has to curb finance', *Financial Times*, 21 May, at http://www.ft.com/cms/s/0/24bfcb30–4636–11de-803f-00144feabdc0.html?ftcamp=rss#axzz1MXPSpLPd (accessed 5 February 2011).

Wolf, M. (2010a) 'Mistakes that drained the fiscal reservoir', *Financial Times*, 24 March, at http://www.ft.com/cms/s/0/e32dc8d4–3757–11df-9176–00144feabdc0.html?ftcamp=rss#axzz1MXPSpLPd (accessed 5 February 2011).

Wolf, M. (2010b) 'Why the battle is joined over tightening', *Financial Times*, 18 July, at http://www.ft.com/cms/s/0/f3eb2596–9296–11df-9142–00144feab49a.html#axzz1MXPSpLPd (accessed 5 September 2010).

Wolf, M. (2010c) 'Why the Balls critique is correct', *Financial Times*, 2 September, at http://www.ft.com/cms/s/0/119c59ac-b6c3–11df-b3dd-00144feabdc0.html?ftcamp=rss#axzz1MXPSpLPd (accessed 5 September 2010).

Wolf, M. (2011a) 'A warning shot for the British experiment', *Financial Times*, 27 January at http://www.ft.com/cms/s/0/886ec5a8–2a52–11e0-b906–00144feab49a.html?ftcamp=rss#axzz1MXPSpLPd (accessed 5 February 2011).

Wolf, M. (20011b) 'Britain's experiment in austerity', *Financial Times*, 8 February, at http://www.ft.com/cms/s/0/5e5a6d1e-33c9–11e0-b1ed-00144feabdc0.html?ftcamp=rss#axzz1MXPSpLPd (accessed 15 February 2011).

Wolf, M. (2011c) 'How to avoid 20 lean years', *Financial Times*, 24 March, at http://www.ft.com/cms/s/0/fb409804–5653–11e0–82aa-00144feab49a.html?ftcamp=rss#axzz1MXPSpLPd (accessed 5 February 2011).

Wolf, M. (2011d) 'Why British fiscal policy is a huge gamble', *Financial Times*, 28 April, at http://www.ft.com/cms/s/0/5f2b4b60–71c6–11e0–9adf-00144feabdc0.html?ftcamp=rss#axzz1MXPSpLPd (accessed 5 May 2011).

Yeates, N., Haux, T., Jawad, R. and Kilkey, M. (2011) *In Defence of Welfare: The Impacts of the Spending Review*, Social Policy Organization, at http://www.social-policy.org.uk/downloads/idow.pdf (accessed 15 March 2011).

Zagar, I. Z. (2010) '*Topoi* in critical discourse analysis', *Lodz Papers in Pragmatics* 6(1): 3–27, DOI: 10.2478/v10016–010–0002–1.

Zagar, I. Z. (2011) 'The use and misuse of *Topoi*: critical discourse analysis and discourse-historical approach', in Eeemeren, F. H. van, Garssen, B., Godden, D. and Mitchell, G. (eds) *Proceedings of the 7th Conference of the International Society for the Study of Argumentation*, Amsterdam: SicSat, 2032–2046.

Žižek, S. (2009) *First as Tragedy, Then as Farce*, London: Verso.

Index

Note: page numbers in **bold** refer to main definitions or discussions of an entry. The letter n following a page numbers refers to a note.

activity types 14, 22, **53–4**, 63, 111, **200–3**, 232, 241, 251n; *see also* debate
adjudication 54, 200, 251n
agency–structure dialectic 12, 80, 102, 155, 199, 237, 241–3, 244
appeal to expert opinion 55; *see also* argument from authority
argument from authority 39, 123–4, 126–8, 131, 137, 141–2, 145
argument: conductive **36–7**, 50, 68, 92, 133; deductive 36–8, 50, 67, 71–2; inductive **36–8**, 52, 71–2; plausible **38–9**; versus explanation 110, 116, 134, 250n
Aristotle 1, 5, 14–15, 18–21, 25, 28, 36–7, 56–8, 69–71, 76, 235, 246n, 249n
Audi, R. 36, 39–41, 43, 45, 61, 67–71, 95–9, 108, 113, 115, 131–3, 169–70, 210, 236, 247–9n
Austin, J. L. 249n

Bauman, Z. 28
Beetham, D. 109, 112
Berlin, I. 32, 59, 248n
Bickenbach, J. E. 38
Billig, M. 248n
Blackburn, S. 46, 70–1, 214, 249
Blair, J. A. 52, 57, 250
Blanchflower, D. 153–4, 158
Bohman, J. 33–4
Bourdieu, P. 22, 80, 247n
Bowell, T. 52, 145, 247–50n
burden of proof 55, 67, 93–4, 154, 171, 224–5, 227, 232, 248n, 251n

Cable, V. 9–10, 177–8, 194, 207–9, 211–12, 215, 224–5, 228
Chilton, P. 20–1, 235
Cohen, J. 30, 32, 111

consensus 14, 29, 31–4, 58–9, 63, 111, 222, 239–41, 243; *see also* debate; disagreement
Corbett, E. P. J. 256n
Critical Discourse Analysis (CDA) 1–2, 12–13, 15–16, 60, **78–116**, 155, 237, 241–2
critical discussion **53–4**, 77, 123, 168, **200–2**, **206**, 212, 222, 232, 239, 248n, 251n
critical questions 11, 16, **54–5**, **61–7**, 75–7, 80, 93–4, 98, 102, 111, 116, 120, 129, 154–5, 224–7, 240–4, 248n
Critical Rationalism 53, 68, 236–7
critical social science 78–81, 102–3, 115–16, 242–3
critique 12–13, 16; *see also* explanatory critique; normative critique
Cultural Political Economy (CPE) 84–5, 103–4

debate: as activity type 10, 14, 22, 54, 63, 111, **200–5**, 231–3, 239–41, 245, 251n; parliamentary 222–3, 230–3, 239, 241, 243, 251
deliberation: in Aristotle 1, 5, 14, 19, 20–1, 58–9, 69, 71; and debate *see* debate as activity type; and democracy *see* deliberative democracy; as genre 10, **13–14**, 22, 50, **53–4**, 87, 133, **200–8**, 214, 232–3, *see also* genre; in institutional contexts 16, 18, 22, 54, 111, 153, 200–3, 212–14, 232–3, 241, 245, 249n; instrumental versus non-instrumental 47, 51, 61, 68–9, 90, 130, 146, 156, 165, 168, 174, 226, 232; leading to decision and action 3–5, 11, 17, 20, 22, 27, 63, 89–90, 122, 125, 149, 202–6, 209, 232–3; over goals versus over means *see* instrumental versus non-instrumental; in single-agent and multi-agent contexts 14, 16, 22, 28, 33, 40, 50–1, 62, 87, 92, 106, 133, 156, 200, 202, 204–5; as weighing of reasons 9–11, 14, 26–7, 34, **38**,